BUG!
THE ADVENTURES OF FORAGER

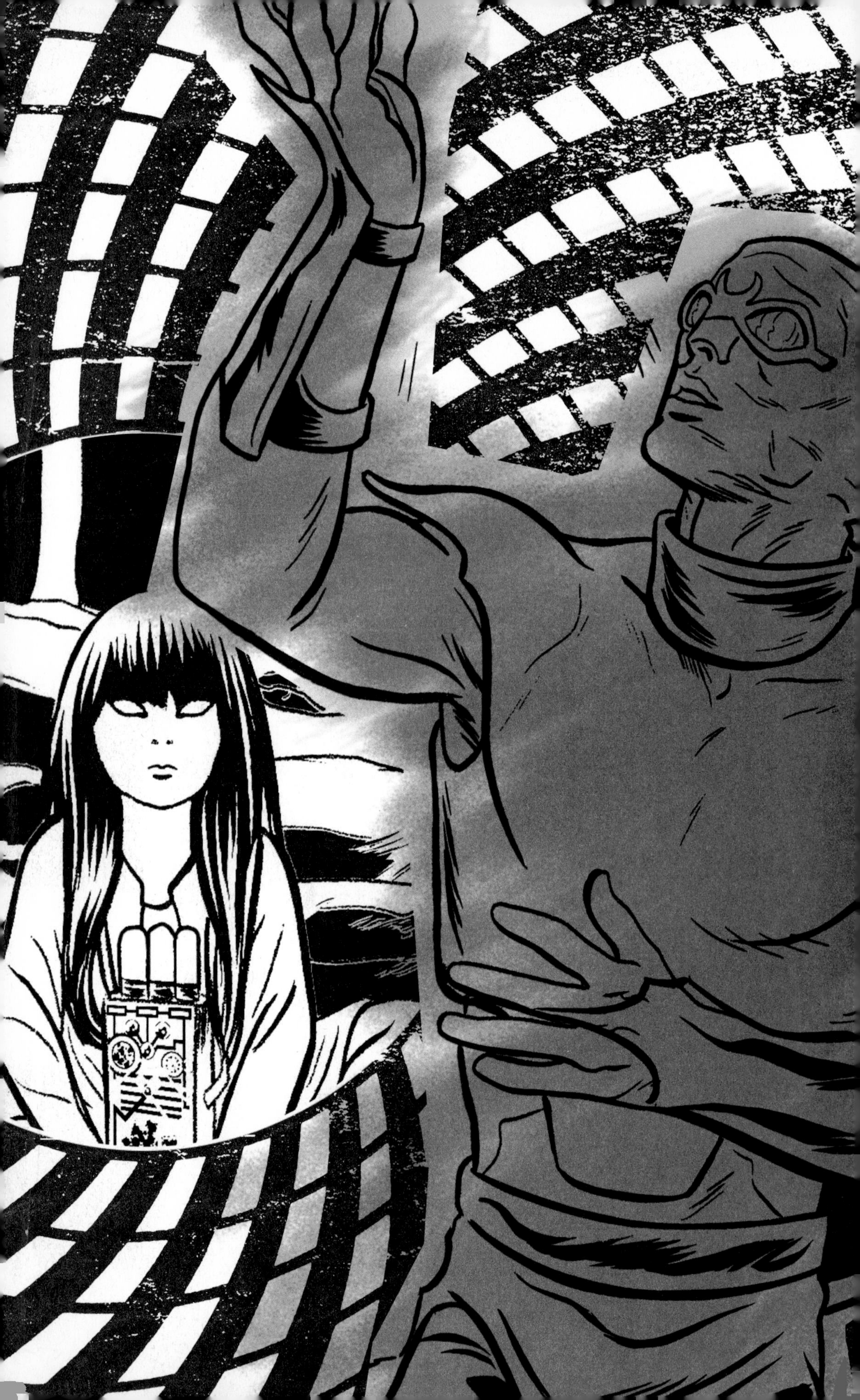

BUG!
THE ADVENTURES OF FORAGER

LEE ALLRED
MICHAEL ALLRED Storytellers
LAURA ALLRED Colorist
NATE PIEKOS OF BLAMBOT® Letterer
MICHAEL ALLRED
LAURA ALLRED Cover Art and Original Series Covers
NEW GODS CREATED BY JACK KIRBY

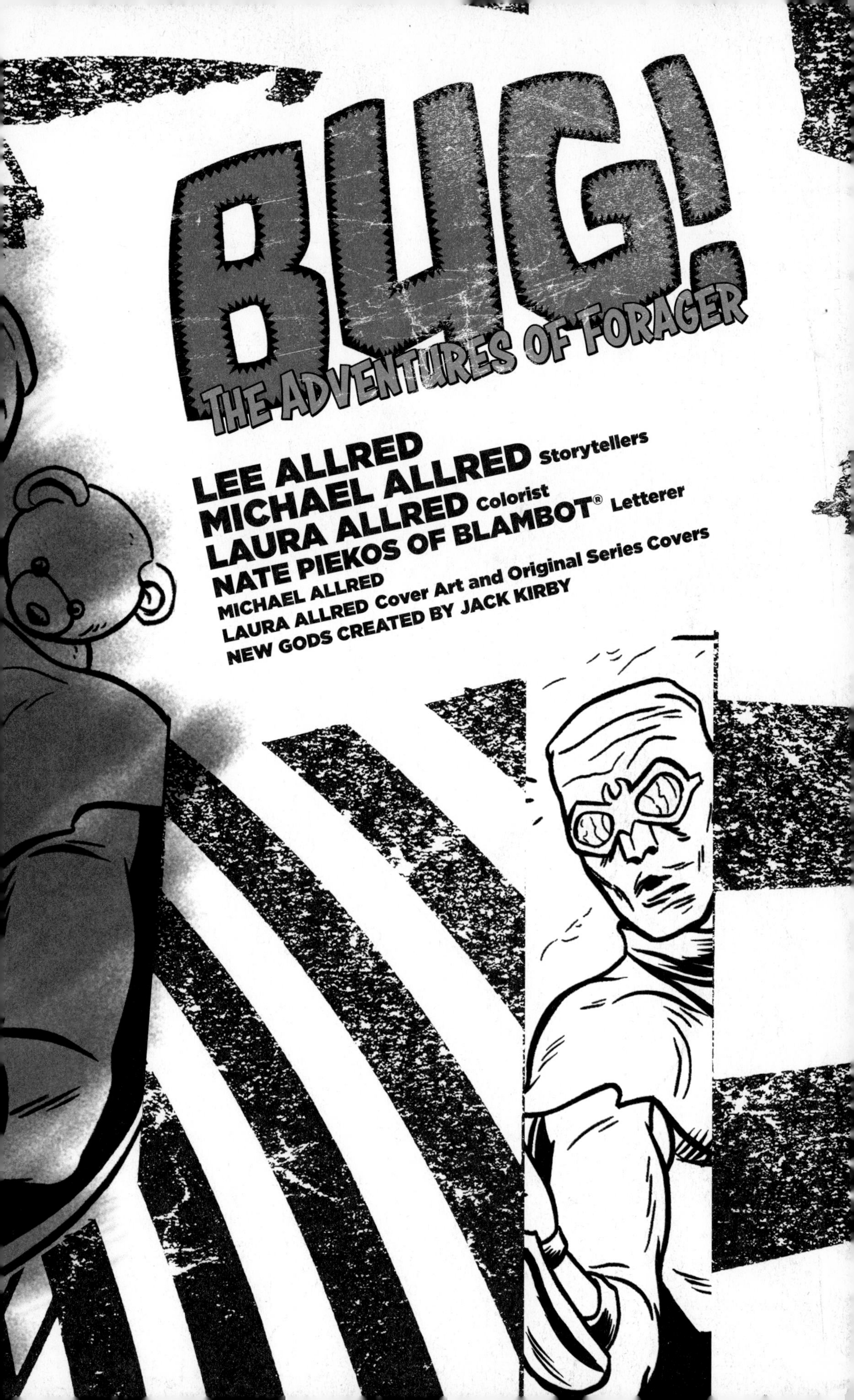

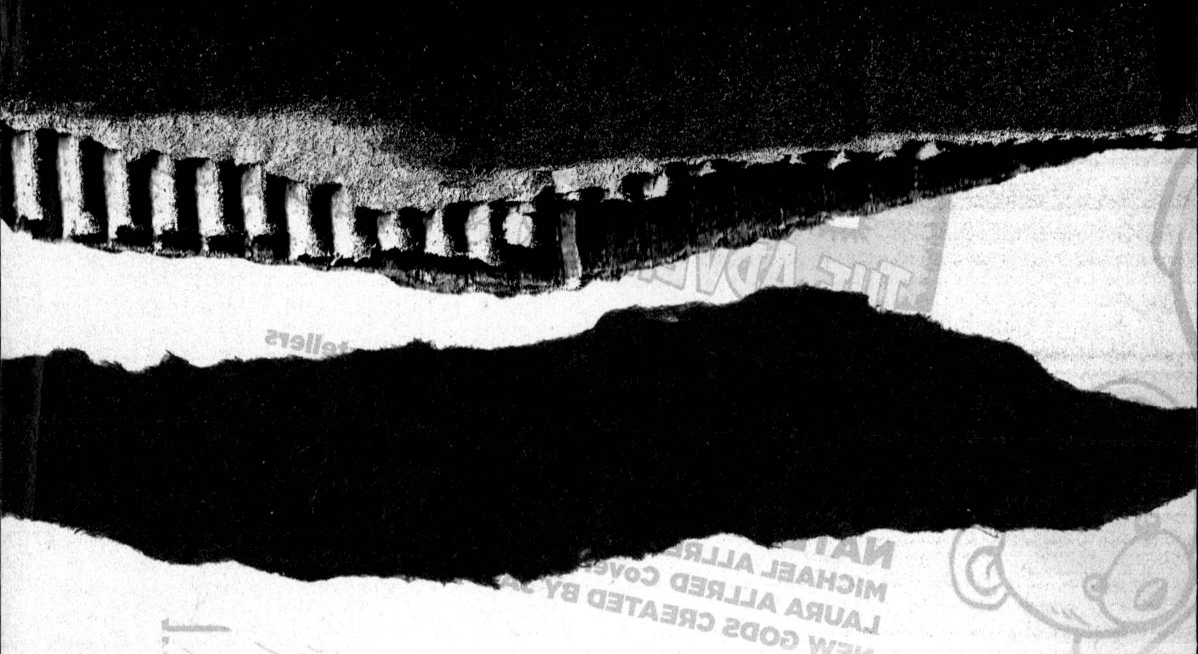

Jamie S. Rich Editor – Original Series and Group Editor – Vertigo Comics
Molly Mahan Associate Editor – Original Series
Maggie Howell Assistant Editor – Original Series
Jeb Woodard Group Editor – Collected Editions
Scott Nybakken Editor – Collected Edition
Steve Cook Design Director – Books
Megen Bellersen Publication Design

Bob Harras Senior VP – Editor-in-Chief, DC Comics
Mark Doyle Executive Editor, Vertigo

Diane Nelson President
Dan DiDio Publisher
Jim Lee Publisher
Geoff Johns President & Chief Creative Officer
Amit Desai Executive VP – Business & Marketing Strategy,
Direct to Consumer & Global Franchise Management
Sam Ades Senior VP & General Manager, Digital Services
Bobbie Chase VP & Executive Editor, Young Reader & Talent Development
Mark Chiarello Senior VP – Art, Design & Collected Editions
John Cunningham Senior VP – Sales & Trade Marketing
Anne DePies Senior VP – Business Strategy, Finance & Administration
Don Falletti VP – Manufacturing Operations
Lawrence Ganem VP – Editorial Administration & Talent Relations
Alison Gill Senior VP – Manufacturing & Operations
Hank Kanalz Senior VP – Editorial Strategy & Administration
Jay Kogan VP – Legal Affairs
Jack Mahan VP – Business Affairs
Nick J. Napolitano VP – Manufacturing Administration
Eddie Scannell VP – Consumer Marketing
Courtney Simmons Senior VP – Publicity & Communications
Jim (Ski) Sokolowski VP – Comic Book Specialty Sales & Trade Marketing
Nancy Spears VP – Mass, Book, Digital Sales & Trade Marketing
Michele R. Wells VP – Content Strategy

BUG! THE ADVENTURES OF FORAGER

DC Comics
2900 West Alameda Avenue
Burbank, CA 91505
Printed by LSC Communications, Owensville, MO, USA. 3/23/18.
First printing.
ISBN: 978-1-4012-7530-3

Library of Congress Cataloging-in-Publication Data is available.

MIX
Paper from
responsible sources
FSC® C132124

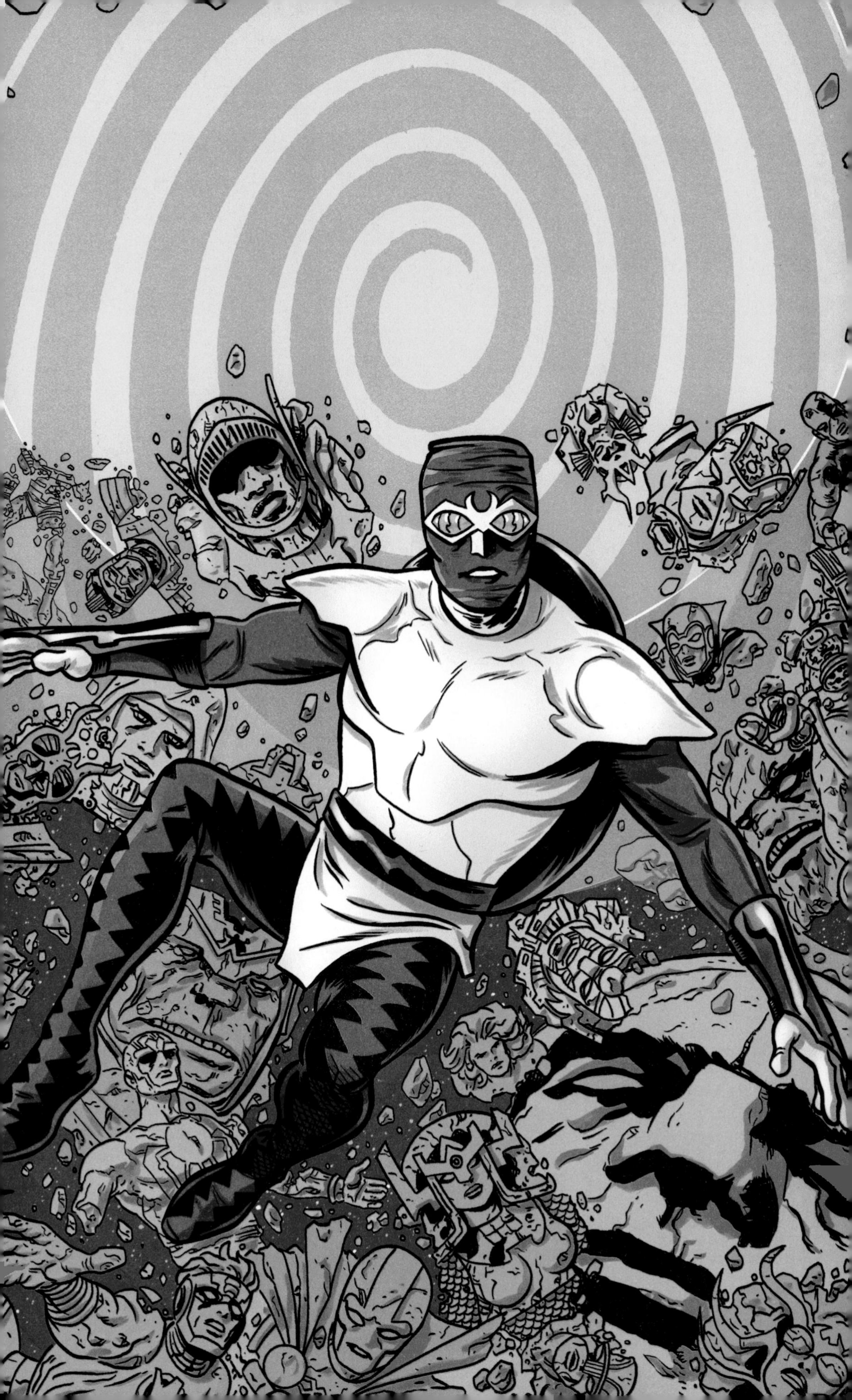

Variant cover art for issue #1 by Paul Pope and Paul Maybury

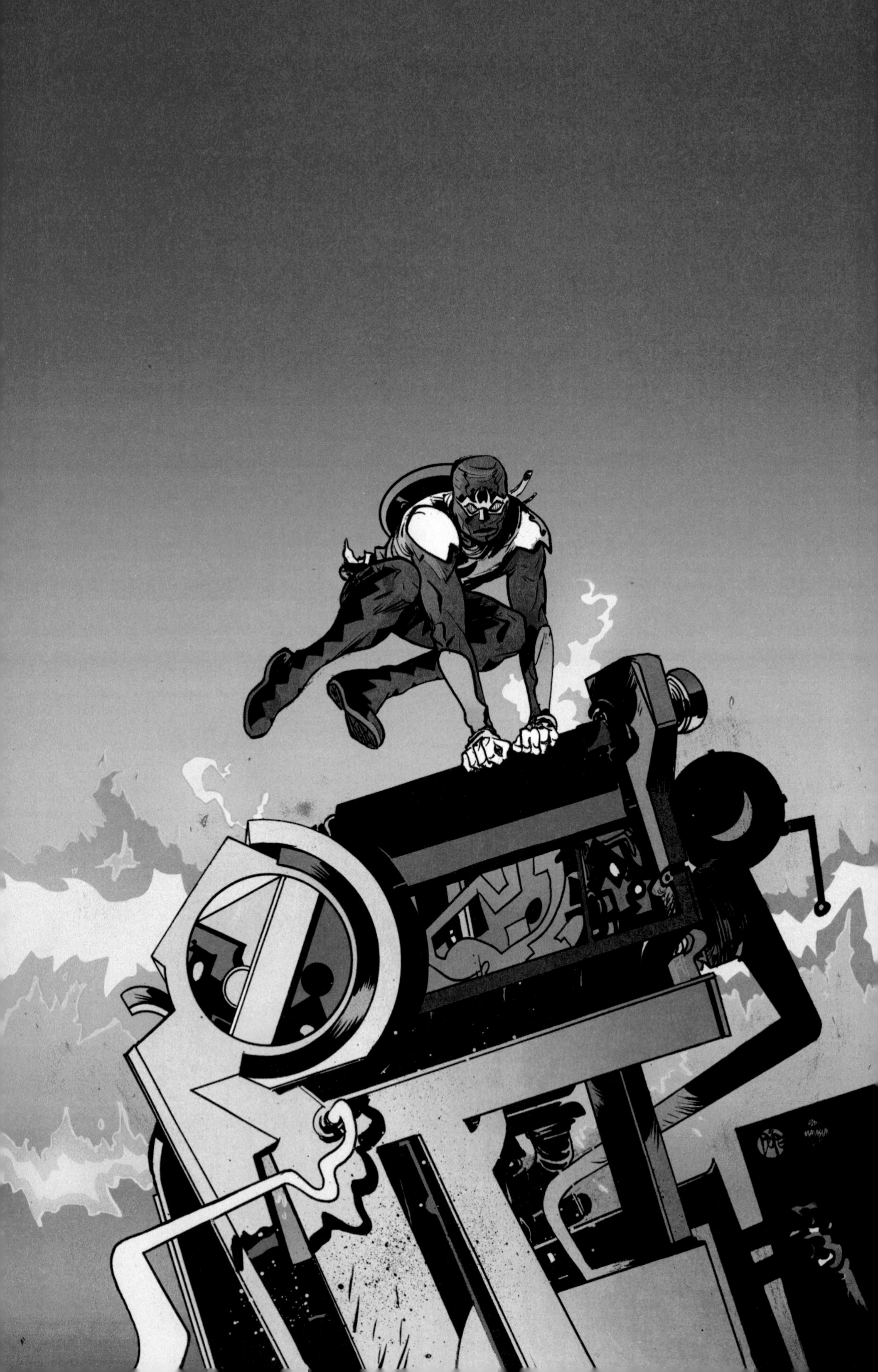

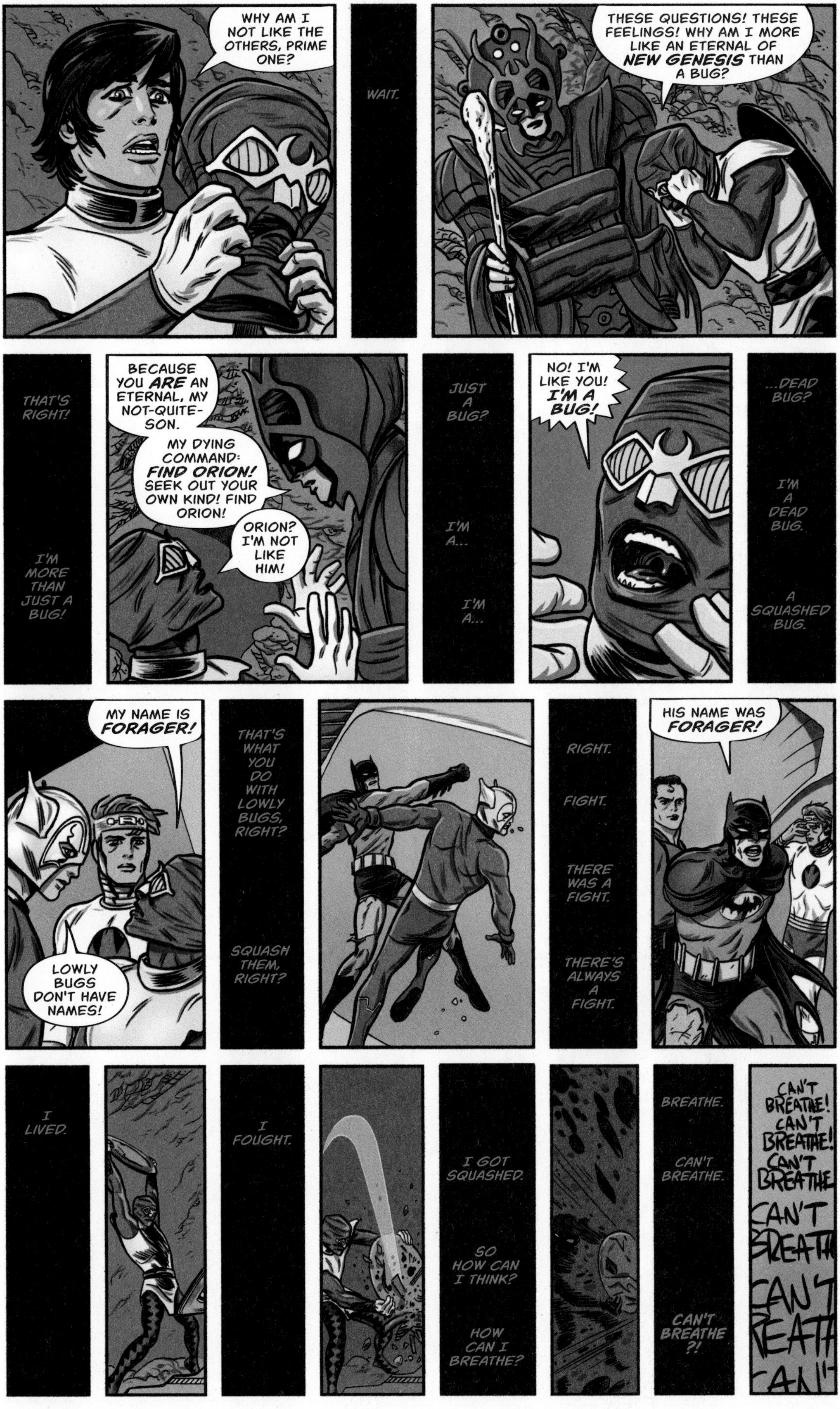
WHY AM I NOT LIKE THE OTHERS, PRIME ONE?
WAIT.
THESE QUESTIONS! THESE FEELINGS! WHY AM I MORE LIKE AN ETERNAL OF NEW GENESIS THAN A BUG?
THAT'S RIGHT!
I'M MORE THAN JUST A BUG!
BECAUSE YOU ARE AN ETERNAL, MY NOT-QUITE-SON.
MY DYING COMMAND: FIND ORION! SEEK OUT YOUR OWN KIND! FIND ORION!
ORION? I'M NOT LIKE HIM!
JUST A BUG?
I'M A...
I'M A...
NO! I'M LIKE YOU! I'M A BUG!
...DEAD BUG?
I'M A DEAD BUG.
A SQUASHED BUG.
MY NAME IS FORAGER!
LOWLY BUGS DON'T HAVE NAMES!
THAT'S WHAT YOU DO WITH LOWLY BUGS, RIGHT?
SQUASH THEM, RIGHT?
RIGHT.
FIGHT.
THERE WAS A FIGHT.
THERE'S ALWAYS A FIGHT.
HIS NAME WAS FORAGER!
I LIVED.
I FOUGHT.
I GOT SQUASHED.
SO HOW CAN I THINK?
HOW CAN I BREATHE?
BREATHE.
CAN'T BREATHE.
CAN'T BREATHE?!
CAN'T BREATHE! CAN'T BREATHE! CAN'T BREATHE

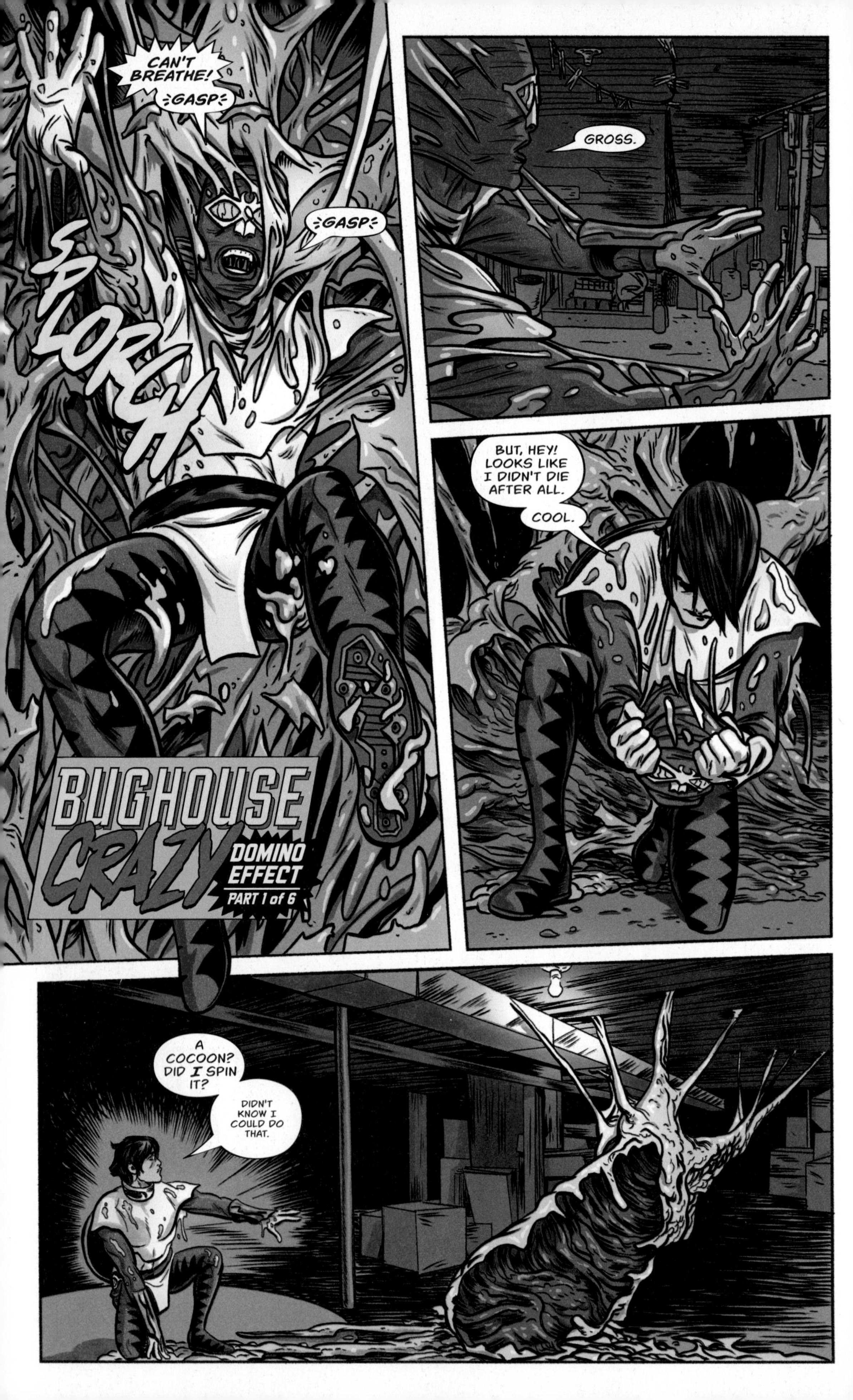

CAN'T BREATHE!
GASP
GASP
SPLORCH
BUGHOUSE CRAZY
DOMINO EFFECT
PART 1 of 6
GROSS.
BUT, HEY! LOOKS LIKE I DIDN'T DIE AFTER ALL.
COOL.
A COCOON? DID I SPIN IT?
DIDN'T KNOW I COULD DO THAT.

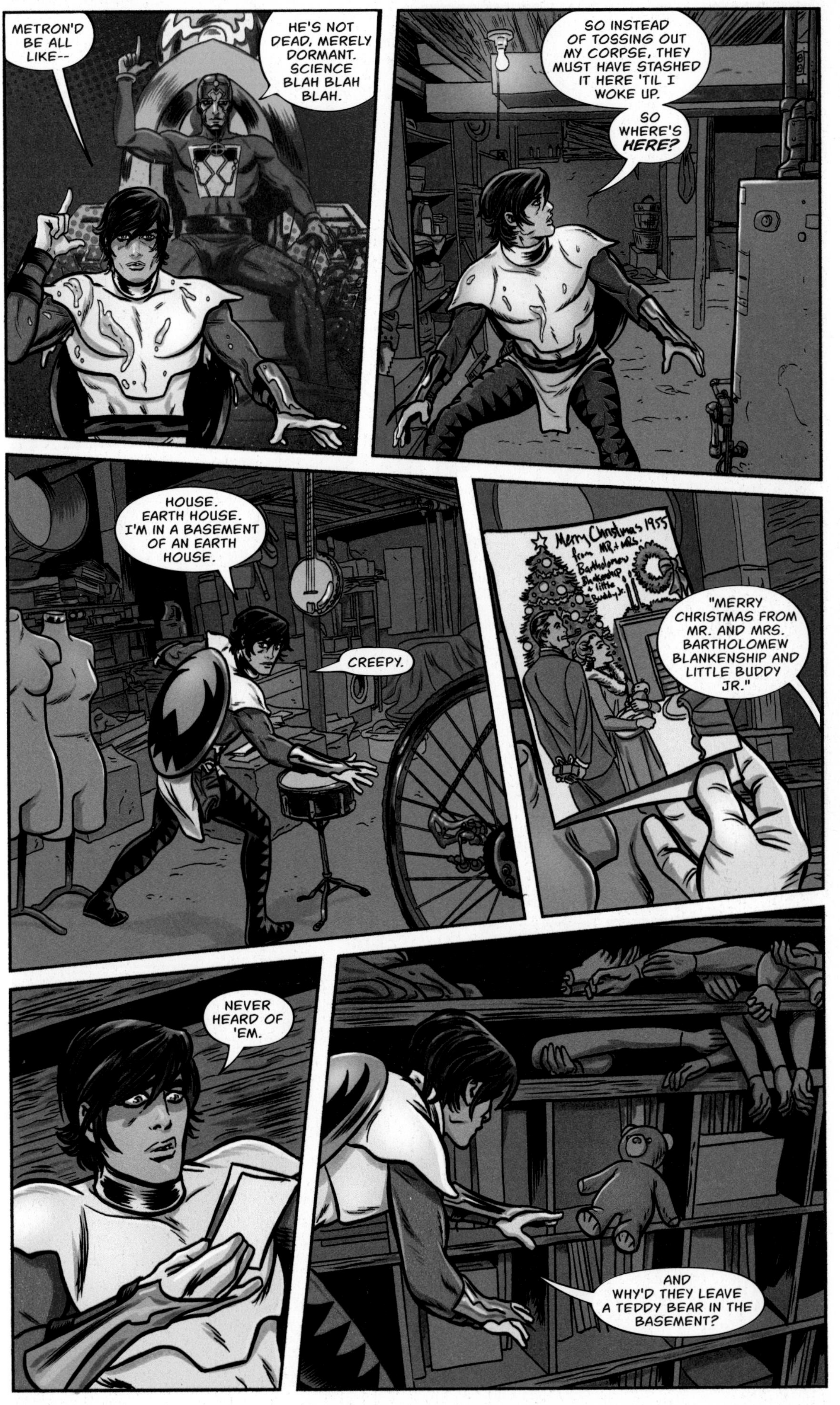

METRON'D BE ALL LIKE--
HE'S NOT DEAD, MERELY DORMANT. SCIENCE BLAH BLAH BLAH.
SO INSTEAD OF TOSSING OUT MY CORPSE, THEY MUST HAVE STASHED IT HERE 'TIL I WOKE UP.
SO WHERE'S HERE?
HOUSE. EARTH HOUSE. I'M IN A BASEMENT OF AN EARTH HOUSE.
CREEPY.
Merry Christmas 1955 from MR. & MRS. Bartholomew Blankenship & little Buddy Jr.
"MERRY CHRISTMAS FROM MR. AND MRS. BARTHOLOMEW BLANKENSHIP AND LITTLE BUDDY JR."
NEVER HEARD OF 'EM.
AND WHY'D THEY LEAVE A TEDDY BEAR IN THE BASEMENT?

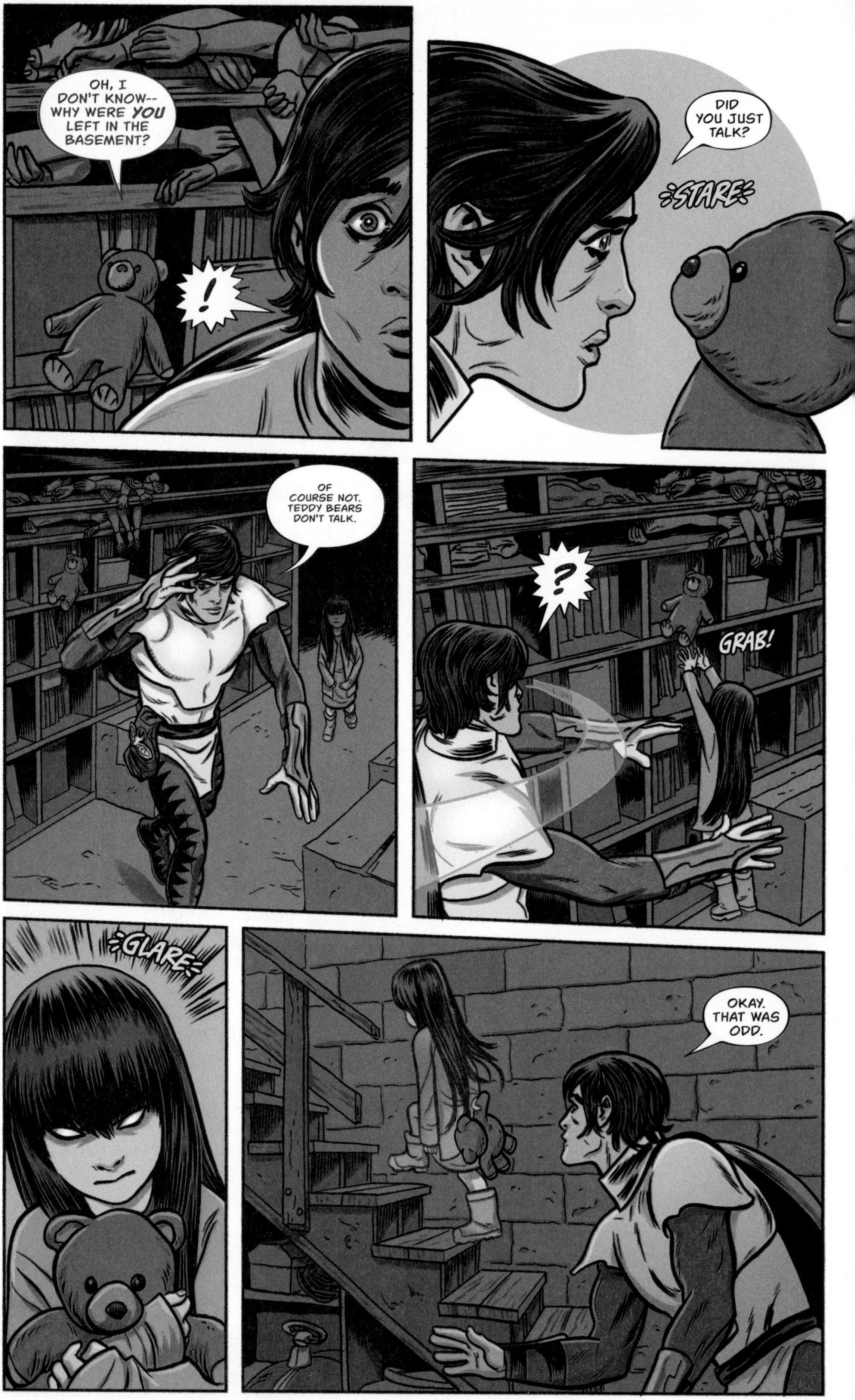
OH, I DON'T KNOW-- WHY WERE YOU LEFT IN THE BASEMENT?
!
DID YOU JUST TALK?
STARE
OF COURSE NOT. TEDDY BEARS DON'T TALK.
?
GRAB!
GLARE
OKAY. THAT WAS ODD.

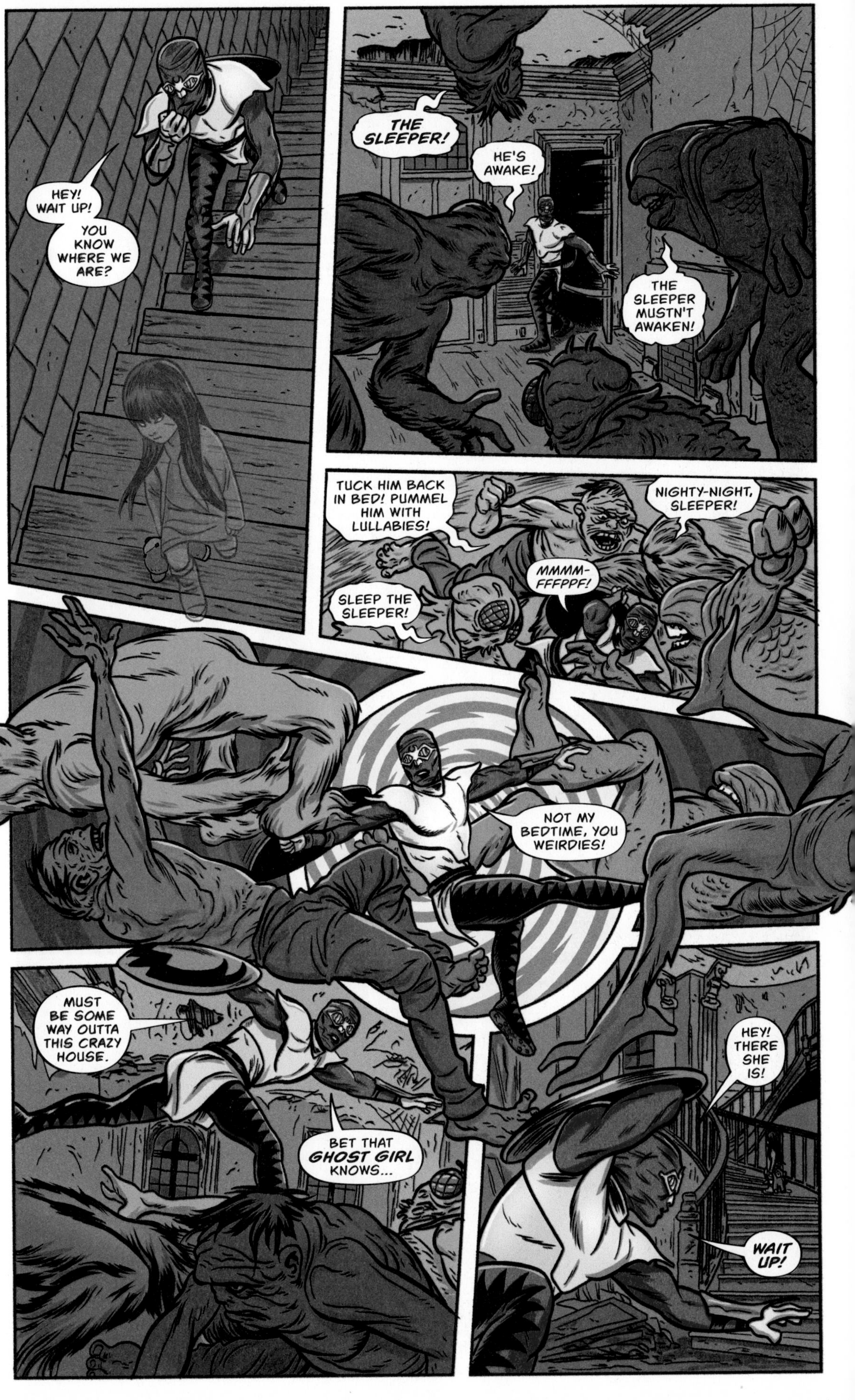
HEY! WAIT UP!
YOU KNOW WHERE WE ARE?
THE SLEEPER!
HE'S AWAKE!
THE SLEEPER MUSTN'T AWAKEN!
TUCK HIM BACK IN BED! PUMMEL HIM WITH LULLABIES!
NIGHTY-NIGHT, SLEEPER!
MMMM-FFFPPF!
SLEEP THE SLEEPER!
NOT MY BEDTIME, YOU WEIRDIES!
MUST BE SOME WAY OUTTA THIS CRAZY HOUSE.
BET THAT GHOST GIRL KNOWS...
HEY! THERE SHE IS!
WAIT UP!

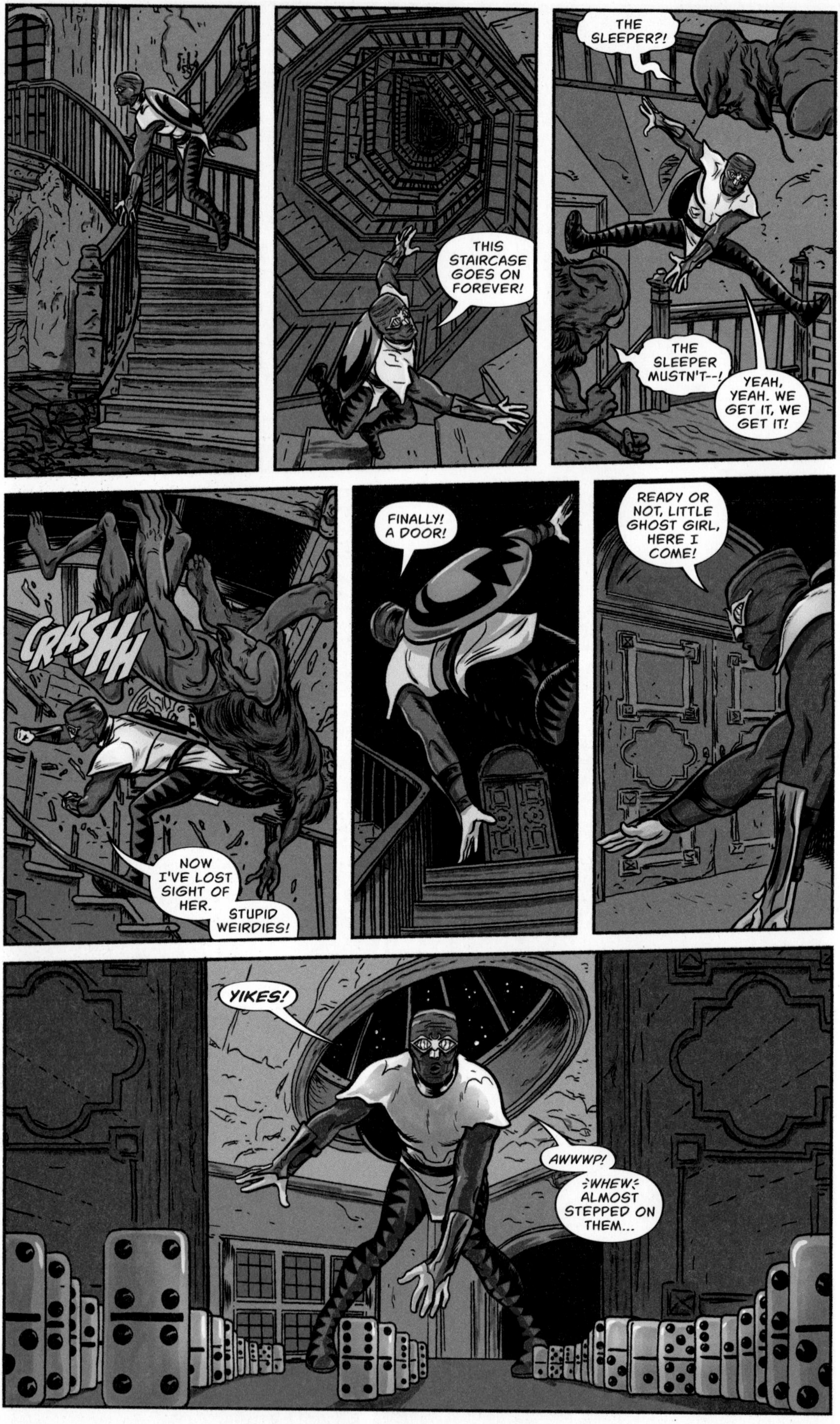
THIS STAIRCASE GOES ON FOREVER!
THE SLEEPER?!
THE SLEEPER MUSTN'T--!
YEAH, YEAH. WE GET IT, WE GET IT!
CRASHH
NOW I'VE LOST SIGHT OF HER.
STUPID WEIRDIES!
FINALLY! A DOOR!
READY OR NOT, LITTLE GHOST GIRL, HERE I COME!
YIKES!
AWWWP!
WHEW
ALMOST STEPPED ON THEM...

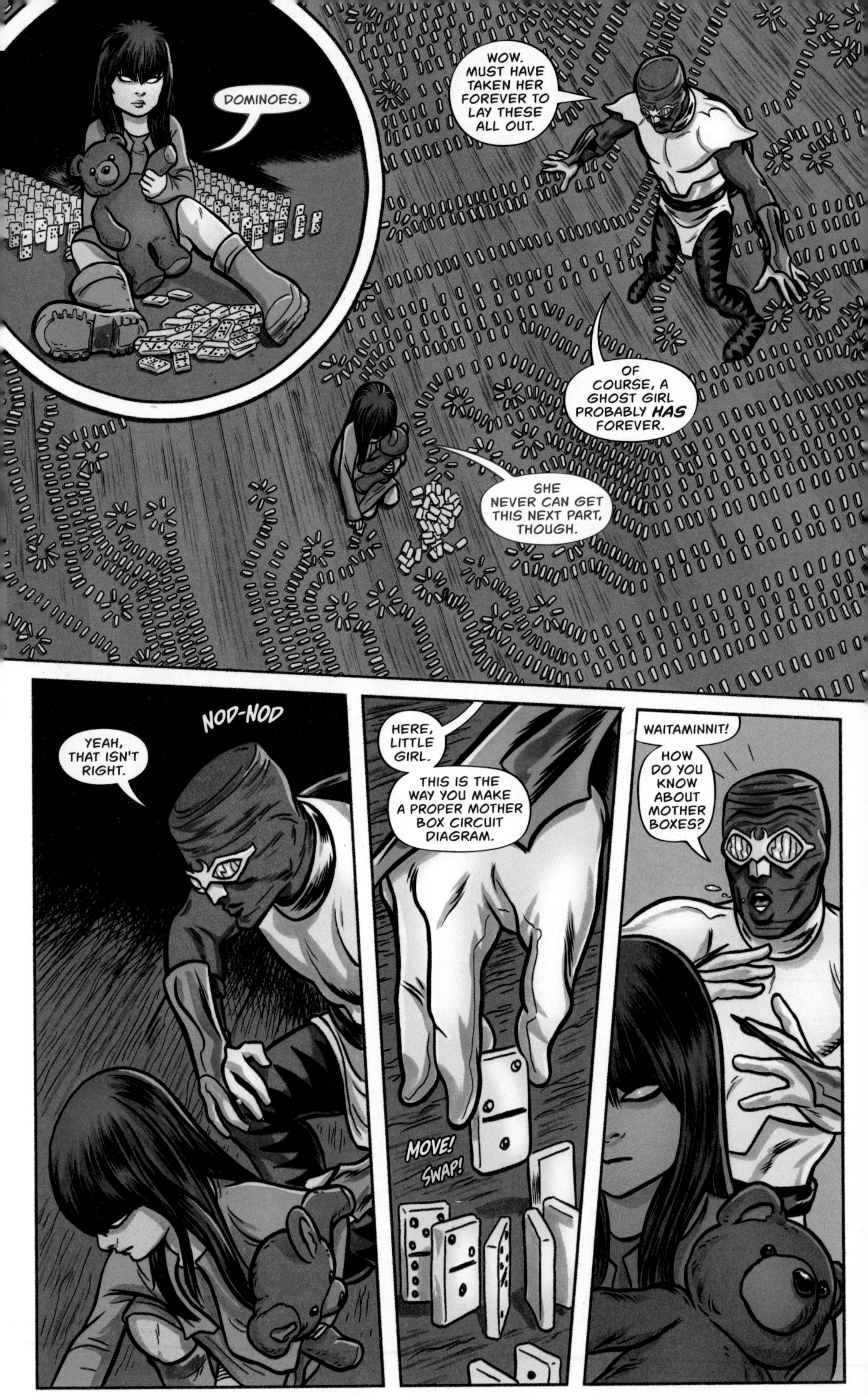
DOMINOES.
WOW. MUST HAVE TAKEN HER FOREVER TO LAY THESE ALL OUT.
OF COURSE, A GHOST GIRL PROBABLY HAS FOREVER.
SHE NEVER CAN GET THIS NEXT PART, THOUGH.
NOD-NOD
YEAH, THAT ISN'T RIGHT.
HERE, LITTLE GIRL.
THIS IS THE WAY YOU MAKE A PROPER MOTHER BOX CIRCUIT DIAGRAM.
MOVE!
SWAP!
WAITAMINNIT!
HOW DO YOU KNOW ABOUT MOTHER BOXES?

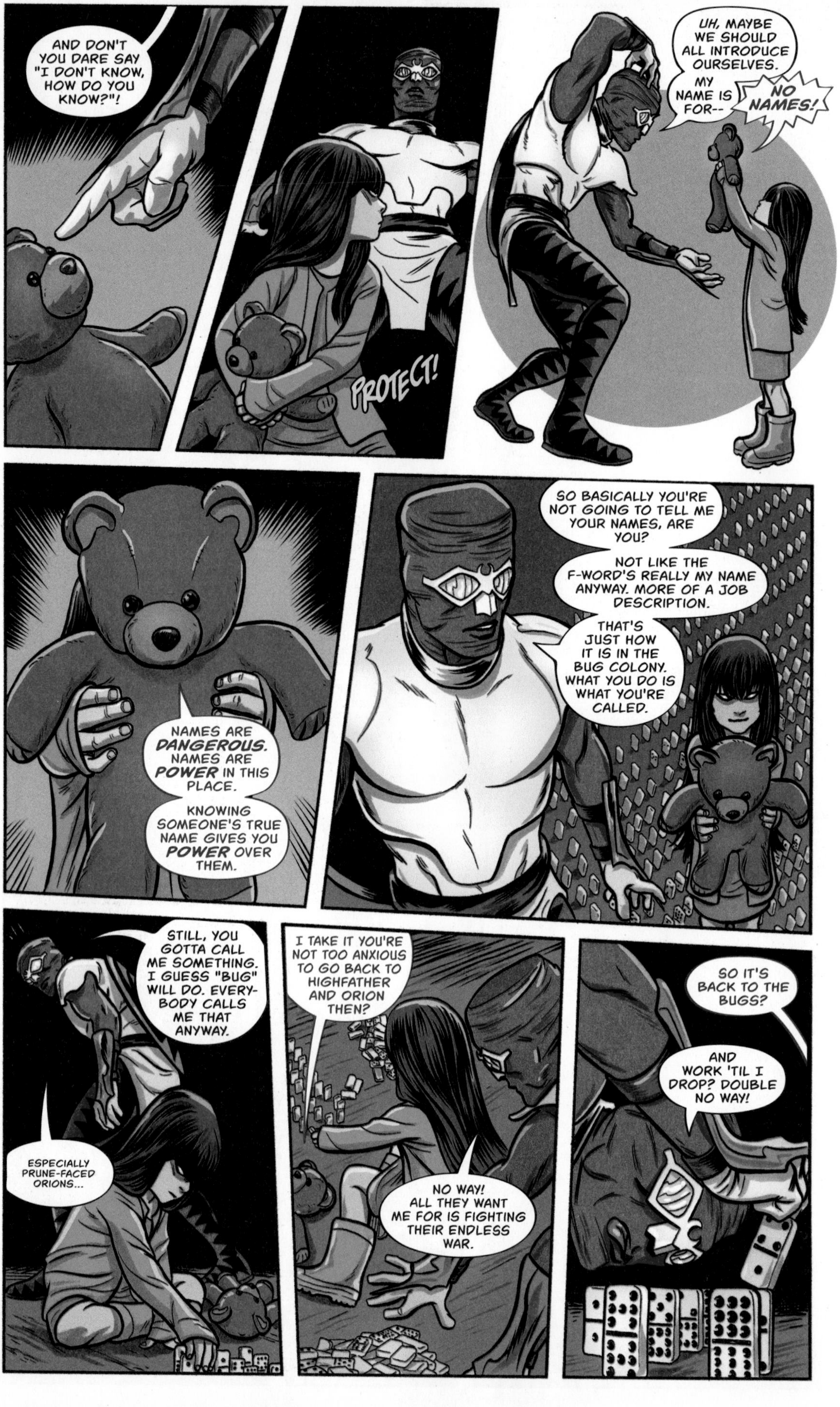
AND DON'T YOU DARE SAY "I DON'T KNOW, HOW DO YOU KNOW?"!
PROTECT!
UH, MAYBE WE SHOULD ALL INTRODUCE OURSELVES.
MY NAME IS FOR--
NO NAMES!
NAMES ARE DANGEROUS. NAMES ARE POWER IN THIS PLACE.
KNOWING SOMEONE'S TRUE NAME GIVES YOU POWER OVER THEM.
SO BASICALLY YOU'RE NOT GOING TO TELL ME YOUR NAMES, ARE YOU?
NOT LIKE THE F-WORD'S REALLY MY NAME ANYWAY. MORE OF A JOB DESCRIPTION.
THAT'S JUST HOW IT IS IN THE BUG COLONY. WHAT YOU DO IS WHAT YOU'RE CALLED.
STILL, YOU GOTTA CALL ME SOMETHING. I GUESS "BUG" WILL DO. EVERY-BODY CALLS ME THAT ANYWAY.
ESPECIALLY PRUNE-FACED ORIONS...
I TAKE IT YOU'RE NOT TOO ANXIOUS TO GO BACK TO HIGHFATHER AND ORION THEN?
NO WAY! ALL THEY WANT ME FOR IS FIGHTING THEIR ENDLESS WAR.
SO IT'S BACK TO THE BUGS?
AND WORK 'TIL I DROP? DOUBLE NO WAY!

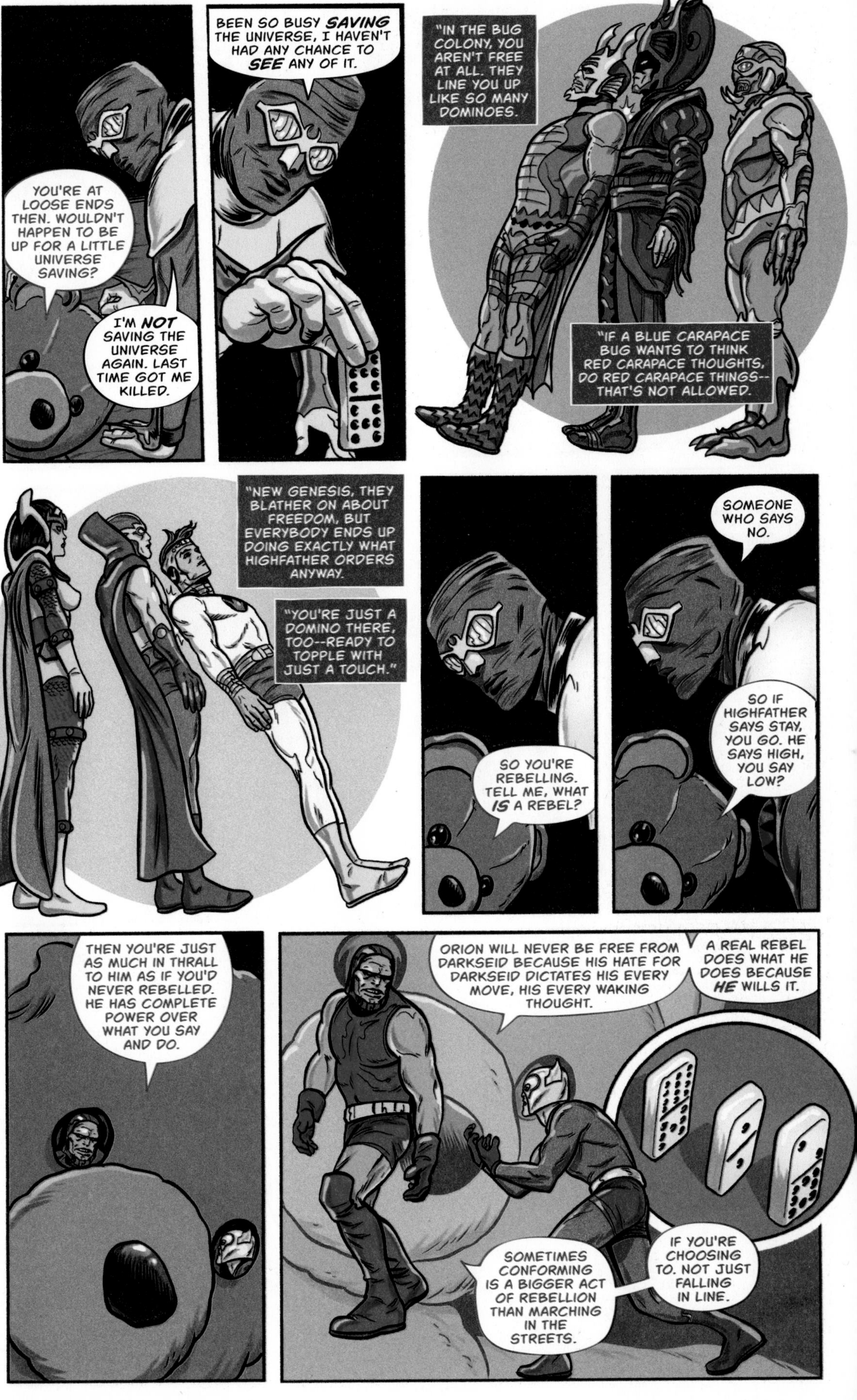
YOU'RE AT LOOSE ENDS THEN. WOULDN'T HAPPEN TO BE UP FOR A LITTLE UNIVERSE SAVING?
I'M NOT SAVING THE UNIVERSE AGAIN. LAST TIME GOT ME KILLED.
BEEN SO BUSY SAVING THE UNIVERSE, I HAVEN'T HAD ANY CHANCE TO SEE ANY OF IT.
"IN THE BUG COLONY, YOU AREN'T FREE AT ALL. THEY LINE YOU UP LIKE SO MANY DOMINOES.
"IF A BLUE CARAPACE BUG WANTS TO THINK RED CARAPACE THOUGHTS, DO RED CARAPACE THINGS-- THAT'S NOT ALLOWED.
"NEW GENESIS, THEY BLATHER ON ABOUT FREEDOM, BUT EVERYBODY ENDS UP DOING EXACTLY WHAT HIGHFATHER ORDERS ANYWAY.
"YOU'RE JUST A DOMINO THERE, TOO--READY TO TOPPLE WITH JUST A TOUCH."
SO YOU'RE REBELLING. TELL ME, WHAT IS A REBEL?
SOMEONE WHO SAYS NO.
SO IF HIGHFATHER SAYS STAY, YOU GO. HE SAYS HIGH, YOU SAY LOW?
THEN YOU'RE JUST AS MUCH IN THRALL TO HIM AS IF YOU'D NEVER REBELLED. HE HAS COMPLETE POWER OVER WHAT YOU SAY AND DO.
ORION WILL NEVER BE FREE FROM DARKSEID BECAUSE HIS HATE FOR DARKSEID DICTATES HIS EVERY MOVE, HIS EVERY WAKING THOUGHT.
A REAL REBEL DOES WHAT HE DOES BECAUSE HE WILLS IT.
SOMETIMES CONFORMING IS A BIGGER ACT OF REBELLION THAN MARCHING IN THE STREETS.
IF YOU'RE CHOOSING TO. NOT JUST FALLING IN LINE.

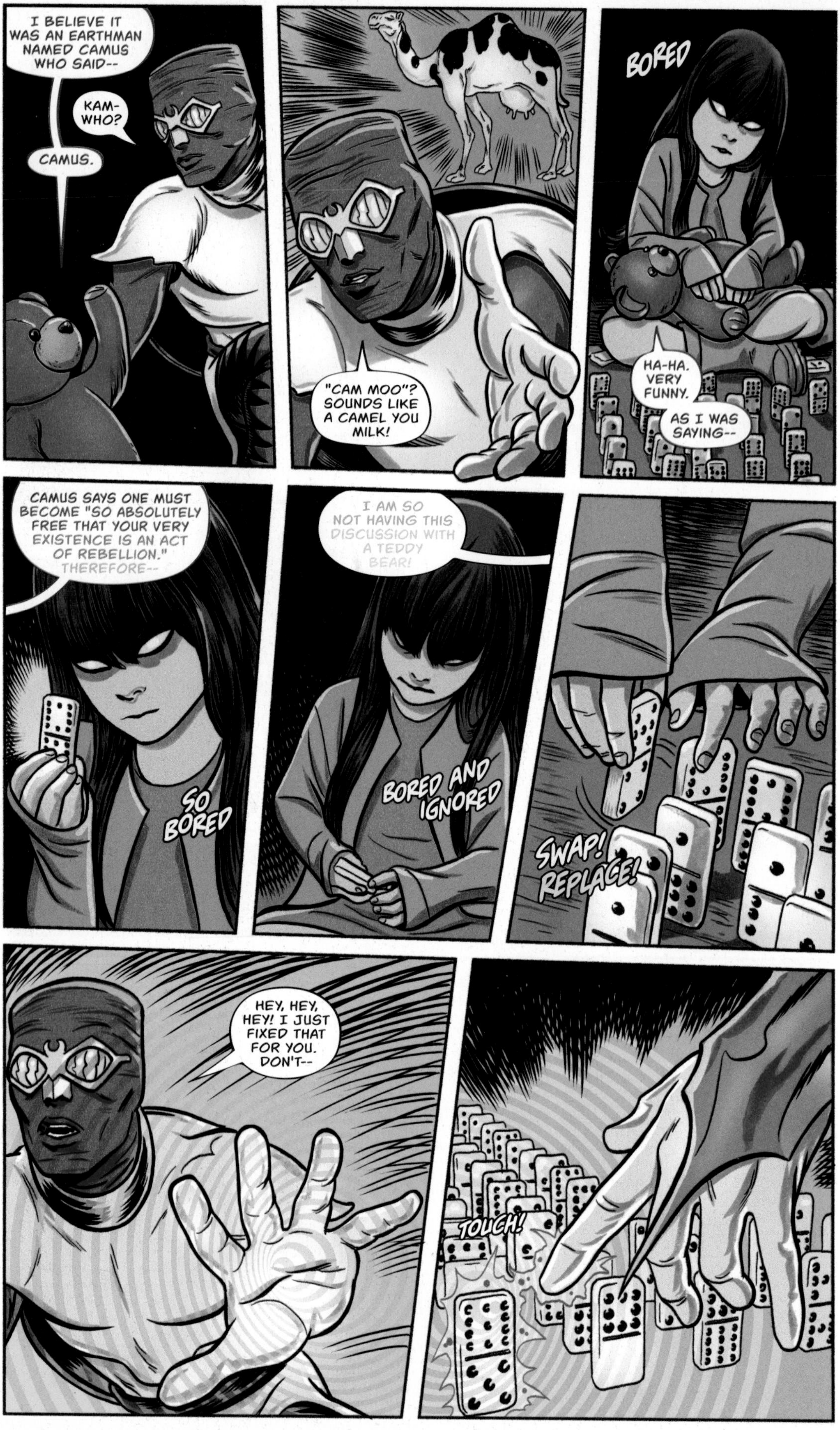
I BELIEVE IT WAS AN EARTHMAN NAMED CAMUS WHO SAID--
KAM-WHO?
CAMUS.
"CAM MOO"? SOUNDS LIKE A CAMEL YOU MILK!
BORED
HA-HA. VERY FUNNY.
AS I WAS SAYING--
CAMUS SAYS ONE MUST BECOME "SO ABSOLUTELY FREE THAT YOUR VERY EXISTENCE IS AN ACT OF REBELLION." THEREFORE--
SO BORED
I AM SO NOT HAVING THIS DISCUSSION WITH A TEDDY BEAR!
BORED AND IGNORED
SWAP! REPLACE!
HEY, HEY, HEY! I JUST FIXED THAT FOR YOU. DON'T--
TOUCH!

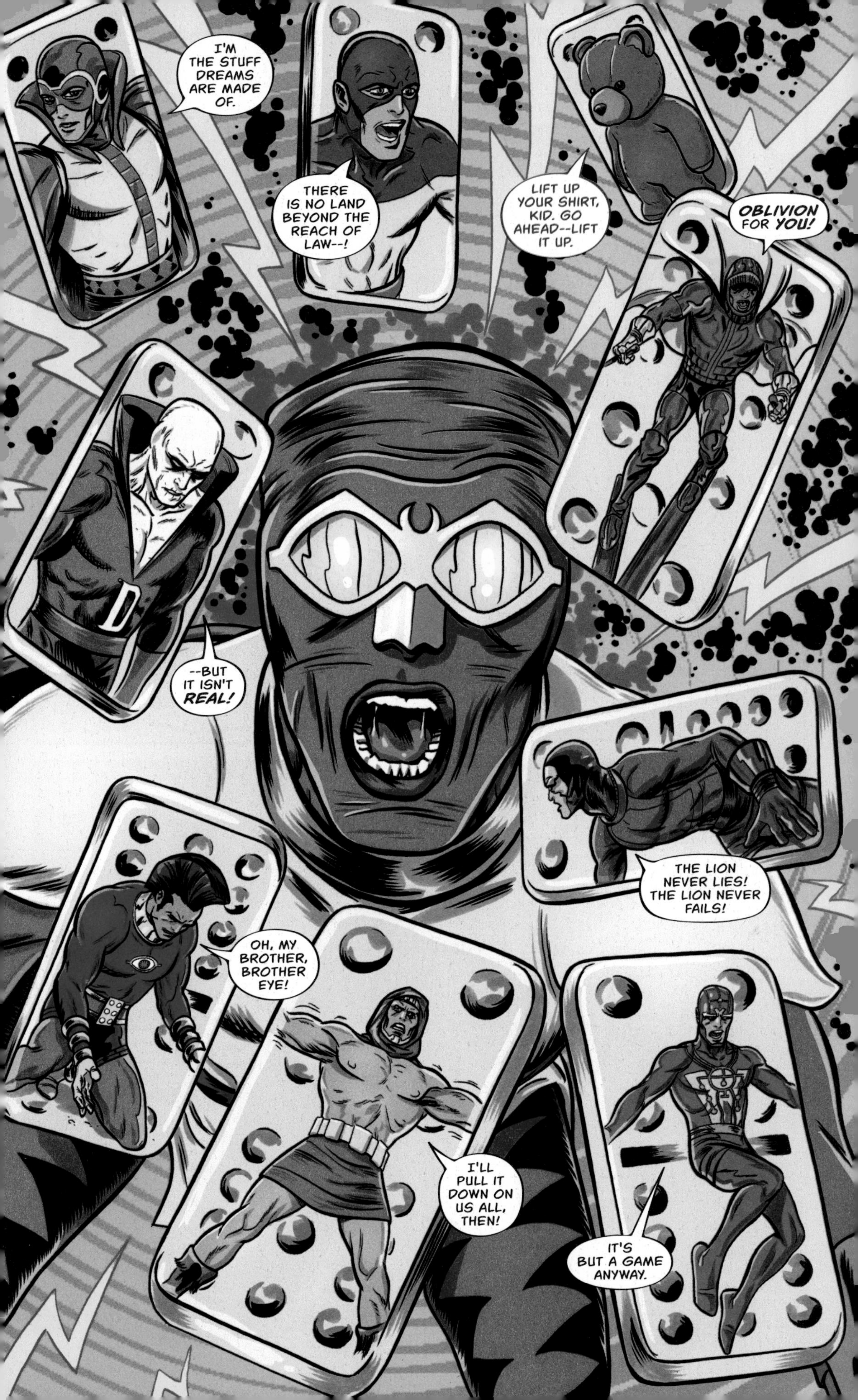
I'M THE STUFF DREAMS ARE MADE OF.
THERE IS NO LAND BEYOND THE REACH OF LAW--!
LIFT UP YOUR SHIRT, KID. GO AHEAD--LIFT IT UP.
OBLIVION FOR YOU!
--BUT IT ISN'T REAL!
THE LION NEVER LIES! THE LION NEVER FAILS!
OH, MY BROTHER, BROTHER EYE!
I'LL PULL IT DOWN ON US ALL, THEN!
IT'S BUT A GAME ANYWAY.

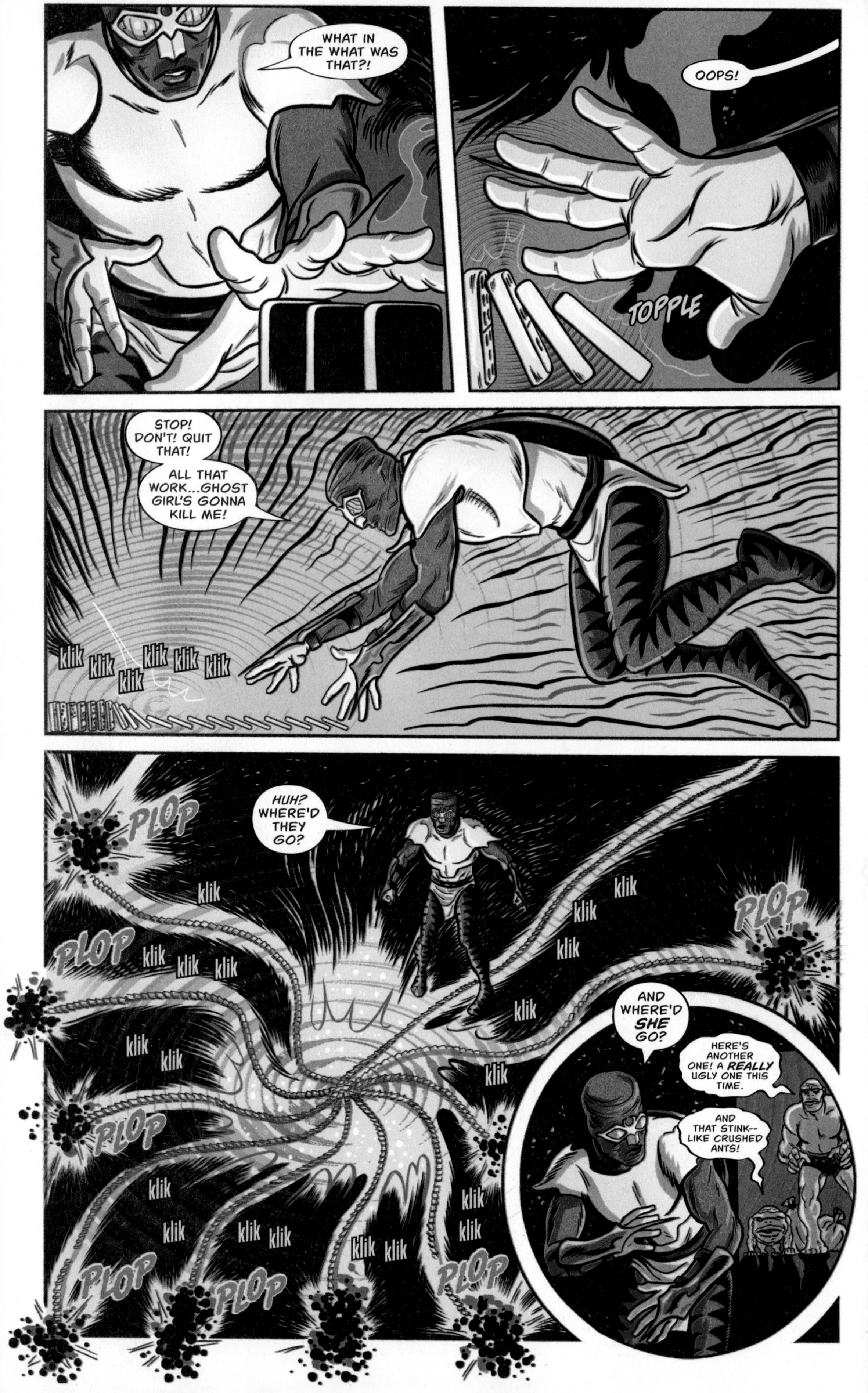
WHAT IN THE WHAT WAS THAT?!
OOPS!
TOPPLE
STOP! DON'T! QUIT THAT!
ALL THAT WORK...GHOST GIRL'S GONNA KILL ME!
klik klik klik klik klik klik
HUH? WHERE'D THEY GO?
PLOP
klik
klik
PLOP
PLOP
klik klik klik
klik
klik
klik
klik
klik
klik
PLOP
klik
klik
klik klik
klik klik
klik
klik
PLOP
PLOP
PLOP
AND WHERE'D SHE GO?
HERE'S ANOTHER ONE! A REALLY UGLY ONE THIS TIME.
AND THAT STINK--LIKE CRUSHED ANTS!

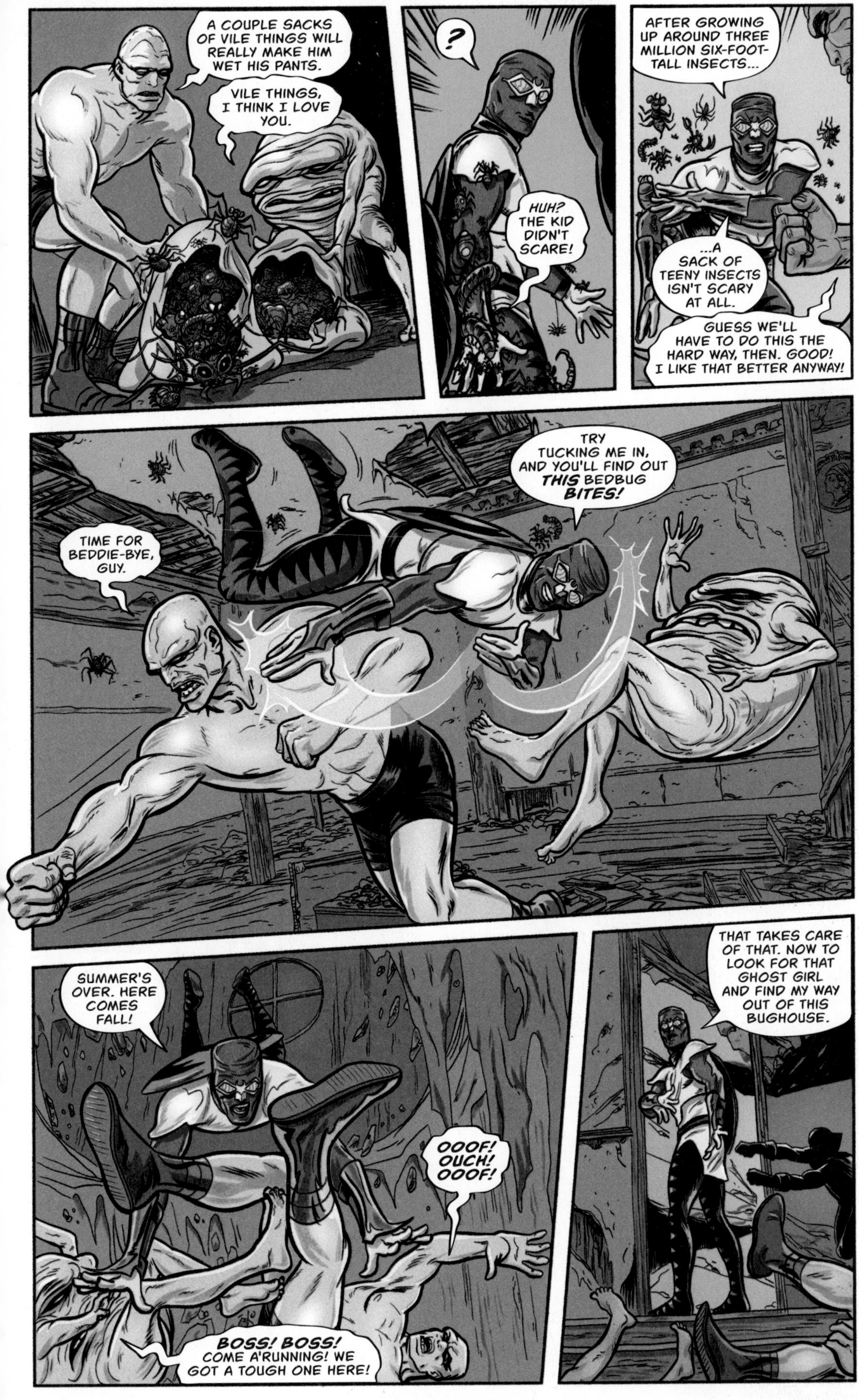
A COUPLE SACKS OF VILE THINGS WILL REALLY MAKE HIM WET HIS PANTS.
VILE THINGS, I THINK I LOVE YOU.
?
HUH? THE KID DIDN'T SCARE!
AFTER GROWING UP AROUND THREE MILLION SIX-FOOT-TALL INSECTS...
...A SACK OF TEENY INSECTS ISN'T SCARY AT ALL.
GUESS WE'LL HAVE TO DO THIS THE HARD WAY, THEN. GOOD! I LIKE THAT BETTER ANYWAY!
TIME FOR BEDDIE-BYE, GUY.
TRY TUCKING ME IN, AND YOU'LL FIND OUT THIS BEDBUG BITES!
SUMMER'S OVER. HERE COMES FALL!
OOOF! OUCH! OOOF!
BOSS! BOSS! COME A'RUNNING! WE GOT A TOUGH ONE HERE!
THAT TAKES CARE OF THAT. NOW TO LOOK FOR THAT GHOST GIRL AND FIND MY WAY OUT OF THIS BUGHOUSE.

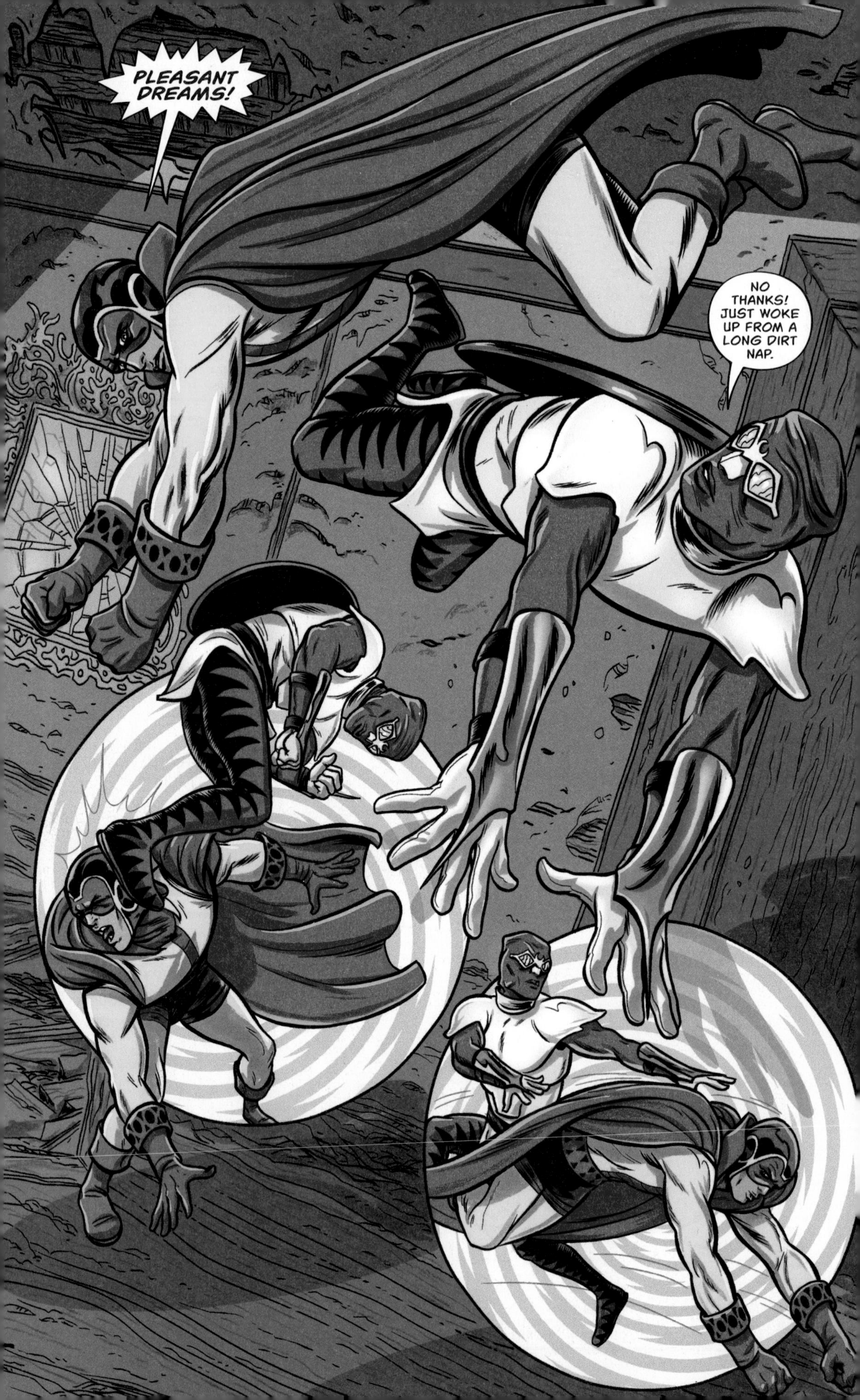
PLEASANT DREAMS!
NO THANKS! JUST WOKE UP FROM A LONG DIRT NAP.

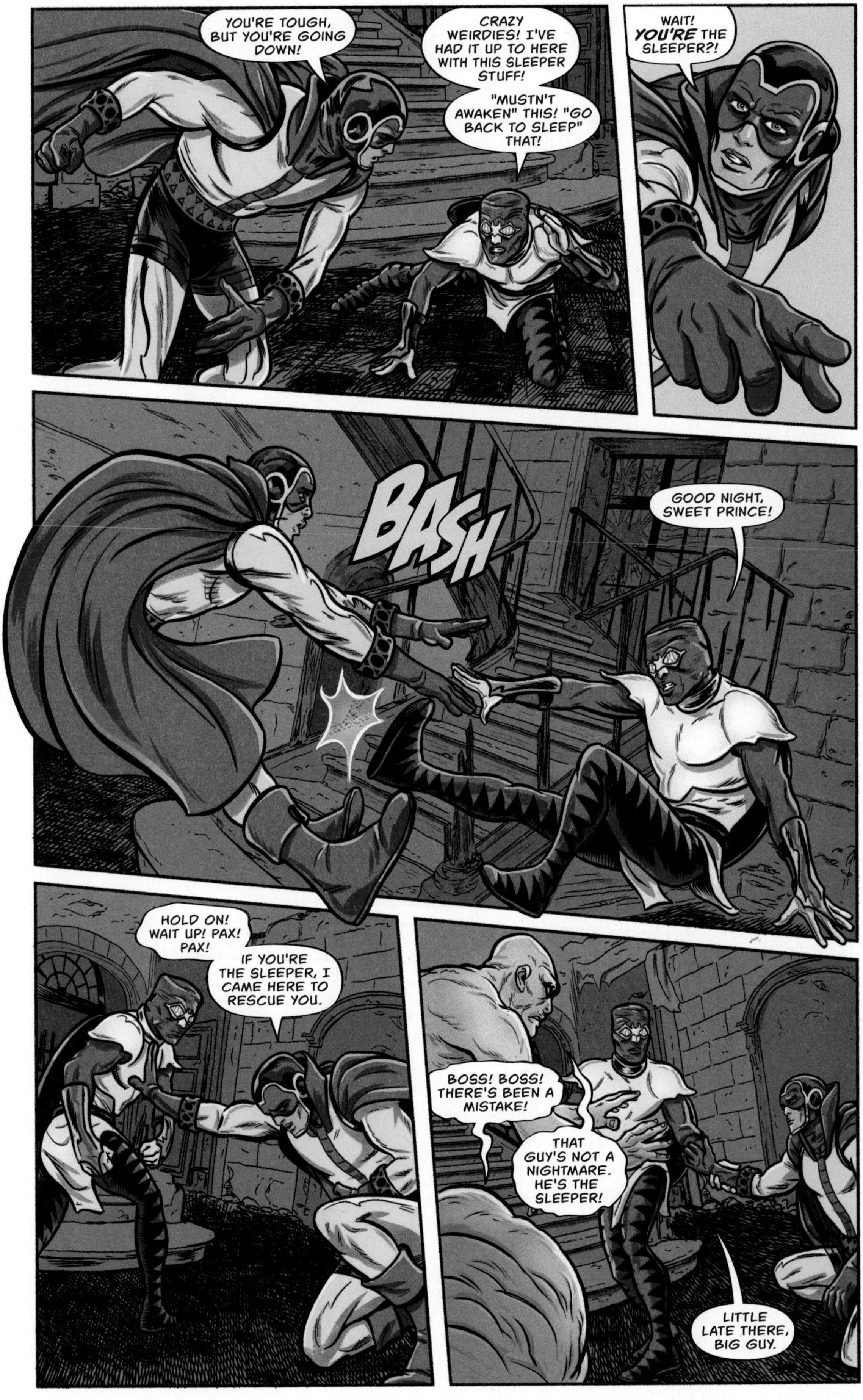
YOU'RE TOUGH, BUT YOU'RE GOING DOWN!
CRAZY WEIRDIES! I'VE HAD IT UP TO HERE WITH THIS SLEEPER STUFF!
"MUSTN'T AWAKEN" THIS! "GO BACK TO SLEEP" THAT!
WAIT! YOU'RE THE SLEEPER?!
BASH
GOOD NIGHT, SWEET PRINCE!
HOLD ON! WAIT UP! PAX! PAX!
IF YOU'RE THE SLEEPER, I CAME HERE TO RESCUE YOU.
BOSS! BOSS! THERE'S BEEN A MISTAKE!
THAT GUY'S NOT A NIGHTMARE. HE'S THE SLEEPER!
LITTLE LATE THERE, BIG GUY.

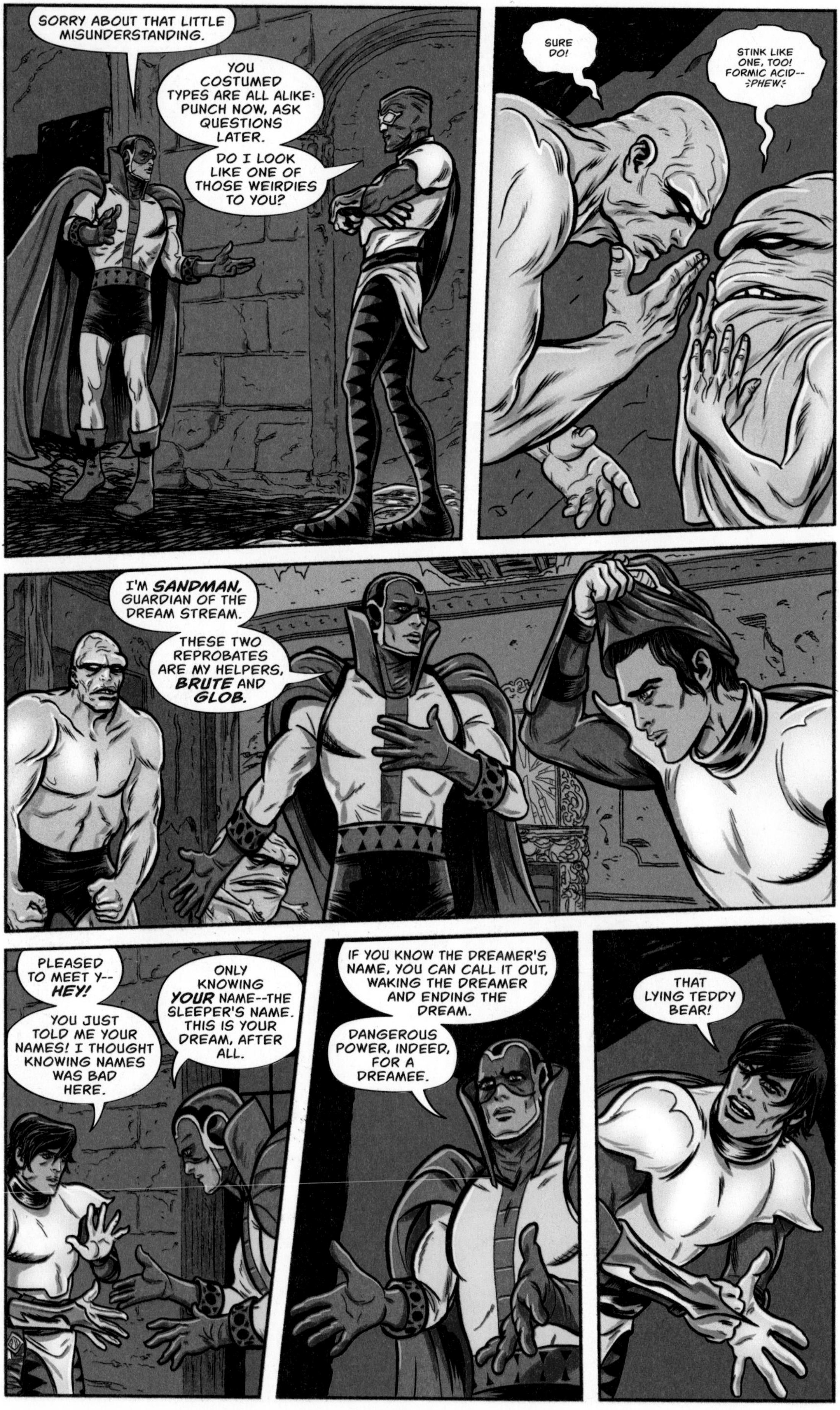
SORRY ABOUT THAT LITTLE MISUNDERSTANDING.
YOU COSTUMED TYPES ARE ALL ALIKE: PUNCH NOW, ASK QUESTIONS LATER.
DO I LOOK LIKE ONE OF THOSE WEIRDIES TO YOU?
SURE DO!
STINK LIKE ONE, TOO! FORMIC ACID-- PHEW
I'M SANDMAN, GUARDIAN OF THE DREAM STREAM.
THESE TWO REPROBATES ARE MY HELPERS, BRUTE AND GLOB.
PLEASED TO MEET Y-- HEY!
YOU JUST TOLD ME YOUR NAMES! I THOUGHT KNOWING NAMES WAS BAD HERE.
ONLY KNOWING YOUR NAME--THE SLEEPER'S NAME. THIS IS YOUR DREAM, AFTER ALL.
IF YOU KNOW THE DREAMER'S NAME, YOU CAN CALL IT OUT, WAKING THE DREAMER AND ENDING THE DREAM.
DANGEROUS POWER, INDEED, FOR A DREAMEE.
THAT LYING TEDDY BEAR!

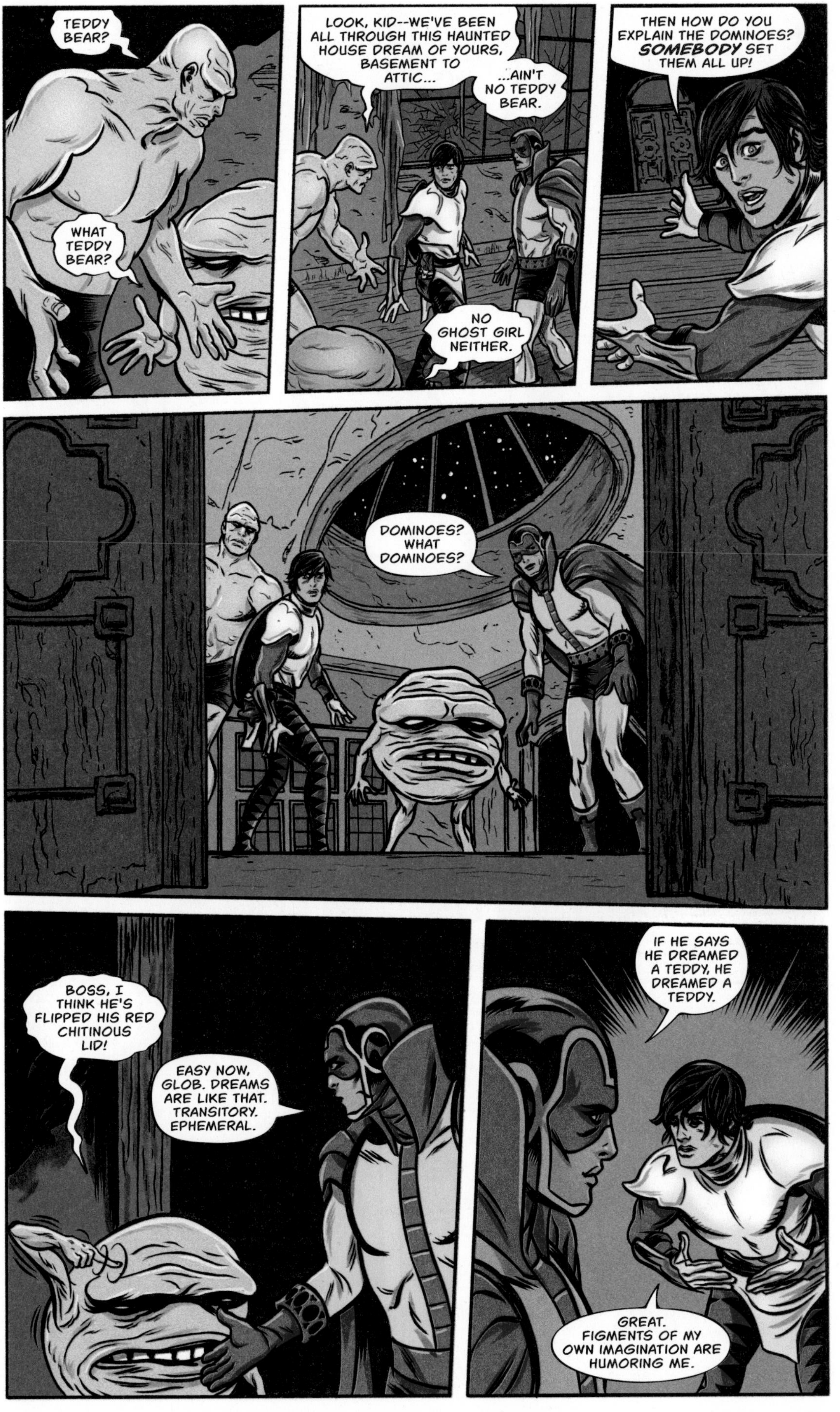
TEDDY BEAR?
WHAT TEDDY BEAR?
LOOK, KID--WE'VE BEEN ALL THROUGH THIS HAUNTED HOUSE DREAM OF YOURS, BASEMENT TO ATTIC...
...AIN'T NO TEDDY BEAR.
NO GHOST GIRL NEITHER.
THEN HOW DO YOU EXPLAIN THE DOMINOES? *SOMEBODY* SET THEM ALL UP!
DOMINOES? WHAT DOMINOES?
BOSS, I THINK HE'S FLIPPED HIS RED CHITINOUS LID!
EASY NOW, GLOB. DREAMS ARE LIKE THAT. TRANSITORY. EPHEMERAL.
IF HE SAYS HE DREAMED A TEDDY, HE DREAMED A TEDDY.
GREAT. FIGMENTS OF MY OWN IMAGINATION ARE HUMORING ME.

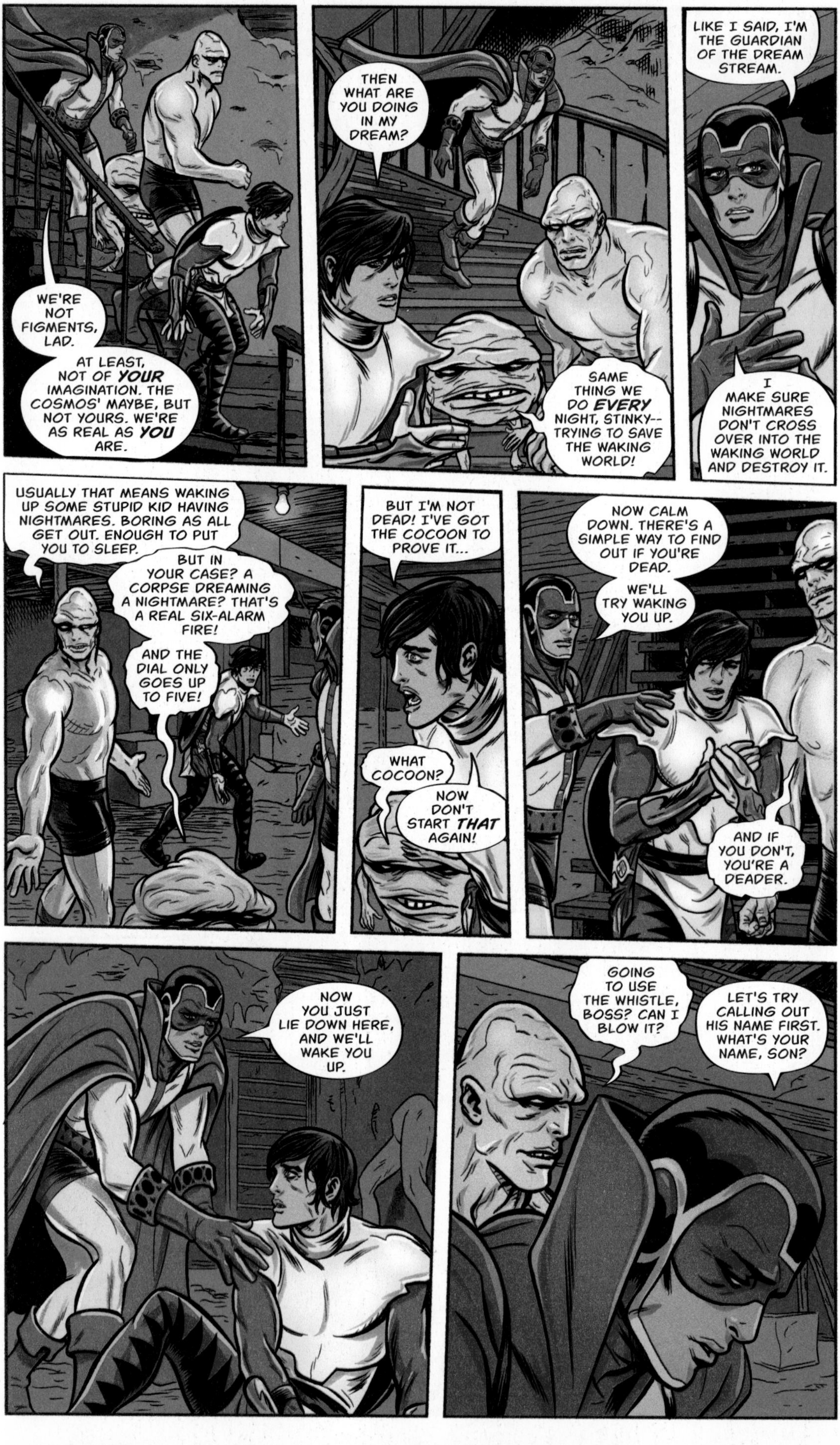
WE'RE NOT FIGMENTS, LAD.
AT LEAST, NOT OF YOUR IMAGINATION. THE COSMOS' MAYBE, BUT NOT YOURS. WE'RE AS REAL AS YOU ARE.
THEN WHAT ARE YOU DOING IN MY DREAM?
SAME THING WE DO EVERY NIGHT, STINKY-- TRYING TO SAVE THE WAKING WORLD!
LIKE I SAID, I'M THE GUARDIAN OF THE DREAM STREAM.
I MAKE SURE NIGHTMARES DON'T CROSS OVER INTO THE WAKING WORLD AND DESTROY IT.
USUALLY THAT MEANS WAKING UP SOME STUPID KID HAVING NIGHTMARES. BORING AS ALL GET OUT. ENOUGH TO PUT YOU TO SLEEP.
BUT IN YOUR CASE? A CORPSE DREAMING A NIGHTMARE? THAT'S A REAL SIX-ALARM FIRE!
AND THE DIAL ONLY GOES UP TO FIVE!
BUT I'M NOT DEAD! I'VE GOT THE COCOON TO PROVE IT...
WHAT COCOON?
NOW DON'T START THAT AGAIN!
NOW CALM DOWN. THERE'S A SIMPLE WAY TO FIND OUT IF YOU'RE DEAD.
WE'LL TRY WAKING YOU UP.
AND IF YOU DON'T, YOU'RE A DEADER.
NOW YOU JUST LIE DOWN HERE, AND WE'LL WAKE YOU UP.
GOING TO USE THE WHISTLE, BOSS? CAN I BLOW IT?
LET'S TRY CALLING OUT HIS NAME FIRST. WHAT'S YOUR NAME, SON?

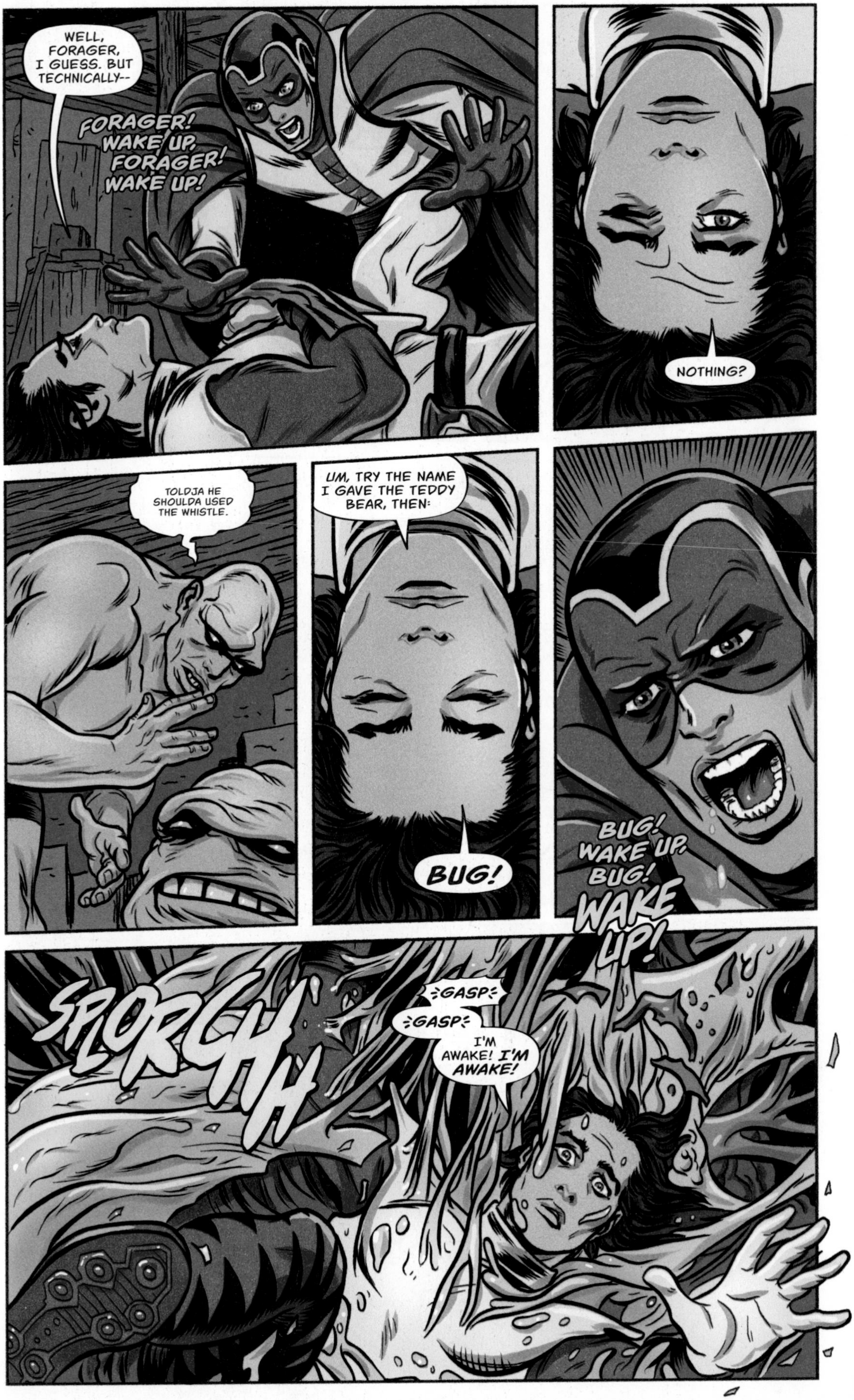
WELL, FORAGER, I GUESS. BUT TECHNICALLY--
FORAGER! WAKE UP, FORAGER! WAKE UP!
NOTHING?
TOLDJA HE SHOULDA USED THE WHISTLE.
UM, TRY THE NAME I GAVE THE TEDDY BEAR, THEN:
BUG!
BUG! WAKE UP, BUG! WAKE UP!
SPLORCHH
GASP
GASP
I'M AWAKE! I'M AWAKE!

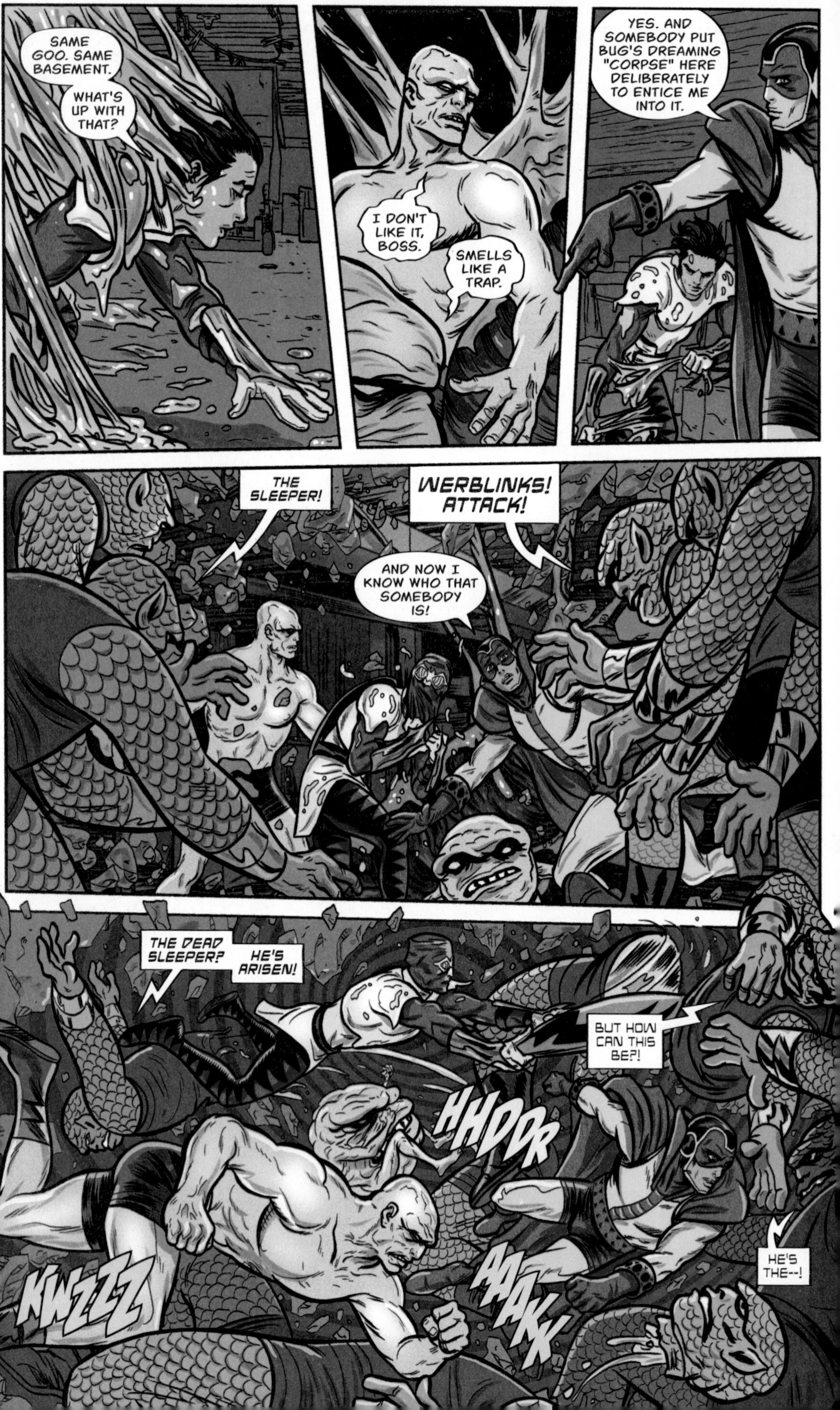
SAME GOO. SAME BASEMENT.
WHAT'S UP WITH THAT?
I DON'T LIKE IT, BOSS.
SMELLS LIKE A TRAP.
YES. AND SOMEBODY PUT BUG'S DREAMING "CORPSE" HERE DELIBERATELY TO ENTICE ME INTO IT.
THE SLEEPER!
WERBLINKS! ATTACK!
AND NOW I KNOW WHO THAT SOMEBODY IS!
THE DEAD SLEEPER?
HE'S ARISEN!
BUT HOW CAN THIS BE?!
HHDDR
KWZZZZ
AAAKK
HE'S THE--!

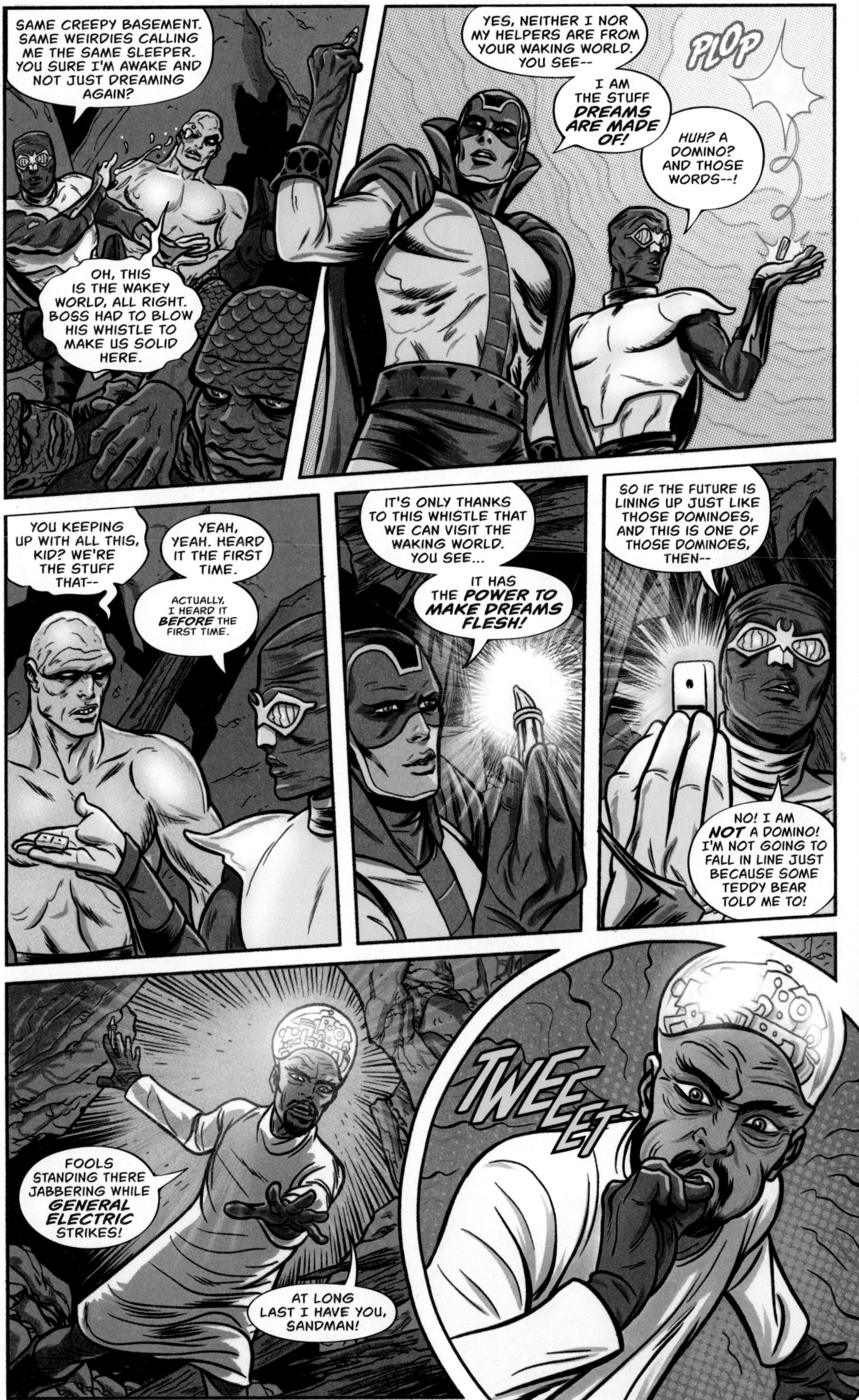
SAME CREEPY BASEMENT. SAME WEIRDIES CALLING ME THE SAME SLEEPER. YOU SURE I'M AWAKE AND NOT JUST DREAMING AGAIN?
OH, THIS IS THE WAKEY WORLD, ALL RIGHT. BOSS HAD TO BLOW HIS WHISTLE TO MAKE US SOLID HERE.
YES, NEITHER I NOR MY HELPERS ARE FROM YOUR WAKING WORLD. YOU SEE--
I AM THE STUFF DREAMS ARE MADE OF!
PLOP
HUH? A DOMINO? AND THOSE WORDS--!
YOU KEEPING UP WITH ALL THIS, KID? WE'RE THE STUFF THAT--
YEAH, YEAH. HEARD IT THE FIRST TIME.
ACTUALLY, I HEARD IT BEFORE THE FIRST TIME.
IT'S ONLY THANKS TO THIS WHISTLE THAT WE CAN VISIT THE WAKING WORLD. YOU SEE...
IT HAS THE POWER TO MAKE DREAMS FLESH!
SO IF THE FUTURE IS LINING UP JUST LIKE THOSE DOMINOES, AND THIS IS ONE OF THOSE DOMINOES, THEN--
NO! I AM NOT A DOMINO! I'M NOT GOING TO FALL IN LINE JUST BECAUSE SOME TEDDY BEAR TOLD ME TO!
FOOLS STANDING THERE JABBERING WHILE GENERAL ELECTRIC STRIKES!
AT LONG LAST I HAVE YOU, SANDMAN!
TWEEEET

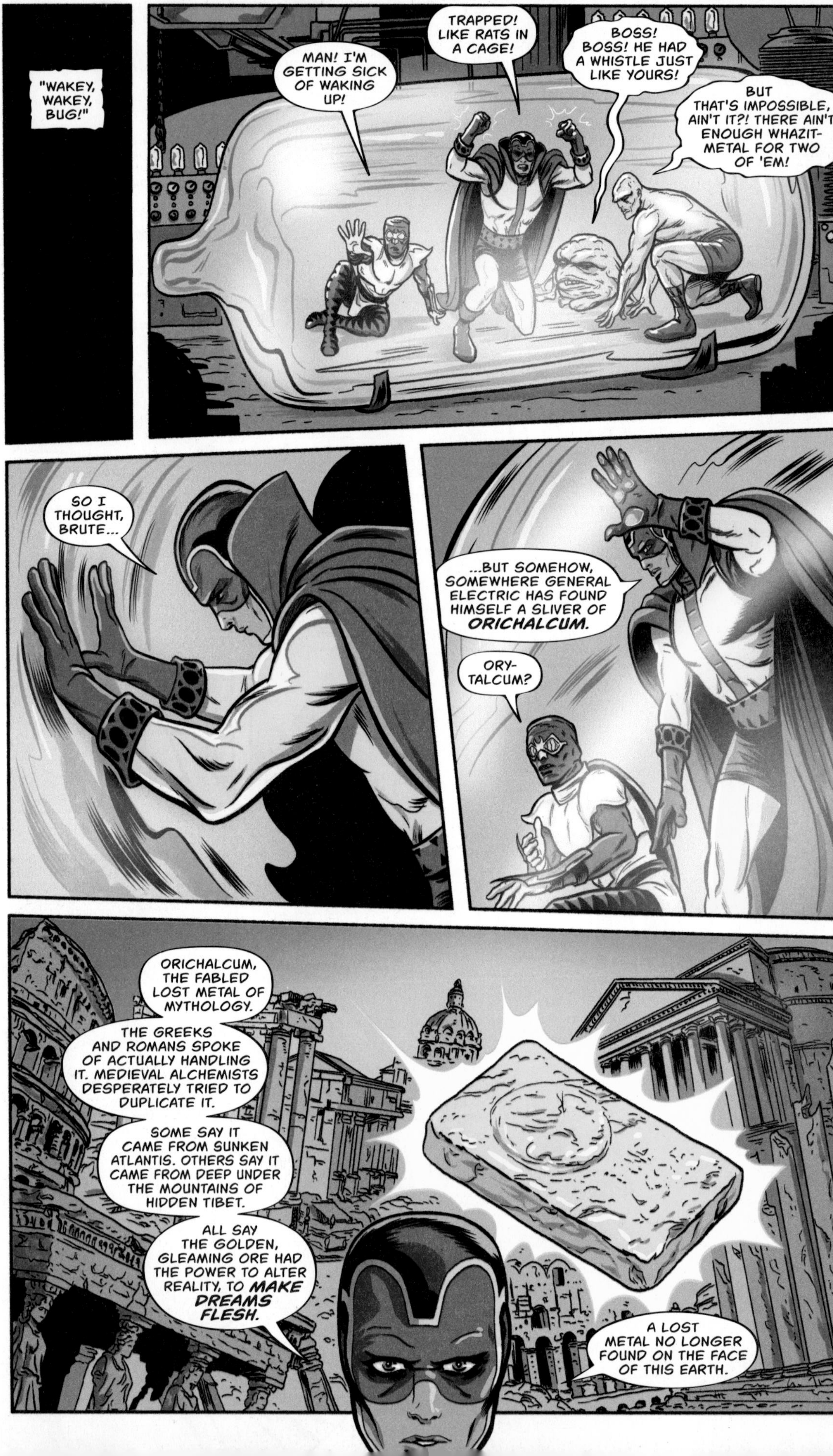
"WAKEY, WAKEY, BUG!"
MAN! I'M GETTING SICK OF WAKING UP!
TRAPPED! LIKE RATS IN A CAGE!
BOSS! BOSS! HE HAD A WHISTLE JUST LIKE YOURS!
BUT THAT'S IMPOSSIBLE, AIN'T IT?! THERE AIN'T ENOUGH WHAZIT-METAL FOR TWO OF 'EM!
SO I THOUGHT, BRUTE...
...BUT SOMEHOW, SOMEWHERE GENERAL ELECTRIC HAS FOUND HIMSELF A SLIVER OF ORICHALCUM.
ORY-TALCUM?
ORICHALCUM, THE FABLED LOST METAL OF MYTHOLOGY.
THE GREEKS AND ROMANS SPOKE OF ACTUALLY HANDLING IT. MEDIEVAL ALCHEMISTS DESPERATELY TRIED TO DUPLICATE IT.
SOME SAY IT CAME FROM SUNKEN ATLANTIS. OTHERS SAY IT CAME FROM DEEP UNDER THE MOUNTAINS OF HIDDEN TIBET.
ALL SAY THE GOLDEN, GLEAMING ORE HAD THE POWER TO ALTER REALITY, TO MAKE DREAMS FLESH.
A LOST METAL NO LONGER FOUND ON THE FACE OF THIS EARTH.

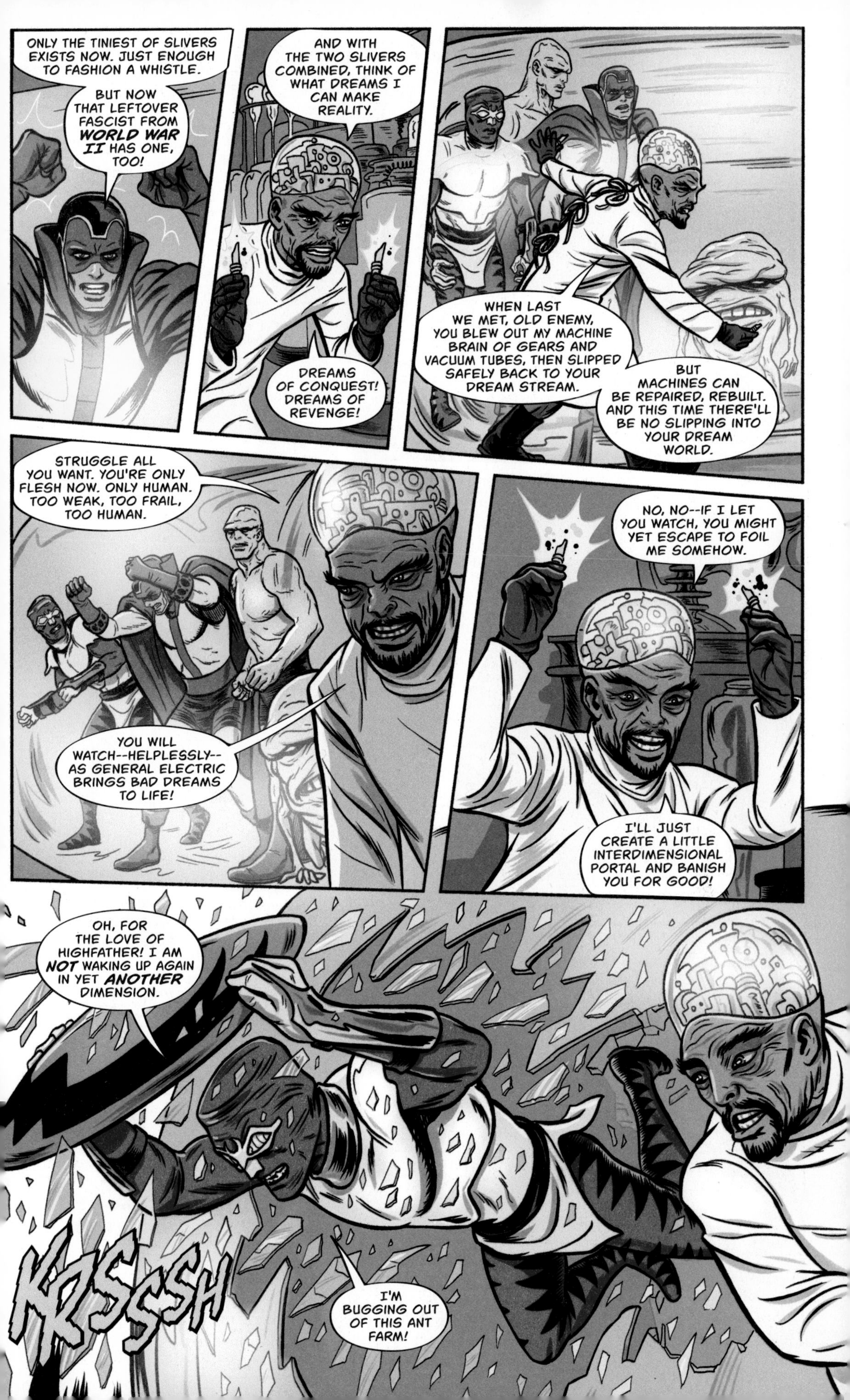
ONLY THE TINIEST OF SLIVERS EXISTS NOW. JUST ENOUGH TO FASHION A WHISTLE.
BUT NOW THAT LEFTOVER FASCIST FROM WORLD WAR II HAS ONE, TOO!
AND WITH THE TWO SLIVERS COMBINED, THINK OF WHAT DREAMS I CAN MAKE REALITY.
DREAMS OF CONQUEST! DREAMS OF REVENGE!
WHEN LAST WE MET, OLD ENEMY, YOU BLEW OUT MY MACHINE BRAIN OF GEARS AND VACUUM TUBES, THEN SLIPPED SAFELY BACK TO YOUR DREAM STREAM.
BUT MACHINES CAN BE REPAIRED, REBUILT. AND THIS TIME THERE'LL BE NO SLIPPING INTO YOUR DREAM WORLD.
STRUGGLE ALL YOU WANT. YOU'RE ONLY FLESH NOW. ONLY HUMAN. TOO WEAK, TOO FRAIL, TOO HUMAN.
YOU WILL WATCH--HELPLESSLY--AS GENERAL ELECTRIC BRINGS BAD DREAMS TO LIFE!
NO, NO--IF I LET YOU WATCH, YOU MIGHT YET ESCAPE TO FOIL ME SOMEHOW.
I'LL JUST CREATE A LITTLE INTERDIMENSIONAL PORTAL AND BANISH YOU FOR GOOD!
OH, FOR THE LOVE OF HIGHFATHER! I AM NOT WAKING UP AGAIN IN YET ANOTHER DIMENSION.
KRSSSH
I'M BUGGING OUT OF THIS ANT FARM!

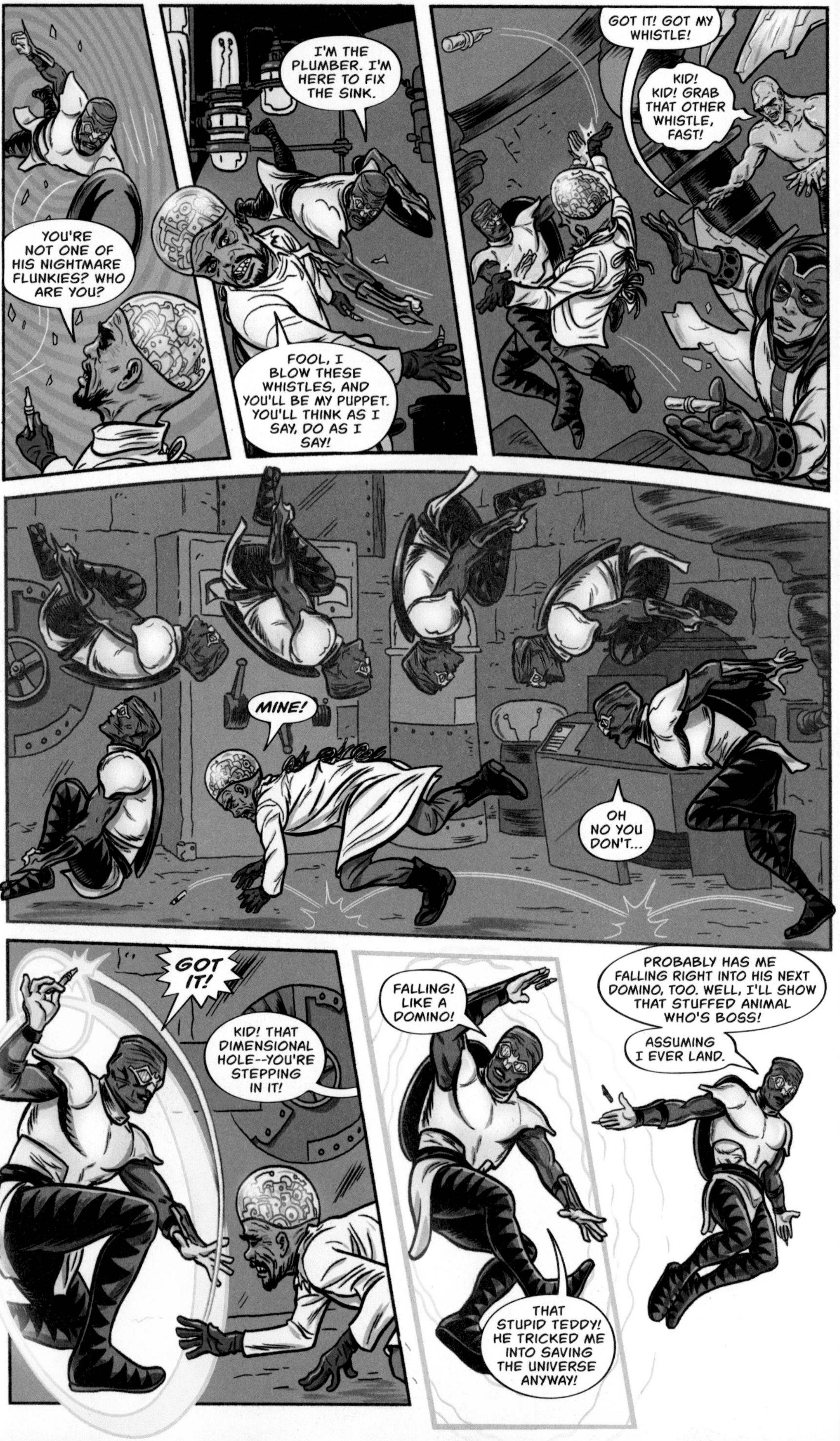
YOU'RE NOT ONE OF HIS NIGHTMARE FLUNKIES? WHO ARE YOU?
I'M THE PLUMBER. I'M HERE TO FIX THE SINK.
FOOL, I BLOW THESE WHISTLES, AND YOU'LL BE MY PUPPET. YOU'LL THINK AS I SAY, DO AS I SAY!
GOT IT! GOT MY WHISTLE!
KID! KID! GRAB THAT OTHER WHISTLE, FAST!
MINE!
OH NO YOU DON'T...
GOT IT!
KID! THAT DIMENSIONAL HOLE--YOU'RE STEPPING IN IT!
FALLING! LIKE A DOMINO!
THAT STUPID TEDDY! HE TRICKED ME INTO SAVING THE UNIVERSE ANYWAY!
PROBABLY HAS ME FALLING RIGHT INTO HIS NEXT DOMINO, TOO. WELL, I'LL SHOW THAT STUFFED ANIMAL WHO'S BOSS!
ASSUMING I EVER LAND.

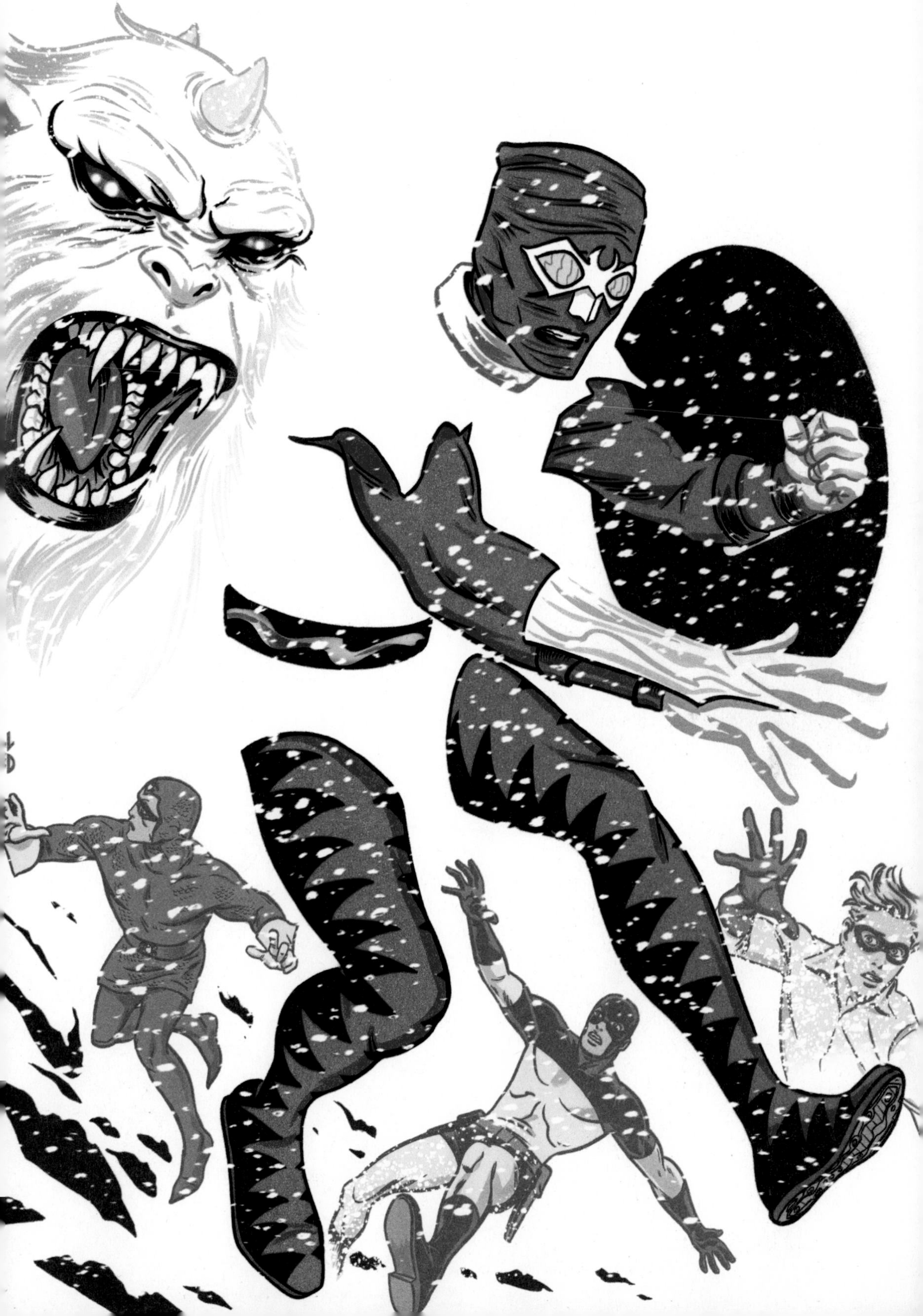

Variant cover art for issue #2 by Evan "Doc" Shaner

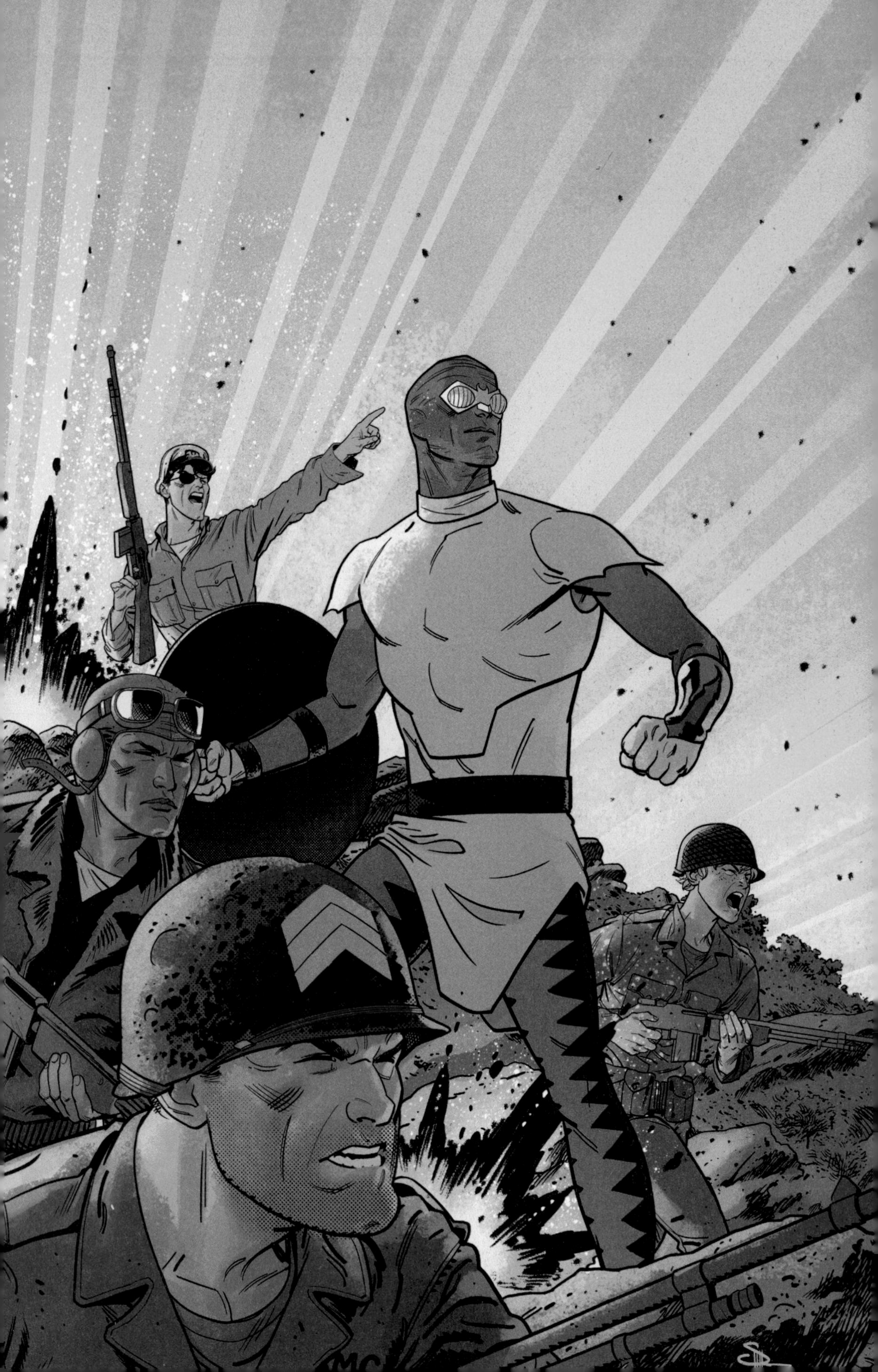

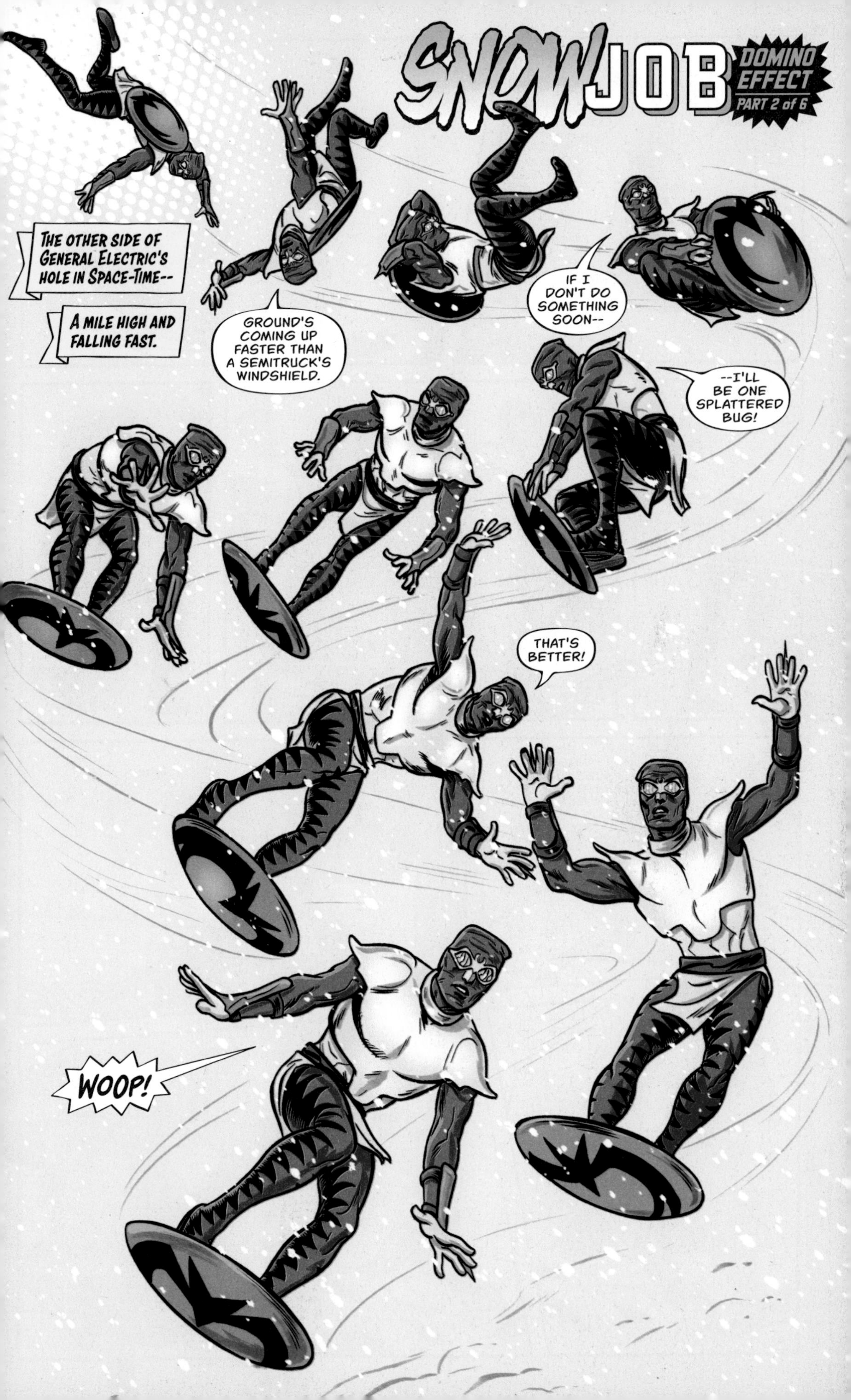
SNOW JOB
DOMINO EFFECT PART 2 of 6
THE OTHER SIDE OF GENERAL ELECTRIC'S HOLE IN SPACE-TIME--
A MILE HIGH AND FALLING FAST.
GROUND'S COMING UP FASTER THAN A SEMITRUCK'S WINDSHIELD.
IF I DON'T DO SOMETHING SOON--
--I'LL BE ONE SPLATTERED BUG!
THAT'S BETTER!
WOOP!

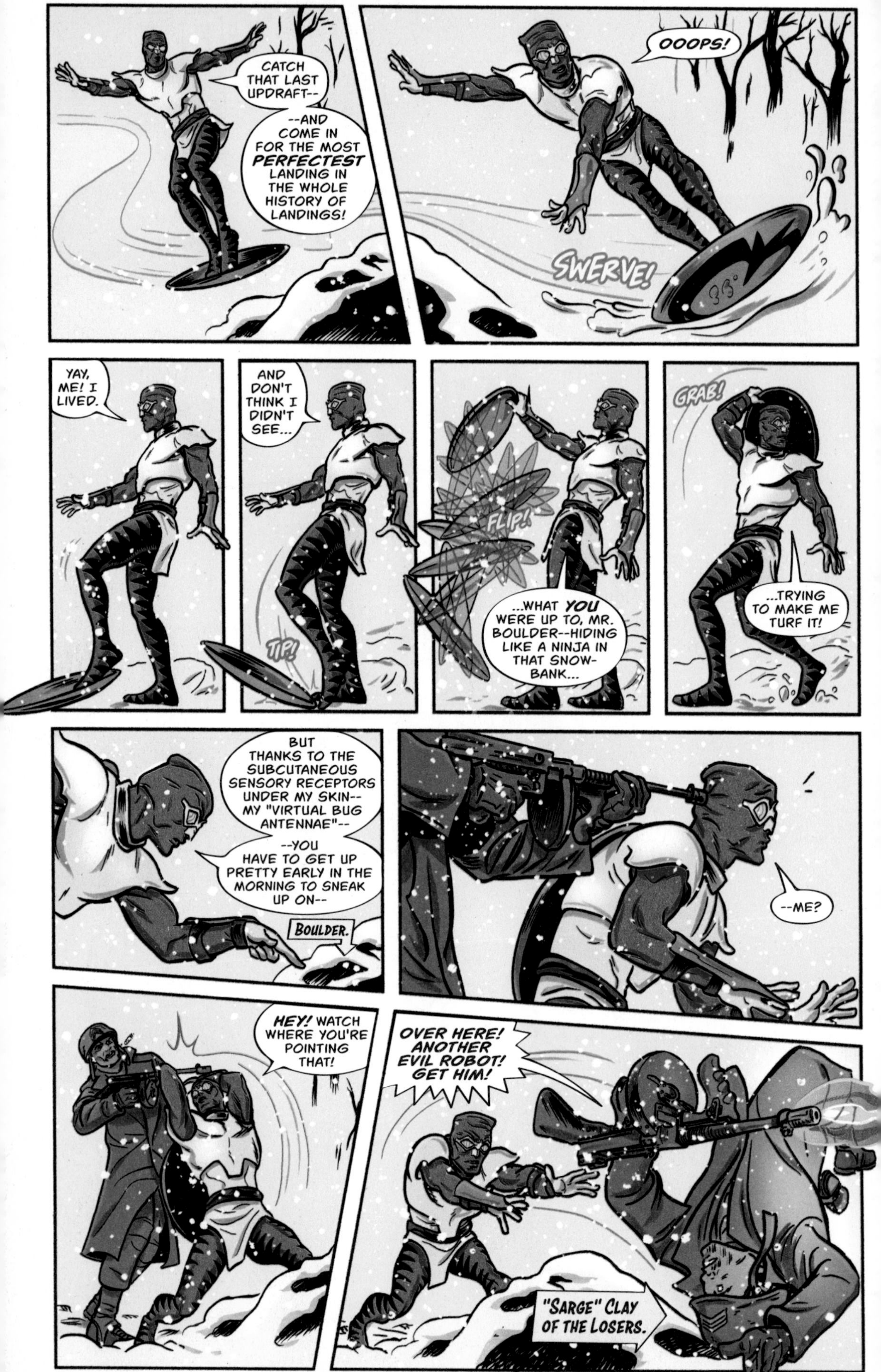
CATCH THAT LAST UPDRAFT--
--AND COME IN FOR THE MOST PERFECTEST LANDING IN THE WHOLE HISTORY OF LANDINGS!
OOOPS!
SWERVE!
YAY, ME! I LIVED.
AND DON'T THINK I DIDN'T SEE...
TIP!
FLIP!
...WHAT YOU WERE UP TO, MR. BOULDER--HIDING LIKE A NINJA IN THAT SNOW-BANK...
GRAB!
...TRYING TO MAKE ME TURF IT!
BUT THANKS TO THE SUBCUTANEOUS SENSORY RECEPTORS UNDER MY SKIN-- MY "VIRTUAL BUG ANTENNAE"--
--YOU HAVE TO GET UP PRETTY EARLY IN THE MORNING TO SNEAK UP ON--
BOULDER.
!
--ME?
HEY! WATCH WHERE YOU'RE POINTING THAT!
OVER HERE! ANOTHER EVIL ROBOT! GET HIM!
"SARGE" CLAY OF THE LOSERS.

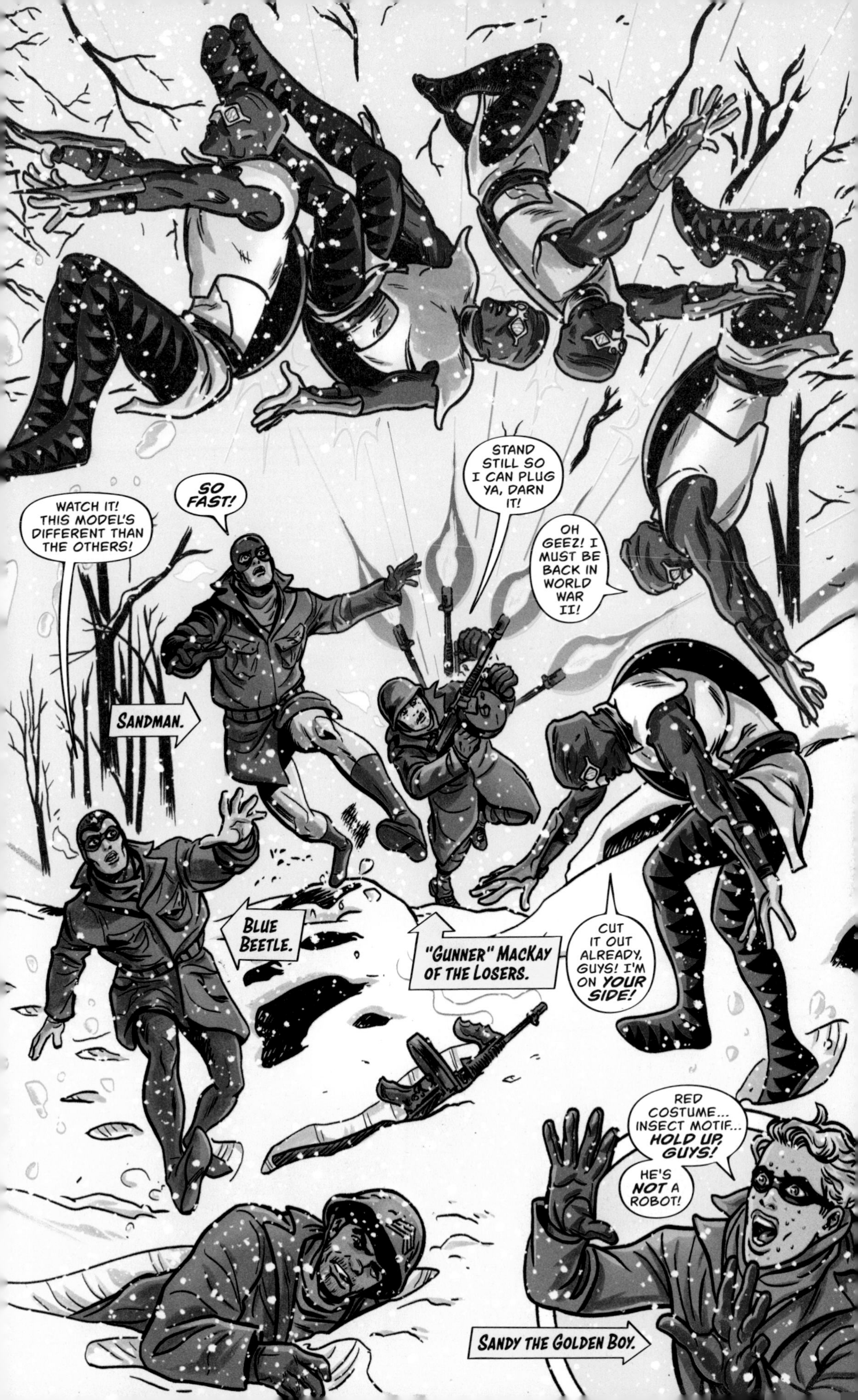

WATCH IT! THIS MODEL'S DIFFERENT THAN THE OTHERS!
SO FAST!
STAND STILL SO I CAN PLUG YA, DARN IT!
OH GEEZ! I MUST BE BACK IN WORLD WAR II!
SANDMAN.
BLUE BEETLE.
"GUNNER" MACKAY OF THE LOSERS.
CUT IT OUT ALREADY, GUYS! I'M ON YOUR SIDE!
RED COSTUME... INSECT MOTIF... HOLD UP, GUYS!
HE'S NOT A ROBOT!
SANDY THE GOLDEN BOY.

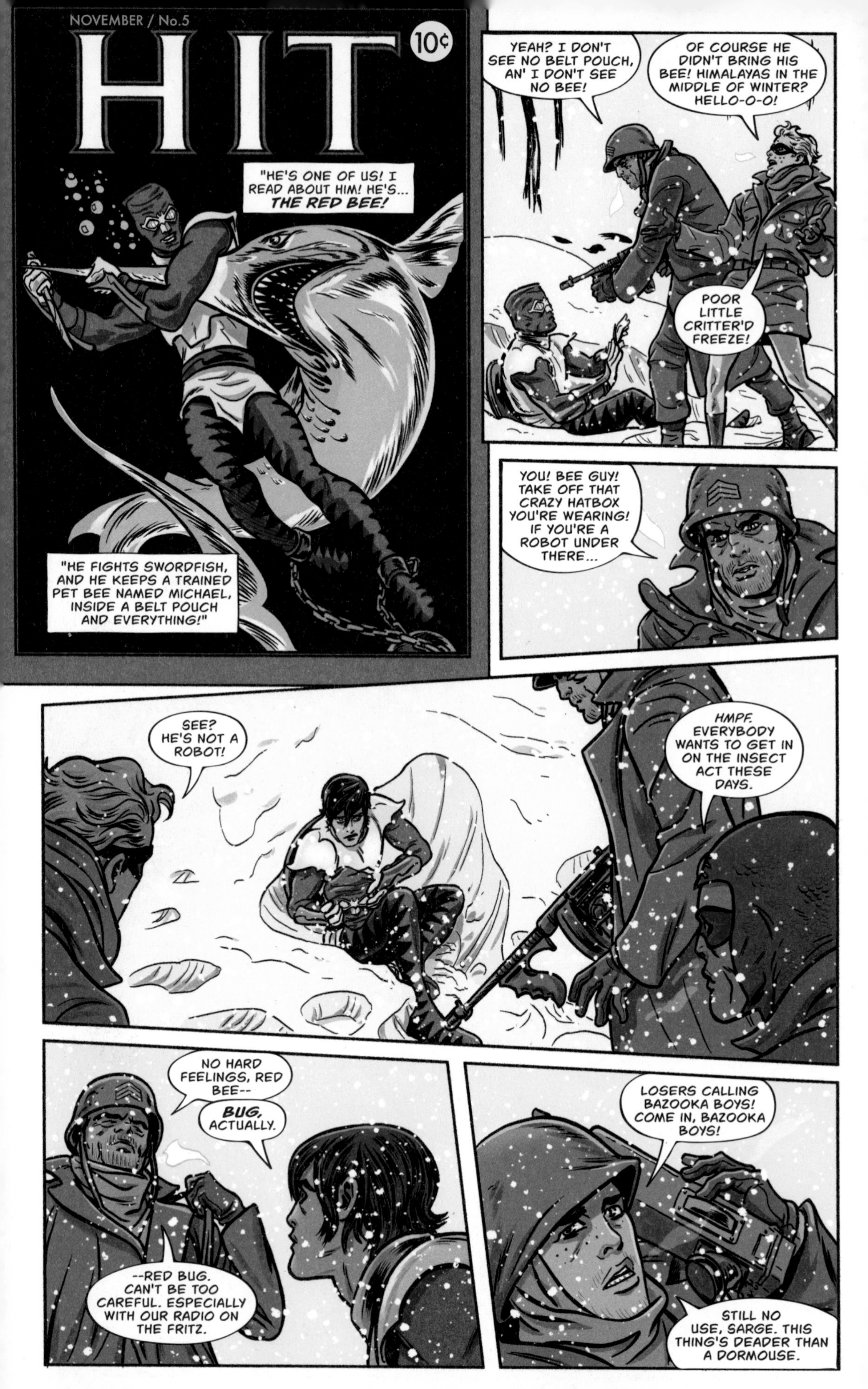
NOVEMBER / No.5
HIT
10¢
"HE'S ONE OF US! I READ ABOUT HIM! HE'S... THE RED BEE!
"HE FIGHTS SWORDFISH, AND HE KEEPS A TRAINED PET BEE NAMED MICHAEL, INSIDE A BELT POUCH AND EVERYTHING!"
YEAH? I DON'T SEE NO BELT POUCH, AN' I DON'T SEE NO BEE!
OF COURSE HE DIDN'T BRING HIS BEE! HIMALAYAS IN THE MIDDLE OF WINTER? HELLO-O-O!
POOR LITTLE CRITTER'D FREEZE!
YOU! BEE GUY! TAKE OFF THAT CRAZY HATBOX YOU'RE WEARING! IF YOU'RE A ROBOT UNDER THERE...
SEE? HE'S NOT A ROBOT!
HMPF. EVERYBODY WANTS TO GET IN ON THE INSECT ACT THESE DAYS.
NO HARD FEELINGS, RED BEE--
BUG, ACTUALLY.
--RED BUG. CAN'T BE TOO CAREFUL. ESPECIALLY WITH OUR RADIO ON THE FRITZ.
LOSERS CALLING BAZOOKA BOYS! COME IN, BAZOOKA BOYS!
STILL NO USE, SARGE. THIS THING'S DEADER THAN A DORMOUSE.

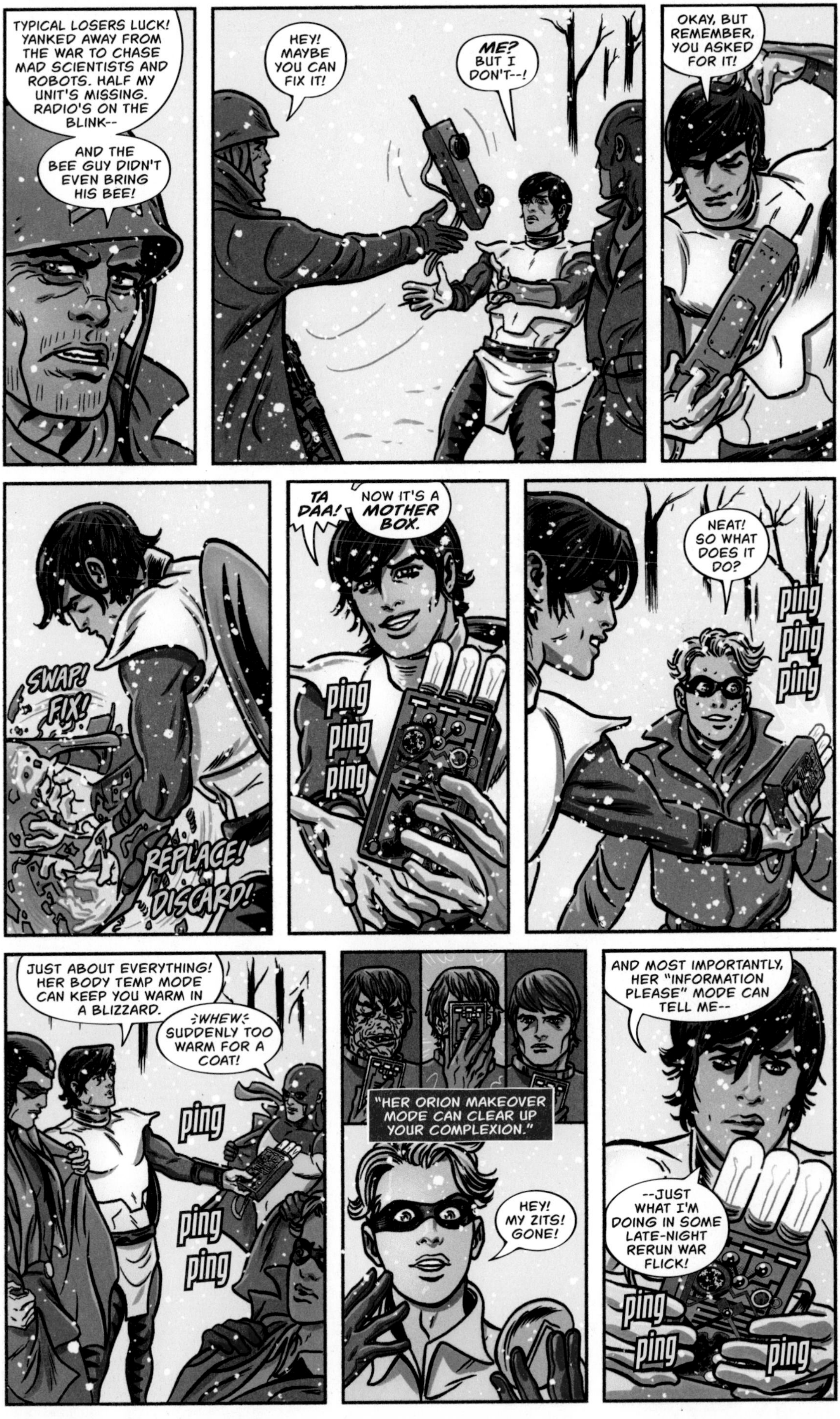
TYPICAL LOSERS LUCK! YANKED AWAY FROM THE WAR TO CHASE MAD SCIENTISTS AND ROBOTS. HALF MY UNIT'S MISSING. RADIO'S ON THE BLINK--
AND THE BEE GUY DIDN'T EVEN BRING HIS BEE!
HEY! MAYBE YOU CAN FIX IT!
ME? BUT I DON'T--!
OKAY, BUT REMEMBER, YOU ASKED FOR IT!
SWAP! FIX!
REPLACE! DISCARD!
TA DAA!
NOW IT'S A MOTHER BOX.
ping ping ping
NEAT! SO WHAT DOES IT DO?
ping ping ping
JUST ABOUT EVERYTHING! HER BODY TEMP MODE CAN KEEP YOU WARM IN A BLIZZARD.
WHEW SUDDENLY TOO WARM FOR A COAT!
ping
ping ping
"HER ORION MAKEOVER MODE CAN CLEAR UP YOUR COMPLEXION."
HEY! MY ZITS! GONE!
AND MOST IMPORTANTLY, HER "INFORMATION PLEASE" MODE CAN TELL ME--
--JUST WHAT I'M DOING IN SOME LATE-NIGHT RERUN WAR FLICK!
ping ping ping

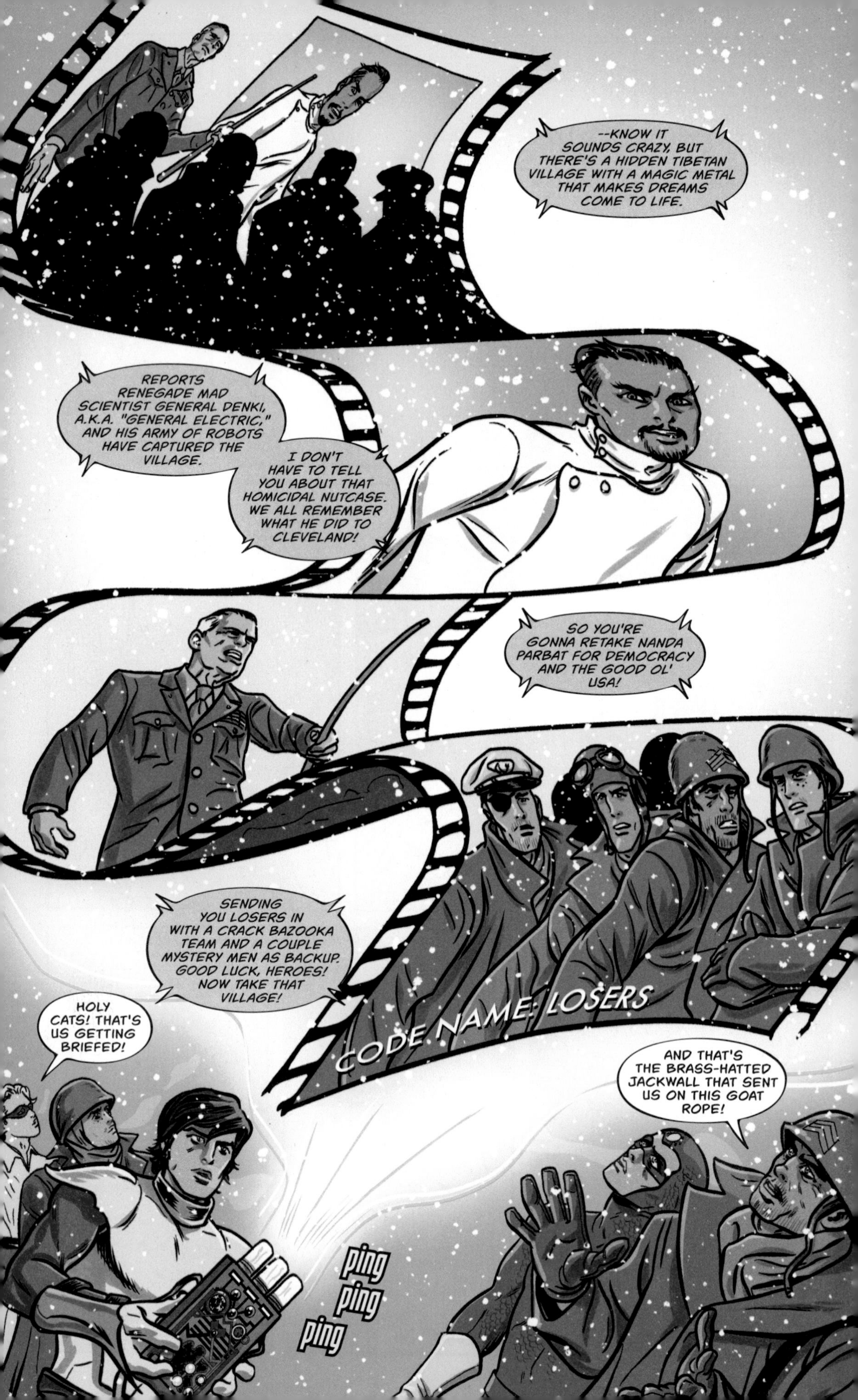
--KNOW IT SOUNDS CRAZY, BUT THERE'S A HIDDEN TIBETAN VILLAGE WITH A MAGIC METAL THAT MAKES DREAMS COME TO LIFE.
REPORTS RENEGADE MAD SCIENTIST GENERAL DENKI, A.K.A. "GENERAL ELECTRIC," AND HIS ARMY OF ROBOTS HAVE CAPTURED THE VILLAGE.
I DON'T HAVE TO TELL YOU ABOUT THAT HOMICIDAL NUTCASE. WE ALL REMEMBER WHAT HE DID TO CLEVELAND!
SO YOU'RE GONNA RETAKE NANDA PARBAT FOR DEMOCRACY AND THE GOOD OL' USA!
SENDING YOU LOSERS IN WITH A CRACK BAZOOKA TEAM AND A COUPLE MYSTERY MEN AS BACKUP. GOOD LUCK, HEROES! NOW TAKE THAT VILLAGE!
CODE NAME: LOSERS
HOLY CATS! THAT'S US GETTING BRIEFED!
AND THAT'S THE BRASS-HATTED JACKWALL THAT SENT US ON THIS GOAT ROPE!
ping ping ping

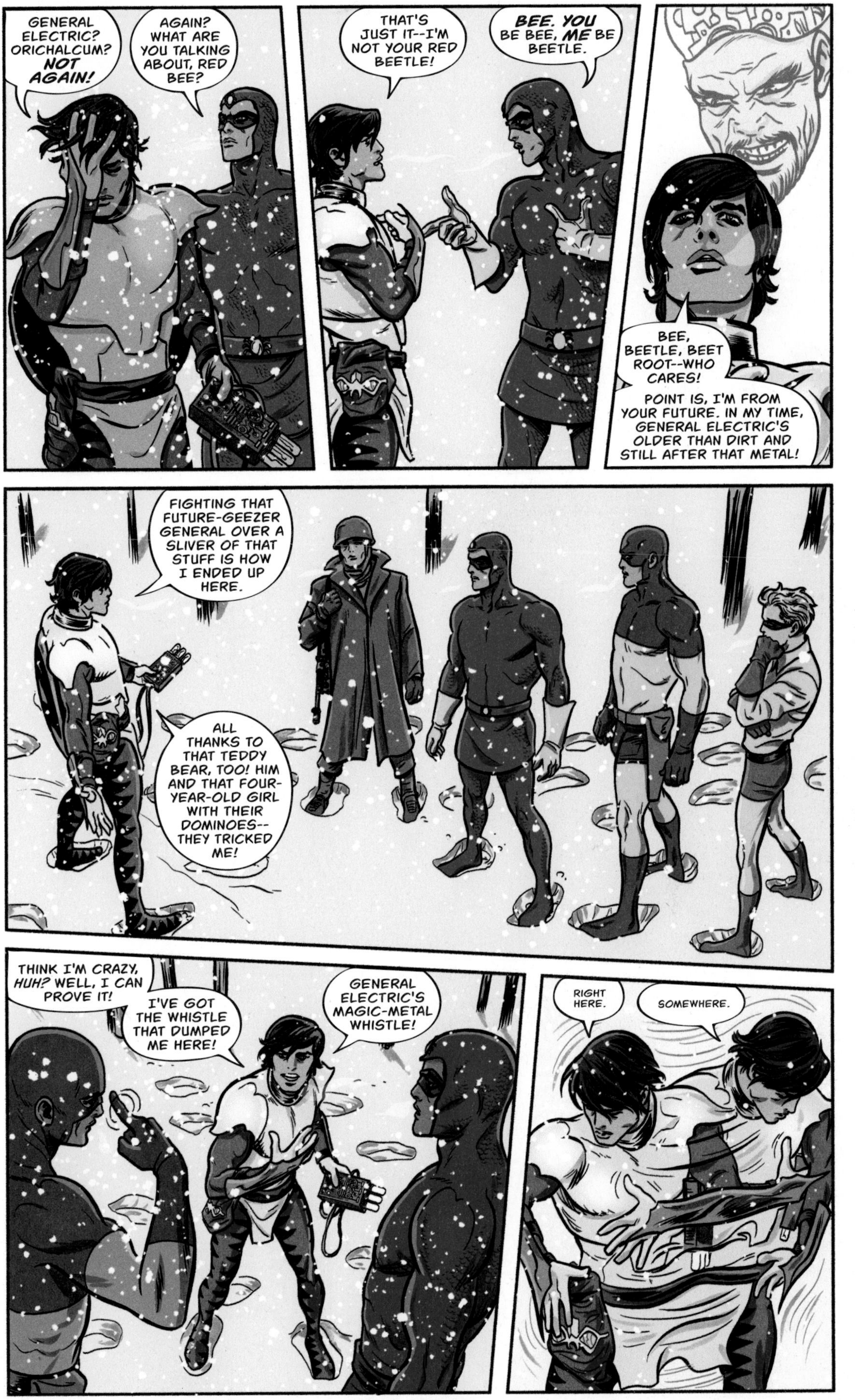
GENERAL ELECTRIC? ORICHALCUM? NOT AGAIN!
AGAIN? WHAT ARE YOU TALKING ABOUT, RED BEE?
THAT'S JUST IT--I'M NOT YOUR RED BEETLE!
BEE. YOU BE BEE, ME BE BEETLE.
BEE, BEETLE, BEET ROOT--WHO CARES!
POINT IS, I'M FROM YOUR FUTURE. IN MY TIME, GENERAL ELECTRIC'S OLDER THAN DIRT AND STILL AFTER THAT METAL!
FIGHTING THAT FUTURE-GEEZER GENERAL OVER A SLIVER OF THAT STUFF IS HOW I ENDED UP HERE.
ALL THANKS TO THAT TEDDY BEAR, TOO! HIM AND THAT FOUR-YEAR-OLD GIRL WITH THEIR DOMINOES--THEY TRICKED ME!
THINK I'M CRAZY, HUH? WELL, I CAN PROVE IT!
I'VE GOT THE WHISTLE THAT DUMPED ME HERE!
GENERAL ELECTRIC'S MAGIC-METAL WHISTLE!
RIGHT HERE.
SOMEWHERE.

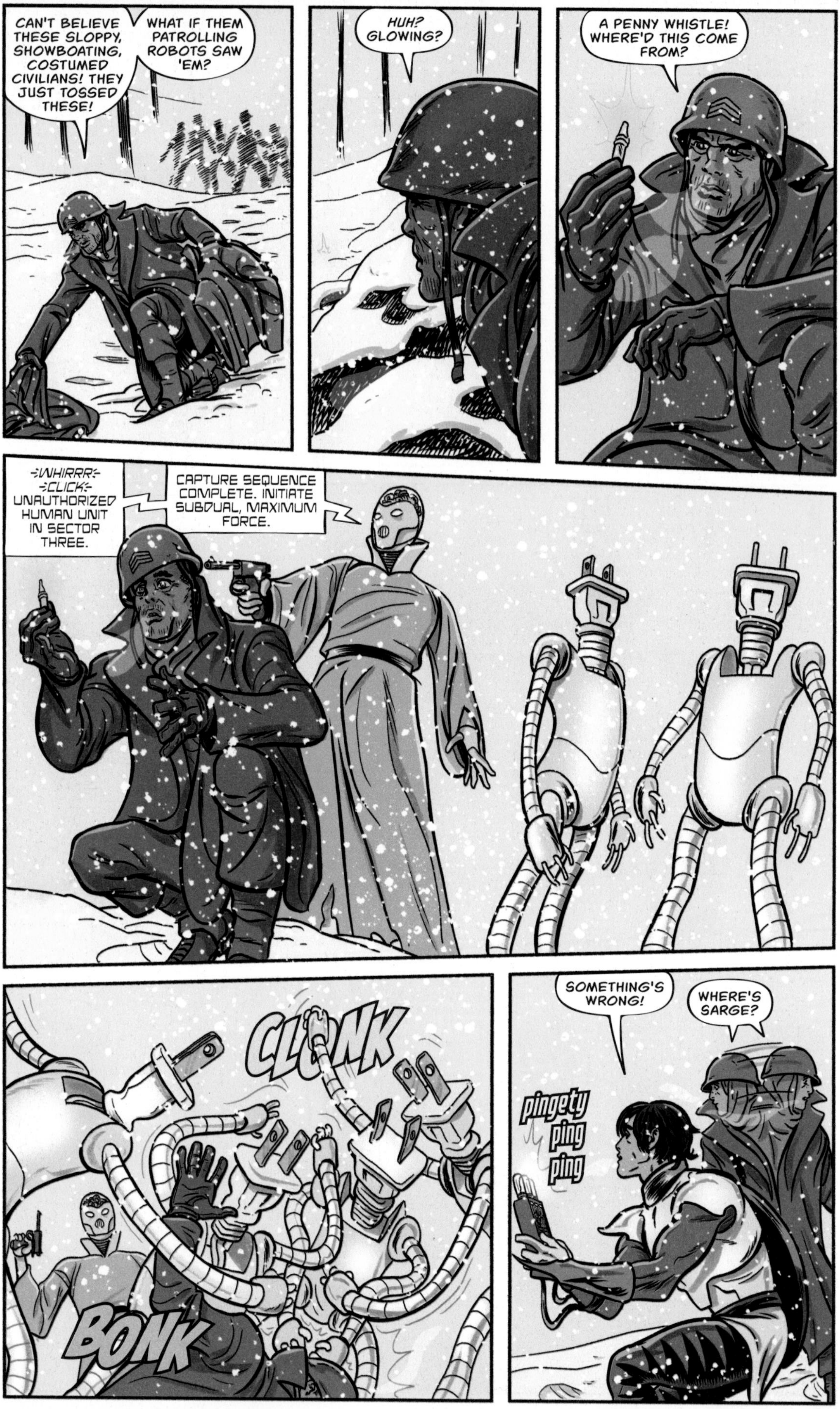
CAN'T BELIEVE THESE SLOPPY, SHOWBOATING, COSTUMED CIVILIANS! THEY JUST TOSSED THESE!
WHAT IF THEM PATROLLING ROBOTS SAW 'EM?
HUH? GLOWING?
A PENNY WHISTLE! WHERE'D THIS COME FROM?
-WHIRRR- -CLICK- UNAUTHORIZED HUMAN UNIT IN SECTOR THREE.
CAPTURE SEQUENCE COMPLETE. INITIATE SUBDUAL, MAXIMUM FORCE.
CLONK
BONK
SOMETHING'S WRONG!
WHERE'S SARGE?
pingety ping ping

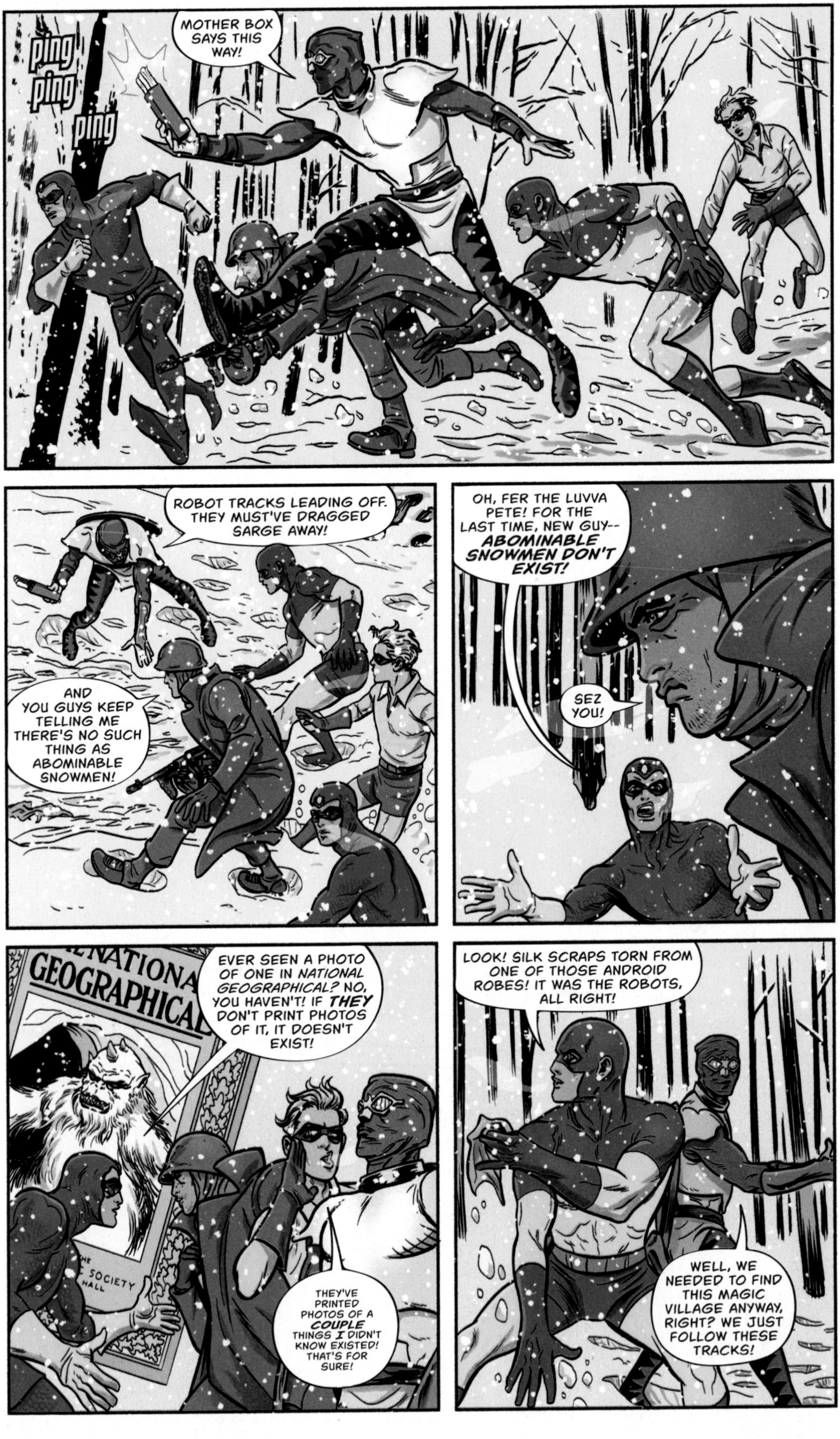
ping
ping
ping
MOTHER BOX SAYS THIS WAY!
ROBOT TRACKS LEADING OFF. THEY MUST'VE DRAGGED SARGE AWAY!
AND YOU GUYS KEEP TELLING ME THERE'S NO SUCH THING AS ABOMINABLE SNOWMEN!
OH, FER THE LUVVA PETE! FOR THE LAST TIME, NEW GUY-- ABOMINABLE SNOWMEN DON'T EXIST!
SEZ YOU!
NATIONAL GEOGRAPHICAL
EVER SEEN A PHOTO OF ONE IN NATIONAL GEOGRAPHICAL? NO, YOU HAVEN'T! IF THEY DON'T PRINT PHOTOS OF IT, IT DOESN'T EXIST!
THEY'VE PRINTED PHOTOS OF A COUPLE THINGS I DIDN'T KNOW EXISTED! THAT'S FOR SURE!
LOOK! SILK SCRAPS TORN FROM ONE OF THOSE ANDROID ROBES! IT WAS THE ROBOTS, ALL RIGHT!
WELL, WE NEEDED TO FIND THIS MAGIC VILLAGE ANYWAY, RIGHT? WE JUST FOLLOW THESE TRACKS!

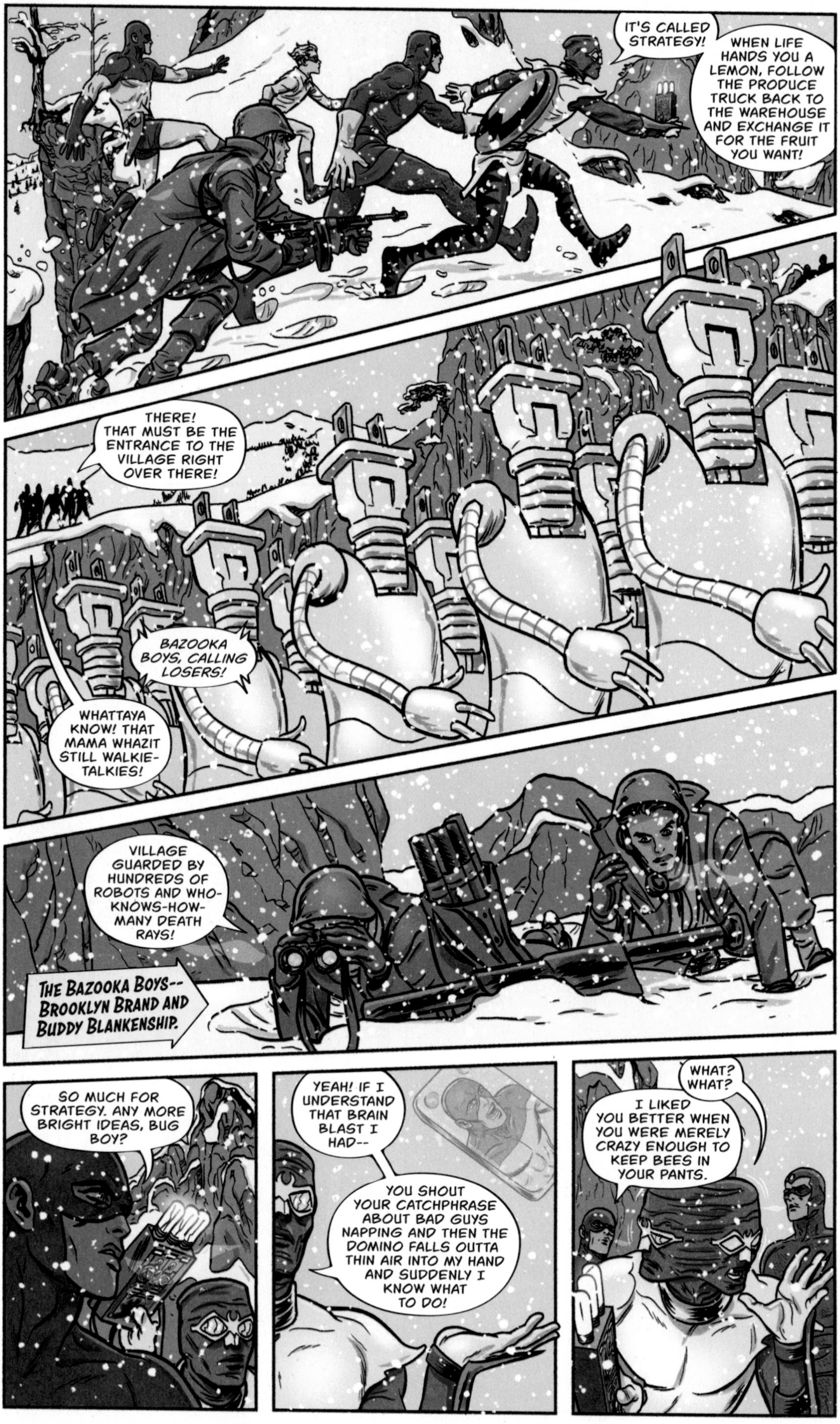
IT'S CALLED STRATEGY!
WHEN LIFE HANDS YOU A LEMON, FOLLOW THE PRODUCE TRUCK BACK TO THE WAREHOUSE AND EXCHANGE IT FOR THE FRUIT YOU WANT!
THERE! THAT MUST BE THE ENTRANCE TO THE VILLAGE RIGHT OVER THERE!
BAZOOKA BOYS, CALLING LOSERS!
WHATTAYA KNOW! THAT MAMA WHAZIT STILL WALKIE-TALKIES!
VILLAGE GUARDED BY HUNDREDS OF ROBOTS AND WHO-KNOWS-HOW-MANY DEATH RAYS!
THE BAZOOKA BOYS-- BROOKLYN BRAND AND BUDDY BLANKENSHIP.
SO MUCH FOR STRATEGY. ANY MORE BRIGHT IDEAS, BUG BOY?
YEAH! IF I UNDERSTAND THAT BRAIN BLAST I HAD--
YOU SHOUT YOUR CATCHPHRASE ABOUT BAD GUYS NAPPING AND THEN THE DOMINO FALLS OUTTA THIN AIR INTO MY HAND AND SUDDENLY I KNOW WHAT TO DO!
WHAT? WHAT?
I LIKED YOU BETTER WHEN YOU WERE MERELY CRAZY ENOUGH TO KEEP BEES IN YOUR PANTS.

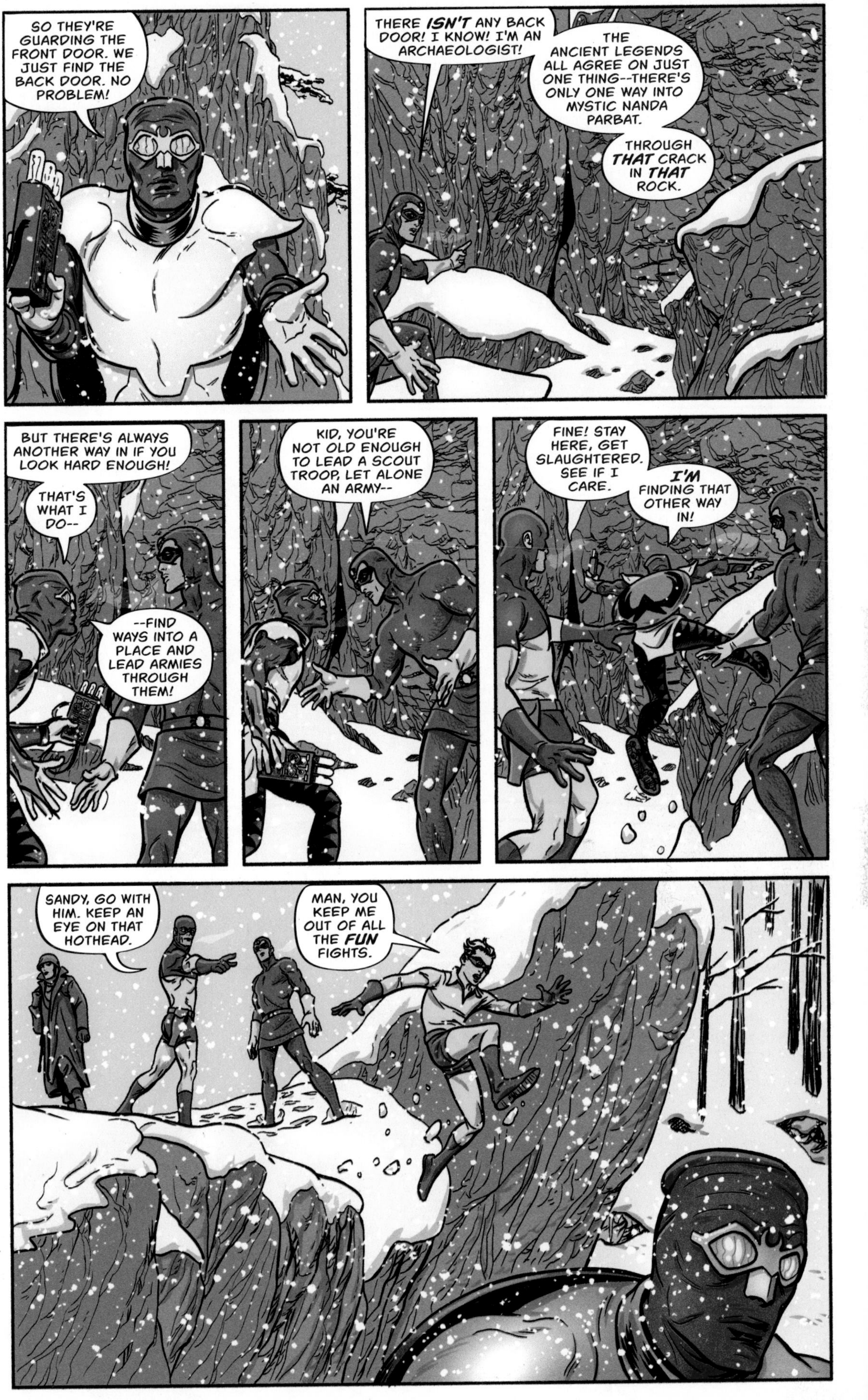
SO THEY'RE GUARDING THE FRONT DOOR. WE JUST FIND THE BACK DOOR. NO PROBLEM!
THERE ISN'T ANY BACK DOOR! I KNOW! I'M AN ARCHAEOLOGIST!
THE ANCIENT LEGENDS ALL AGREE ON JUST ONE THING--THERE'S ONLY ONE WAY INTO MYSTIC NANDA PARBAT.
THROUGH THAT CRACK IN THAT ROCK.
BUT THERE'S ALWAYS ANOTHER WAY IN IF YOU LOOK HARD ENOUGH!
THAT'S WHAT I DO--
--FIND WAYS INTO A PLACE AND LEAD ARMIES THROUGH THEM!
KID, YOU'RE NOT OLD ENOUGH TO LEAD A SCOUT TROOP, LET ALONE AN ARMY--
FINE! STAY HERE, GET SLAUGHTERED. SEE IF I CARE.
I'M FINDING THAT OTHER WAY IN!
SANDY, GO WITH HIM. KEEP AN EYE ON THAT HOTHEAD.
MAN, YOU KEEP ME OUT OF ALL THE FUN FIGHTS.

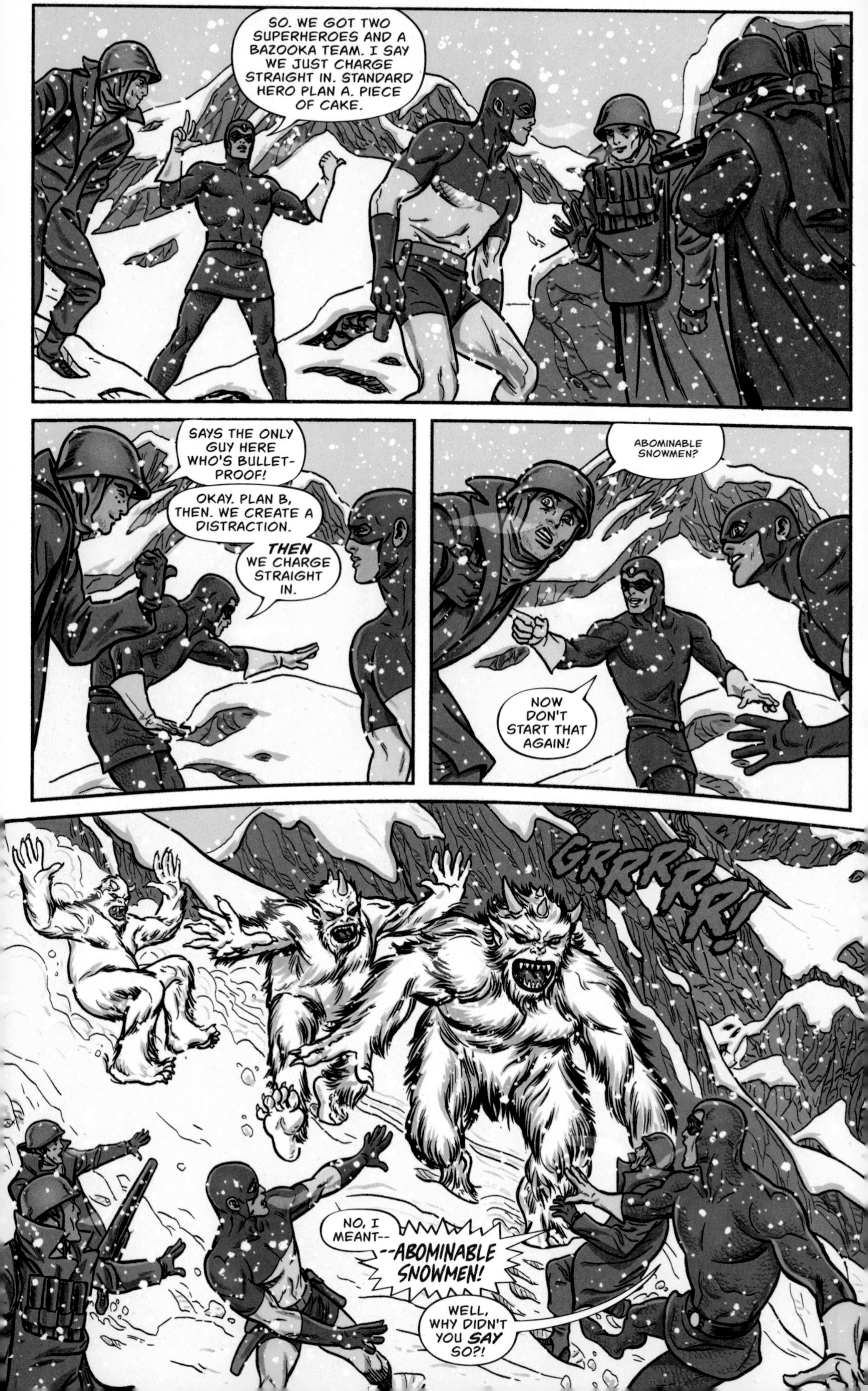
SO. WE GOT TWO SUPERHEROES AND A BAZOOKA TEAM. I SAY WE JUST CHARGE STRAIGHT IN. STANDARD HERO PLAN A. PIECE OF CAKE.
SAYS THE ONLY GUY HERE WHO'S BULLET-PROOF!
OKAY. PLAN B, THEN. WE CREATE A DISTRACTION.
THEN WE CHARGE STRAIGHT IN.
ABOMINABLE SNOWMEN?
NOW DON'T START THAT AGAIN!
GRRRRR!
NO, I MEANT--
--ABOMINABLE SNOWMEN!
WELL, WHY DIDN'T YOU SAY SO?!

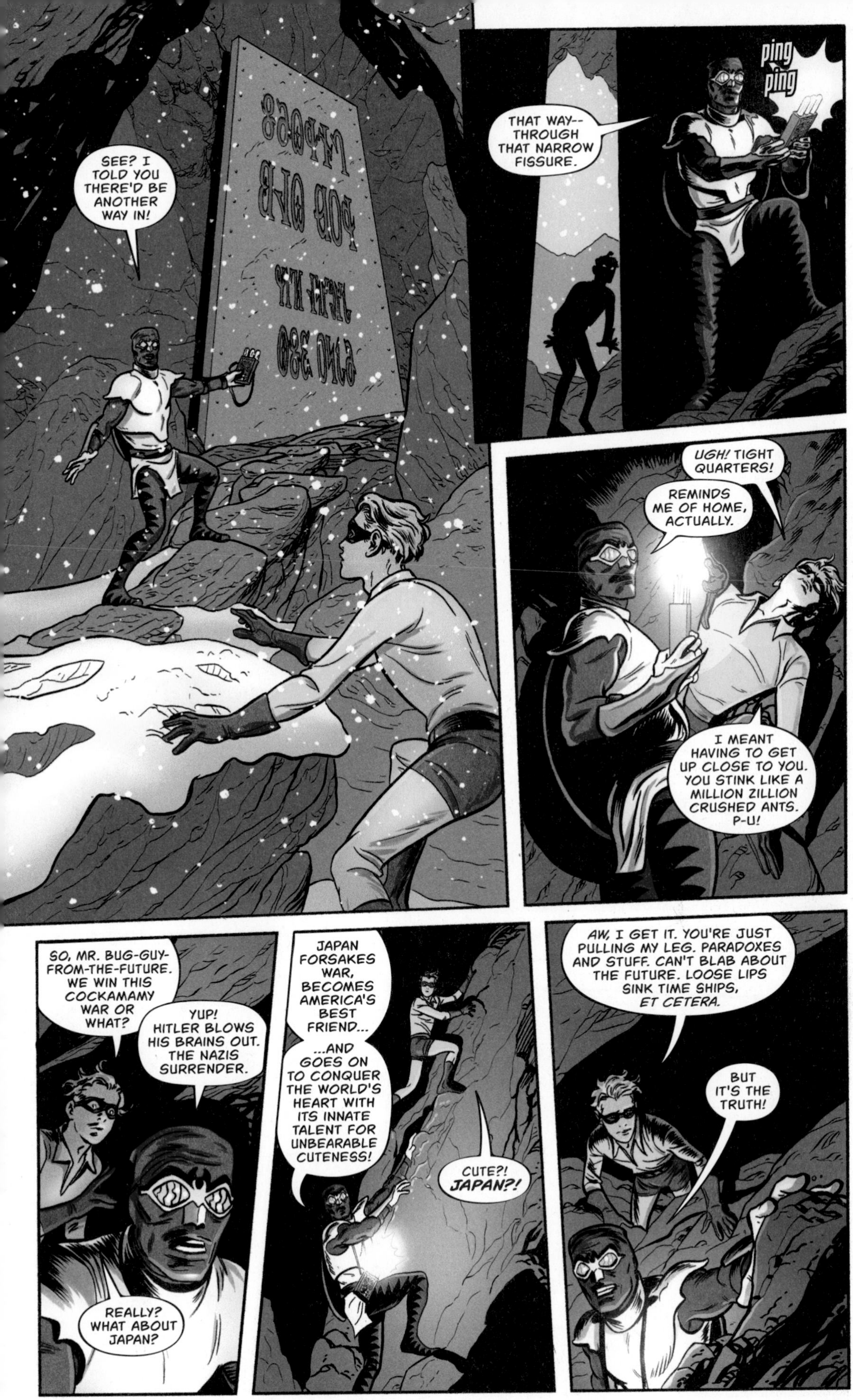
SEE? I TOLD YOU THERE'D BE ANOTHER WAY IN!
ping ping
THAT WAY-- THROUGH THAT NARROW FISSURE.
UGH! TIGHT QUARTERS!
REMINDS ME OF HOME, ACTUALLY.
I MEANT HAVING TO GET UP CLOSE TO YOU. YOU STINK LIKE A MILLION ZILLION CRUSHED ANTS. P-U!
SO, MR. BUG-GUY-FROM-THE-FUTURE. WE WIN THIS COCKAMAMY WAR OR WHAT?
YUP! HITLER BLOWS HIS BRAINS OUT. THE NAZIS SURRENDER.
REALLY? WHAT ABOUT JAPAN?
JAPAN FORSAKES WAR, BECOMES AMERICA'S BEST FRIEND...
...AND GOES ON TO CONQUER THE WORLD'S HEART WITH ITS INNATE TALENT FOR UNBEARABLE CUTENESS!
CUTE?! JAPAN?!
AW, I GET IT. YOU'RE JUST PULLING MY LEG. PARADOXES AND STUFF. CAN'T BLAB ABOUT THE FUTURE. LOOSE LIPS SINK TIME SHIPS, ET CETERA.
BUT IT'S THE TRUTH!

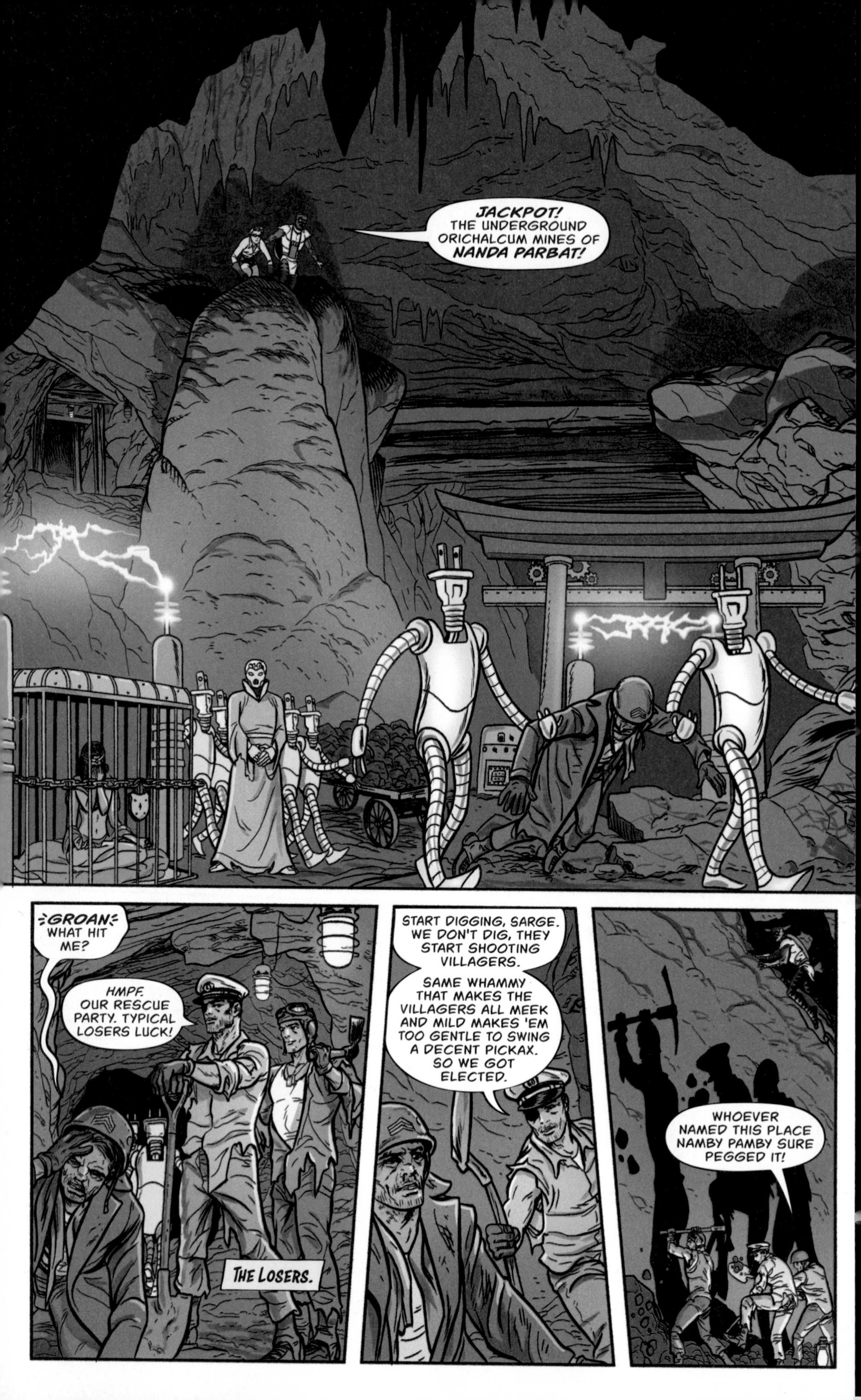
JACKPOT! THE UNDERGROUND ORICHALCUM MINES OF NANDA PARBAT!
GROAN WHAT HIT ME?
HMPF. OUR RESCUE PARTY. TYPICAL LOSERS LUCK!
THE LOSERS.
START DIGGING, SARGE. WE DON'T DIG, THEY START SHOOTING VILLAGERS.
SAME WHAMMY THAT MAKES THE VILLAGERS ALL MEEK AND MILD MAKES 'EM TOO GENTLE TO SWING A DECENT PICKAX. SO WE GOT ELECTED.
WHOEVER NAMED THIS PLACE NAMBY PAMBY SURE PEGGED IT!

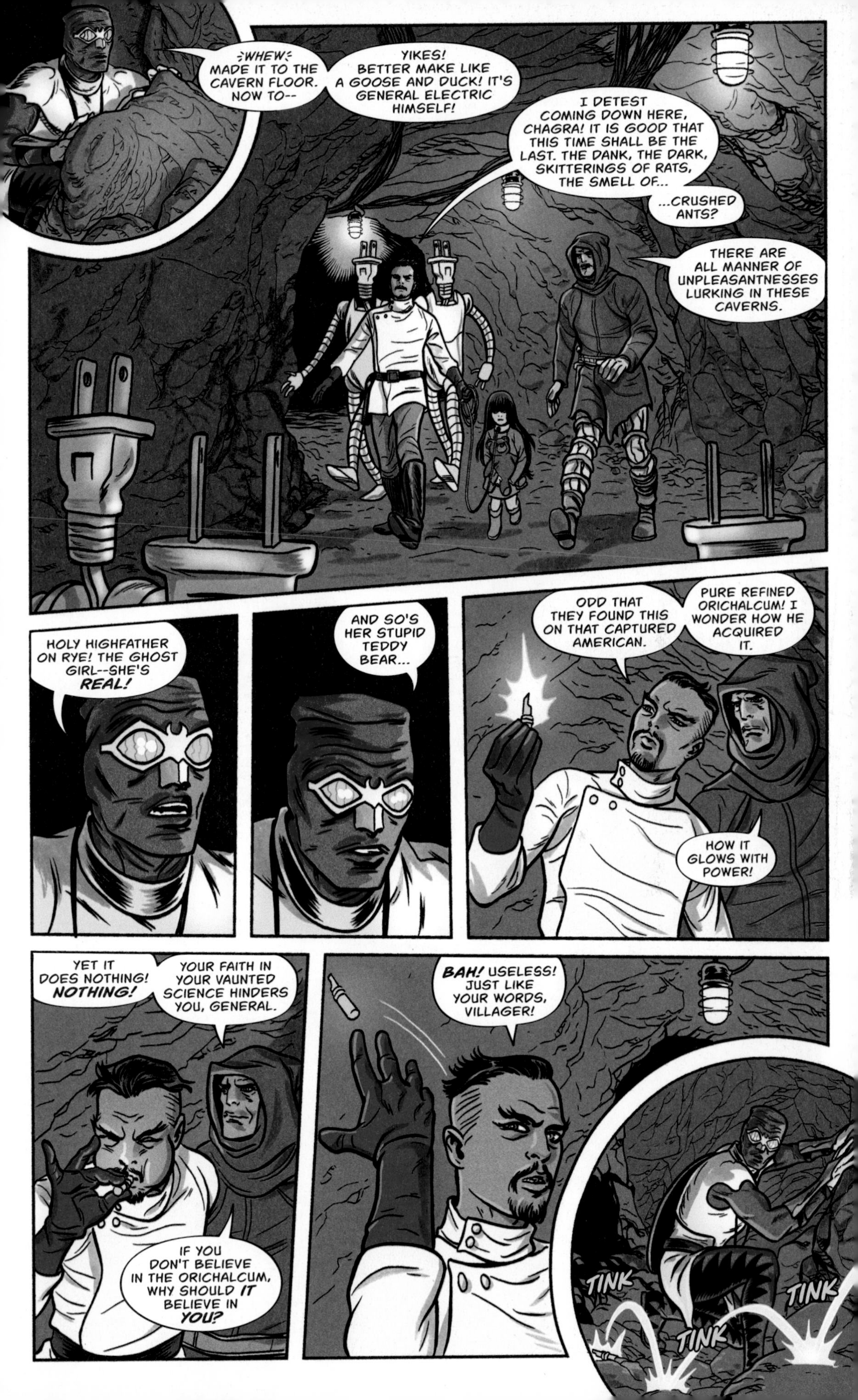

WHEW! MADE IT TO THE CAVERN FLOOR. NOW TO--
YIKES! BETTER MAKE LIKE A GOOSE AND DUCK! IT'S GENERAL ELECTRIC HIMSELF!
I DETEST COMING DOWN HERE, CHAGRA! IT IS GOOD THAT THIS TIME SHALL BE THE LAST. THE DANK, THE DARK, SKITTERINGS OF RATS, THE SMELL OF...
...CRUSHED ANTS?
THERE ARE ALL MANNER OF UNPLEASANTNESSES LURKING IN THESE CAVERNS.
HOLY HIGHFATHER ON RYE! THE GHOST GIRL--SHE'S **REAL!**
AND SO'S HER STUPID TEDDY BEAR...
ODD THAT THEY FOUND THIS ON THAT CAPTURED AMERICAN.
PURE REFINED ORICHALCUM! I WONDER HOW HE ACQUIRED IT.
HOW IT GLOWS WITH POWER!
YET IT DOES NOTHING! **NOTHING!**
YOUR FAITH IN YOUR VAUNTED SCIENCE HINDERS YOU, GENERAL.
IF YOU DON'T BELIEVE IN THE ORICHALCUM, WHY SHOULD ***IT*** BELIEVE IN ***YOU?***
BAH! USELESS! JUST LIKE YOUR WORDS, VILLAGER!
TINK
TINK
TINK

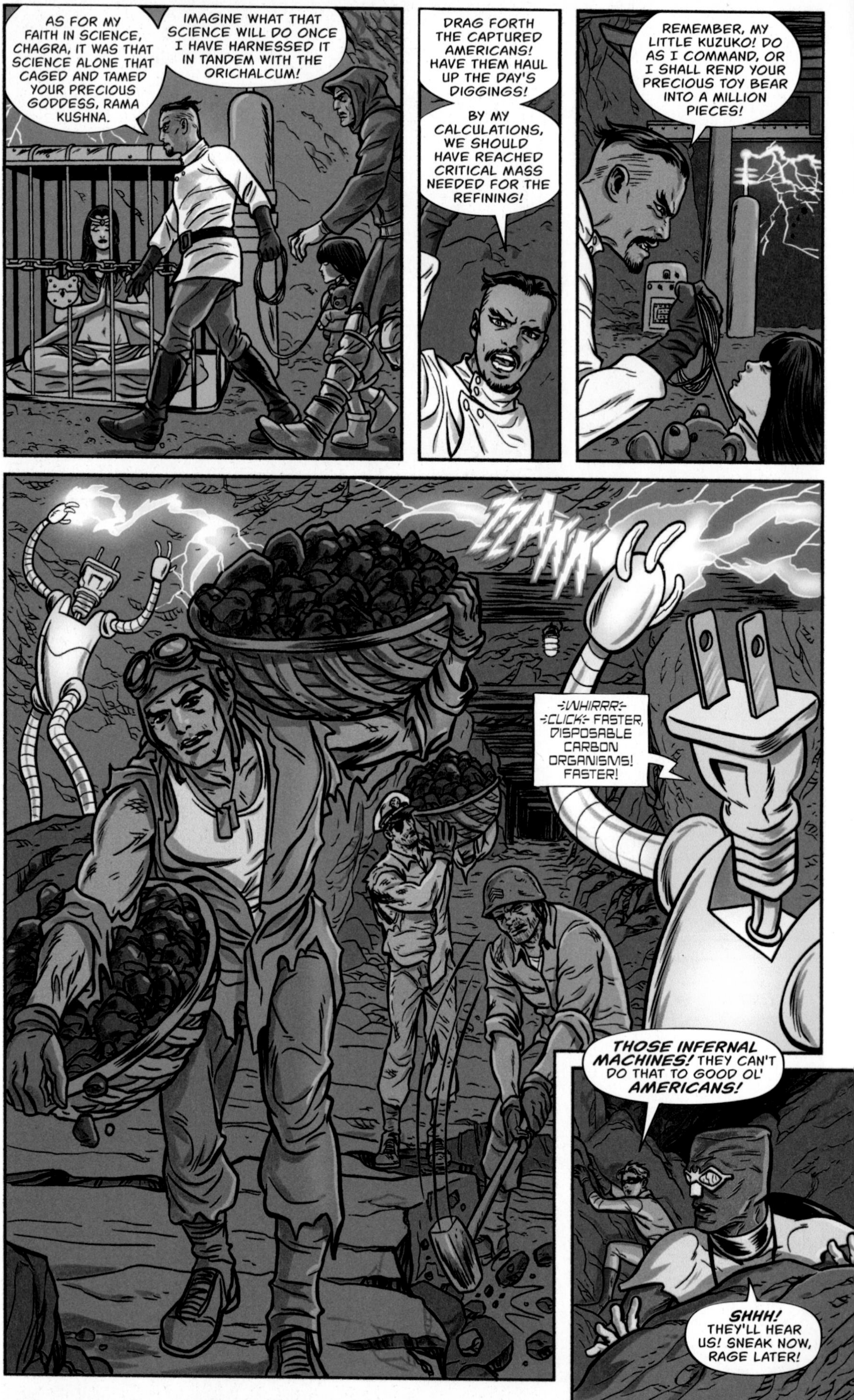
AS FOR MY FAITH IN SCIENCE, CHAGRA, IT WAS THAT SCIENCE ALONE THAT CAGED AND TAMED YOUR PRECIOUS GODDESS, RAMA KUSHNA.
IMAGINE WHAT THAT SCIENCE WILL DO ONCE I HAVE HARNESSED IT IN TANDEM WITH THE ORICHALCUM!
DRAG FORTH THE CAPTURED AMERICANS! HAVE THEM HAUL UP THE DAY'S DIGGINGS!
BY MY CALCULATIONS, WE SHOULD HAVE REACHED CRITICAL MASS NEEDED FOR THE REFINING!
REMEMBER, MY LITTLE KUZUKO! DO AS I COMMAND, OR I SHALL REND YOUR PRECIOUS TOY BEAR INTO A MILLION PIECES!
ZZAKK
-WHIRRR- -CLICK- FASTER, DISPOSABLE CARBON ORGANISMS! FASTER!
THOSE INFERNAL MACHINES! THEY CAN'T DO THAT TO GOOD OL' AMERICANS!
SHHH! THEY'LL HEAR US! SNEAK NOW, RAGE LATER!

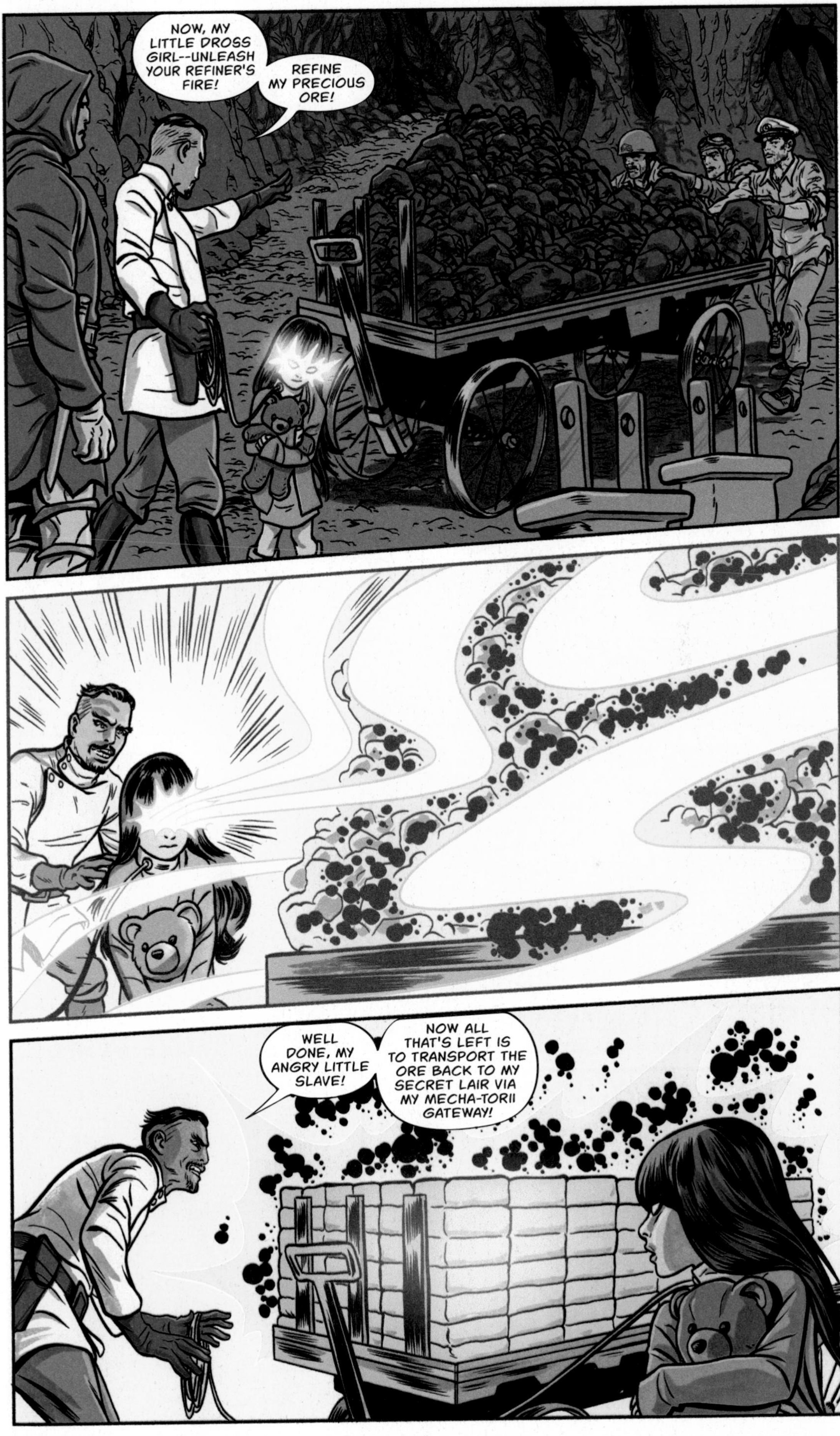
NOW, MY LITTLE DROSS GIRL--UNLEASH YOUR REFINER'S FIRE!
REFINE MY PRECIOUS ORE!
WELL DONE, MY ANGRY LITTLE SLAVE!
NOW ALL THAT'S LEFT IS TO TRANSPORT THE ORE BACK TO MY SECRET LAIR VIA MY MECHA-TORII GATEWAY!

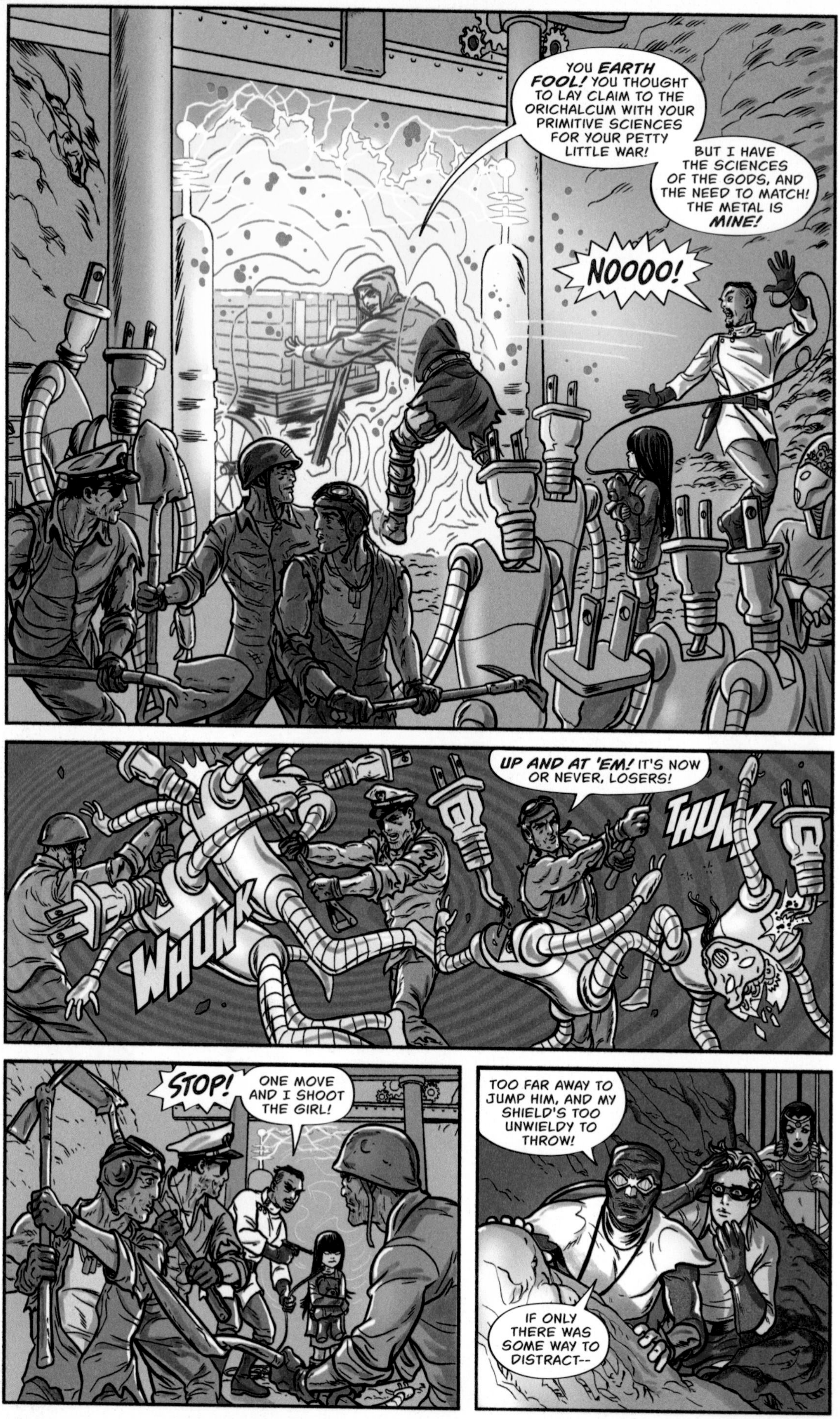
YOU EARTH FOOL! YOU THOUGHT TO LAY CLAIM TO THE ORICHALCUM WITH YOUR PRIMITIVE SCIENCES FOR YOUR PETTY LITTLE WAR!
BUT I HAVE THE SCIENCES OF THE GODS, AND THE NEED TO MATCH! THE METAL IS MINE!
NOOOO!
UP AND AT 'EM! IT'S NOW OR NEVER, LOSERS!
THUNK
WHUNK
STOP!
ONE MOVE AND I SHOOT THE GIRL!
TOO FAR AWAY TO JUMP HIM, AND MY SHIELD'S TOO UNWIELDY TO THROW!
IF ONLY THERE WAS SOME WAY TO DISTRACT--

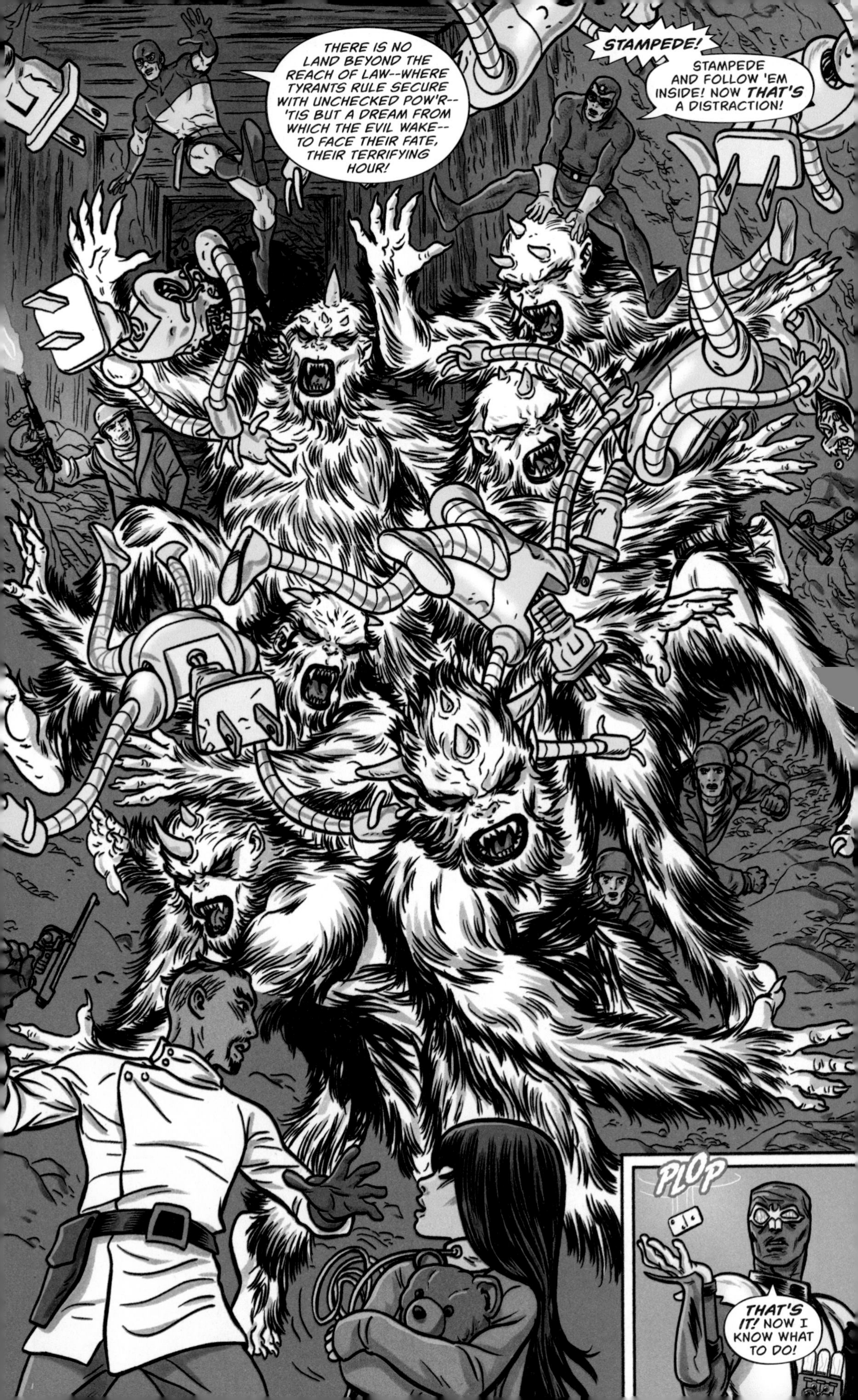
THERE IS NO LAND BEYOND THE REACH OF LAW--WHERE TYRANTS RULE SECURE WITH UNCHECKED POW'R-- 'TIS BUT A DREAM FROM WHICH THE EVIL WAKE-- TO FACE THEIR FATE, THEIR TERRIFYING HOUR!
STAMPEDE!
STAMPEDE AND FOLLOW 'EM INSIDE! NOW THAT'S A DISTRACTION!
PLOP
THAT'S IT! NOW I KNOW WHAT TO DO!

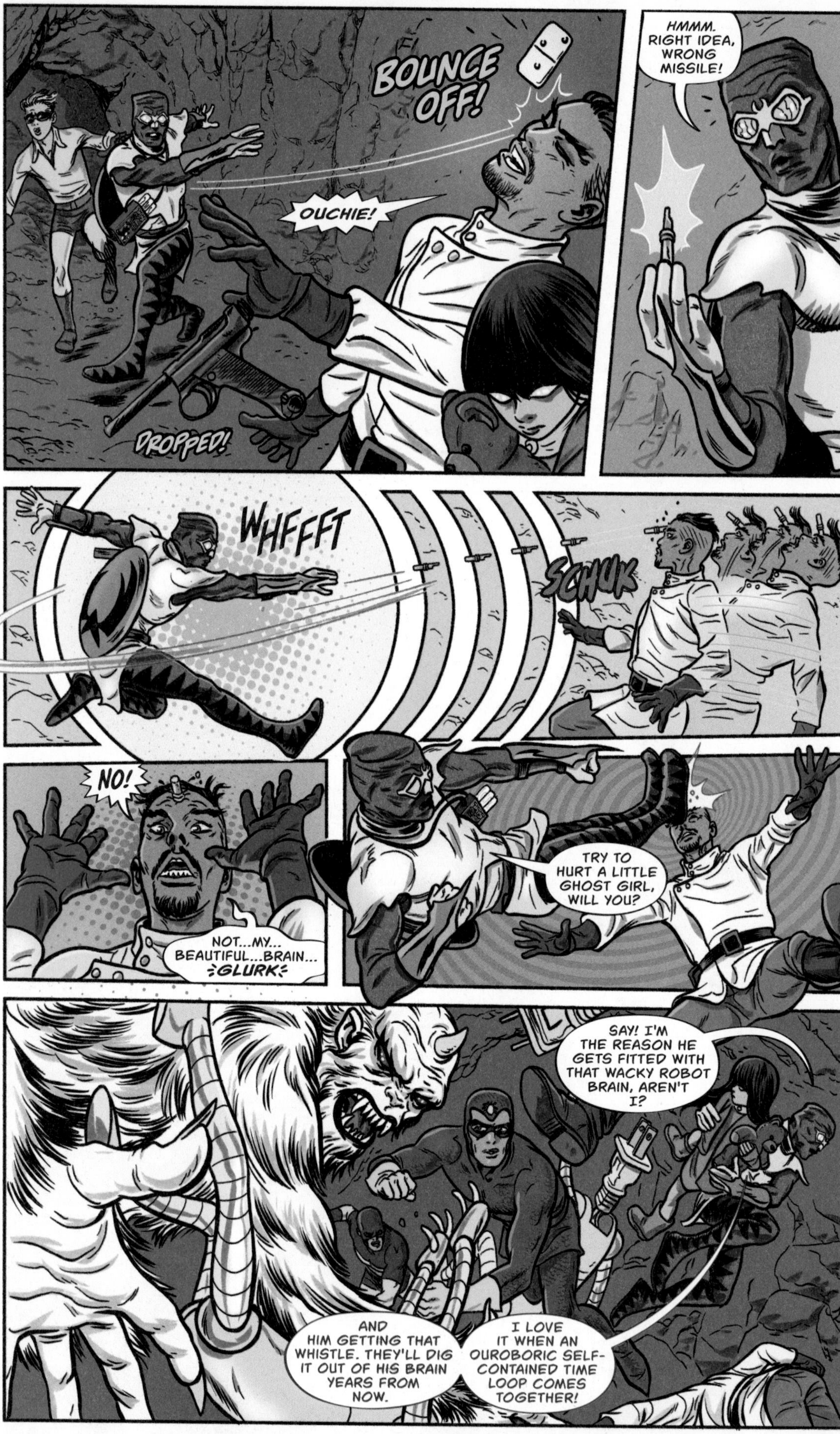
BOUNCE OFF!
OUCHIE!
DROPPED!
HMMM. RIGHT IDEA, WRONG MISSILE!
WHFFFT
SCHUK
NO!
NOT...MY... BEAUTIFUL...BRAIN... GLURK
TRY TO HURT A LITTLE GHOST GIRL, WILL YOU?
SAY! I'M THE REASON HE GETS FITTED WITH THAT WACKY ROBOT BRAIN, AREN'T I?
AND HIM GETTING THAT WHISTLE. THEY'LL DIG IT OUT OF HIS BRAIN YEARS FROM NOW.
I LOVE IT WHEN AN OUROBORIC SELF-CONTAINED TIME LOOP COMES TOGETHER!

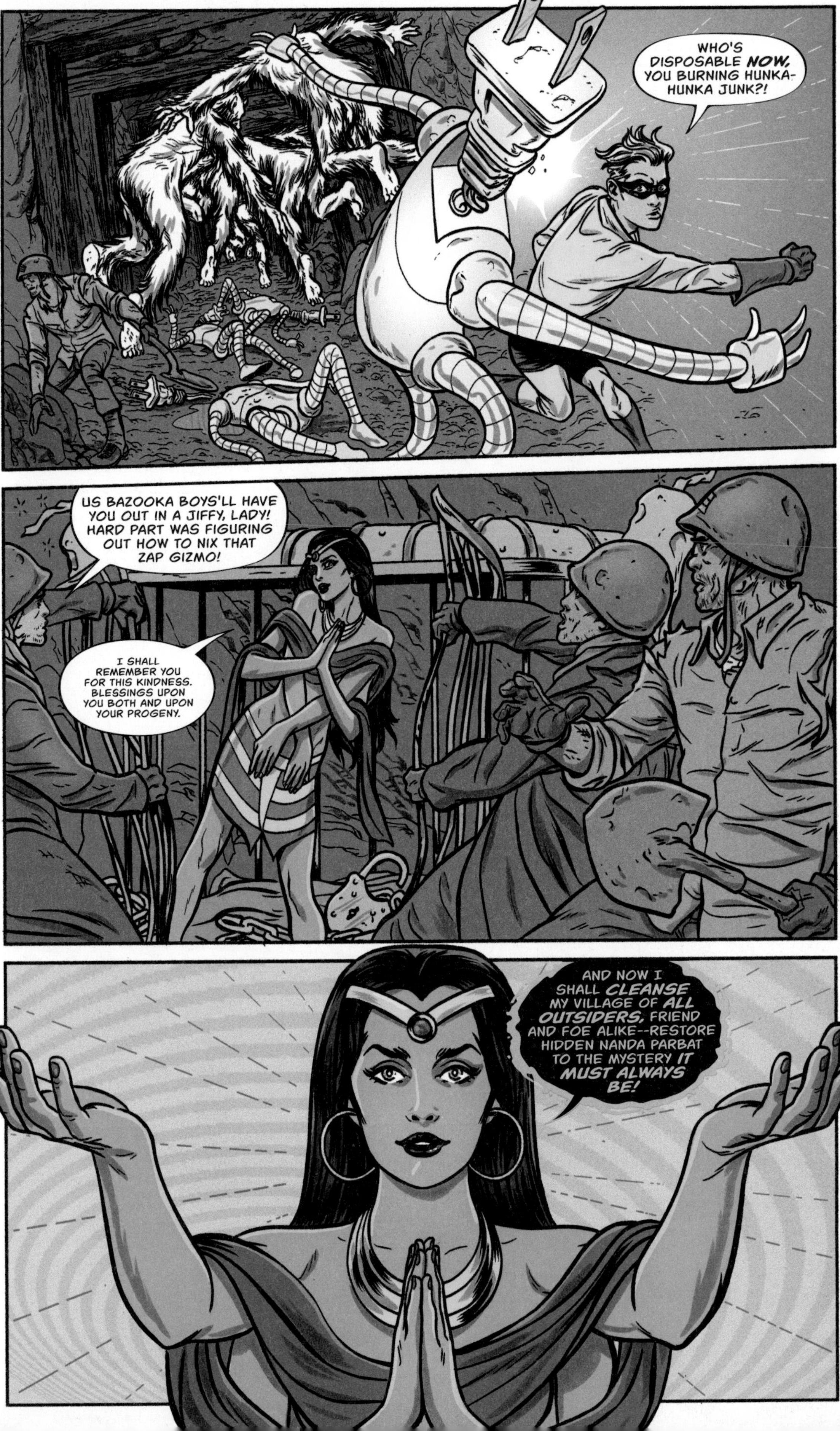

WHO'S DISPOSABLE NOW, YOU BURNING HUNKA-HUNKA JUNK?!
US BAZOOKA BOYS'LL HAVE YOU OUT IN A JIFFY, LADY! HARD PART WAS FIGURING OUT HOW TO NIX THAT ZAP GIZMO!
I SHALL REMEMBER YOU FOR THIS KINDNESS. BLESSINGS UPON YOU BOTH AND UPON YOUR PROGENY.
AND NOW I SHALL CLEANSE MY VILLAGE OF ALL OUTSIDERS, FRIEND AND FOE ALIKE--RESTORE HIDDEN NANDA PARBAT TO THE MYSTERY IT MUST ALWAYS BE!

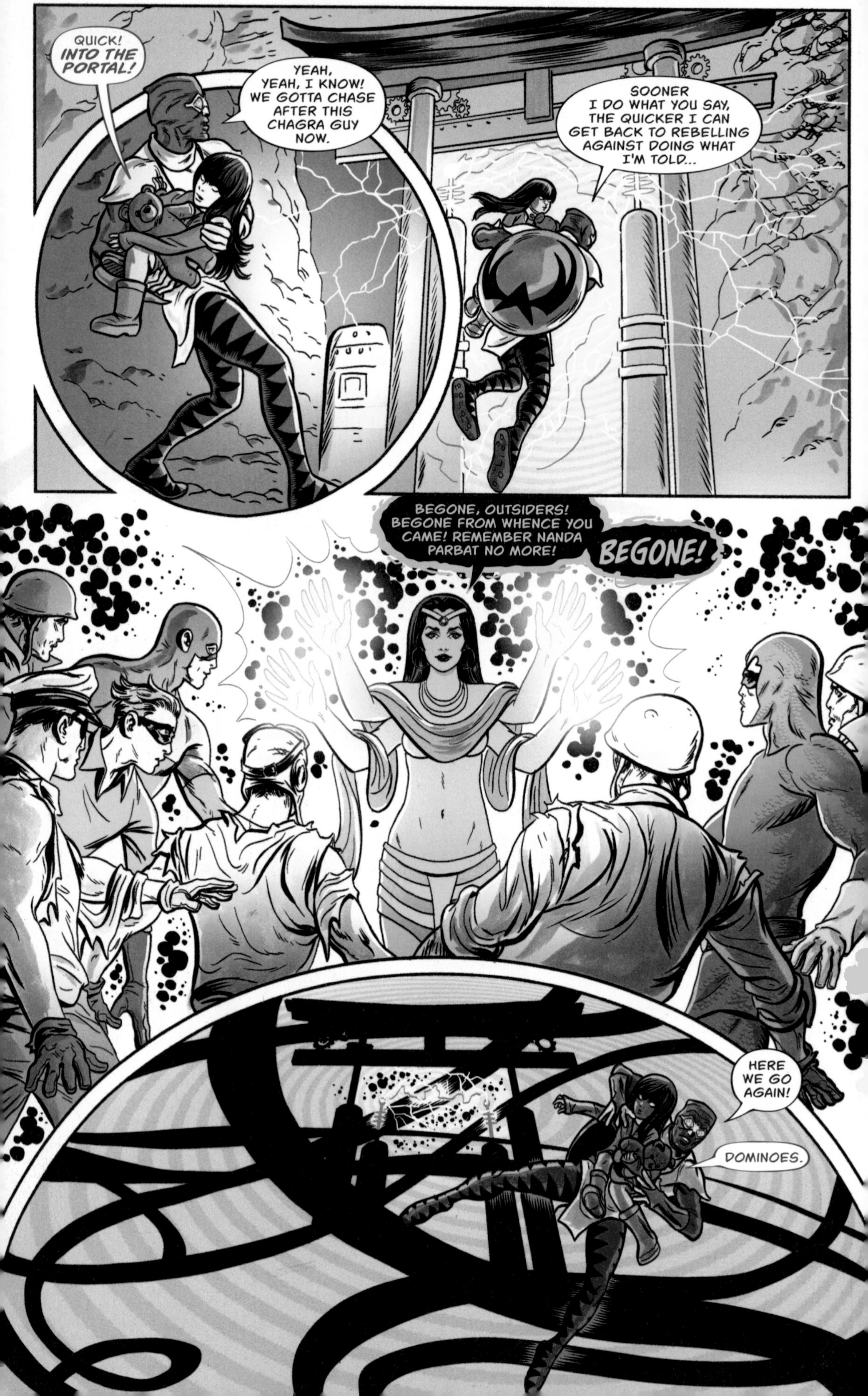
QUICK! INTO THE PORTAL!
YEAH, YEAH, I KNOW! WE GOTTA CHASE AFTER THIS CHAGRA GUY NOW.
SOONER I DO WHAT YOU SAY, THE QUICKER I CAN GET BACK TO REBELLING AGAINST DOING WHAT I'M TOLD...
BEGONE, OUTSIDERS! BEGONE FROM WHENCE YOU CAME! REMEMBER NANDA PARBAT NO MORE!
BEGONE!
HERE WE GO AGAIN!
DOMINOES.

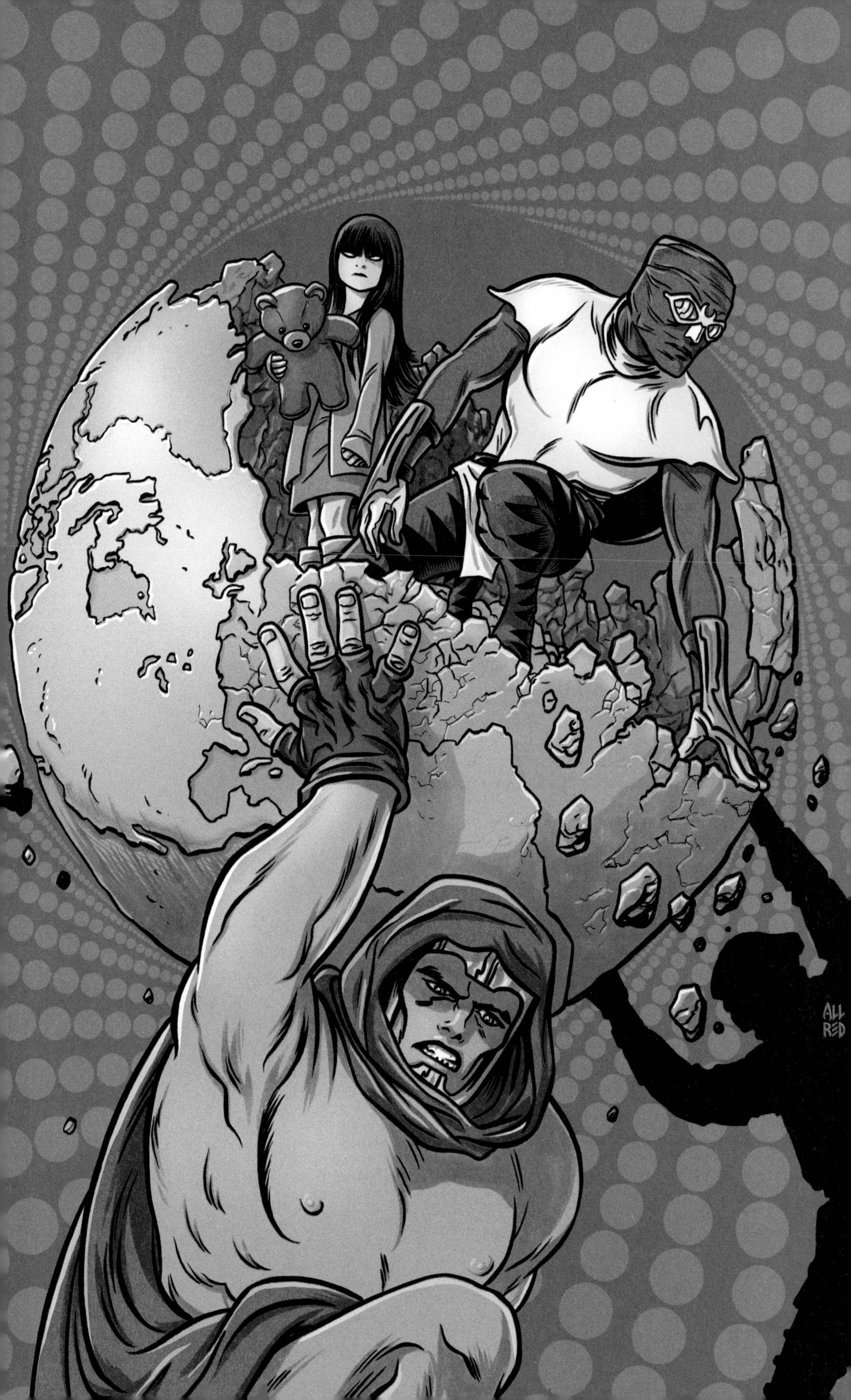
ALL
RED

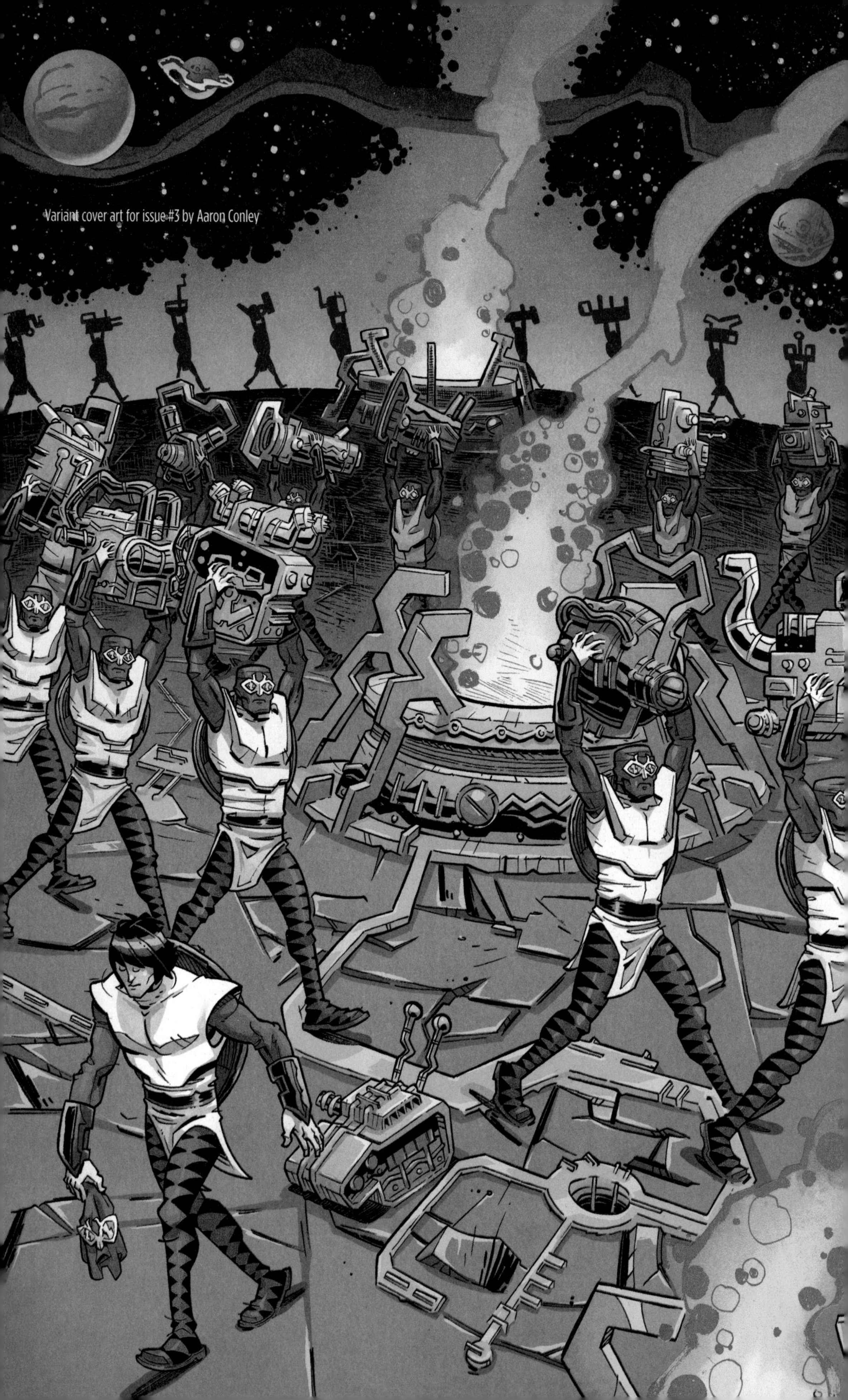
Variant cover art for issue #3 by Aaron Conley

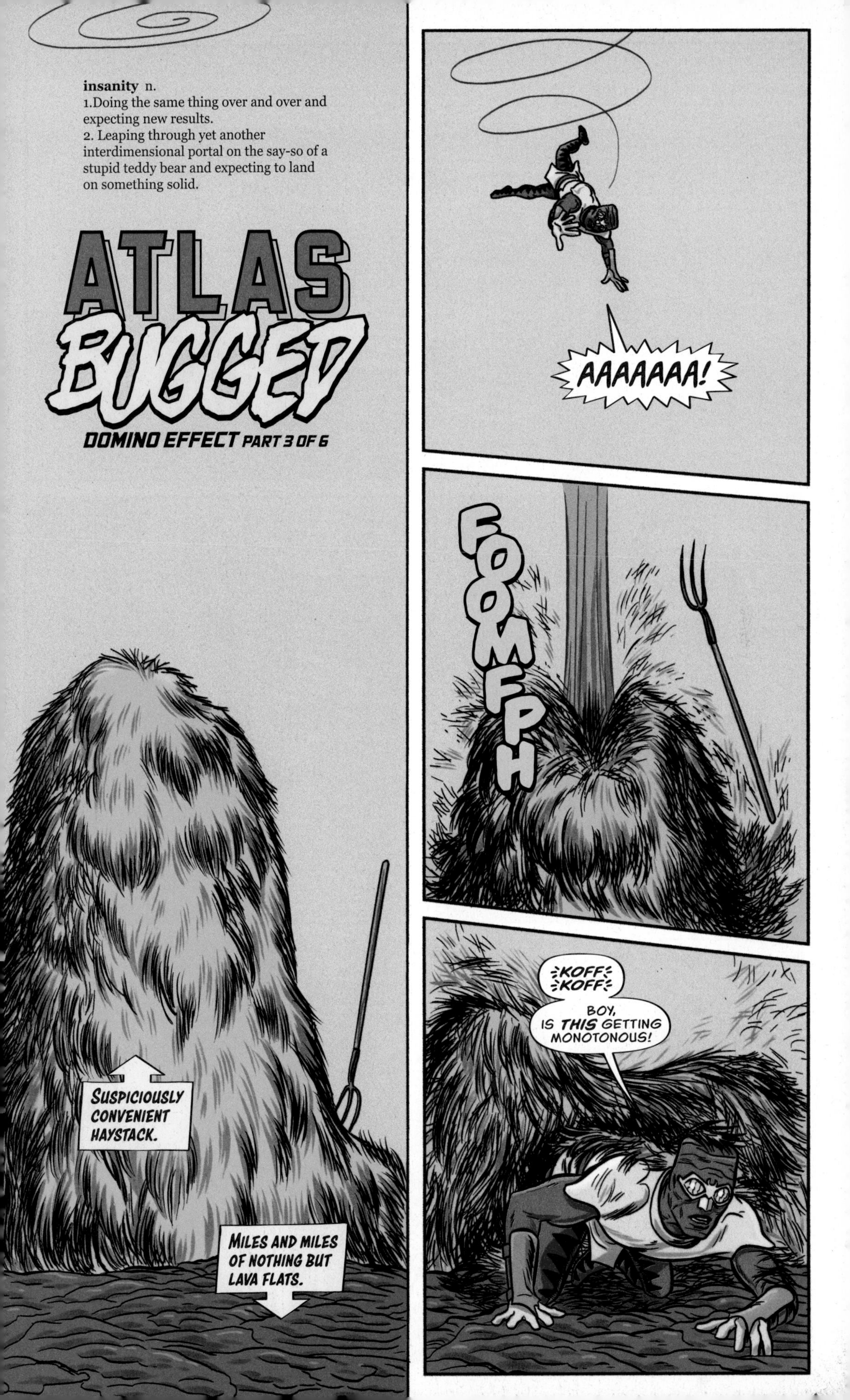
insanity n.
1.Doing the same thing over and over and expecting new results.
2. Leaping through yet another interdimensional portal on the say-so of a stupid teddy bear and expecting to land on something solid.
ATLAS BUGGED
DOMINO EFFECT PART 3 OF 6
SUSPICIOUSLY CONVENIENT HAYSTACK.
MILES AND MILES OF NOTHING BUT LAVA FLATS.
AAAAAAA!
FOOMFPH
KOFF KOFF
BOY, IS THIS GETTING MONOTONOUS!

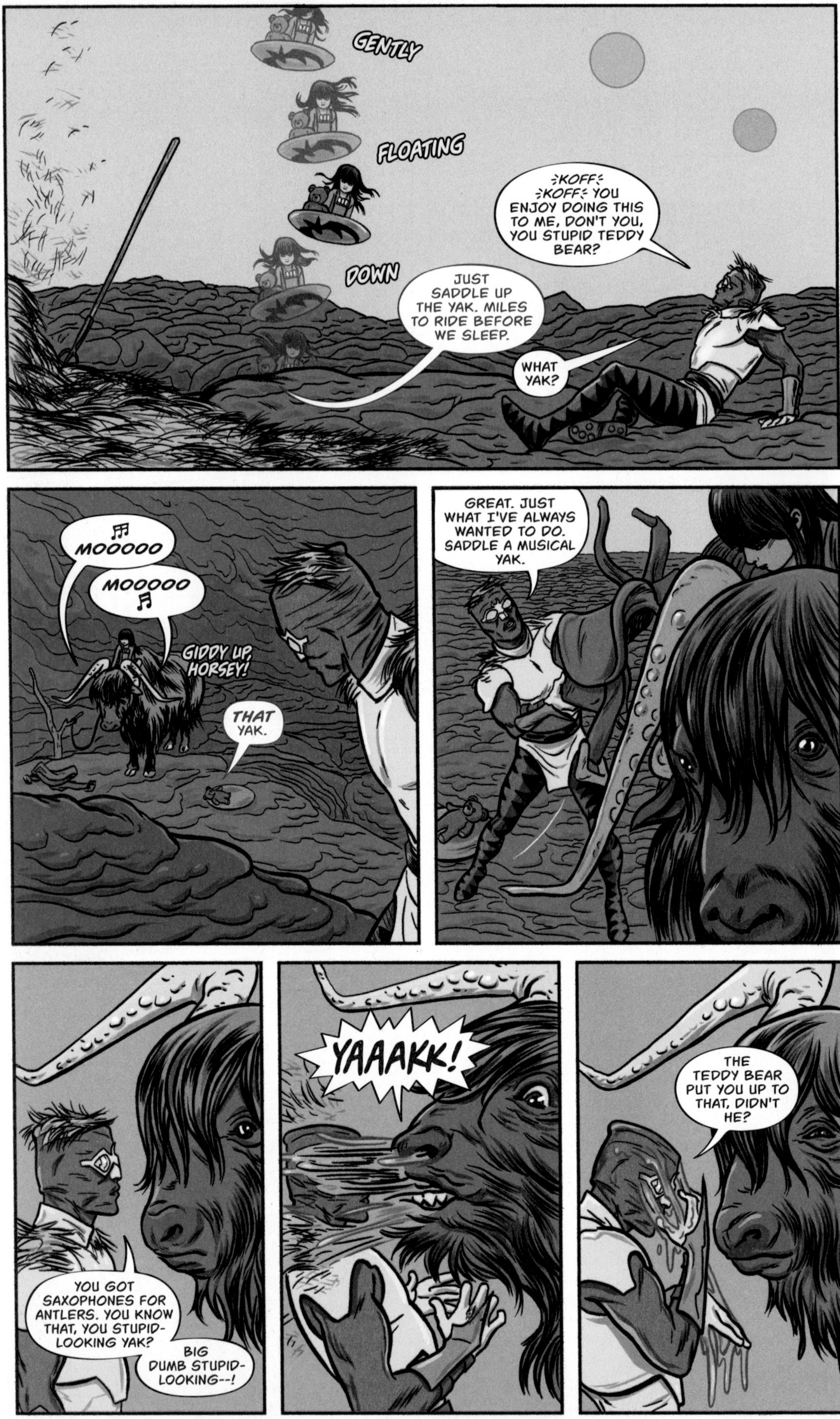
GENTLY
FLOATING
DOWN
≈KOFF≈ ≈KOFF≈ YOU ENJOY DOING THIS TO ME, DON'T YOU, YOU STUPID TEDDY BEAR?
JUST SADDLE UP THE YAK. MILES TO RIDE BEFORE WE SLEEP.
WHAT YAK?
♬ MOOOOO
MOOOOO ♬
GIDDY UP, HORSEY!
THAT YAK.
GREAT. JUST WHAT I'VE ALWAYS WANTED TO DO. SADDLE A MUSICAL YAK.
YOU GOT SAXOPHONES FOR ANTLERS. YOU KNOW THAT, YOU STUPID-LOOKING YAK?
BIG DUMB STUPID-LOOKING--!
YAAAKK!
THE TEDDY BEAR PUT YOU UP TO THAT, DIDN'T HE?

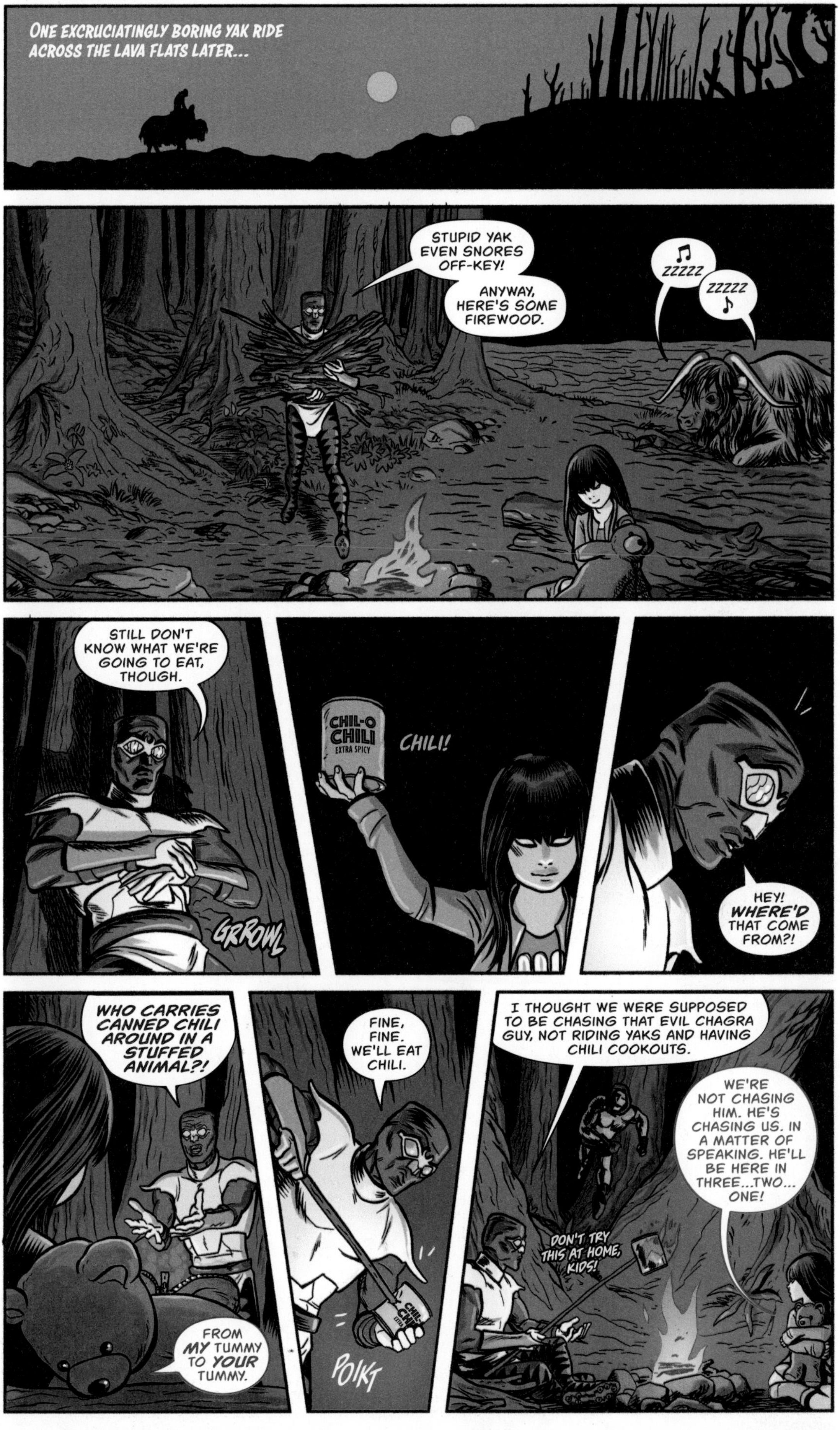
ONE EXCRUCIATINGLY BORING YAK RIDE ACROSS THE LAVA FLATS LATER...
STUPID YAK EVEN SNORES OFF-KEY!
ANYWAY, HERE'S SOME FIREWOOD.
♫ ZZZZZ
ZZZZZ ♪
STILL DON'T KNOW WHAT WE'RE GOING TO EAT, THOUGH.
GRROWL
CHIL-O CHILI EXTRA SPICY
CHILI!
HEY! WHERE'D THAT COME FROM?!
WHO CARRIES CANNED CHILI AROUND IN A STUFFED ANIMAL?!
FROM MY TUMMY TO YOUR TUMMY.
FINE, FINE. WE'LL EAT CHILI.
POIKT
I THOUGHT WE WERE SUPPOSED TO BE CHASING THAT EVIL CHAGRA GUY, NOT RIDING YAKS AND HAVING CHILI COOKOUTS.
DON'T TRY THIS AT HOME, KIDS!
WE'RE NOT CHASING HIM. HE'S CHASING US. IN A MATTER OF SPEAKING. HE'LL BE HERE IN THREE...TWO... ONE!

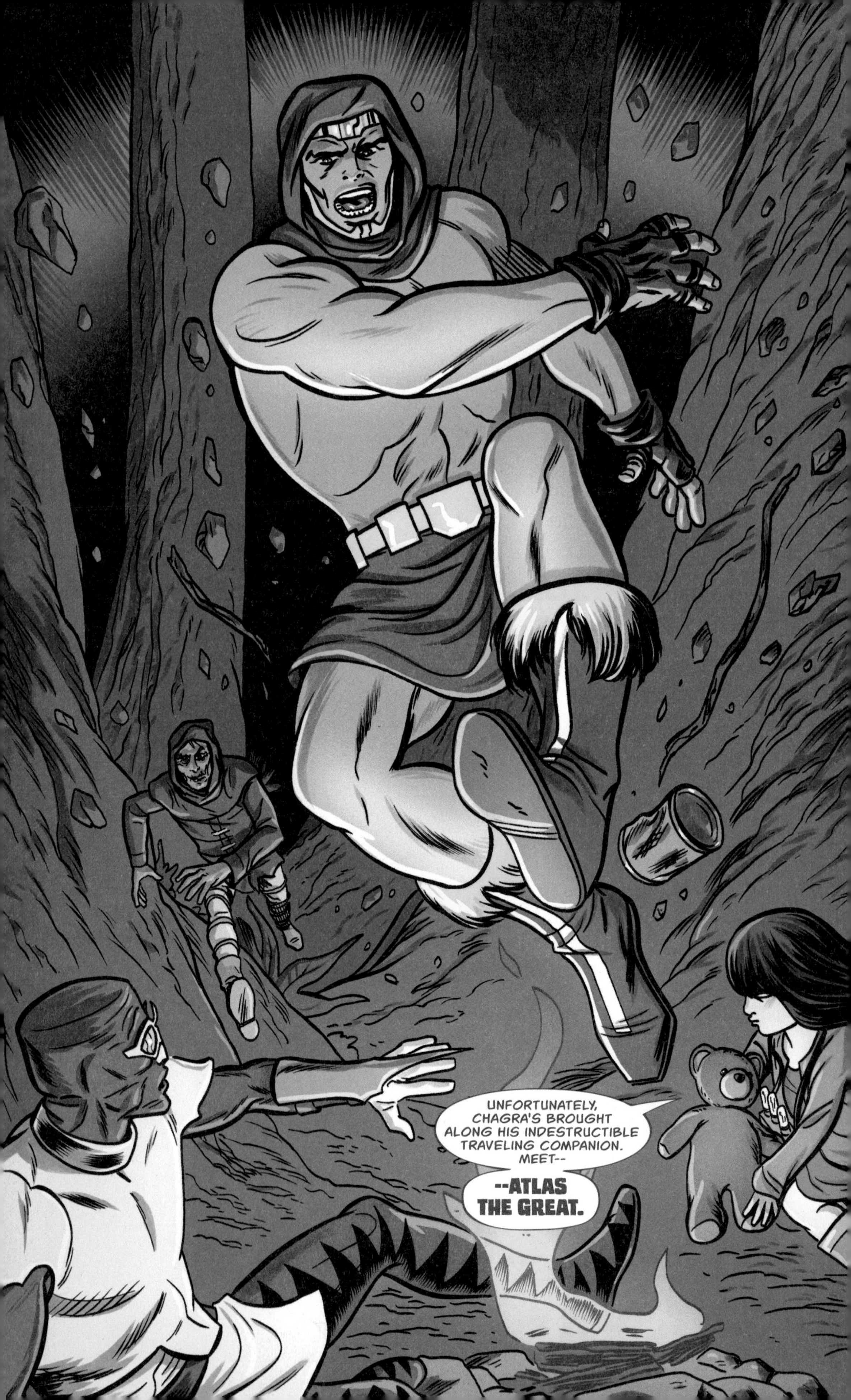
UNFORTUNATELY, CHAGRA'S BROUGHT ALONG HIS INDESTRUCTIBLE TRAVELING COMPANION. MEET--
--ATLAS THE GREAT.

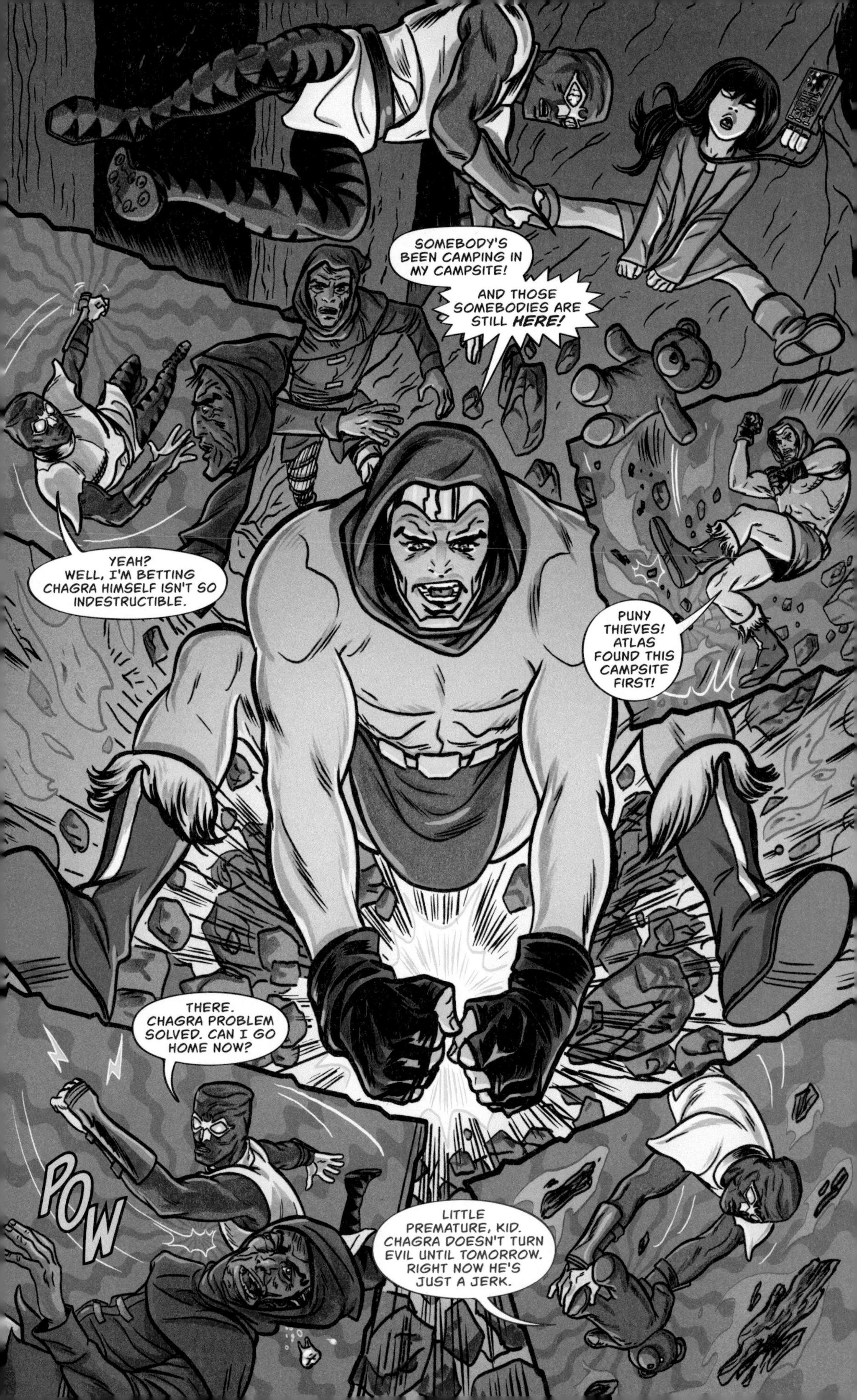
SOMEBODY'S BEEN CAMPING IN MY CAMPSITE!
AND THOSE SOMEBODIES ARE STILL HERE!
YEAH? WELL, I'M BETTING CHAGRA HIMSELF ISN'T SO INDESTRUCTIBLE.
PUNY THIEVES! ATLAS FOUND THIS CAMPSITE FIRST!
THERE. CHAGRA PROBLEM SOLVED. CAN I GO HOME NOW?
POW
LITTLE PREMATURE, KID. CHAGRA DOESN'T TURN EVIL UNTIL TOMORROW. RIGHT NOW HE'S JUST A JERK.

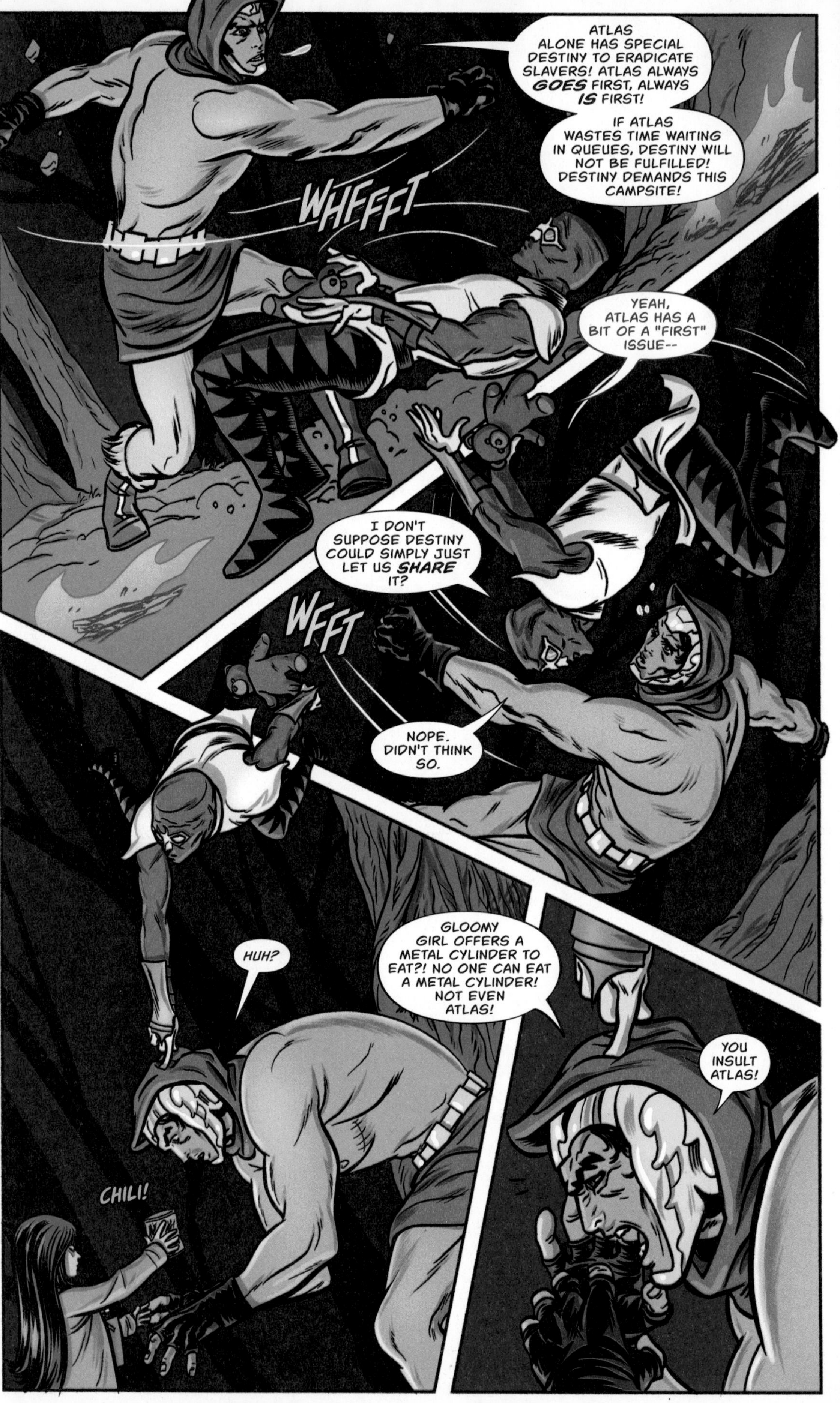
ATLAS ALONE HAS SPECIAL DESTINY TO ERADICATE SLAVERS! ATLAS ALWAYS GOES FIRST, ALWAYS IS FIRST!
IF ATLAS WASTES TIME WAITING IN QUEUES, DESTINY WILL NOT BE FULFILLED! DESTINY DEMANDS THIS CAMPSITE!
WHFFFT
YEAH, ATLAS HAS A BIT OF A "FIRST" ISSUE--
I DON'T SUPPOSE DESTINY COULD SIMPLY JUST LET US SHARE IT?
WFFT
NOPE. DIDN'T THINK SO.
HUH?
CHILI!
GLOOMY GIRL OFFERS A METAL CYLINDER TO EAT?! NO ONE CAN EAT A METAL CYLINDER! NOT EVEN ATLAS!
YOU INSULT ATLAS!

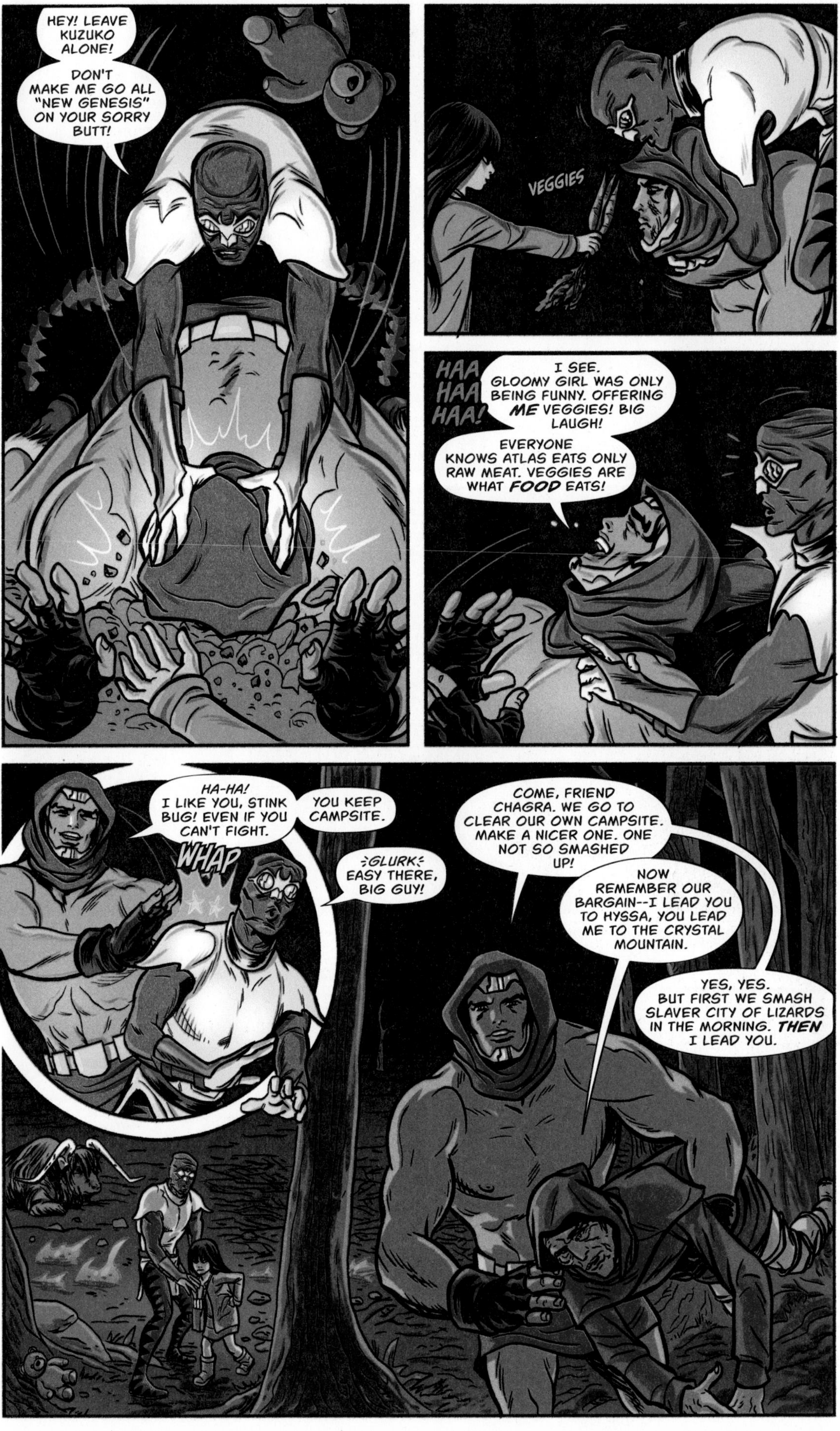
HEY! LEAVE KUZUKO ALONE!
DON'T MAKE ME GO ALL "NEW GENESIS" ON YOUR SORRY BUTT!
VEGGIES
HAA HAA HAA!
I SEE. GLOOMY GIRL WAS ONLY BEING FUNNY. OFFERING ME VEGGIES! BIG LAUGH!
EVERYONE KNOWS ATLAS EATS ONLY RAW MEAT. VEGGIES ARE WHAT FOOD EATS!
HA-HA! I LIKE YOU, STINK BUG! EVEN IF YOU CAN'T FIGHT.
YOU KEEP CAMPSITE.
WHAP
GLURK EASY THERE, BIG GUY!
COME, FRIEND CHAGRA. WE GO TO CLEAR OUR OWN CAMPSITE. MAKE A NICER ONE. ONE NOT SO SMASHED UP!
NOW REMEMBER OUR BARGAIN--I LEAD YOU TO HYSSA, YOU LEAD ME TO THE CRYSTAL MOUNTAIN.
YES, YES. BUT FIRST WE SMASH SLAVER CITY OF LIZARDS IN THE MORNING. THEN I LEAD YOU.

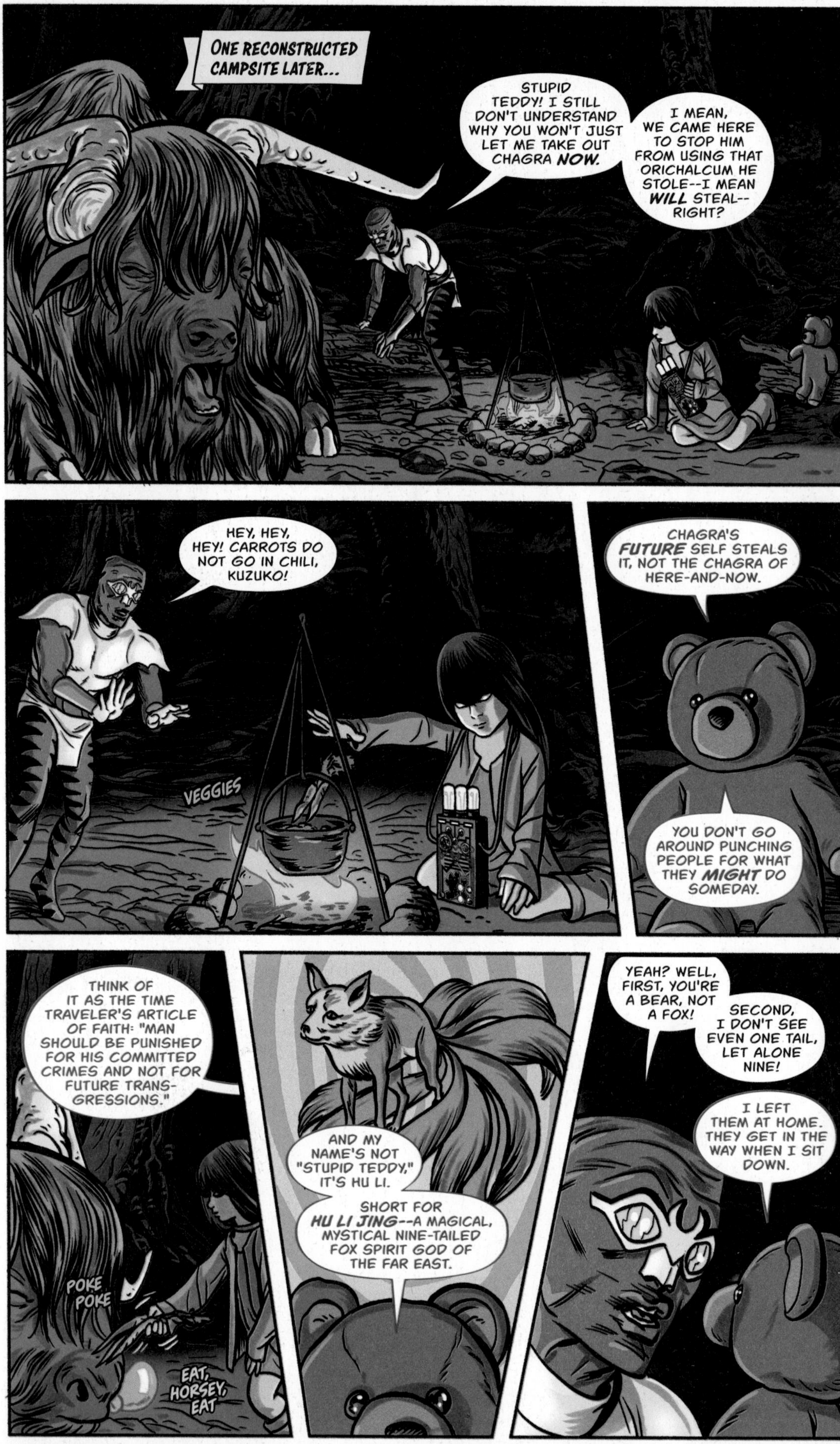
ONE RECONSTRUCTED CAMPSITE LATER...
STUPID TEDDY! I STILL DON'T UNDERSTAND WHY YOU WON'T JUST LET ME TAKE OUT CHAGRA NOW.
I MEAN, WE CAME HERE TO STOP HIM FROM USING THAT ORICHALCUM HE STOLE--I MEAN WILL STEAL--RIGHT?
HEY, HEY, HEY! CARROTS DO NOT GO IN CHILI, KUZUKO!
VEGGIES
CHAGRA'S FUTURE SELF STEALS IT, NOT THE CHAGRA OF HERE-AND-NOW.
YOU DON'T GO AROUND PUNCHING PEOPLE FOR WHAT THEY MIGHT DO SOMEDAY.
THINK OF IT AS THE TIME TRAVELER'S ARTICLE OF FAITH: "MAN SHOULD BE PUNISHED FOR HIS COMMITTED CRIMES AND NOT FOR FUTURE TRANS-GRESSIONS."
POKE POKE
EAT, HORSEY, EAT
AND MY NAME'S NOT "STUPID TEDDY," IT'S HU LI.
SHORT FOR HU LI JING--A MAGICAL, MYSTICAL NINE-TAILED FOX SPIRIT GOD OF THE FAR EAST.
YEAH? WELL, FIRST, YOU'RE A BEAR, NOT A FOX!
SECOND, I DON'T SEE EVEN ONE TAIL, LET ALONE NINE!
I LEFT THEM AT HOME. THEY GET IN THE WAY WHEN I SIT DOWN.

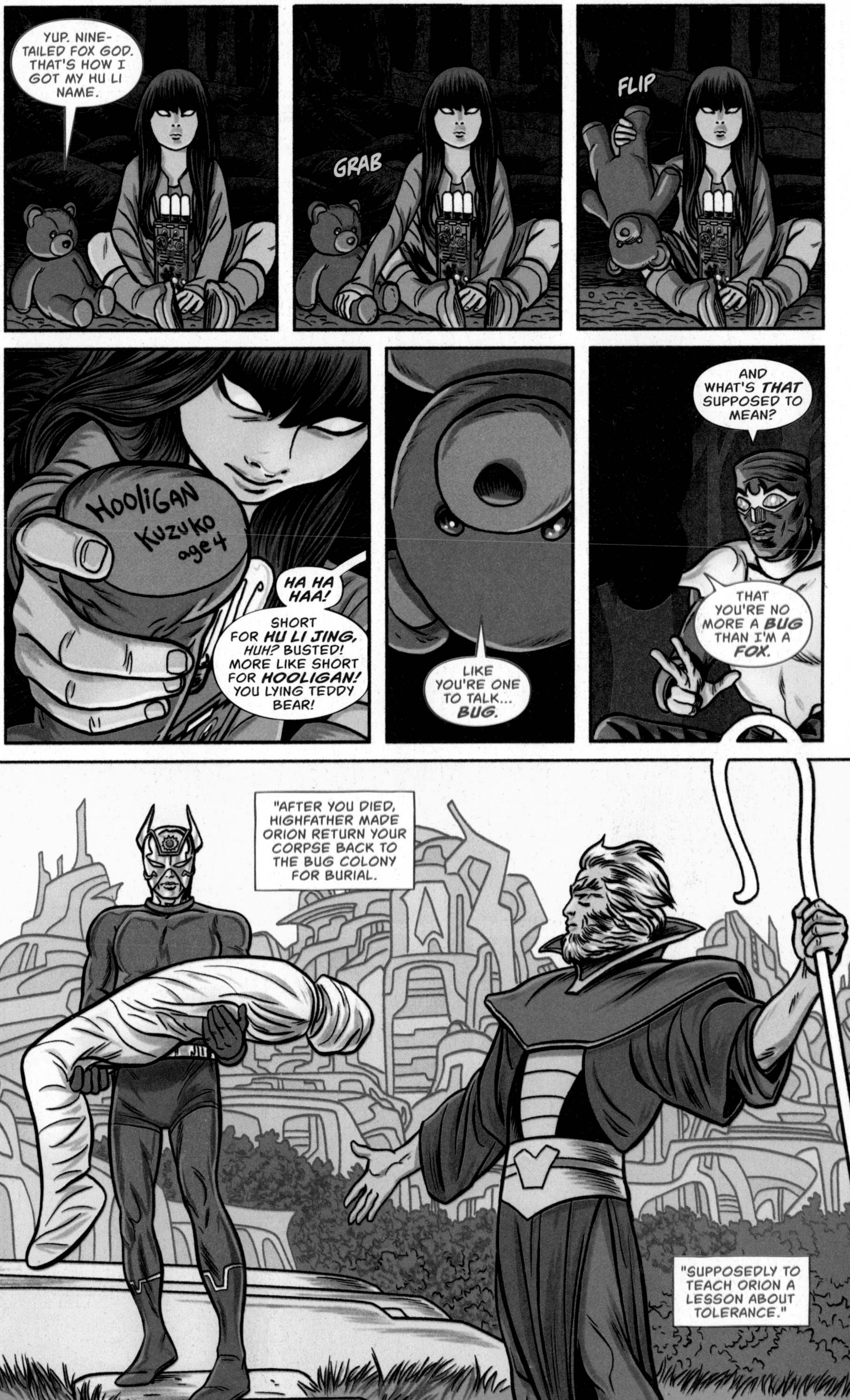
YUP. NINE-TAILED FOX GOD. THAT'S HOW I GOT MY HU LI NAME.
GRAB
FLIP
HOOLIGAN KUZUKO age 4
HA HA HAA!
SHORT FOR HU LI JING, HUH? BUSTED! MORE LIKE SHORT FOR HOOLIGAN! YOU LYING TEDDY BEAR!
LIKE YOU'RE ONE TO TALK... BUG.
AND WHAT'S THAT SUPPOSED TO MEAN?
THAT YOU'RE NO MORE A BUG THAN I'M A FOX.
"AFTER YOU DIED, HIGHFATHER MADE ORION RETURN YOUR CORPSE BACK TO THE BUG COLONY FOR BURIAL.
"SUPPOSEDLY TO TEACH ORION A LESSON ABOUT TOLERANCE."

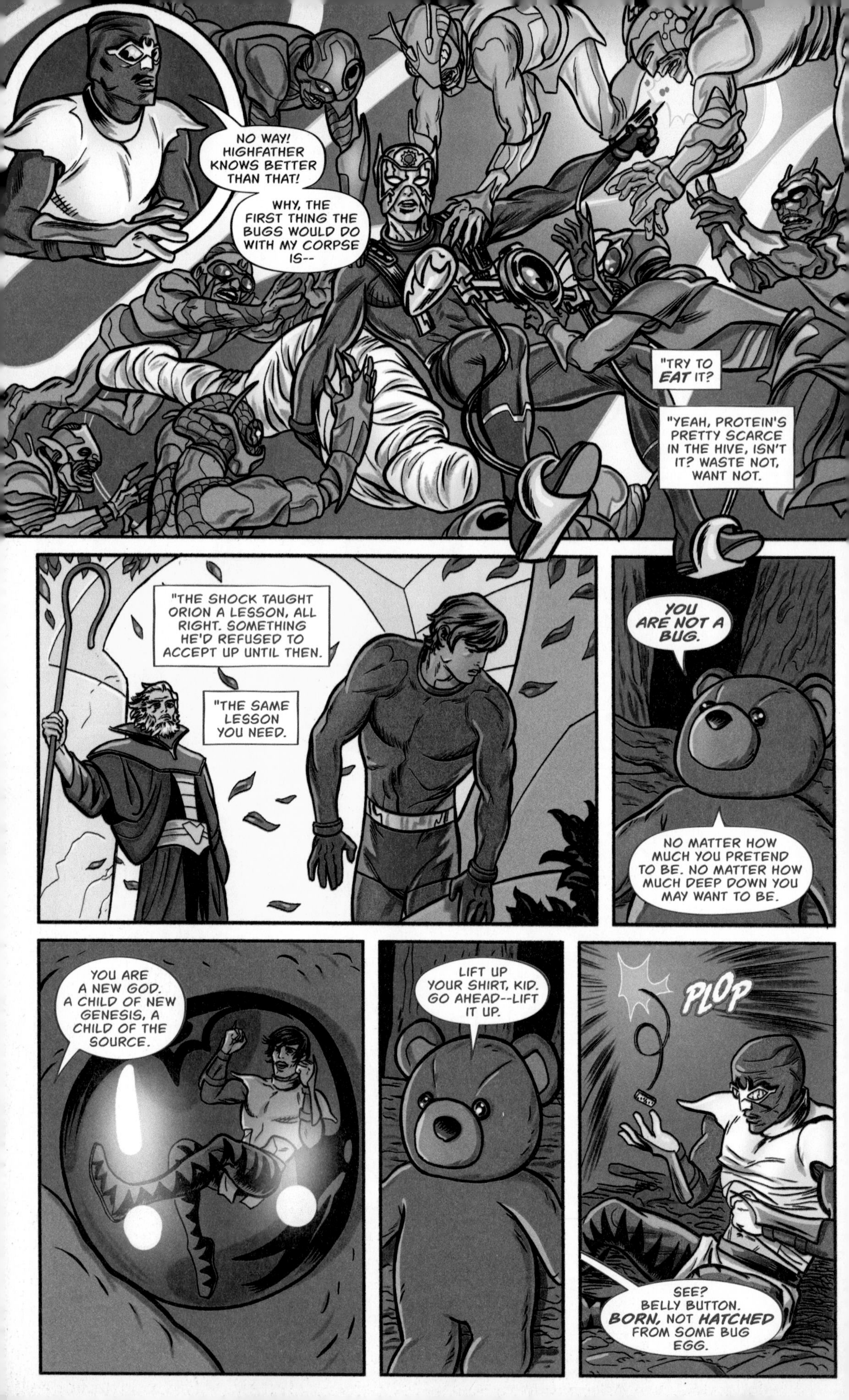
NO WAY! HIGHFATHER KNOWS BETTER THAN THAT!
WHY, THE FIRST THING THE BUGS WOULD DO WITH MY CORPSE IS--
"TRY TO EAT IT?
"YEAH, PROTEIN'S PRETTY SCARCE IN THE HIVE, ISN'T IT? WASTE NOT, WANT NOT.
"THE SHOCK TAUGHT ORION A LESSON, ALL RIGHT. SOMETHING HE'D REFUSED TO ACCEPT UP UNTIL THEN.
"THE SAME LESSON YOU NEED.
YOU ARE NOT A BUG.
NO MATTER HOW MUCH YOU PRETEND TO BE. NO MATTER HOW MUCH DEEP DOWN YOU MAY WANT TO BE.
YOU ARE A NEW GOD. A CHILD OF NEW GENESIS, A CHILD OF THE SOURCE.
LIFT UP YOUR SHIRT, KID. GO AHEAD--LIFT IT UP.
PLOP
SEE? BELLY BUTTON. BORN, NOT HATCHED FROM SOME BUG EGG.

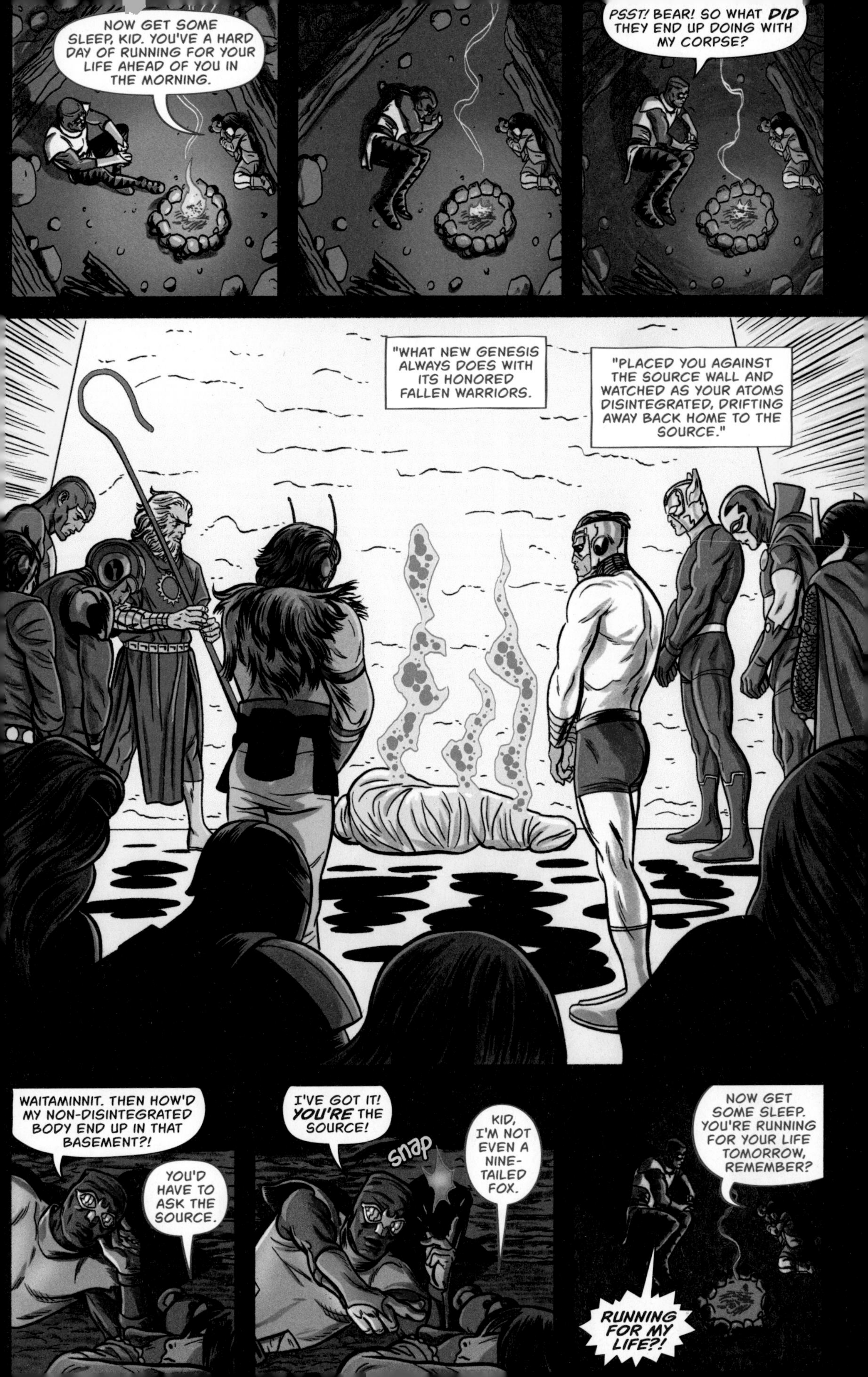
NOW GET SOME SLEEP, KID. YOU'VE A HARD DAY OF RUNNING FOR YOUR LIFE AHEAD OF YOU IN THE MORNING.
PSST! BEAR! SO WHAT DID THEY END UP DOING WITH MY CORPSE?
"WHAT NEW GENESIS ALWAYS DOES WITH ITS HONORED FALLEN WARRIORS.
"PLACED YOU AGAINST THE SOURCE WALL AND WATCHED AS YOUR ATOMS DISINTEGRATED, DRIFTING AWAY BACK HOME TO THE SOURCE."
WAITAMINNIT. THEN HOW'D MY NON-DISINTEGRATED BODY END UP IN THAT BASEMENT?!
YOU'D HAVE TO ASK THE SOURCE.
I'VE GOT IT! YOU'RE THE SOURCE!
SNAP
KID, I'M NOT EVEN A NINE-TAILED FOX.
NOW GET SOME SLEEP. YOU'RE RUNNING FOR YOUR LIFE TOMORROW, REMEMBER?
RUNNING FOR MY LIFE?!

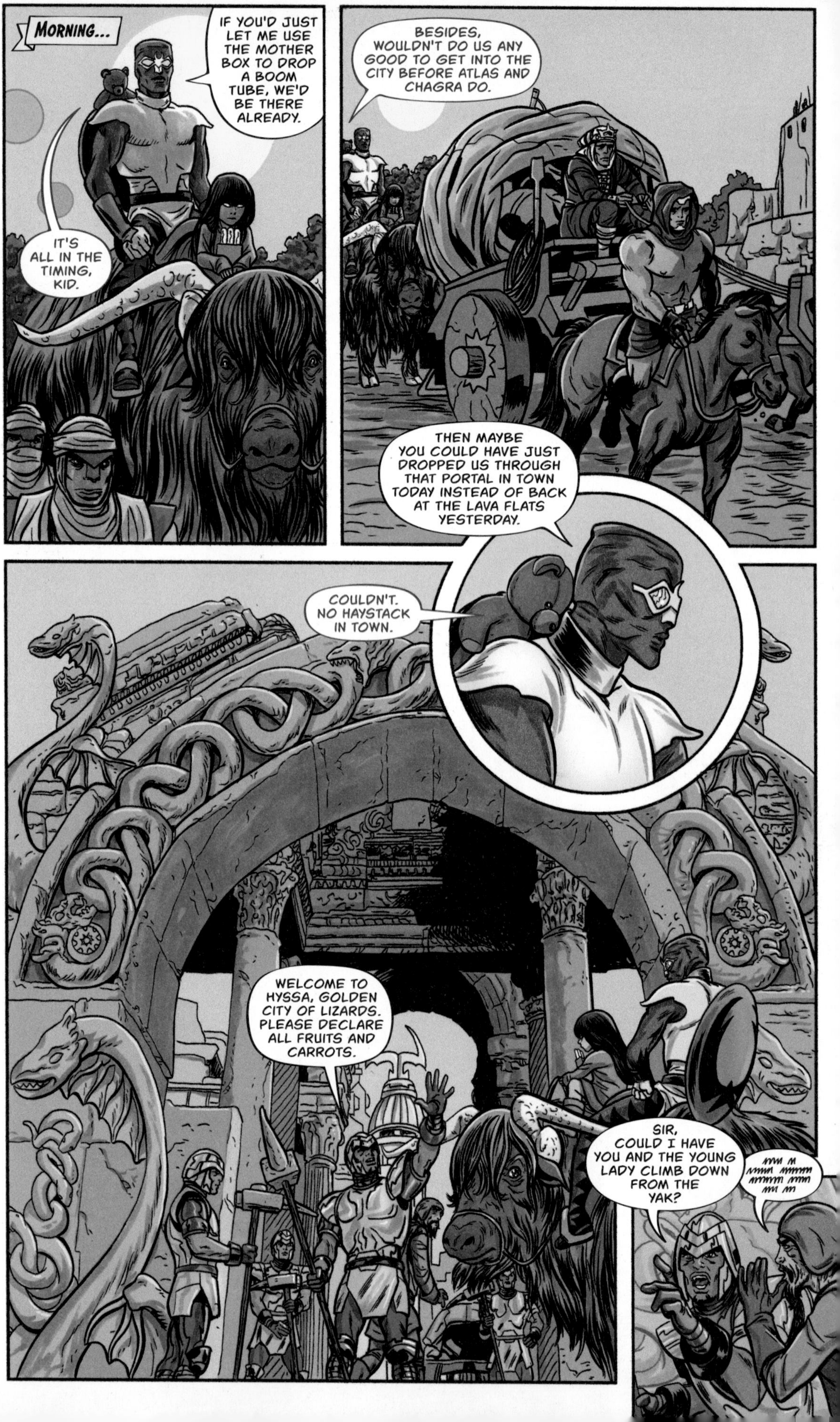
MORNING...
IF YOU'D JUST LET ME USE THE MOTHER BOX TO DROP A BOOM TUBE, WE'D BE THERE ALREADY.
IT'S ALL IN THE TIMING, KID.
BESIDES, WOULDN'T DO US ANY GOOD TO GET INTO THE CITY BEFORE ATLAS AND CHAGRA DO.
THEN MAYBE YOU COULD HAVE JUST DROPPED US THROUGH THAT PORTAL IN TOWN TODAY INSTEAD OF BACK AT THE LAVA FLATS YESTERDAY.
COULDN'T. NO HAYSTACK IN TOWN.
WELCOME TO HYSSA, GOLDEN CITY OF LIZARDS. PLEASE DECLARE ALL FRUITS AND CARROTS.
SIR, COULD I HAVE YOU AND THE YOUNG LADY CLIMB DOWN FROM THE YAK?

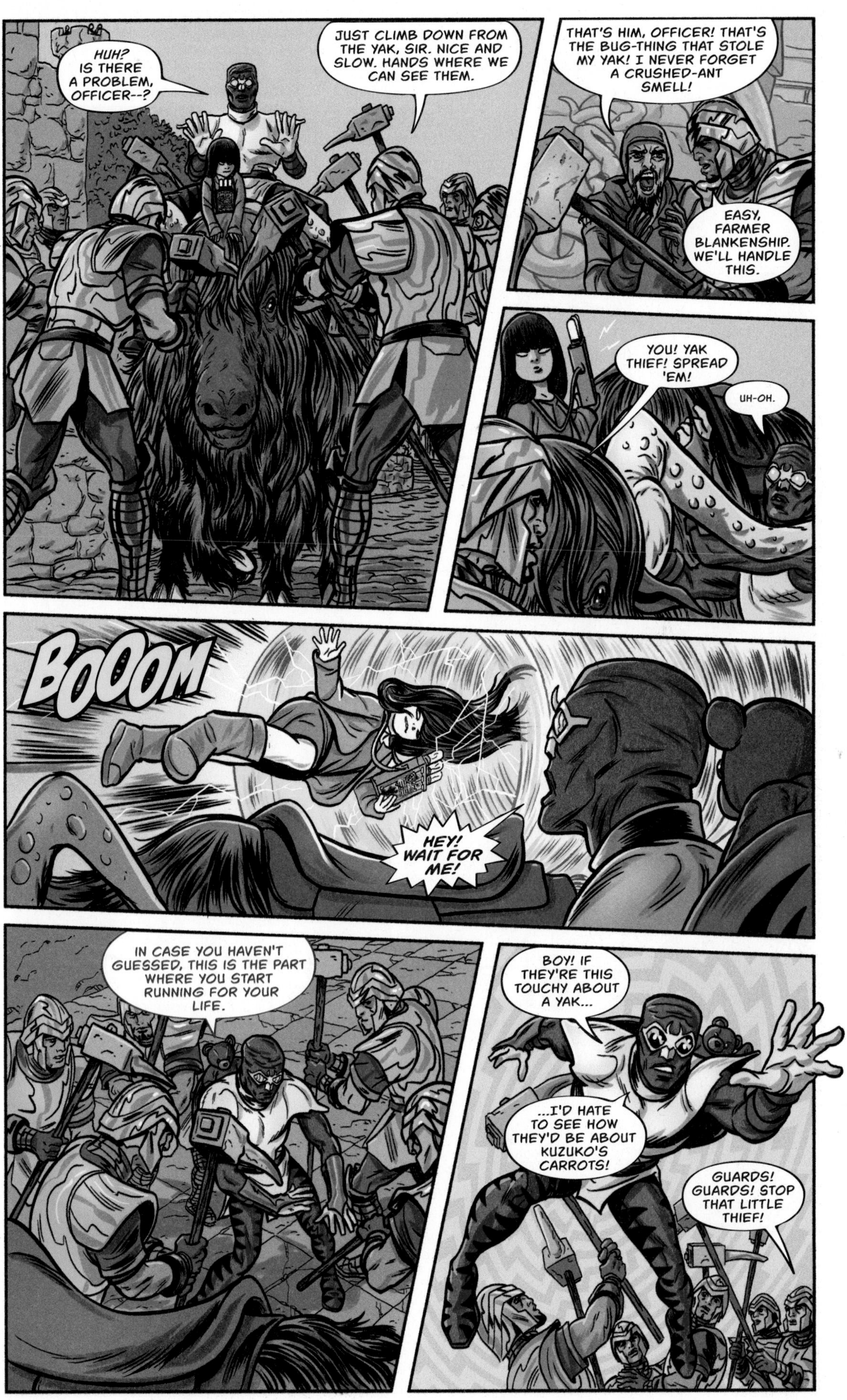
HUH? IS THERE A PROBLEM, OFFICER--?
JUST CLIMB DOWN FROM THE YAK, SIR. NICE AND SLOW. HANDS WHERE WE CAN SEE THEM.
THAT'S HIM, OFFICER! THAT'S THE BUG-THING THAT STOLE MY YAK! I NEVER FORGET A CRUSHED-ANT SMELL!
EASY, FARMER BLANKENSHIP. WE'LL HANDLE THIS.
YOU! YAK THIEF! SPREAD 'EM!
UH-OH.
BOOOM
HEY! WAIT FOR ME!
IN CASE YOU HAVEN'T GUESSED, THIS IS THE PART WHERE YOU START RUNNING FOR YOUR LIFE.
BOY! IF THEY'RE THIS TOUCHY ABOUT A YAK...
...I'D HATE TO SEE HOW THEY'D BE ABOUT KUZUKO'S CARROTS!
GUARDS! GUARDS! STOP THAT LITTLE THIEF!

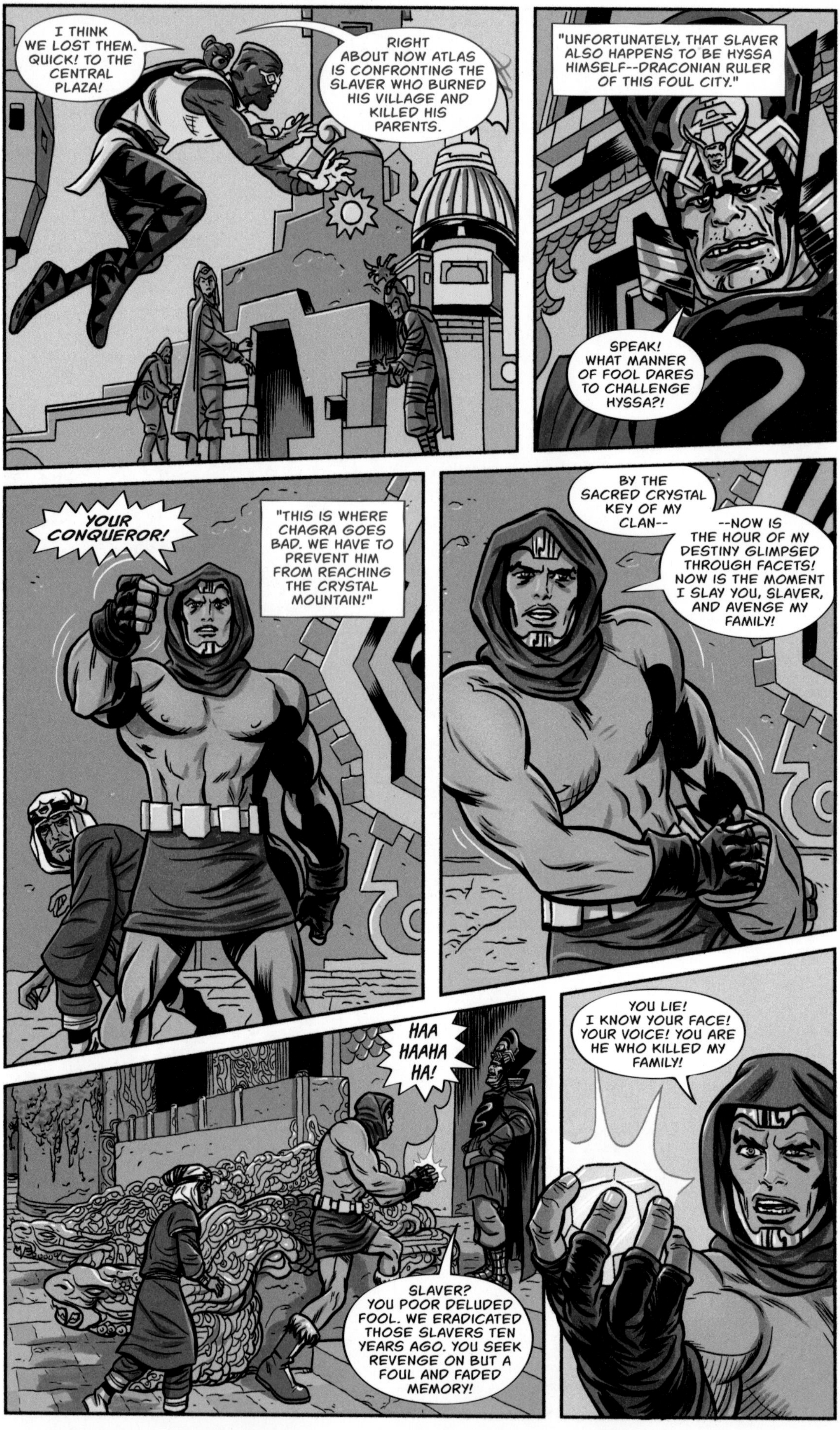
I THINK WE LOST THEM. QUICK! TO THE CENTRAL PLAZA!
RIGHT ABOUT NOW ATLAS IS CONFRONTING THE SLAVER WHO BURNED HIS VILLAGE AND KILLED HIS PARENTS.
"UNFORTUNATELY, THAT SLAVER ALSO HAPPENS TO BE HYSSA HIMSELF--DRACONIAN RULER OF THIS FOUL CITY."
SPEAK! WHAT MANNER OF FOOL DARES TO CHALLENGE HYSSA?!
YOUR CONQUEROR!
"THIS IS WHERE CHAGRA GOES BAD. WE HAVE TO PREVENT HIM FROM REACHING THE CRYSTAL MOUNTAIN!"
BY THE SACRED CRYSTAL KEY OF MY CLAN--
--NOW IS THE HOUR OF MY DESTINY GLIMPSED THROUGH FACETS! NOW IS THE MOMENT I SLAY YOU, SLAVER, AND AVENGE MY FAMILY!
HAA HAAHA HA!
SLAVER? YOU POOR DELUDED FOOL. WE ERADICATED THOSE SLAVERS TEN YEARS AGO. YOU SEEK REVENGE ON BUT A FOUL AND FADED MEMORY!
YOU LIE! I KNOW YOUR FACE! YOUR VOICE! YOU ARE HE WHO KILLED MY FAMILY!

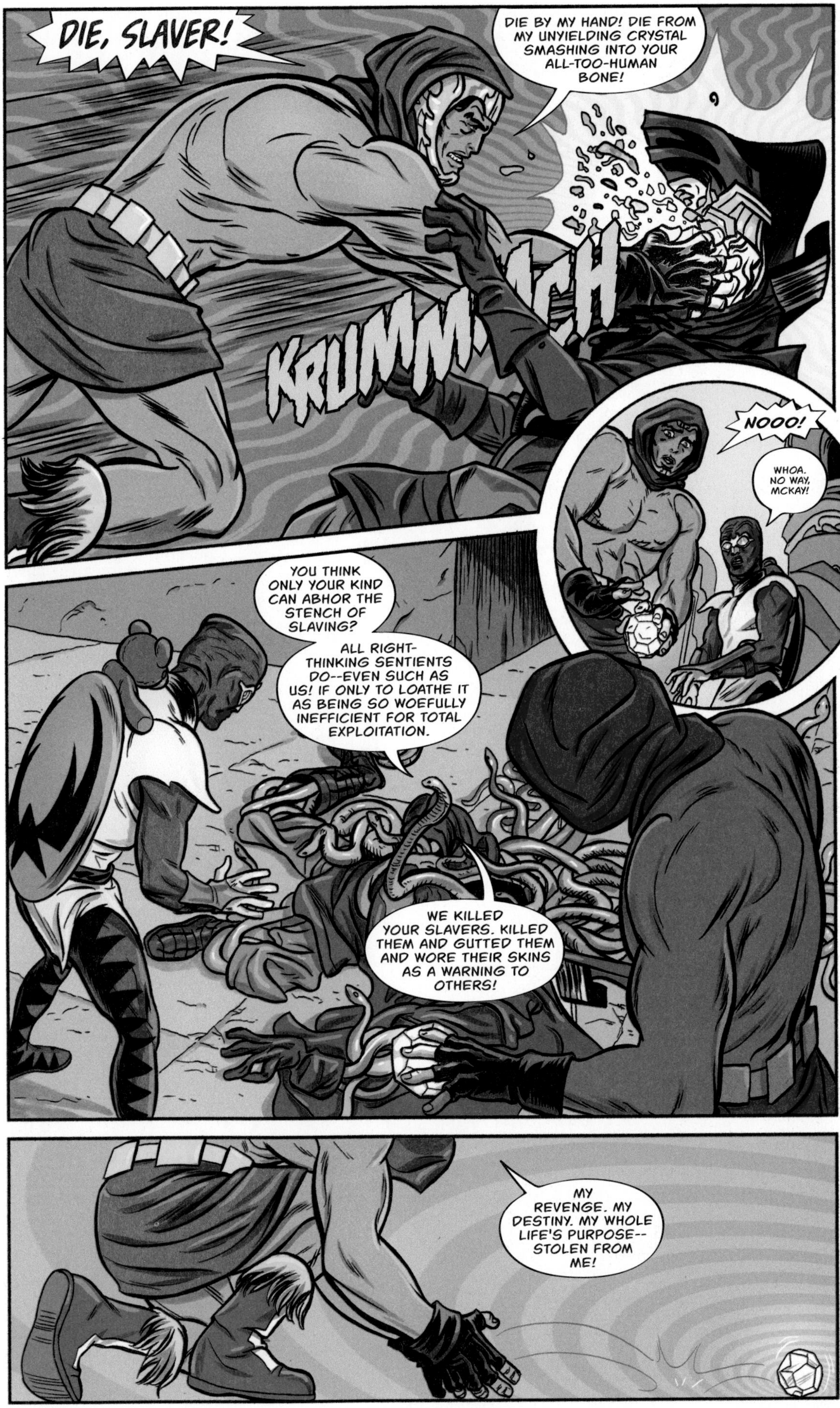
DIE, SLAVER!
DIE BY MY HAND! DIE FROM MY UNYIELDING CRYSTAL SMASHING INTO YOUR ALL-TOO-HUMAN BONE!
KRUMMMMCH
NOOO!
WHOA. NO WAY, MCKAY!
YOU THINK ONLY YOUR KIND CAN ABHOR THE STENCH OF SLAVING?
ALL RIGHT-THINKING SENTIENTS DO--EVEN SUCH AS US! IF ONLY TO LOATHE IT AS BEING SO WOEFULLY INEFFICIENT FOR TOTAL EXPLOITATION.
WE KILLED YOUR SLAVERS. KILLED THEM AND GUTTED THEM AND WORE THEIR SKINS AS A WARNING TO OTHERS!
MY REVENGE. MY DESTINY. MY WHOLE LIFE'S PURPOSE--STOLEN FROM ME!

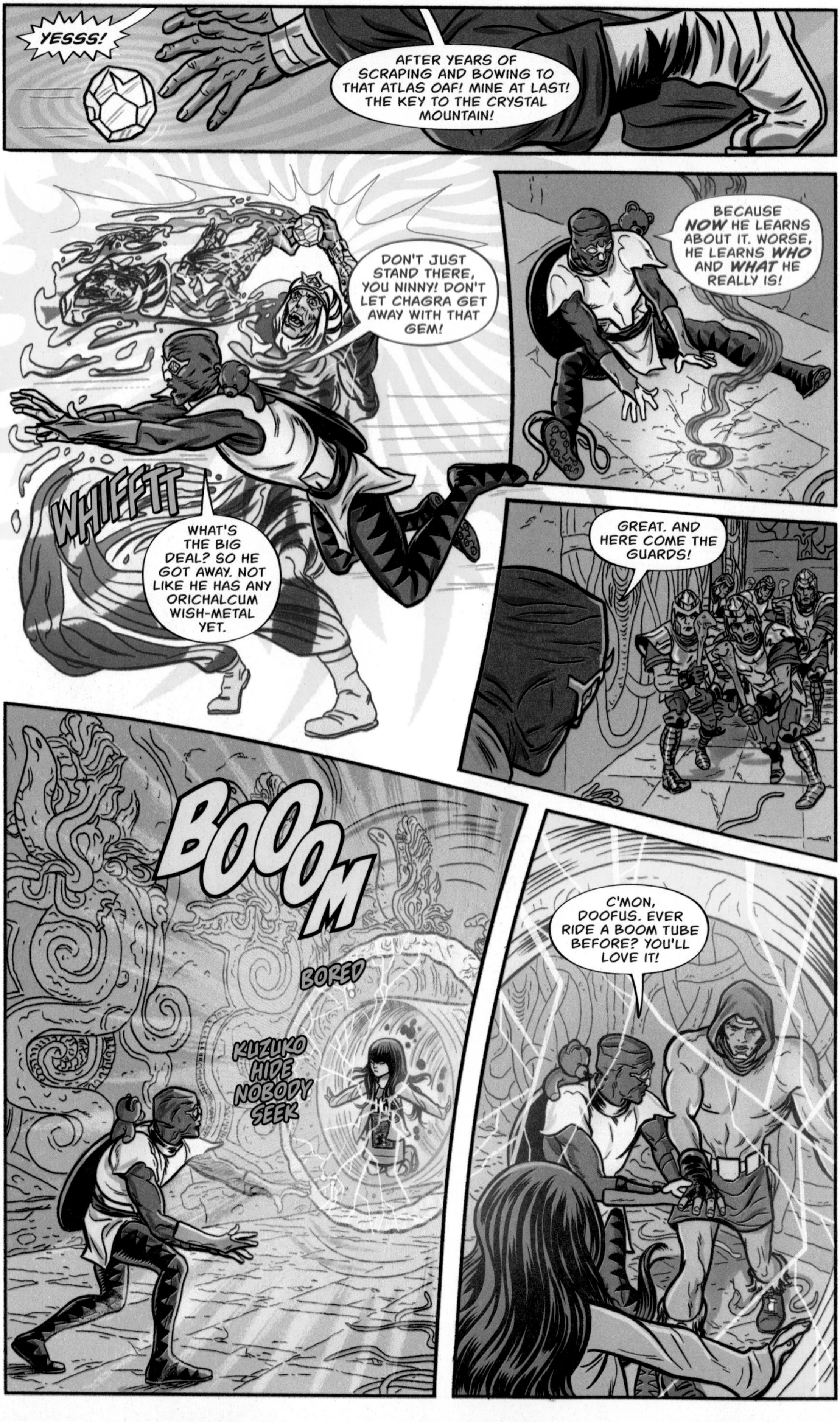
YESSS!
AFTER YEARS OF SCRAPING AND BOWING TO THAT ATLAS OAF! MINE AT LAST! THE KEY TO THE CRYSTAL MOUNTAIN!
DON'T JUST STAND THERE, YOU NINNY! DON'T LET CHAGRA GET AWAY WITH THAT GEM!
WHIFFTT
WHAT'S THE BIG DEAL? SO HE GOT AWAY. NOT LIKE HE HAS ANY ORICHALCUM WISH-METAL YET.
BECAUSE NOW HE LEARNS ABOUT IT. WORSE, HE LEARNS WHO AND WHAT HE REALLY IS!
GREAT. AND HERE COME THE GUARDS!
BOOOM
BORED
KUZUKO HIDE NOBODY SEEK
C'MON, DOOFUS. EVER RIDE A BOOM TUBE BEFORE? YOU'LL LOVE IT!

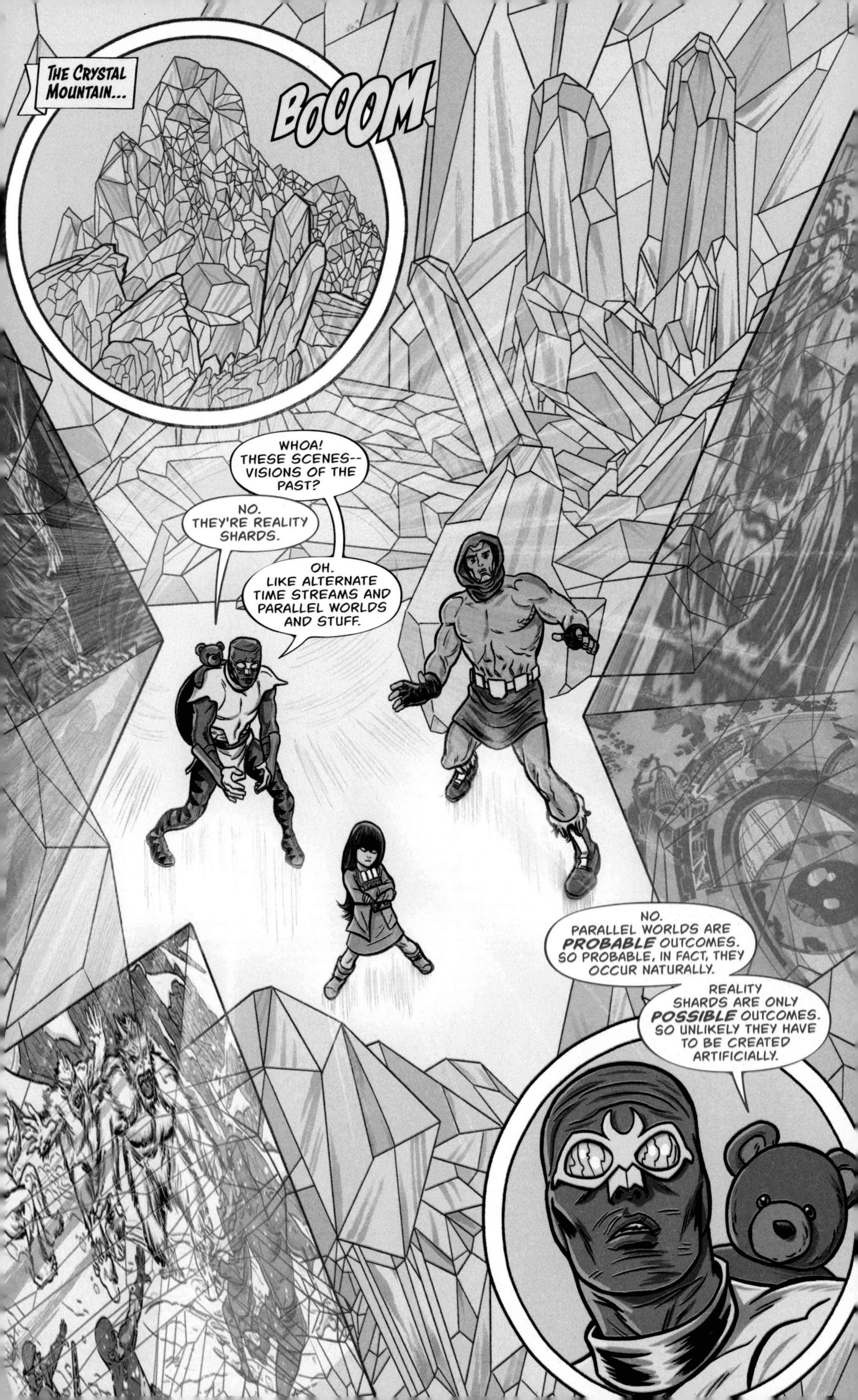
THE CRYSTAL MOUNTAIN...
BOOOM
WHOA! THESE SCENES-- VISIONS OF THE PAST?
NO. THEY'RE REALITY SHARDS.
OH. LIKE ALTERNATE TIME STREAMS AND PARALLEL WORLDS AND STUFF.
NO. PARALLEL WORLDS ARE PROBABLE OUTCOMES. SO PROBABLE, IN FACT, THEY OCCUR NATURALLY.
REALITY SHARDS ARE ONLY POSSIBLE OUTCOMES. SO UNLIKELY THEY HAVE TO BE CREATED ARTIFICIALLY.

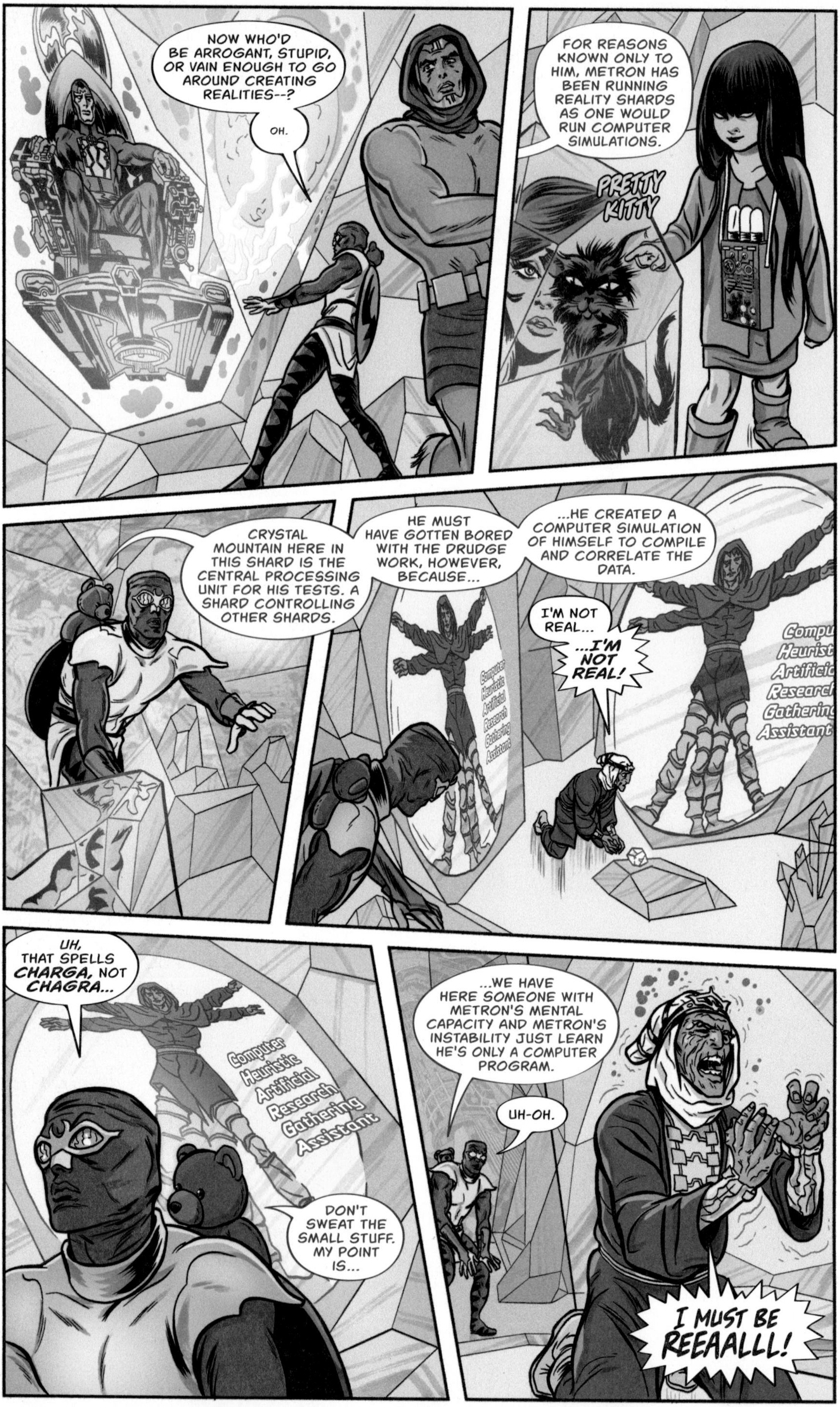
NOW WHO'D BE ARROGANT, STUPID, OR VAIN ENOUGH TO GO AROUND CREATING REALITIES--?
OH.
FOR REASONS KNOWN ONLY TO HIM, METRON HAS BEEN RUNNING REALITY SHARDS AS ONE WOULD RUN COMPUTER SIMULATIONS.
PRETTY KITTY
CRYSTAL MOUNTAIN HERE IN THIS SHARD IS THE CENTRAL PROCESSING UNIT FOR HIS TESTS. A SHARD CONTROLLING OTHER SHARDS.
HE MUST HAVE GOTTEN BORED WITH THE DRUDGE WORK, HOWEVER, BECAUSE...
...HE CREATED A COMPUTER SIMULATION OF HIMSELF TO COMPILE AND CORRELATE THE DATA.
I'M NOT REAL...
...I'M NOT REAL!
Computer Heuristic Artificial Research Gathering Assistant
UH, THAT SPELLS CHARGA, NOT CHAGRA...
Computer Heuristic Artificial Research Gathering Assistant
DON'T SWEAT THE SMALL STUFF. MY POINT IS...
...WE HAVE HERE SOMEONE WITH METRON'S MENTAL CAPACITY AND METRON'S INSTABILITY JUST LEARN HE'S ONLY A COMPUTER PROGRAM.
UH-OH.
I MUST BE REEAALLL!

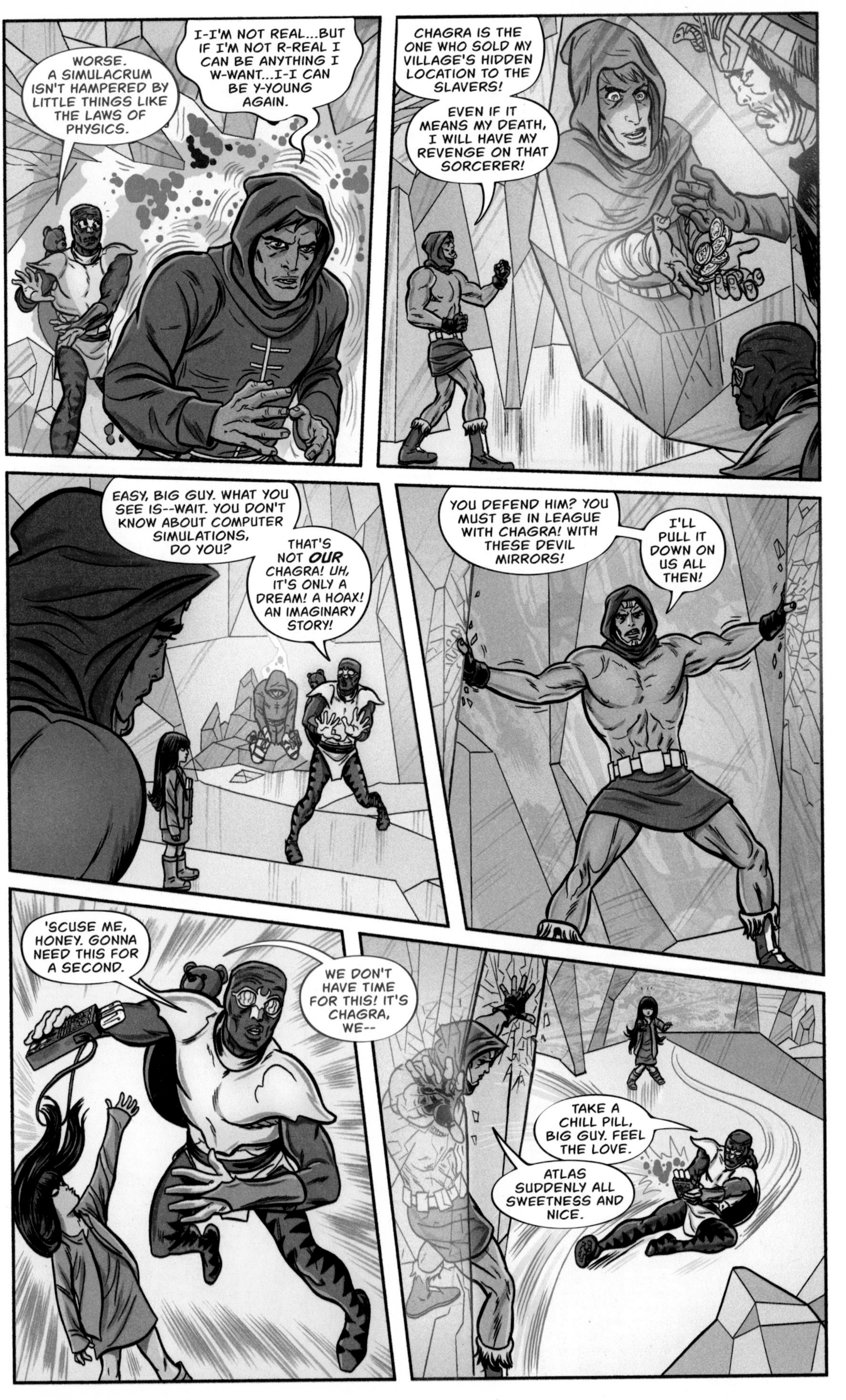
WORSE. A SIMULACRUM ISN'T HAMPERED BY LITTLE THINGS LIKE THE LAWS OF PHYSICS.
I-I'M NOT REAL...BUT IF I'M NOT R-REAL I CAN BE ANYTHING I W-WANT...I-I CAN BE Y-YOUNG AGAIN.
CHAGRA IS THE ONE WHO SOLD MY VILLAGE'S HIDDEN LOCATION TO THE SLAVERS!
EVEN IF IT MEANS MY DEATH, I WILL HAVE MY REVENGE ON THAT SORCERER!
EASY, BIG GUY. WHAT YOU SEE IS--WAIT. YOU DON'T KNOW ABOUT COMPUTER SIMULATIONS, DO YOU?
THAT'S NOT **OUR** CHAGRA! UH, IT'S ONLY A DREAM! A HOAX! AN IMAGINARY STORY!
YOU DEFEND HIM? YOU MUST BE IN LEAGUE WITH CHAGRA! WITH THESE DEVIL MIRRORS!
I'LL PULL IT DOWN ON US ALL THEN!
'SCUSE ME, HONEY. GONNA NEED THIS FOR A SECOND.
WE DON'T HAVE TIME FOR THIS! IT'S CHAGRA, WE--
TAKE A CHILL PILL, BIG GUY. FEEL THE LOVE.
ATLAS SUDDENLY ALL SWEETNESS AND NICE.

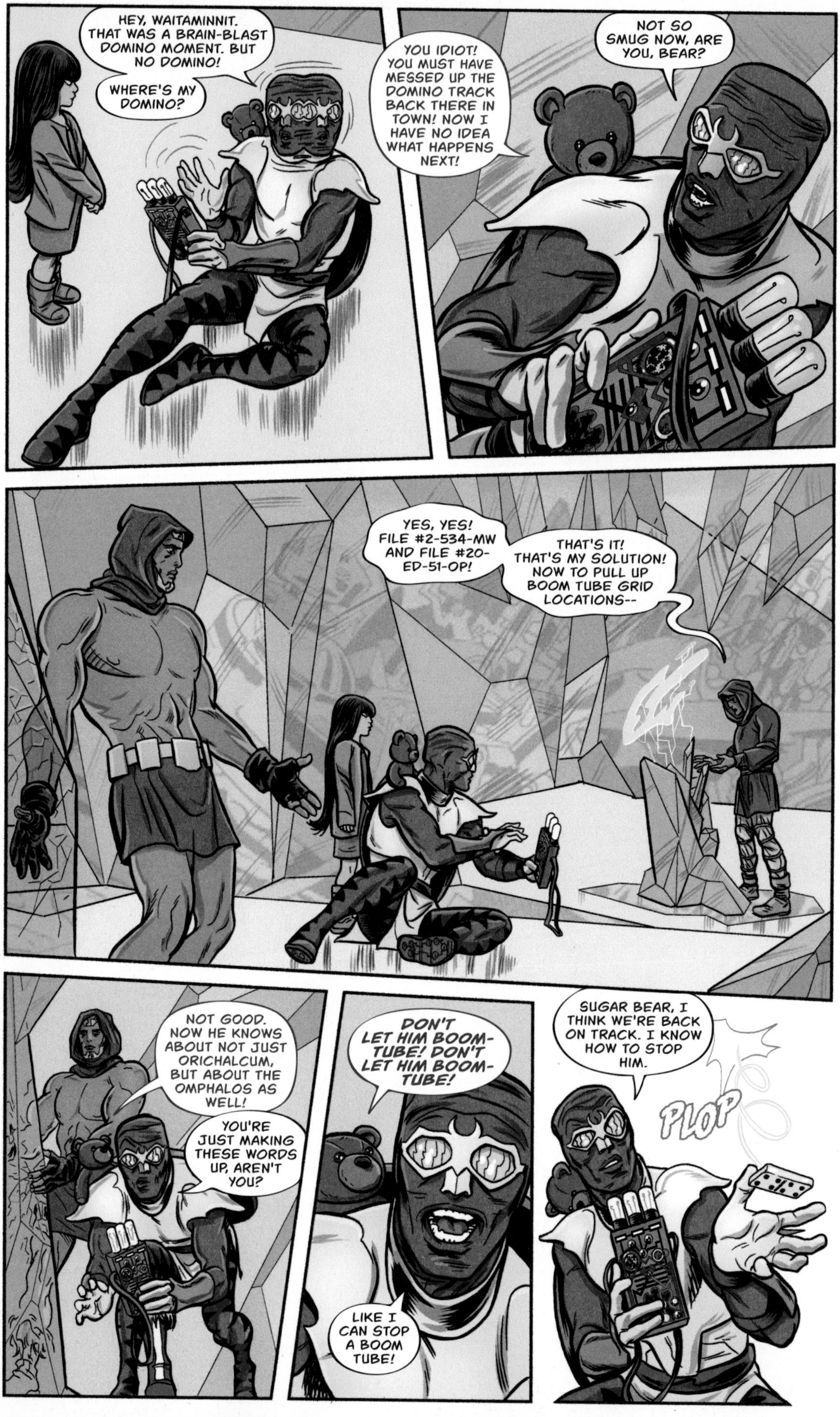
HEY, WAITAMINNIT. THAT WAS A BRAIN-BLAST DOMINO MOMENT. BUT NO DOMINO!
WHERE'S MY DOMINO?
YOU IDIOT! YOU MUST HAVE MESSED UP THE DOMINO TRACK BACK THERE IN TOWN! NOW I HAVE NO IDEA WHAT HAPPENS NEXT!
NOT SO SMUG NOW, ARE YOU, BEAR?
YES, YES! FILE #2-534-MW AND FILE #20-ED-51-OP!
THAT'S IT! THAT'S MY SOLUTION! NOW TO PULL UP BOOM TUBE GRID LOCATIONS--
NOT GOOD. NOW HE KNOWS ABOUT NOT JUST ORICHALCUM, BUT ABOUT THE OMPHALOS AS WELL!
YOU'RE JUST MAKING THESE WORDS UP, AREN'T YOU?
DON'T LET HIM BOOM-TUBE! DON'T LET HIM BOOM-TUBE!
LIKE I CAN STOP A BOOM TUBE!
SUGAR BEAR, I THINK WE'RE BACK ON TRACK. I KNOW HOW TO STOP HIM.
PLOP

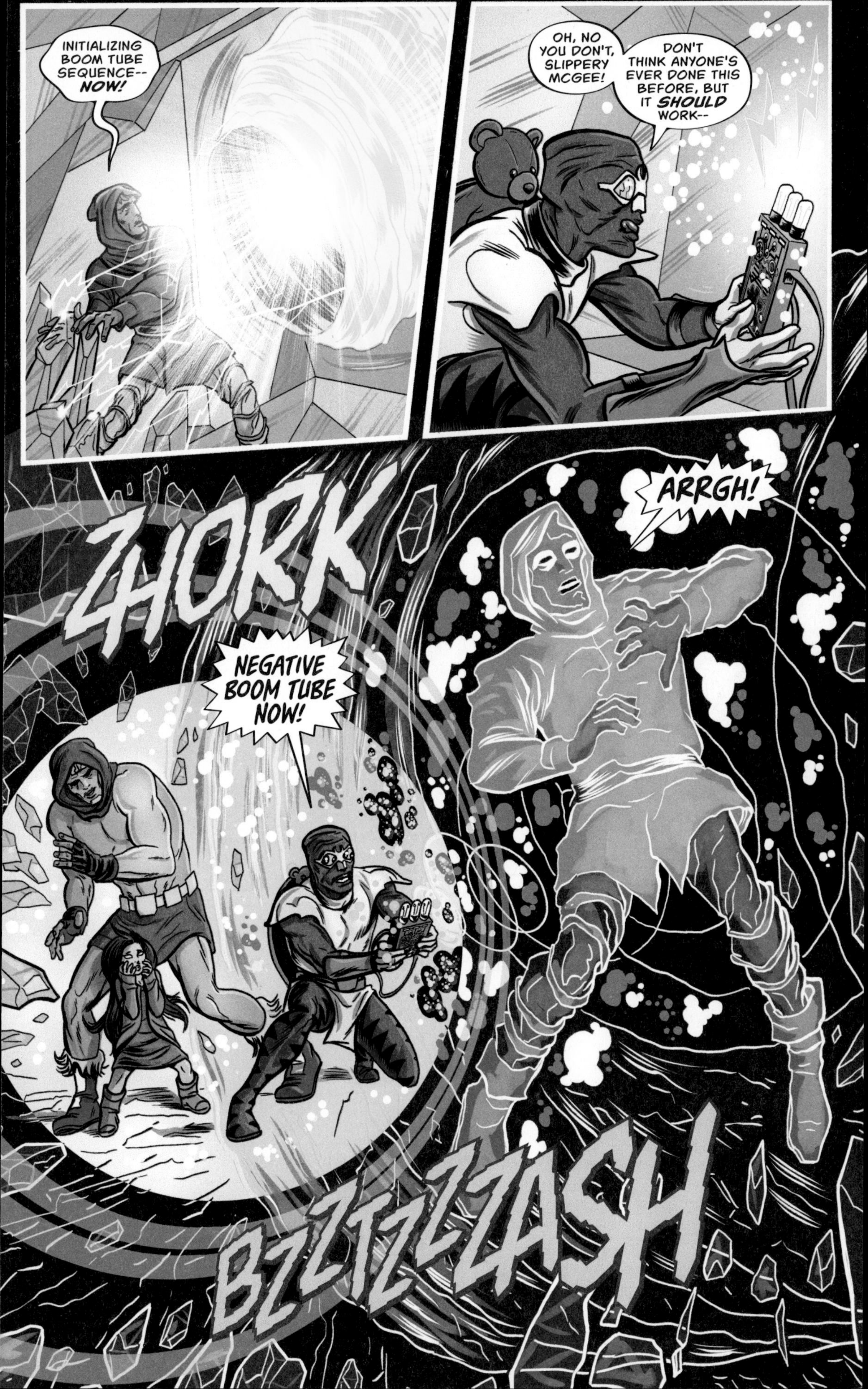
INITIALIZING BOOM TUBE SEQUENCE-- NOW!
OH, NO YOU DON'T, SLIPPERY MCGEE!
DON'T THINK ANYONE'S EVER DONE THIS BEFORE, BUT IT SHOULD WORK--
ZHORK
ARRGH!
NEGATIVE BOOM TUBE NOW!
BZZTZZZASH

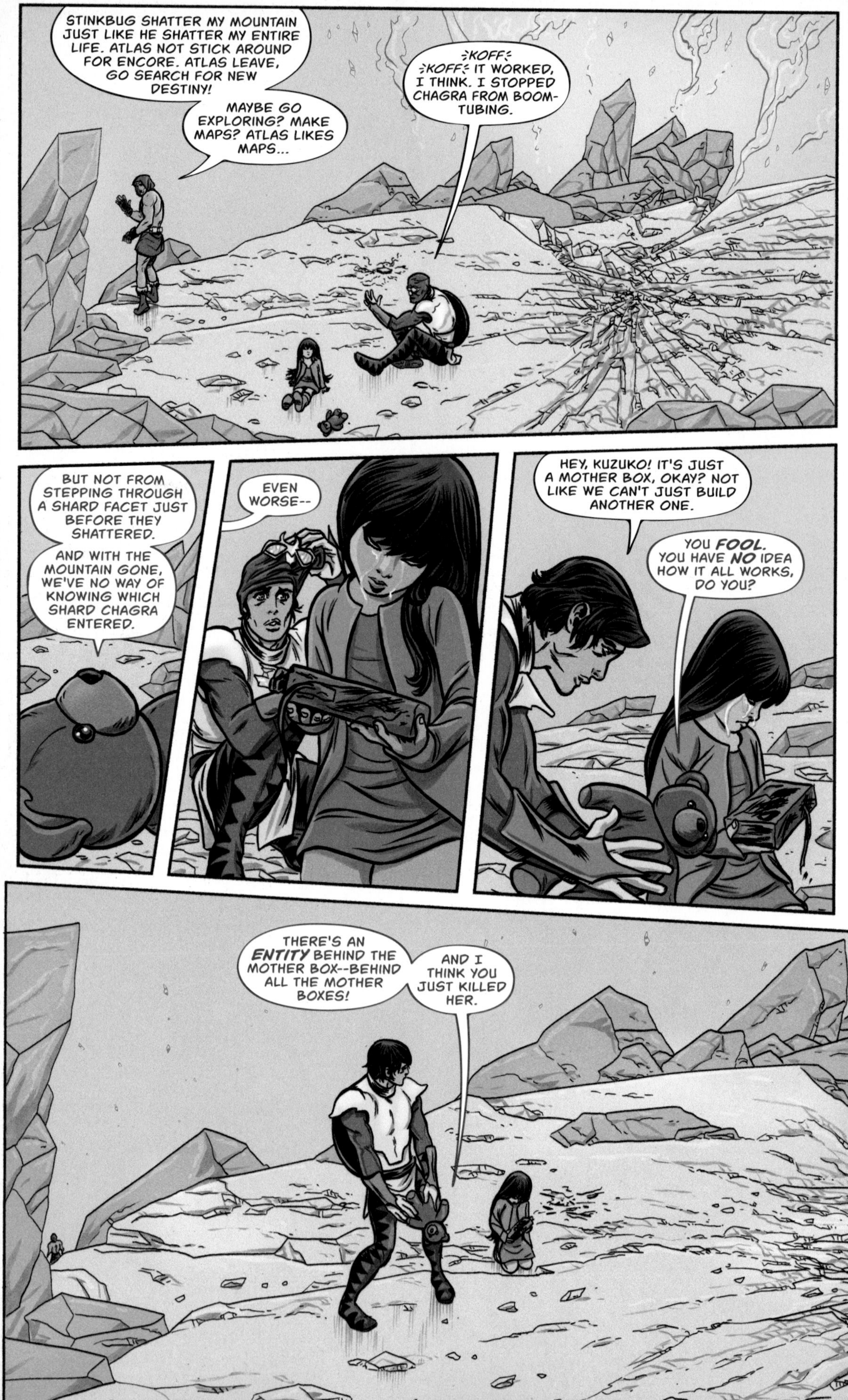
STINKBUG SHATTER MY MOUNTAIN JUST LIKE HE SHATTER MY ENTIRE LIFE. ATLAS NOT STICK AROUND FOR ENCORE. ATLAS LEAVE, GO SEARCH FOR NEW DESTINY!
MAYBE GO EXPLORING? MAKE MAPS? ATLAS LIKES MAPS...
KOFF KOFF IT WORKED, I THINK. I STOPPED CHAGRA FROM BOOM-TUBING.
BUT NOT FROM STEPPING THROUGH A SHARD FACET JUST BEFORE THEY SHATTERED.
AND WITH THE MOUNTAIN GONE, WE'VE NO WAY OF KNOWING WHICH SHARD CHAGRA ENTERED.
EVEN WORSE--
HEY, KUZUKO! IT'S JUST A MOTHER BOX, OKAY? NOT LIKE WE CAN'T JUST BUILD ANOTHER ONE.
YOU FOOL. YOU HAVE NO IDEA HOW IT ALL WORKS, DO YOU?
THERE'S AN ENTITY BEHIND THE MOTHER BOX--BEHIND ALL THE MOTHER BOXES!
AND I THINK YOU JUST KILLED HER.

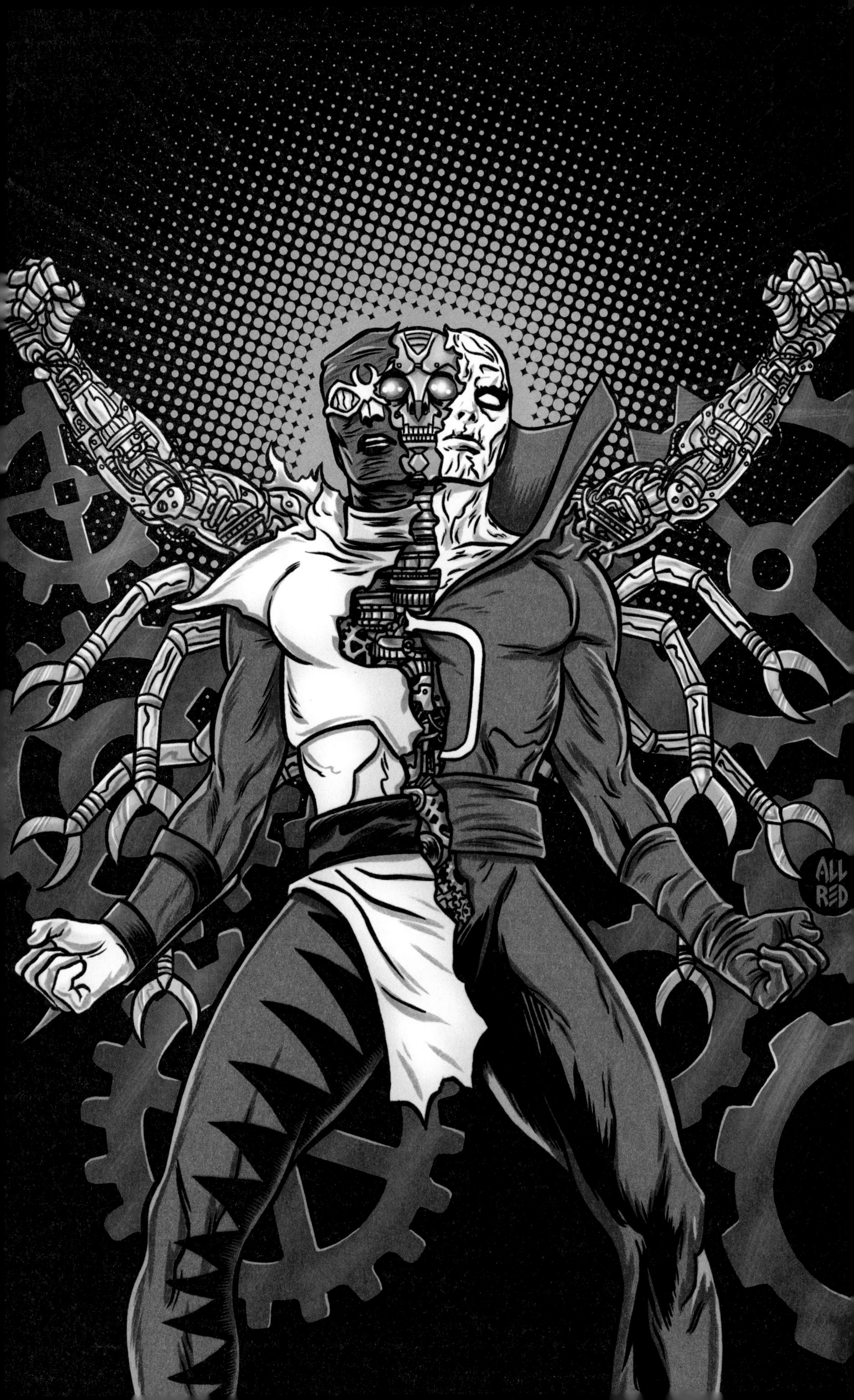
ALL
RED

Variant cover art for issue #4 by Andrew MacLean and Jordie Bellaire

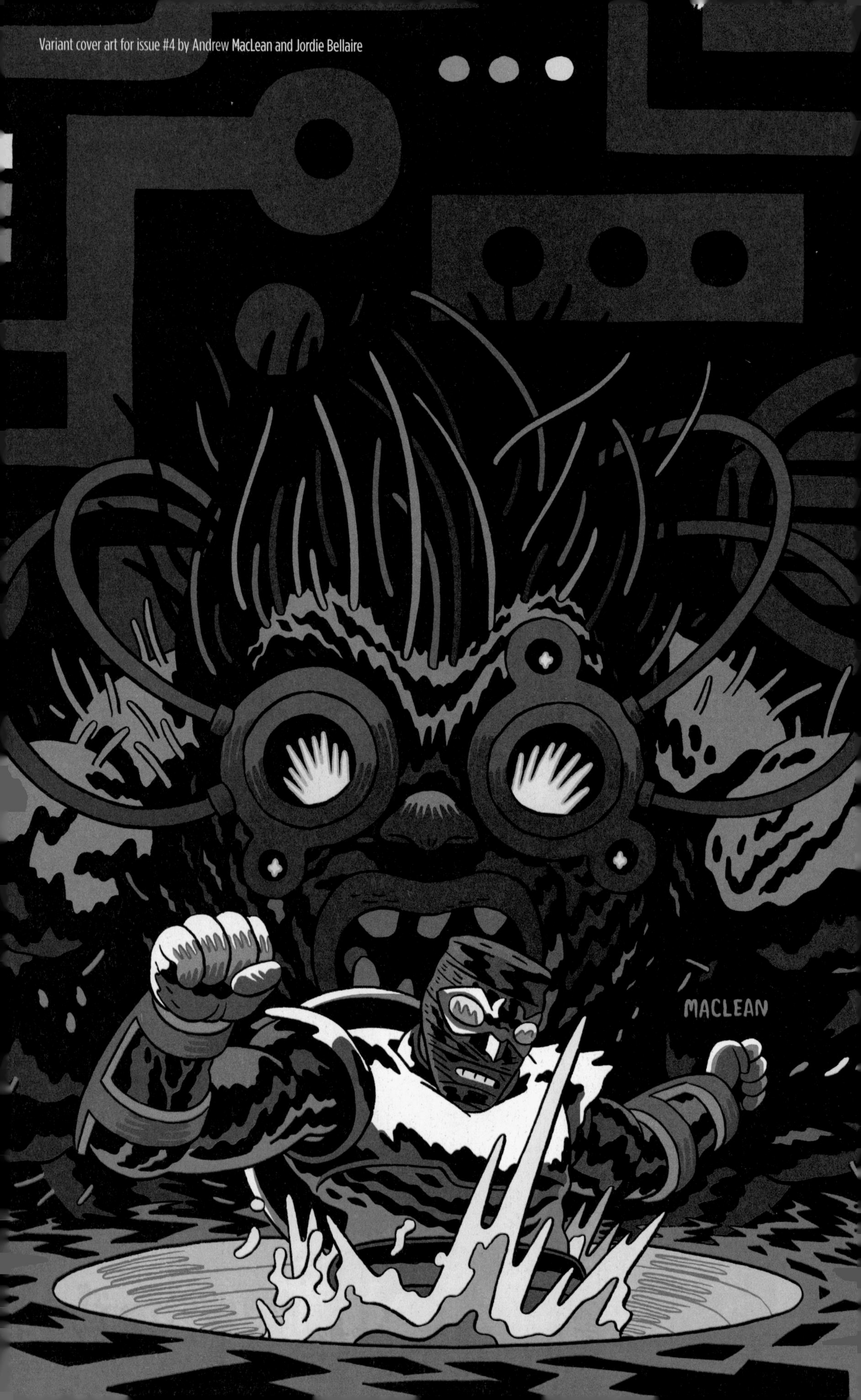
MACLEAN

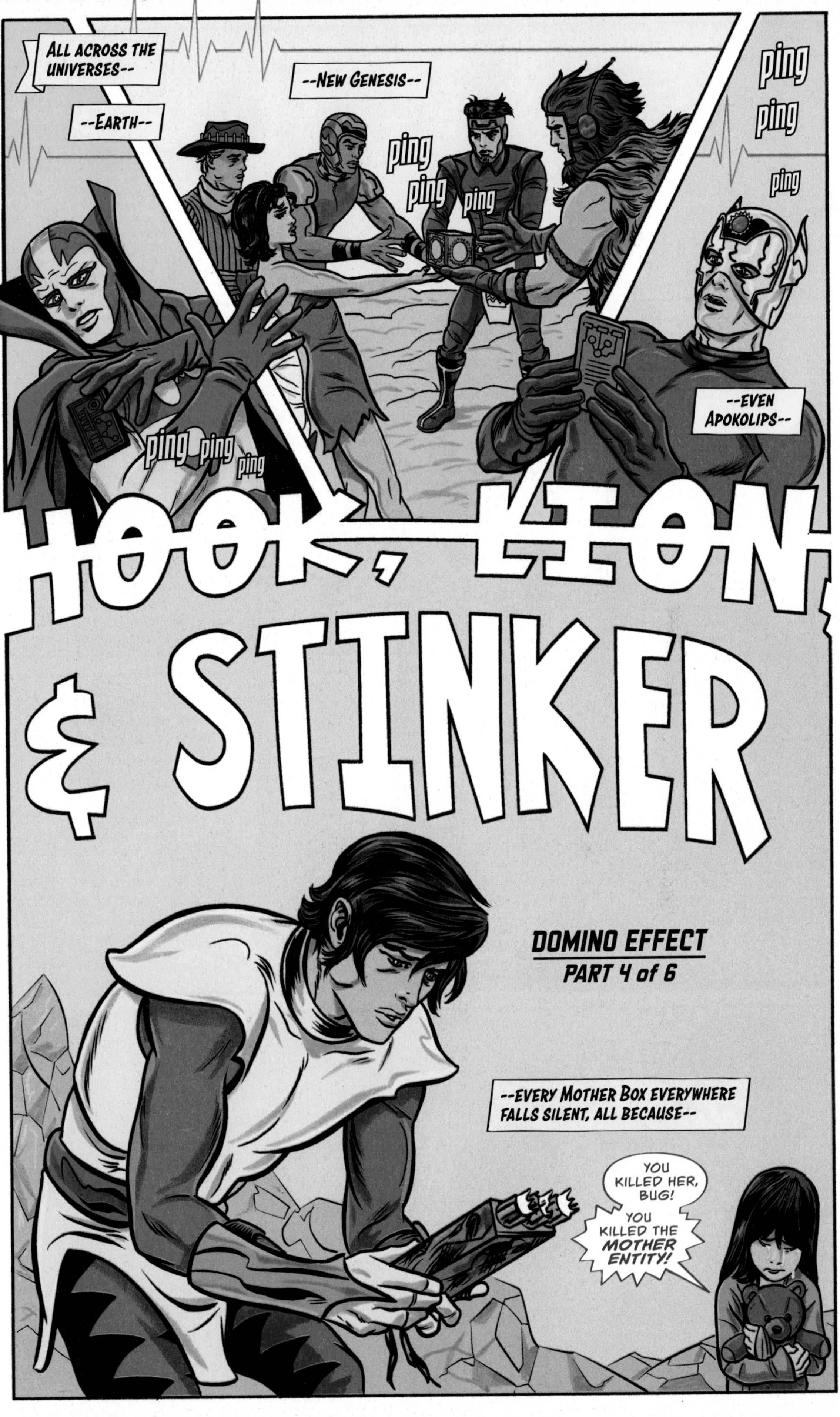

ALL ACROSS THE UNIVERSES--
--EARTH--
--NEW GENESIS--
ping
ping
ping
ping
ping
ping
ping ping ping
--EVEN APOKOLIPS--
HOOK, LION, & STINKER
DOMINO EFFECT
PART 4 of 6
--EVERY MOTHER BOX EVERYWHERE FALLS SILENT, ALL BECAUSE--
YOU KILLED HER, BUG!
YOU KILLED THE MOTHER ENTITY!

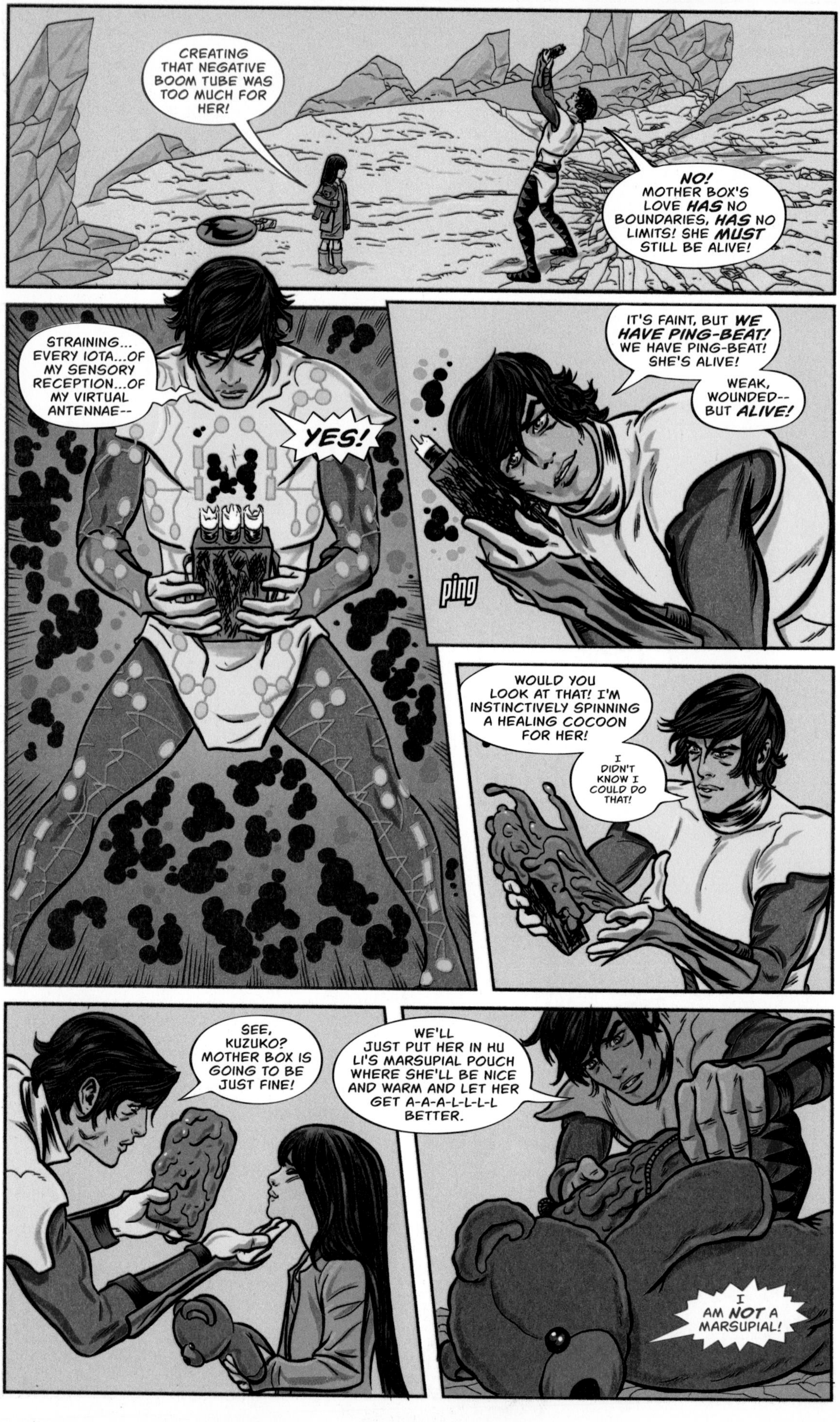
CREATING THAT NEGATIVE BOOM TUBE WAS TOO MUCH FOR HER!
NO! MOTHER BOX'S LOVE HAS NO BOUNDARIES, HAS NO LIMITS! SHE MUST STILL BE ALIVE!
STRAINING... EVERY IOTA...OF MY SENSORY RECEPTION...OF MY VIRTUAL ANTENNAE--
YES!
IT'S FAINT, BUT WE HAVE PING-BEAT! WE HAVE PING-BEAT! SHE'S ALIVE!
WEAK, WOUNDED-- BUT ALIVE!
ping
WOULD YOU LOOK AT THAT! I'M INSTINCTIVELY SPINNING A HEALING COCOON FOR HER!
I DIDN'T KNOW I COULD DO THAT!
SEE, KUZUKO? MOTHER BOX IS GOING TO BE JUST FINE!
WE'LL JUST PUT HER IN HU LI'S MARSUPIAL POUCH WHERE SHE'LL BE NICE AND WARM AND LET HER GET A-A-A-L-L-L-L BETTER.
I AM NOT A MARSUPIAL!

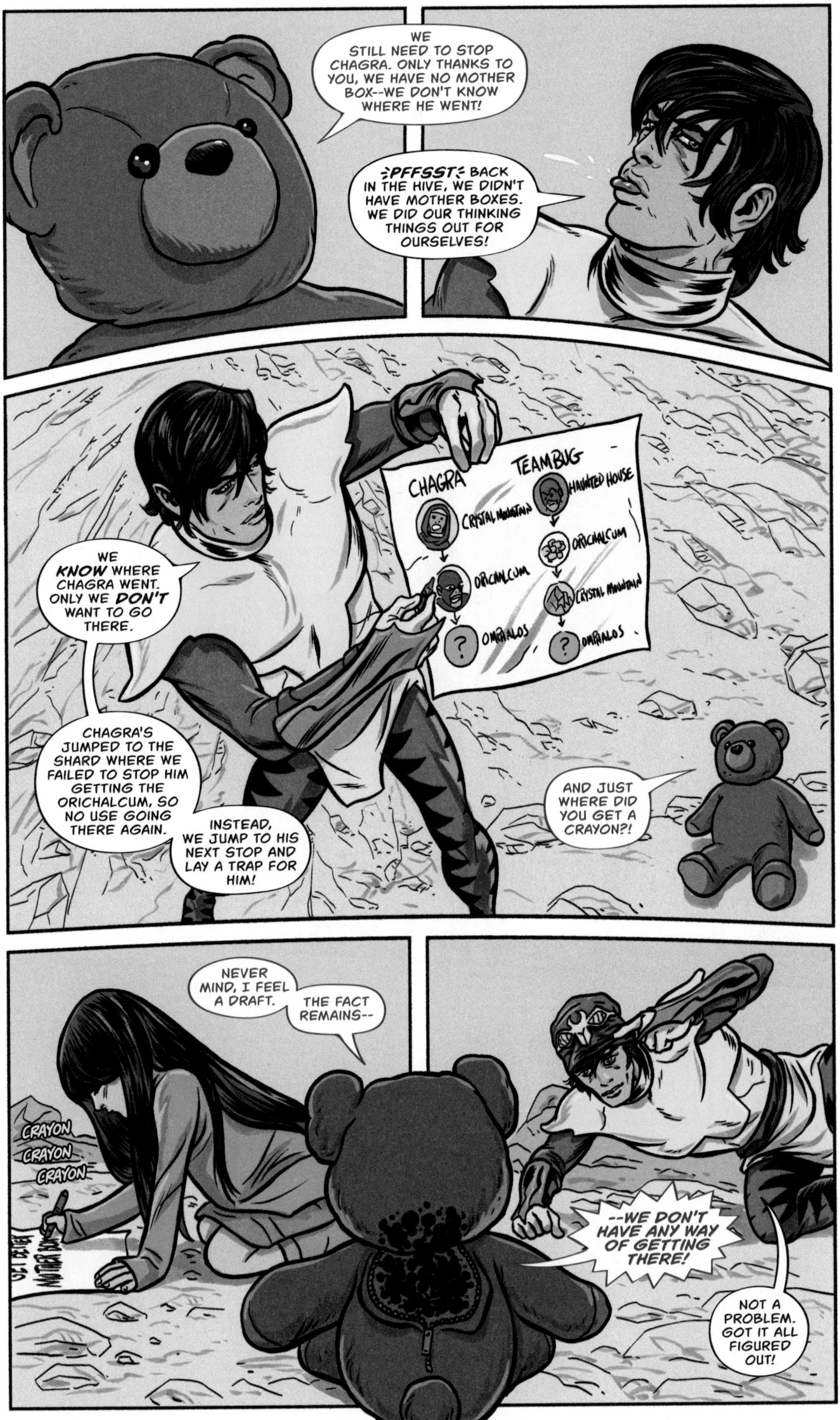
WE STILL NEED TO STOP CHAGRA. ONLY THANKS TO YOU, WE HAVE NO MOTHER BOX--WE DON'T KNOW WHERE HE WENT!
PFFSST BACK IN THE HIVE, WE DIDN'T HAVE MOTHER BOXES. WE DID OUR THINKING THINGS OUT FOR OURSELVES!
CHAGRA
TEAMBUG
HAUNTED HOUSE
CRYSTAL MOUNTAIN
ORICHALCUM
ORICHALCUM
CRYSTAL MOUNTAIN
OMPHALOS
OMPHALOS
WE KNOW WHERE CHAGRA WENT. ONLY WE DON'T WANT TO GO THERE.
CHAGRA'S JUMPED TO THE SHARD WHERE WE FAILED TO STOP HIM GETTING THE ORICHALCUM, SO NO USE GOING THERE AGAIN.
INSTEAD, WE JUMP TO HIS NEXT STOP AND LAY A TRAP FOR HIM!
AND JUST WHERE DID YOU GET A CRAYON?!
NEVER MIND, I FEEL A DRAFT.
THE FACT REMAINS--
CRAYON
CRAYON
CRAYON
GET BETTER MOTHER BOX
--WE DON'T HAVE ANY WAY OF GETTING THERE!
NOT A PROBLEM. GOT IT ALL FIGURED OUT!

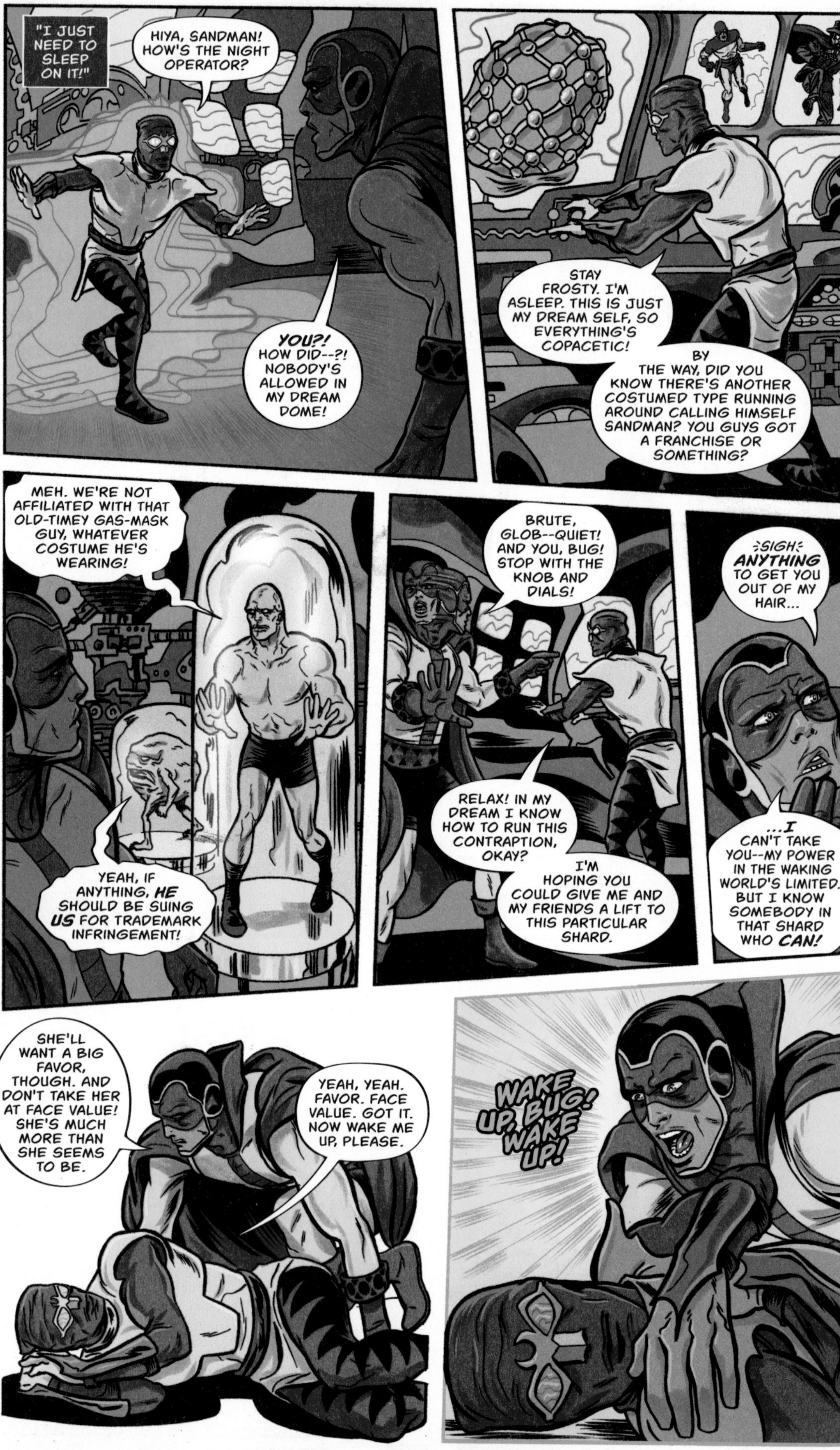
"I JUST NEED TO SLEEP ON IT!"
HIYA, SANDMAN! HOW'S THE NIGHT OPERATOR?
YOU?! HOW DID--?! NOBODY'S ALLOWED IN MY DREAM DOME!
STAY FROSTY. I'M ASLEEP. THIS IS JUST MY DREAM SELF, SO EVERYTHING'S COPACETIC!
BY THE WAY, DID YOU KNOW THERE'S ANOTHER COSTUMED TYPE RUNNING AROUND CALLING HIMSELF SANDMAN? YOU GUYS GOT A FRANCHISE OR SOMETHING?
MEH. WE'RE NOT AFFILIATED WITH THAT OLD-TIMEY GAS-MASK GUY, WHATEVER COSTUME HE'S WEARING!
YEAH, IF ANYTHING, HE SHOULD BE SUING US FOR TRADEMARK INFRINGEMENT!
BRUTE, GLOB--QUIET! AND YOU, BUG! STOP WITH THE KNOB AND DIALS!
RELAX! IN MY DREAM I KNOW HOW TO RUN THIS CONTRAPTION, OKAY?
I'M HOPING YOU COULD GIVE ME AND MY FRIENDS A LIFT TO THIS PARTICULAR SHARD.
SIGH ANYTHING TO GET YOU OUT OF MY HAIR...
...I CAN'T TAKE YOU--MY POWER IN THE WAKING WORLD'S LIMITED. BUT I KNOW SOMEBODY IN THAT SHARD WHO CAN!
SHE'LL WANT A BIG FAVOR, THOUGH. AND DON'T TAKE HER AT FACE VALUE! SHE'S MUCH MORE THAN SHE SEEMS TO BE.
YEAH, YEAH. FAVOR. FACE VALUE. GOT IT. NOW WAKE ME UP, PLEASE.
WAKE UP, BUG! WAKE UP!

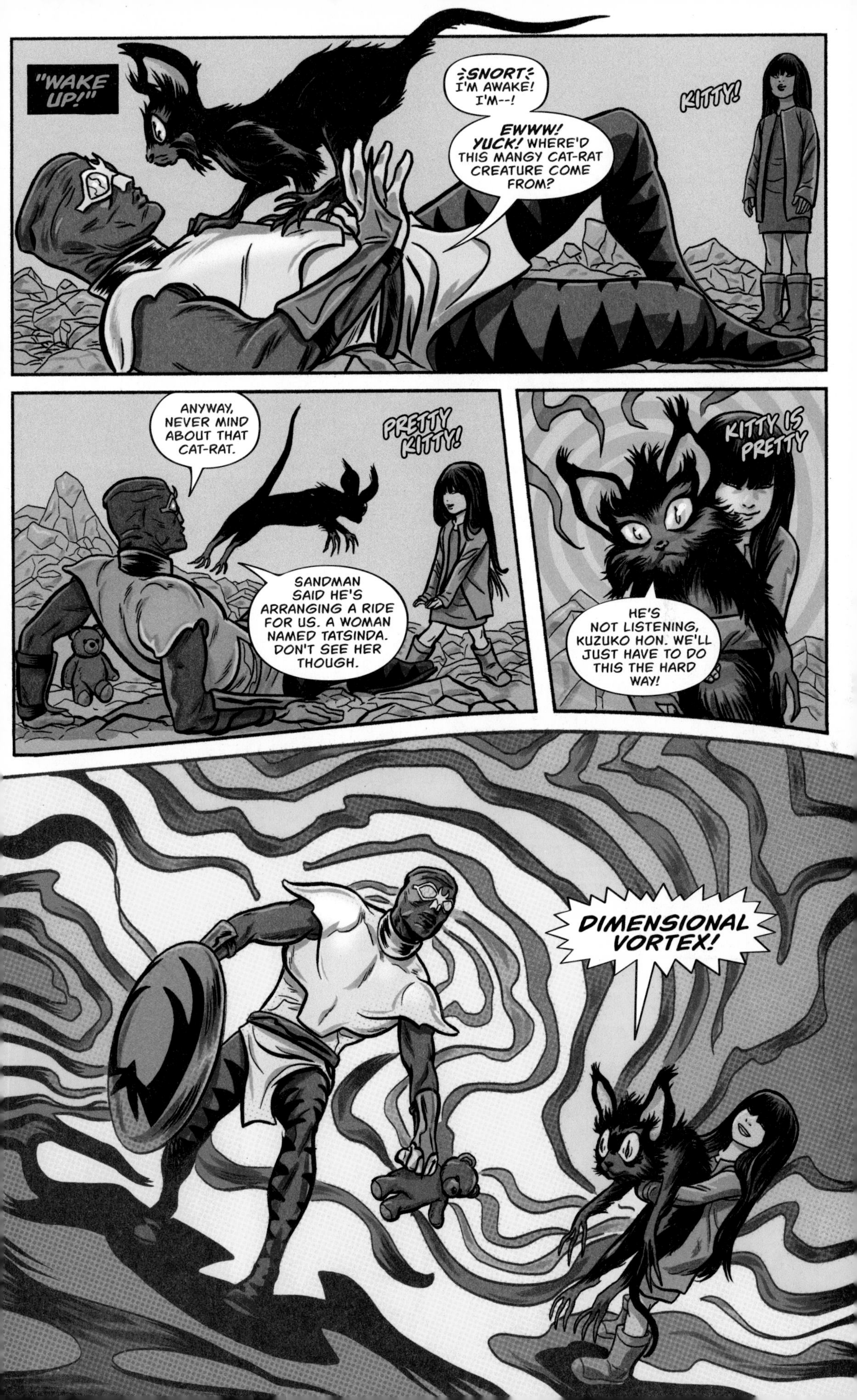
"WAKE UP!"
SNORT I'M AWAKE! I'M--!
EWWW! YUCK! WHERE'D THIS MANGY CAT-RAT CREATURE COME FROM?
KITTY!
ANYWAY, NEVER MIND ABOUT THAT CAT-RAT.
PRETTY KITTY!
SANDMAN SAID HE'S ARRANGING A RIDE FOR US. A WOMAN NAMED TATSINDA. DON'T SEE HER THOUGH.
KITTY IS PRETTY
HE'S NOT LISTENING, KUZUKO HON. WE'LL JUST HAVE TO DO THIS THE HARD WAY!
DIMENSIONAL VORTEX!

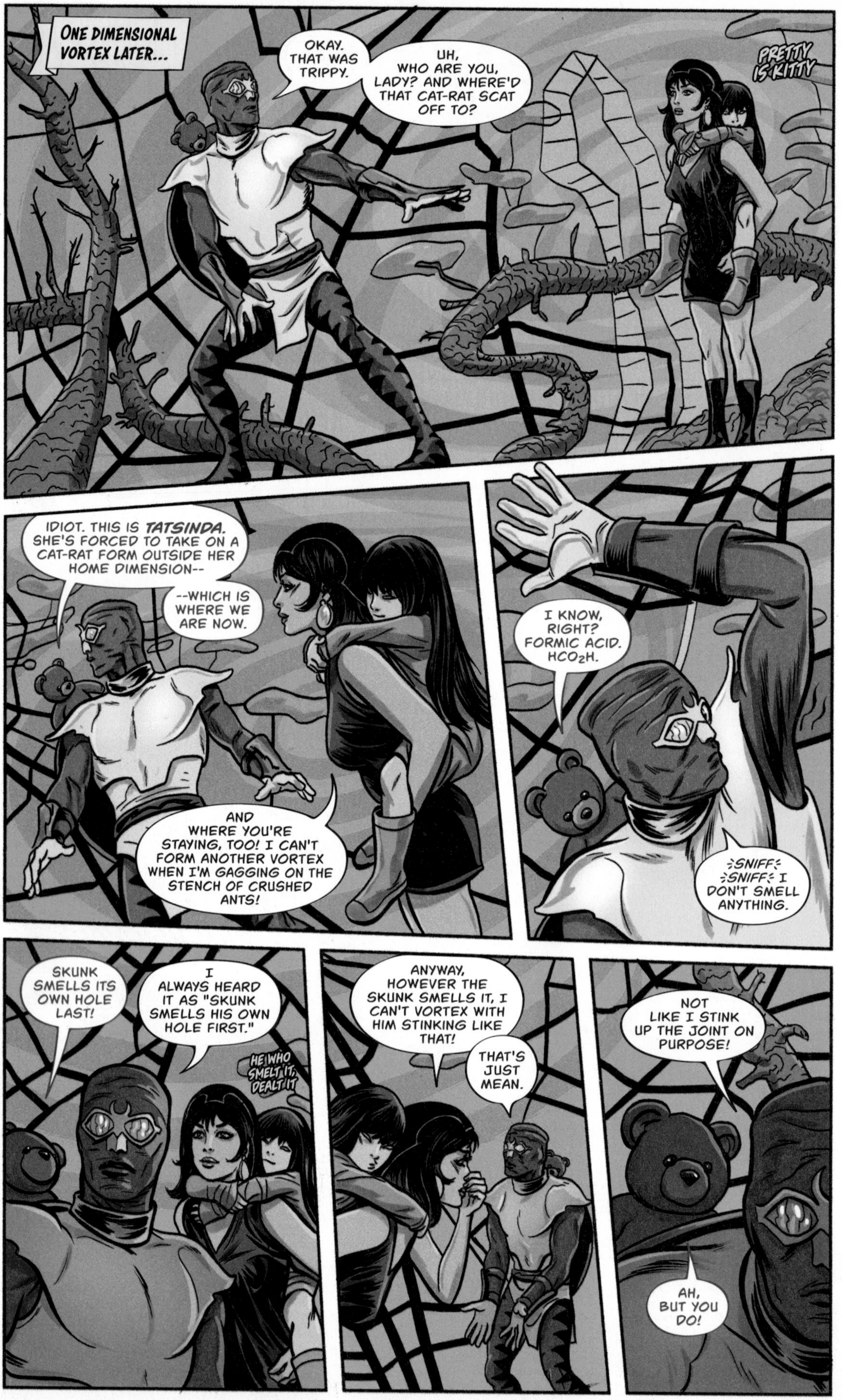
ONE DIMENSIONAL VORTEX LATER...
OKAY. THAT WAS TRIPPY.
UH, WHO ARE YOU, LADY? AND WHERE'D THAT CAT-RAT SCAT OFF TO?
PRETTY IS KITTY
IDIOT. THIS IS TATSINDA. SHE'S FORCED TO TAKE ON A CAT-RAT FORM OUTSIDE HER HOME DIMENSION--
--WHICH IS WHERE WE ARE NOW.
AND WHERE YOU'RE STAYING, TOO! I CAN'T FORM ANOTHER VORTEX WHEN I'M GAGGING ON THE STENCH OF CRUSHED ANTS!
I KNOW, RIGHT? FORMIC ACID. HCO2H.
SNIFF SNIFF I DON'T SMELL ANYTHING.
SKUNK SMELLS ITS OWN HOLE LAST!
I ALWAYS HEARD IT AS "SKUNK SMELLS HIS OWN HOLE FIRST."
HE WHO SMELT IT, DEALT IT
ANYWAY, HOWEVER THE SKUNK SMELLS IT, I CAN'T VORTEX WITH HIM STINKING LIKE THAT!
THAT'S JUST MEAN.
NOT LIKE I STINK UP THE JOINT ON PURPOSE!
AH, BUT YOU DO!

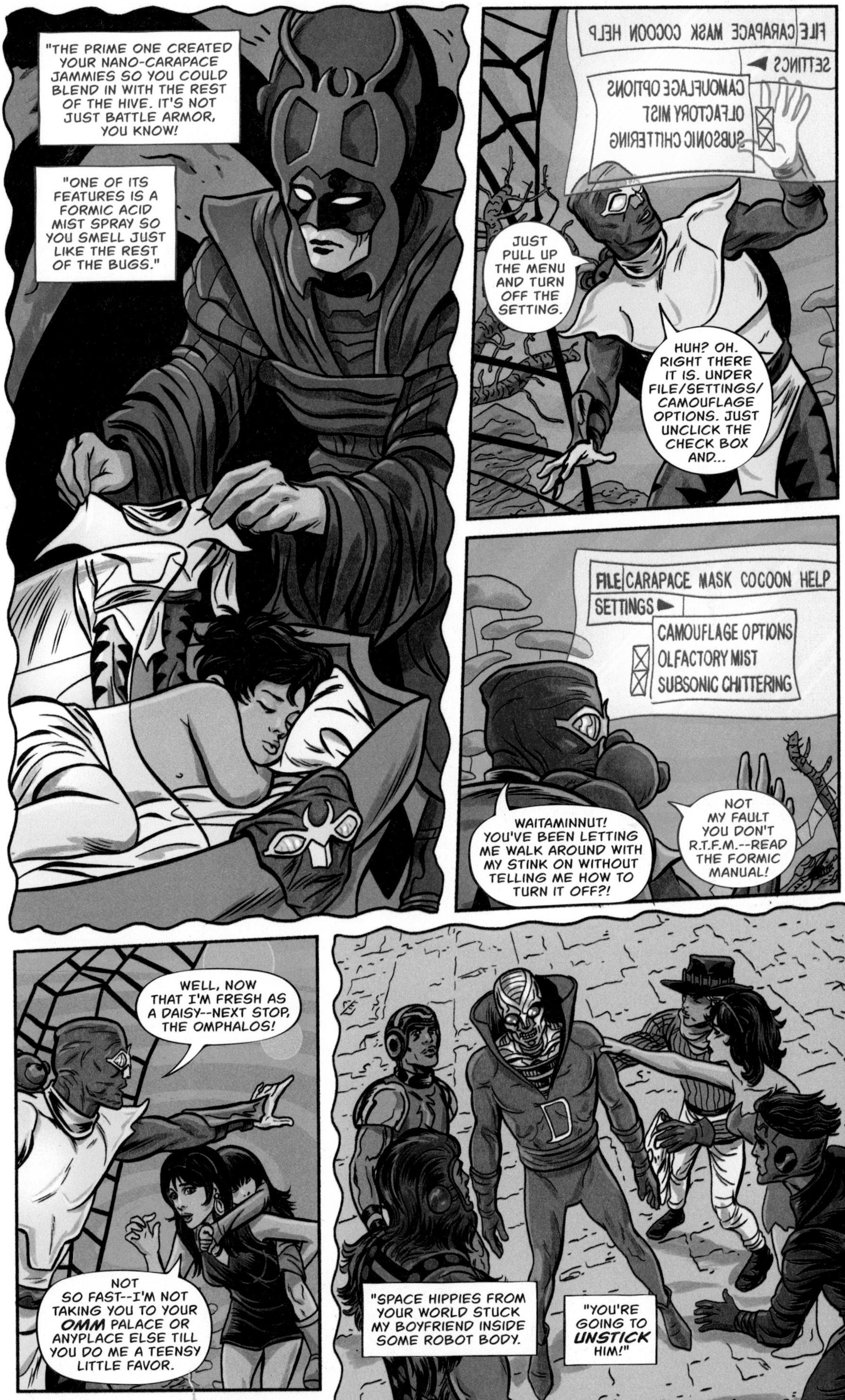
"THE PRIME ONE CREATED YOUR NANO-CARAPACE JAMMIES SO YOU COULD BLEND IN WITH THE REST OF THE HIVE. IT'S NOT JUST BATTLE ARMOR, YOU KNOW!
"ONE OF ITS FEATURES IS A FORMIC ACID MIST SPRAY SO YOU SMELL JUST LIKE THE REST OF THE BUGS."
JUST PULL UP THE MENU AND TURN OFF THE SETTING.
HUH? OH. RIGHT THERE IT IS. UNDER FILE/SETTINGS/ CAMOUFLAGE OPTIONS. JUST UNCLICK THE CHECK BOX AND...
FILE CARAPACE MASK COCOON HELP
SETTINGS ►
CAMOUFLAGE OPTIONS
OLFACTORY MIST
SUBSONIC CHITTERING
WAITAMINNUT! YOU'VE BEEN LETTING ME WALK AROUND WITH MY STINK ON WITHOUT TELLING ME HOW TO TURN IT OFF?!
NOT MY FAULT YOU DON'T R.T.F.M.--READ THE FORMIC MANUAL!
WELL, NOW THAT I'M FRESH AS A DAISY--NEXT STOP, THE OMPHALOS!
NOT SO FAST--I'M NOT TAKING YOU TO YOUR OMM PALACE OR ANYPLACE ELSE TILL YOU DO ME A TEENSY LITTLE FAVOR.
"SPACE HIPPIES FROM YOUR WORLD STUCK MY BOYFRIEND INSIDE SOME ROBOT BODY.
"YOU'RE GOING TO UNSTICK HIM!"

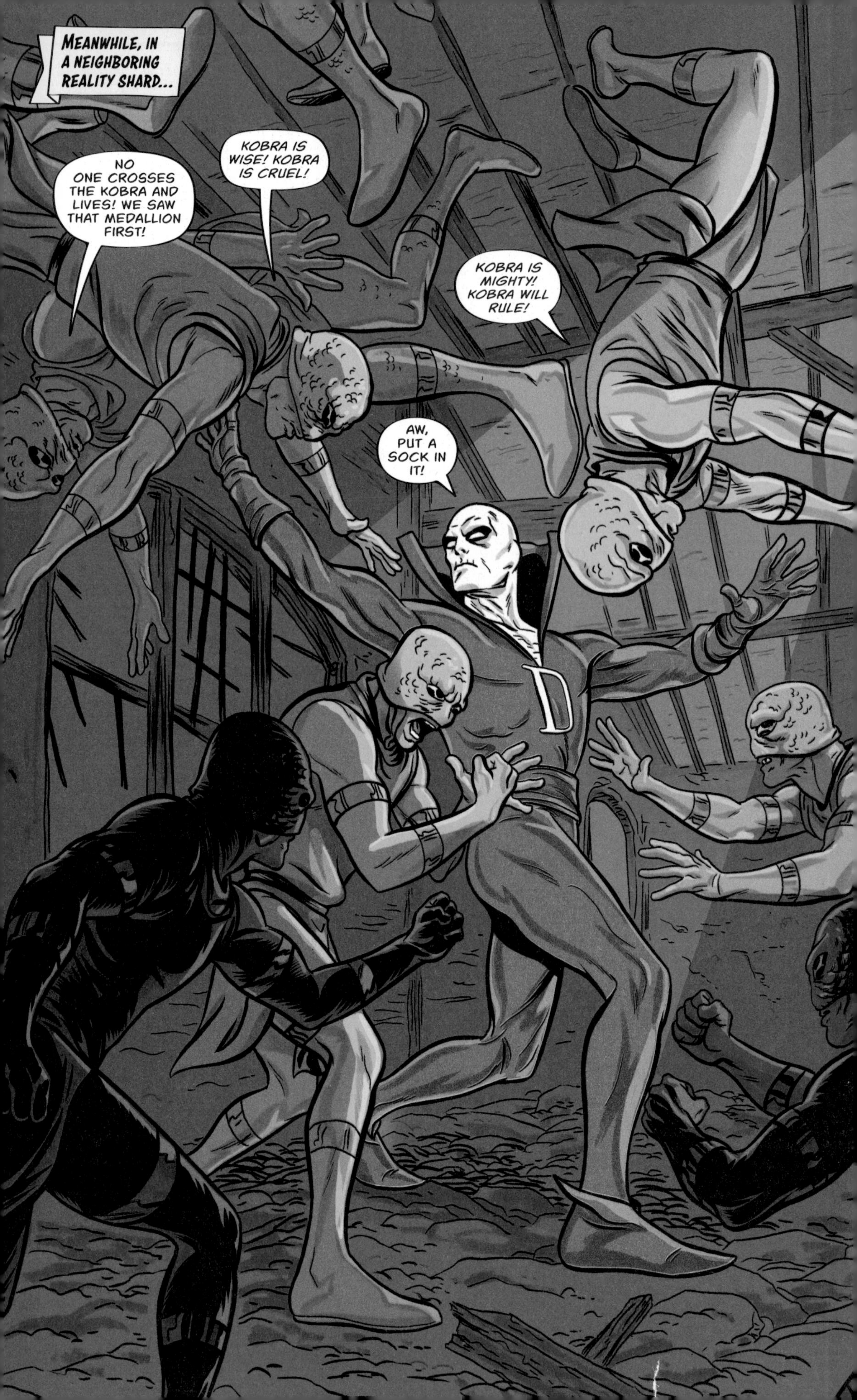
MEANWHILE, IN A NEIGHBORING REALITY SHARD...
NO ONE CROSSES THE KOBRA AND LIVES! WE SAW THAT MEDALLION FIRST!
KOBRA IS WISE! KOBRA IS CRUEL!
KOBRA IS MIGHTY! KOBRA WILL RULE!
AW, PUT A SOCK IN IT!

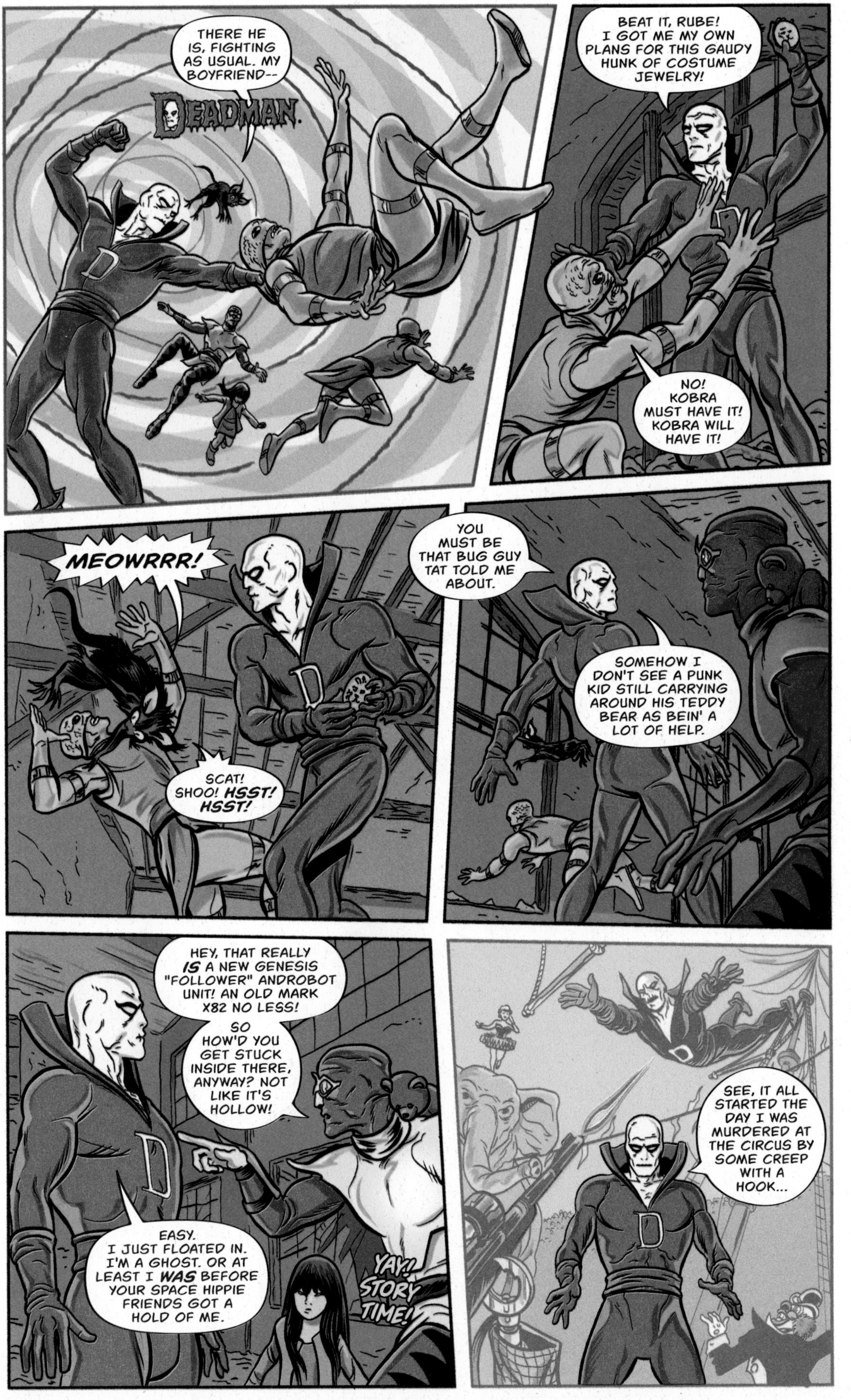
THERE HE IS, FIGHTING AS USUAL. MY BOYFRIEND--
DEADMAN.
BEAT IT, RUBE! I GOT ME MY OWN PLANS FOR THIS GAUDY HUNK OF COSTUME JEWELRY!
NO! KOBRA MUST HAVE IT! KOBRA WILL HAVE IT!
MEOWRRR!
SCAT! SHOO! HSST! HSST!
YOU MUST BE THAT BUG GUY TAT TOLD ME ABOUT.
SOMEHOW I DON'T SEE A PUNK KID STILL CARRYING AROUND HIS TEDDY BEAR AS BEIN' A LOT OF HELP.
HEY, THAT REALLY IS A NEW GENESIS "FOLLOWER" ANDROBOT UNIT! AN OLD MARK X82 NO LESS!
SO HOW'D YOU GET STUCK INSIDE THERE, ANYWAY? NOT LIKE IT'S HOLLOW!
EASY. I JUST FLOATED IN. I'M A GHOST. OR AT LEAST I WAS BEFORE YOUR SPACE HIPPIE FRIENDS GOT A HOLD OF ME.
YAY! STORY TIME!
SEE, IT ALL STARTED THE DAY I WAS MURDERED AT THE CIRCUS BY SOME CREEP WITH A HOOK...

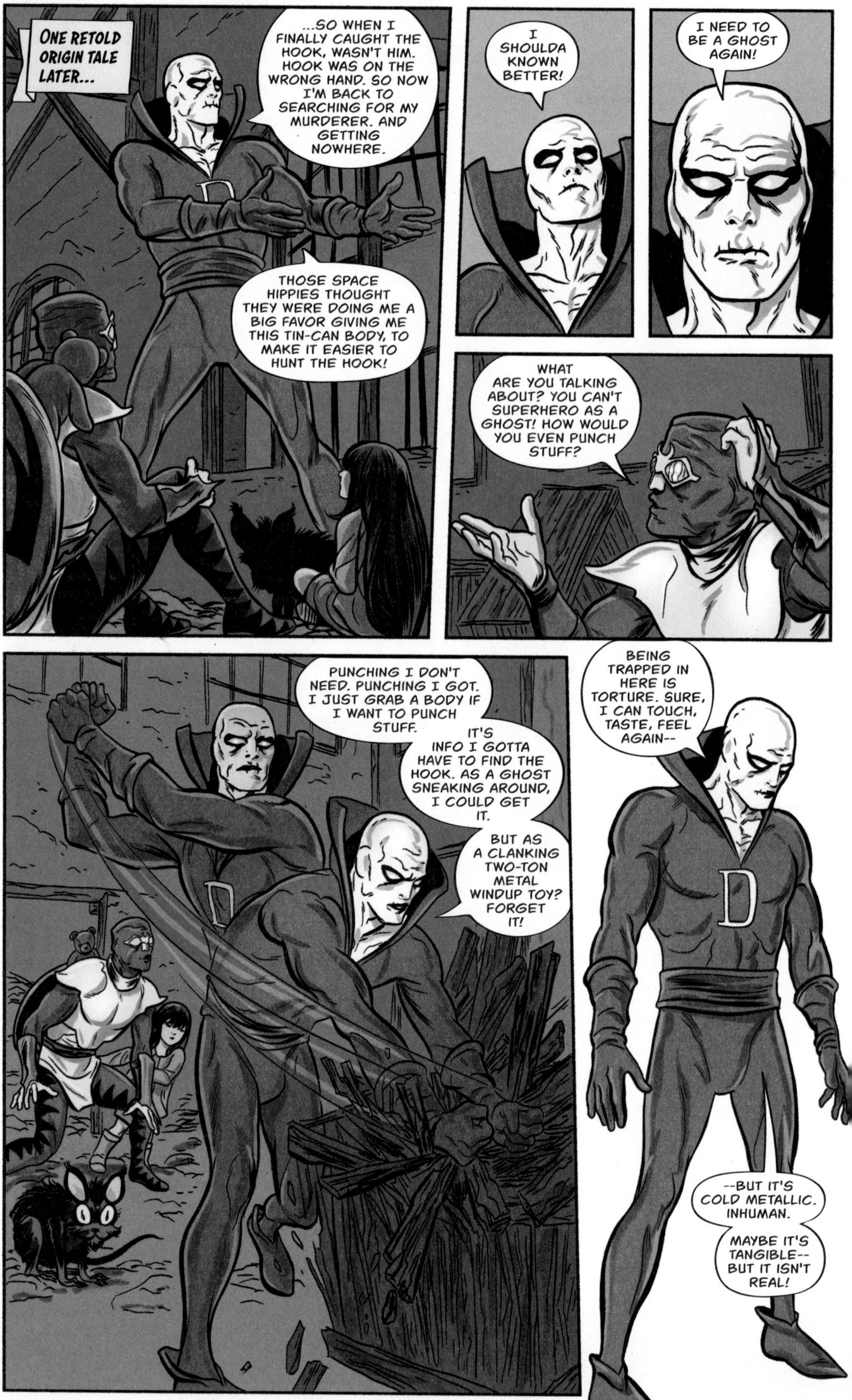
ONE RETOLD ORIGIN TALE LATER...
...SO WHEN I FINALLY CAUGHT THE HOOK, WASN'T HIM. HOOK WAS ON THE WRONG HAND. SO NOW I'M BACK TO SEARCHING FOR MY MURDERER. AND GETTING NOWHERE.
THOSE SPACE HIPPIES THOUGHT THEY WERE DOING ME A BIG FAVOR GIVING ME THIS TIN-CAN BODY, TO MAKE IT EASIER TO HUNT THE HOOK!
I SHOULDA KNOWN BETTER!
I NEED TO BE A GHOST AGAIN!
WHAT ARE YOU TALKING ABOUT? YOU CAN'T SUPERHERO AS A GHOST! HOW WOULD YOU EVEN PUNCH STUFF?
PUNCHING I DON'T NEED. PUNCHING I GOT. I JUST GRAB A BODY IF I WANT TO PUNCH STUFF.
IT'S INFO I GOTTA HAVE TO FIND THE HOOK. AS A GHOST SNEAKING AROUND, I COULD GET IT.
BUT AS A CLANKING TWO-TON METAL WINDUP TOY? FORGET IT!
BEING TRAPPED IN HERE IS TORTURE. SURE, I CAN TOUCH, TASTE, FEEL AGAIN--
--BUT IT'S COLD METALLIC. INHUMAN.
MAYBE IT'S TANGIBLE-- BUT IT ISN'T REAL!

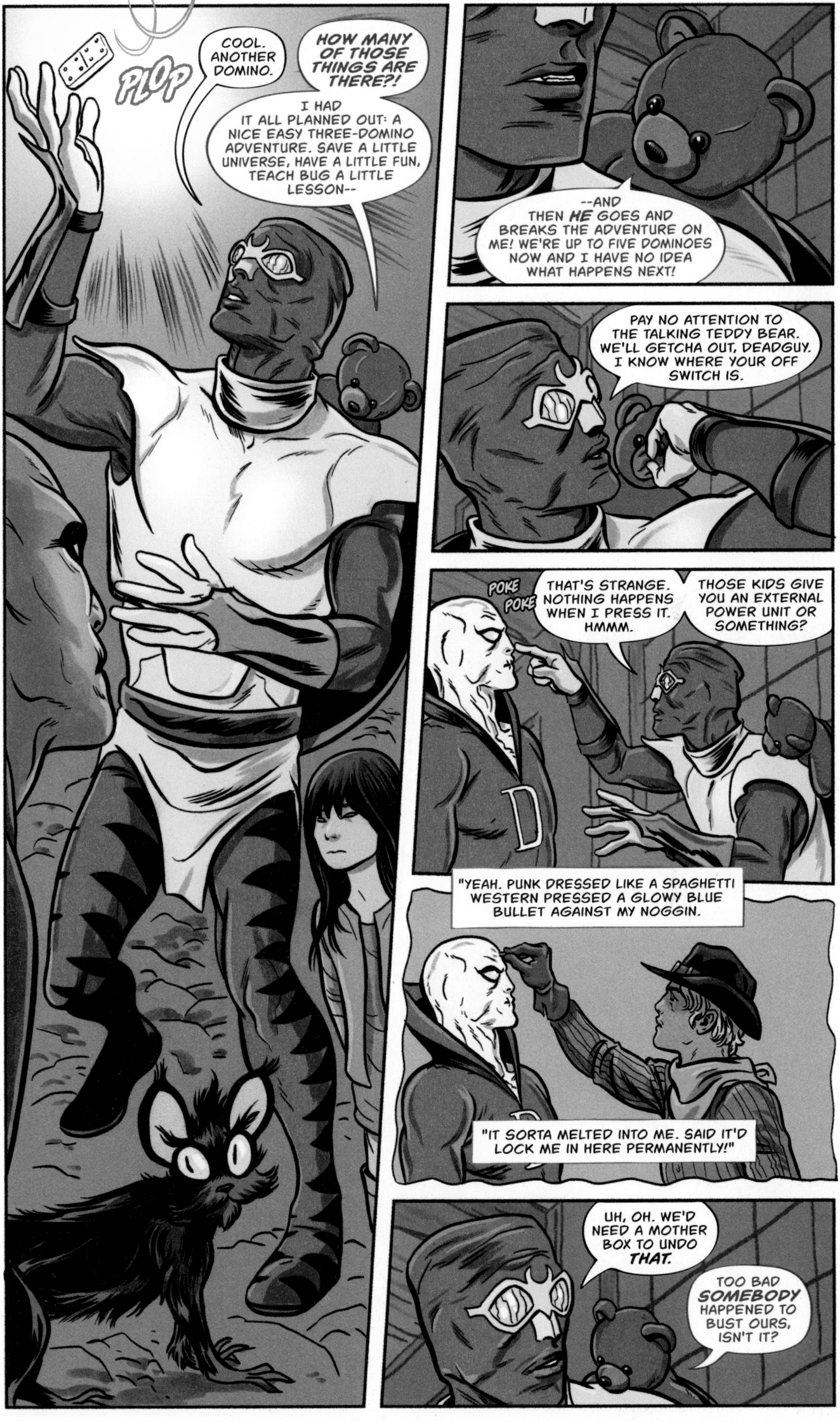
PLOP
COOL. ANOTHER DOMINO.
HOW MANY OF THOSE THINGS ARE THERE?!
I HAD IT ALL PLANNED OUT: A NICE EASY THREE-DOMINO ADVENTURE. SAVE A LITTLE UNIVERSE, HAVE A LITTLE FUN, TEACH BUG A LITTLE LESSON--
--AND THEN HE GOES AND BREAKS THE ADVENTURE ON ME! WE'RE UP TO FIVE DOMINOES NOW AND I HAVE NO IDEA WHAT HAPPENS NEXT!
PAY NO ATTENTION TO THE TALKING TEDDY BEAR. WE'LL GETCHA OUT, DEADGUY. I KNOW WHERE YOUR OFF SWITCH IS.
POKE POKE
THAT'S STRANGE. NOTHING HAPPENS WHEN I PRESS IT. HMMM.
THOSE KIDS GIVE YOU AN EXTERNAL POWER UNIT OR SOMETHING?
"YEAH. PUNK DRESSED LIKE A SPAGHETTI WESTERN PRESSED A GLOWY BLUE BULLET AGAINST MY NOGGIN.
"IT SORTA MELTED INTO ME. SAID IT'D LOCK ME IN HERE PERMANENTLY!"
UH, OH. WE'D NEED A MOTHER BOX TO UNDO THAT.
TOO BAD SOMEBODY HAPPENED TO BUST OURS, ISN'T IT?

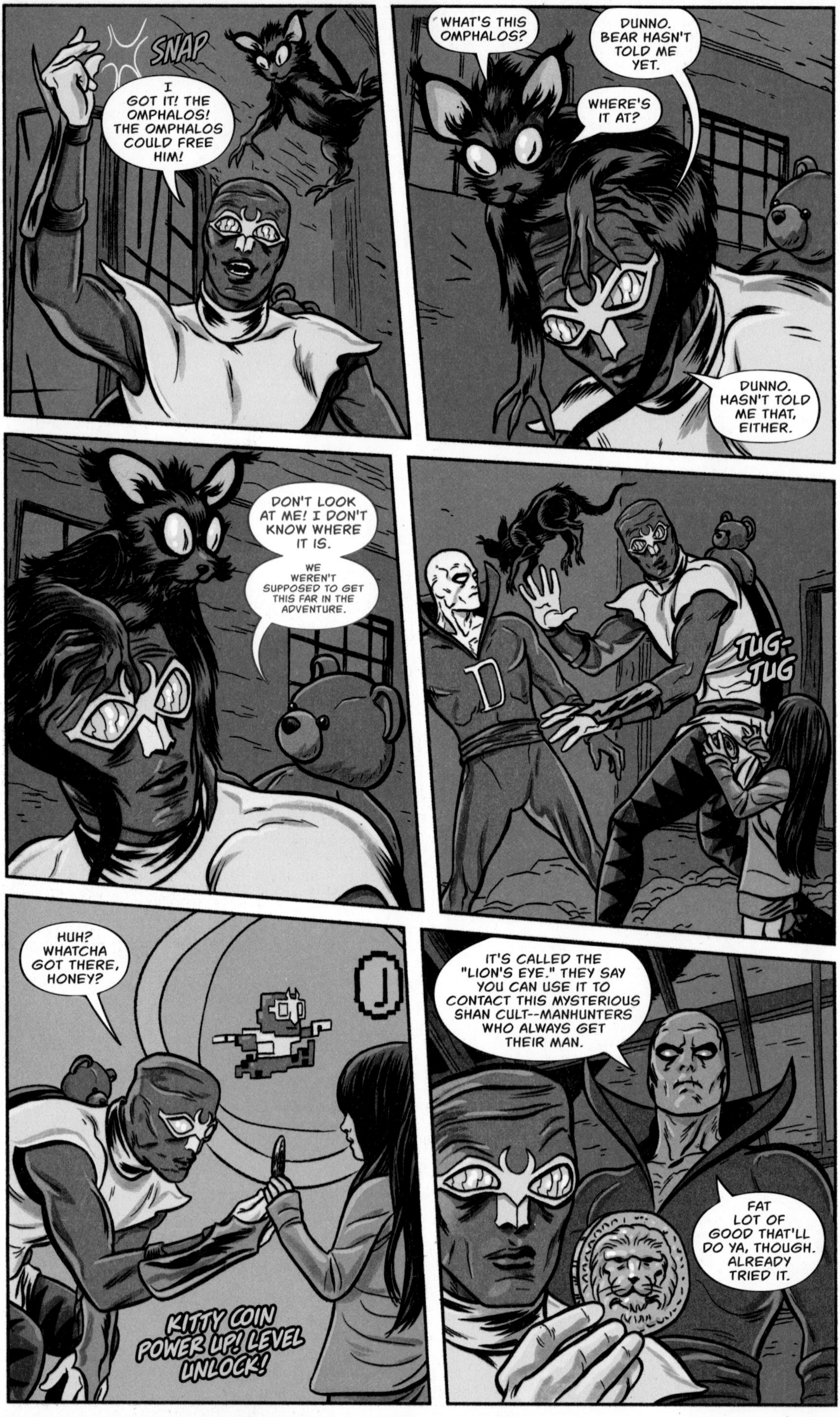
SNAP
I GOT IT! THE OMPHALOS! THE OMPHALOS COULD FREE HIM!
WHAT'S THIS OMPHALOS?
DUNNO. BEAR HASN'T TOLD ME YET.
WHERE'S IT AT?
DUNNO. HASN'T TOLD ME THAT, EITHER.
DON'T LOOK AT ME! I DON'T KNOW WHERE IT IS.
WE WEREN'T SUPPOSED TO GET THIS FAR IN THE ADVENTURE.
TUG-TUG
HUH? WHATCHA GOT THERE, HONEY?
KITTY COIN POWER UP! LEVEL UNLOCK!
IT'S CALLED THE "LION'S EYE." THEY SAY YOU CAN USE IT TO CONTACT THIS MYSTERIOUS SHAN CULT--MANHUNTERS WHO ALWAYS GET THEIR MAN.
FAT LOT OF GOOD THAT'LL DO YA, THOUGH. ALREADY TRIED IT.

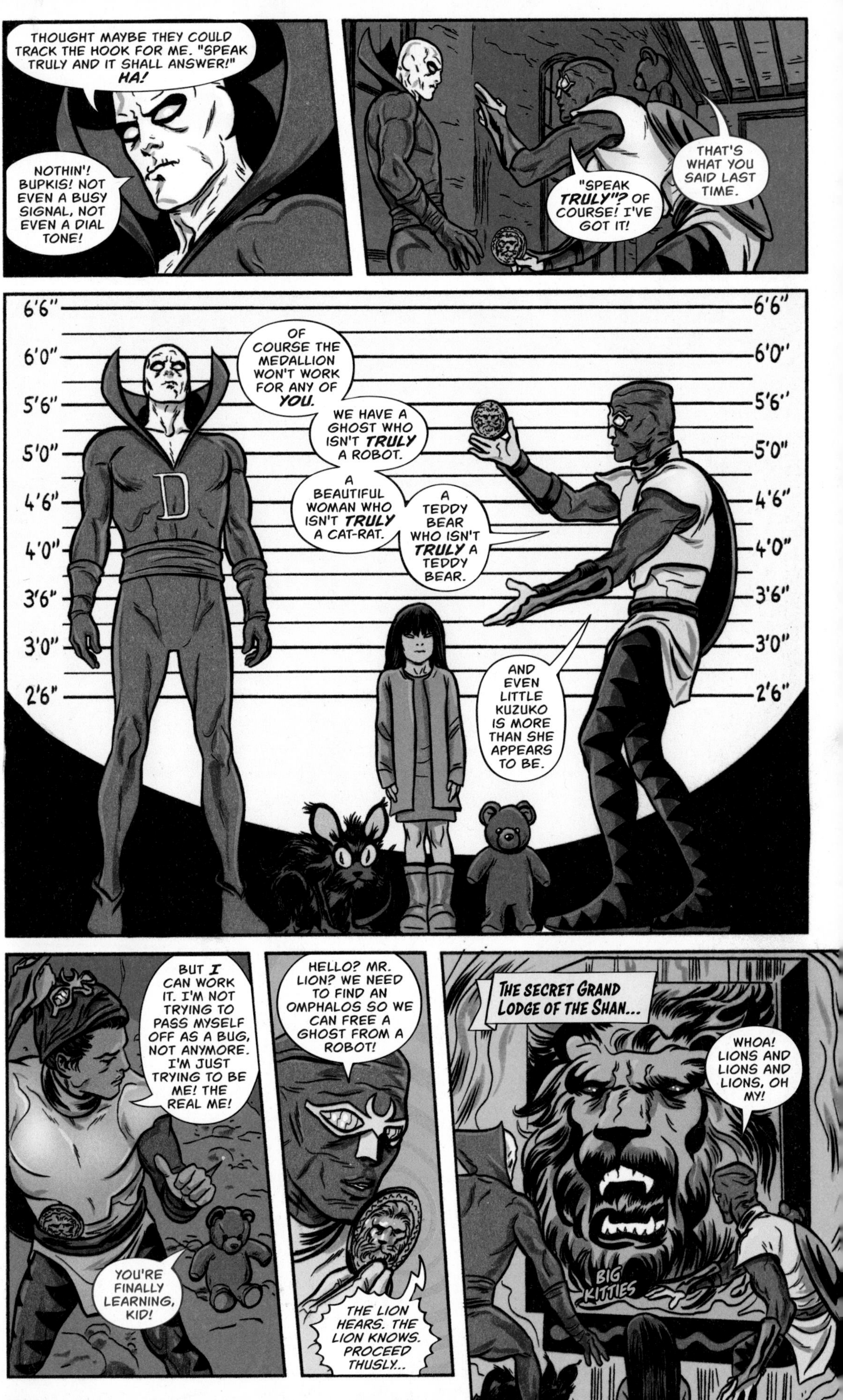
THOUGHT MAYBE THEY COULD TRACK THE HOOK FOR ME. "SPEAK TRULY AND IT SHALL ANSWER!" HA!
NOTHIN'! BUPKIS! NOT EVEN A BUSY SIGNAL, NOT EVEN A DIAL TONE!
THAT'S WHAT YOU SAID LAST TIME.
"SPEAK TRULY"? OF COURSE! I'VE GOT IT!
6'6"
6'0"
5'6"
5'0"
4'6"
4'0"
3'6"
3'0"
2'6"
OF COURSE THE MEDALLION WON'T WORK FOR ANY OF YOU.
WE HAVE A GHOST WHO ISN'T TRULY A ROBOT.
A BEAUTIFUL WOMAN WHO ISN'T TRULY A CAT-RAT.
A TEDDY BEAR WHO ISN'T TRULY A TEDDY BEAR.
AND EVEN LITTLE KUZUKO IS MORE THAN SHE APPEARS TO BE.
BUT I CAN WORK IT. I'M NOT TRYING TO PASS MYSELF OFF AS A BUG, NOT ANYMORE. I'M JUST TRYING TO BE ME! THE REAL ME!
YOU'RE FINALLY LEARNING, KID!
HELLO? MR. LION? WE NEED TO FIND AN OMPHALOS SO WE CAN FREE A GHOST FROM A ROBOT!
THE LION HEARS. THE LION KNOWS. PROCEED THUSLY...
THE SECRET GRAND LODGE OF THE SHAN...
WHOA! LIONS AND LIONS AND LIONS, OH MY!
BIG KITTIES

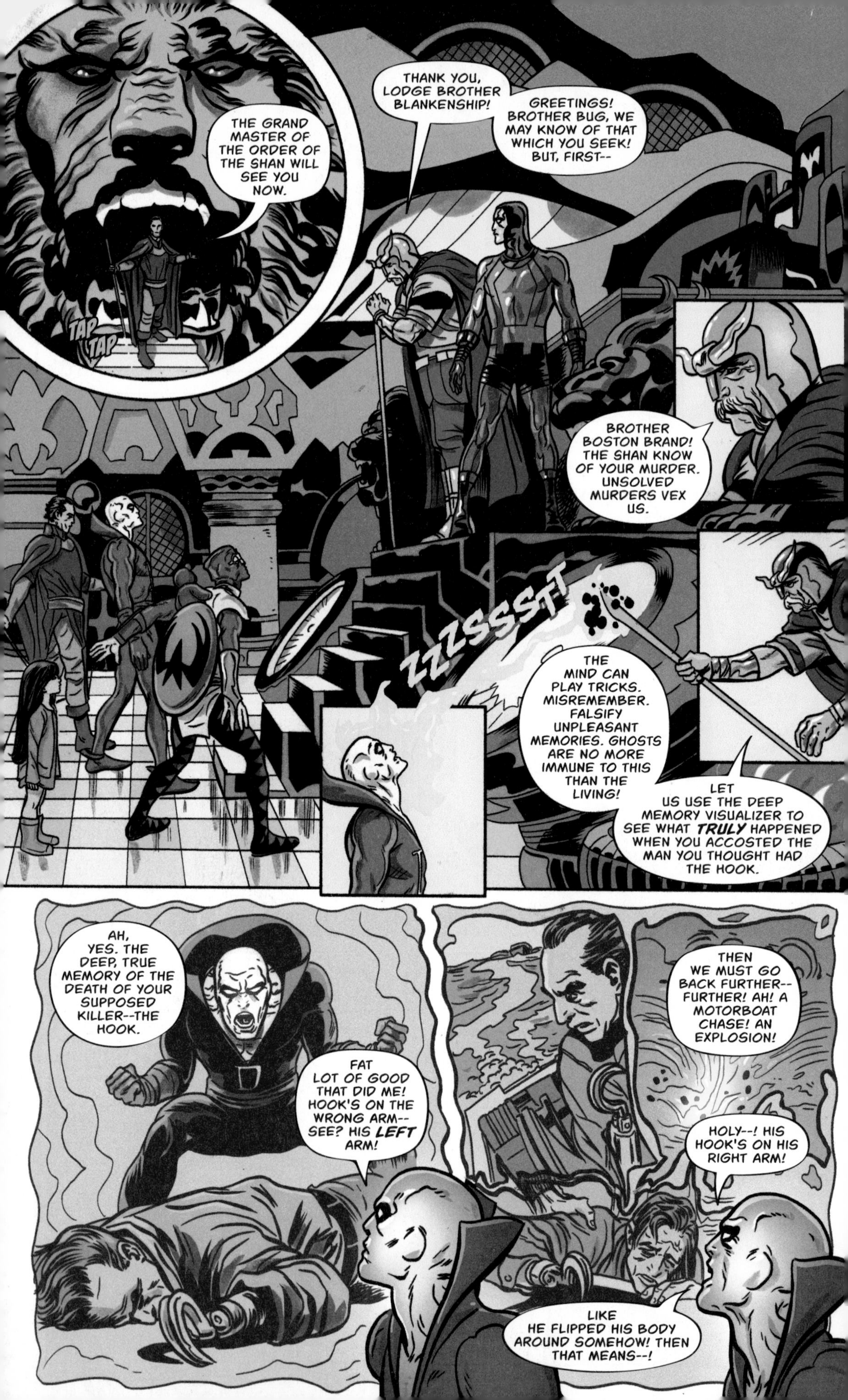
THE GRAND MASTER OF THE ORDER OF THE SHAN WILL SEE YOU NOW.
TAP TAP
THANK YOU, LODGE BROTHER BLANKENSHIP!
GREETINGS! BROTHER BUG, WE MAY KNOW OF THAT WHICH YOU SEEK! BUT, FIRST--
BROTHER BOSTON BRAND! THE SHAN KNOW OF YOUR MURDER. UNSOLVED MURDERS VEX US.
ZZZSSSSTT
THE MIND CAN PLAY TRICKS. MISREMEMBER. FALSIFY UNPLEASANT MEMORIES. GHOSTS ARE NO MORE IMMUNE TO THIS THAN THE LIVING!
LET US USE THE DEEP MEMORY VISUALIZER TO SEE WHAT TRULY HAPPENED WHEN YOU ACCOSTED THE MAN YOU THOUGHT HAD THE HOOK.
AH, YES. THE DEEP, TRUE MEMORY OF THE DEATH OF YOUR SUPPOSED KILLER--THE HOOK.
FAT LOT OF GOOD THAT DID ME! HOOK'S ON THE WRONG ARM-- SEE? HIS LEFT ARM!
THEN WE MUST GO BACK FURTHER-- FURTHER! AH! A MOTORBOAT CHASE! AN EXPLOSION!
HOLY--! HIS HOOK'S ON HIS RIGHT ARM!
LIKE HE FLIPPED HIS BODY AROUND SOMEHOW! THEN THAT MEANS--!

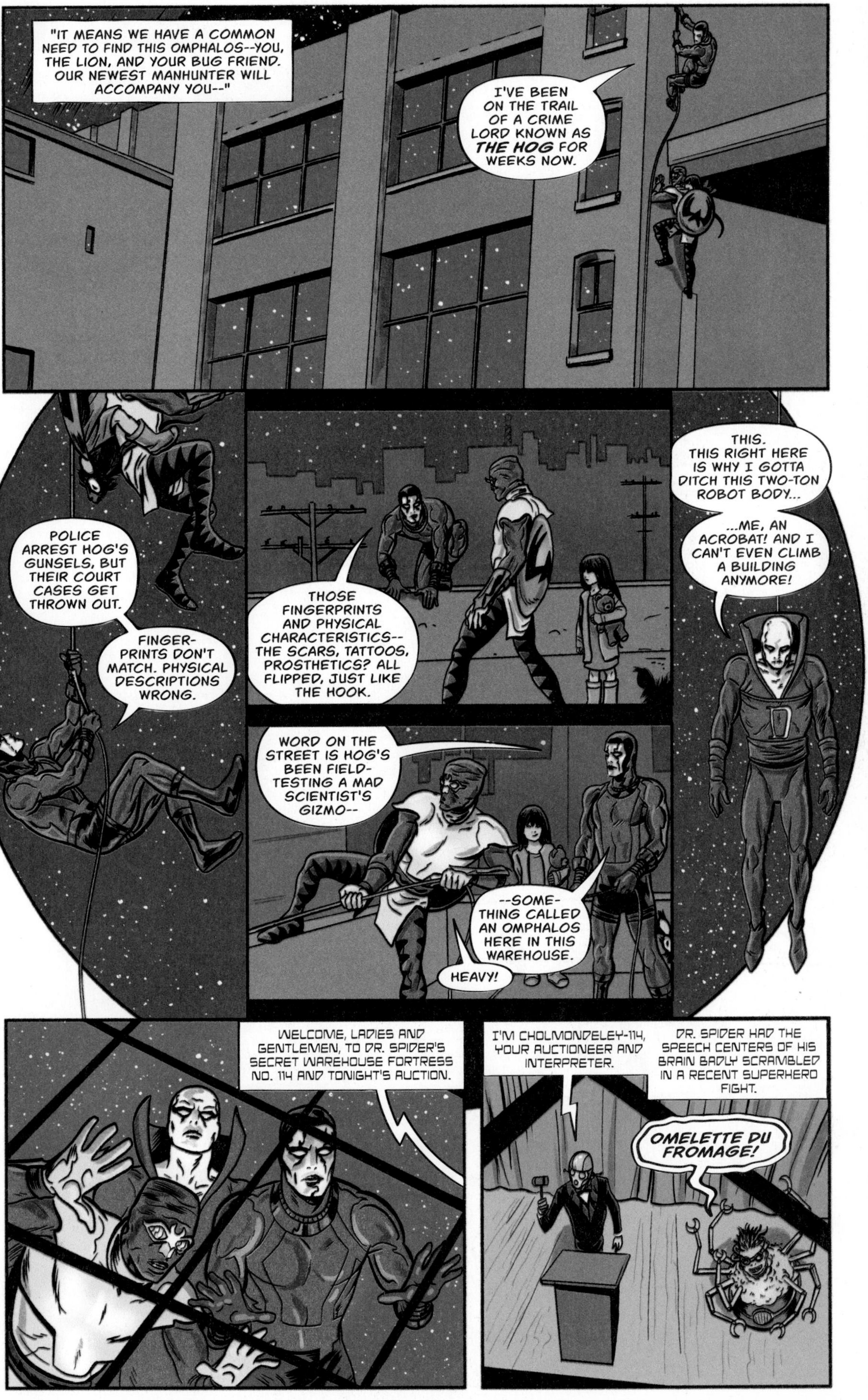
"IT MEANS WE HAVE A COMMON NEED TO FIND THIS OMPHALOS--YOU, THE LION, AND YOUR BUG FRIEND. OUR NEWEST MANHUNTER WILL ACCOMPANY YOU--"
I'VE BEEN ON THE TRAIL OF A CRIME LORD KNOWN AS THE HOG FOR WEEKS NOW.
POLICE ARREST HOG'S GUNSELS, BUT THEIR COURT CASES GET THROWN OUT.
FINGER-PRINTS DON'T MATCH. PHYSICAL DESCRIPTIONS WRONG.
THOSE FINGERPRINTS AND PHYSICAL CHARACTERISTICS-- THE SCARS, TATTOOS, PROSTHETICS? ALL FLIPPED, JUST LIKE THE HOOK.
WORD ON THE STREET IS HOG'S BEEN FIELD-TESTING A MAD SCIENTIST'S GIZMO--
--SOME-THING CALLED AN OMPHALOS HERE IN THIS WAREHOUSE.
HEAVY!
THIS. THIS RIGHT HERE IS WHY I GOTTA DITCH THIS TWO-TON ROBOT BODY...
...ME, AN ACROBAT! AND I CAN'T EVEN CLIMB A BUILDING ANYMORE!
WELCOME, LADIES AND GENTLEMEN, TO DR. SPIDER'S SECRET WAREHOUSE FORTRESS NO. 114 AND TONIGHT'S AUCTION.
I'M CHOLMONDELEY-114, YOUR AUCTIONEER AND INTERPRETER.
DR. SPIDER HAD THE SPEECH CENTERS OF HIS BRAIN BADLY SCRAMBLED IN A RECENT SUPERHERO FIGHT.
OMELETTE DU FROMAGE!

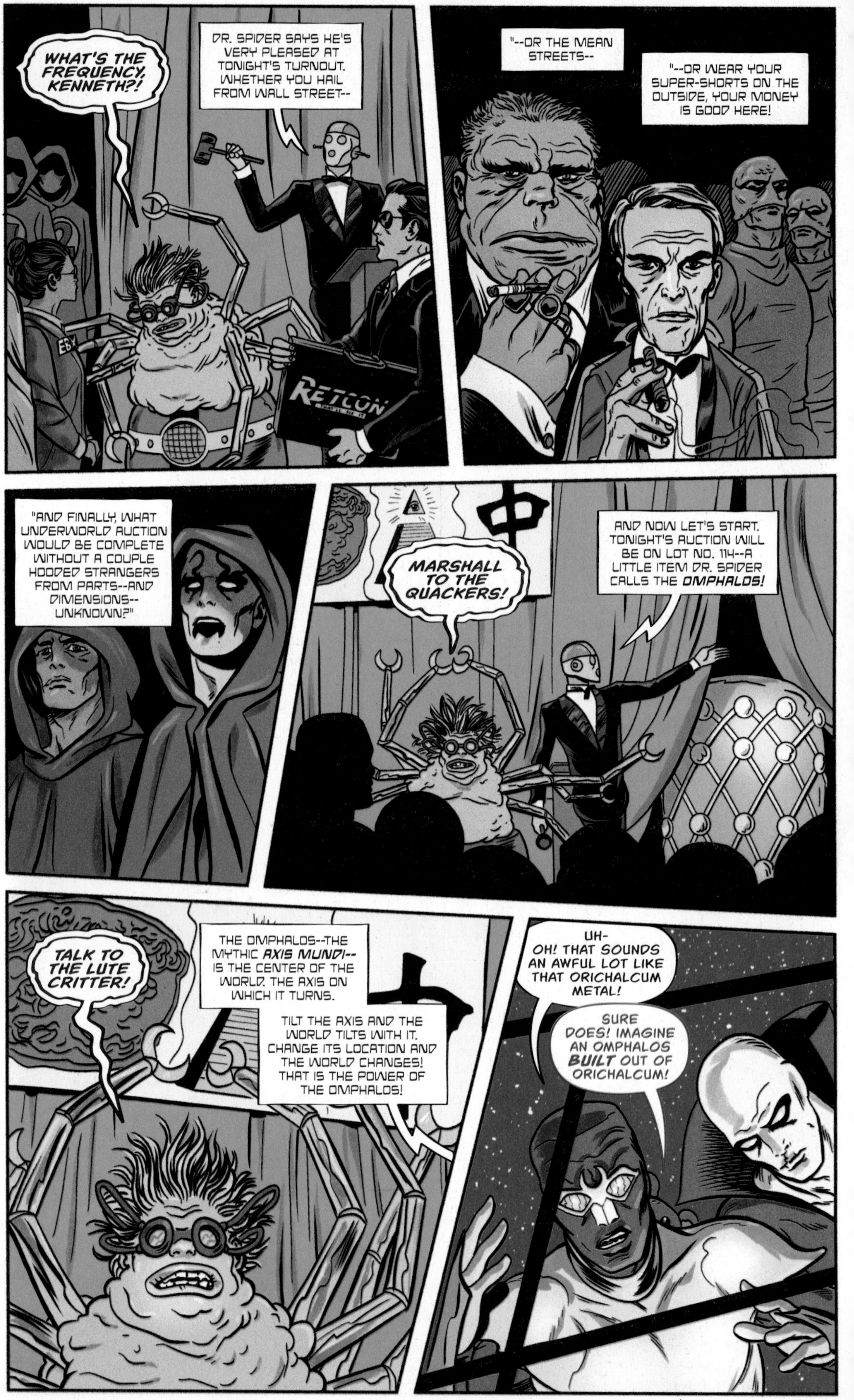
WHAT'S THE FREQUENCY, KENNETH?!
DR. SPIDER SAYS HE'S VERY PLEASED AT TONIGHT'S TURNOUT. WHETHER YOU HAIL FROM WALL STREET--
RETCON
"--OR THE MEAN STREETS--
"--OR WEAR YOUR SUPER-SHORTS ON THE OUTSIDE, YOUR MONEY IS GOOD HERE!
"AND FINALLY, WHAT UNDERWORLD AUCTION WOULD BE COMPLETE WITHOUT A COUPLE HOODED STRANGERS FROM PARTS--AND DIMENSIONS--UNKNOWN?"
MARSHALL TO THE QUACKERS!
AND NOW LET'S START. TONIGHT'S AUCTION WILL BE ON LOT NO. 114--A LITTLE ITEM DR. SPIDER CALLS THE OMPHALOS!
TALK TO THE LUTE CRITTER!
THE OMPHALOS--THE MYTHIC AXIS MUNDI--IS THE CENTER OF THE WORLD. THE AXIS ON WHICH IT TURNS.
TILT THE AXIS AND THE WORLD TILTS WITH IT. CHANGE ITS LOCATION AND THE WORLD CHANGES! THAT IS THE POWER OF THE OMPHALOS!
UH-OH! THAT SOUNDS AN AWFUL LOT LIKE THAT ORICHALCUM METAL!
SURE DOES! IMAGINE AN OMPHALOS BUILT OUT OF ORICHALCUM!

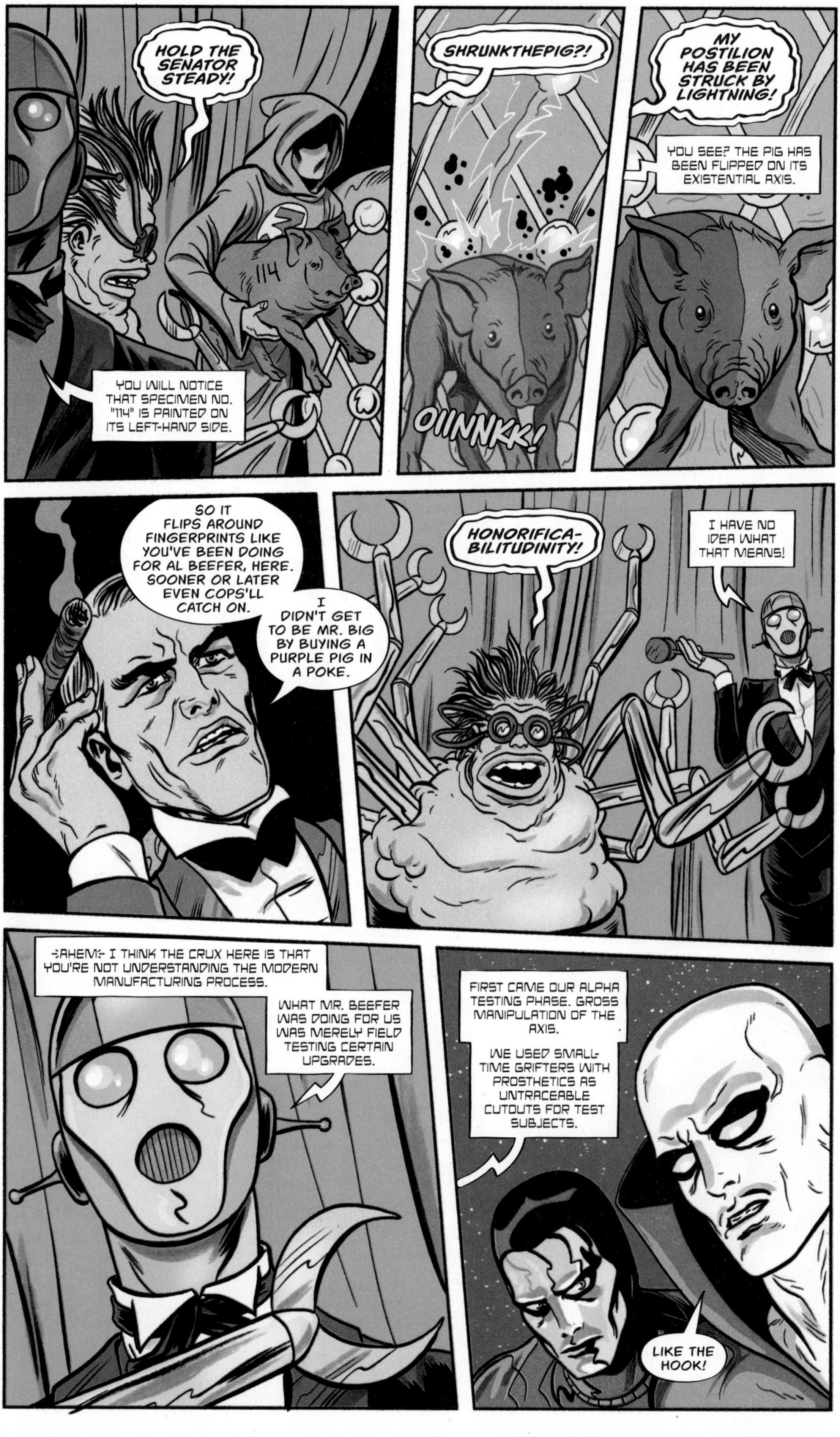
HOLD THE SENATOR STEADY!
YOU WILL NOTICE THAT SPECIMEN NO. "114" IS PAINTED ON ITS LEFT-HAND SIDE.
114
SHRUNKTHEPIG?!
OIINNKK!
MY POSTILION HAS BEEN STRUCK BY LIGHTNING!
YOU SEE? THE PIG HAS BEEN FLIPPED ON ITS EXISTENTIAL AXIS.
SO IT FLIPS AROUND FINGERPRINTS LIKE YOU'VE BEEN DOING FOR AL BEEFER, HERE. SOONER OR LATER EVEN COPS'LL CATCH ON.
I DIDN'T GET TO BE MR. BIG BY BUYING A PURPLE PIG IN A POKE.
HONORIFICA-BILITUDINITY!
I HAVE NO IDEA WHAT THAT MEANS!
=AHEM= I THINK THE CRUX HERE IS THAT YOU'RE NOT UNDERSTANDING THE MODERN MANUFACTURING PROCESS.
WHAT MR. BEEFER WAS DOING FOR US WAS MERELY FIELD TESTING CERTAIN UPGRADES.
FIRST CAME OUR ALPHA TESTING PHASE. GROSS MANIPULATION OF THE AXIS.
WE USED SMALL-TIME GRIFTERS WITH PROSTHETICS AS UNTRACEABLE CUTOUTS FOR TEST SUBJECTS.
LIKE THE HOOK!

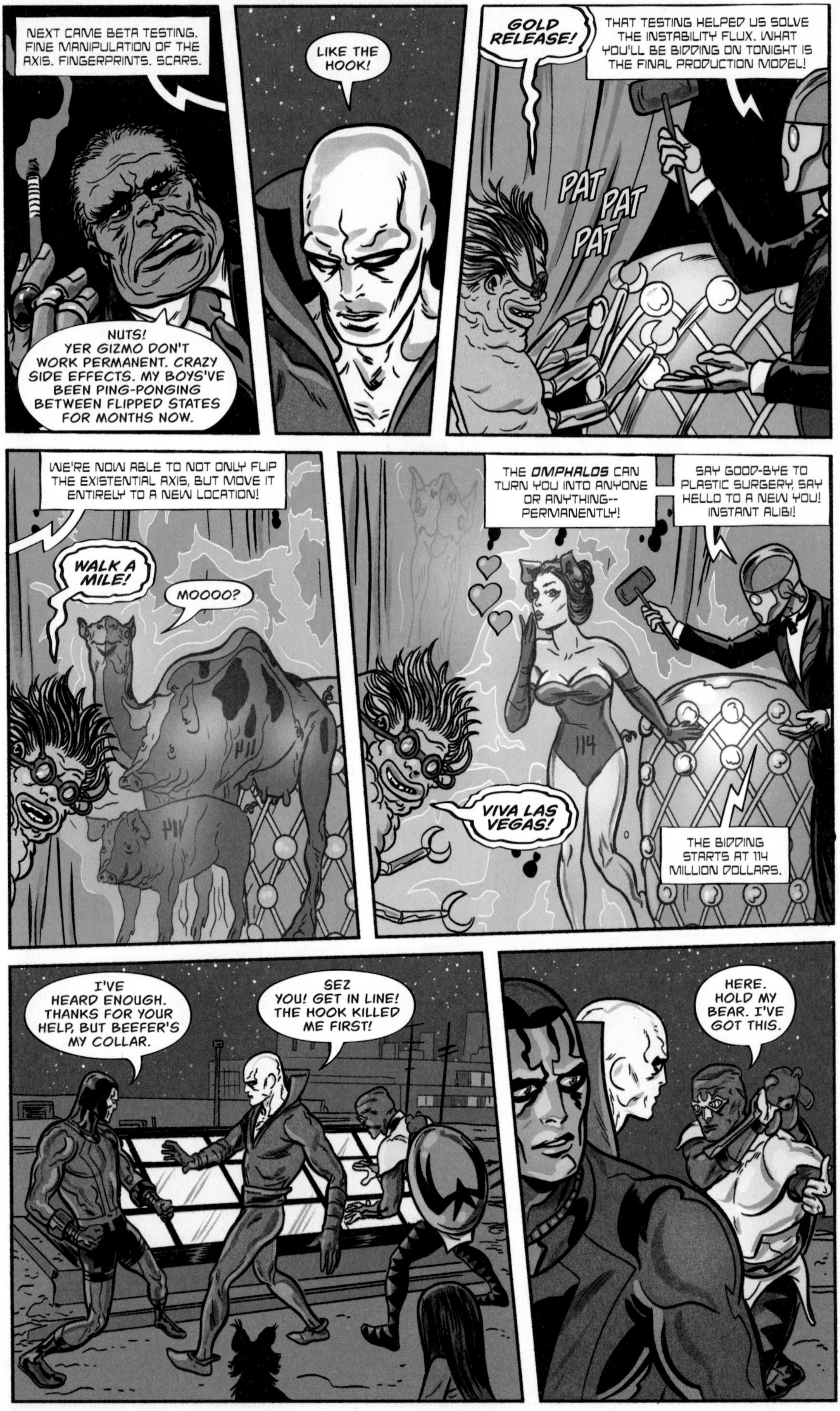
NEXT CAME BETA TESTING. FINE MANIPULATION OF THE AXIS. FINGERPRINTS. SCARS.
NUTS! YER GIZMO DON'T WORK PERMANENT. CRAZY SIDE EFFECTS. MY BOYS'VE BEEN PING-PONGING BETWEEN FLIPPED STATES FOR MONTHS NOW.
LIKE THE HOOK!
GOLD RELEASE!
THAT TESTING HELPED US SOLVE THE INSTABILITY FLUX. WHAT YOU'LL BE BIDDING ON TONIGHT IS THE FINAL PRODUCTION MODEL!
PAT PAT PAT
WE'RE NOW ABLE TO NOT ONLY FLIP THE EXISTENTIAL AXIS, BUT MOVE IT ENTIRELY TO A NEW LOCATION!
WALK A MILE!
MOOOO?
THE OMPHALOS CAN TURN YOU INTO ANYONE OR ANYTHING-- PERMANENTLY!
SAY GOOD-BYE TO PLASTIC SURGERY, SAY HELLO TO A NEW YOU! INSTANT ALIBI!
114
VIVA LAS VEGAS!
THE BIDDING STARTS AT 114 MILLION DOLLARS.
I'VE HEARD ENOUGH. THANKS FOR YOUR HELP, BUT BEEFER'S MY COLLAR.
SEZ YOU! GET IN LINE! THE HOOK KILLED ME FIRST!
HERE. HOLD MY BEAR. I'VE GOT THIS.

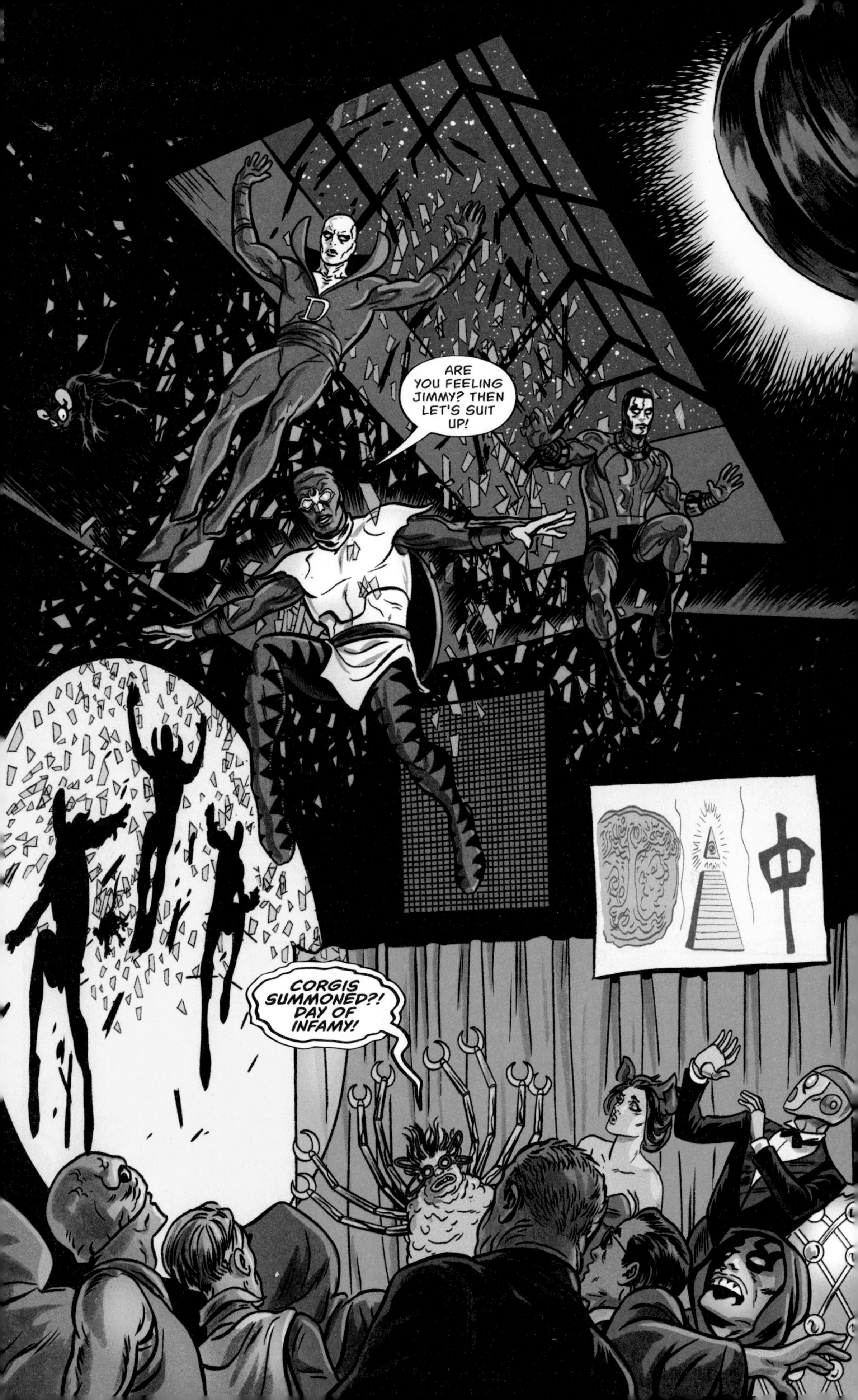
ARE YOU FEELING JIMMY? THEN LET'S SUIT UP!
CORGIS SUMMONED?! DAY OF INFAMY!

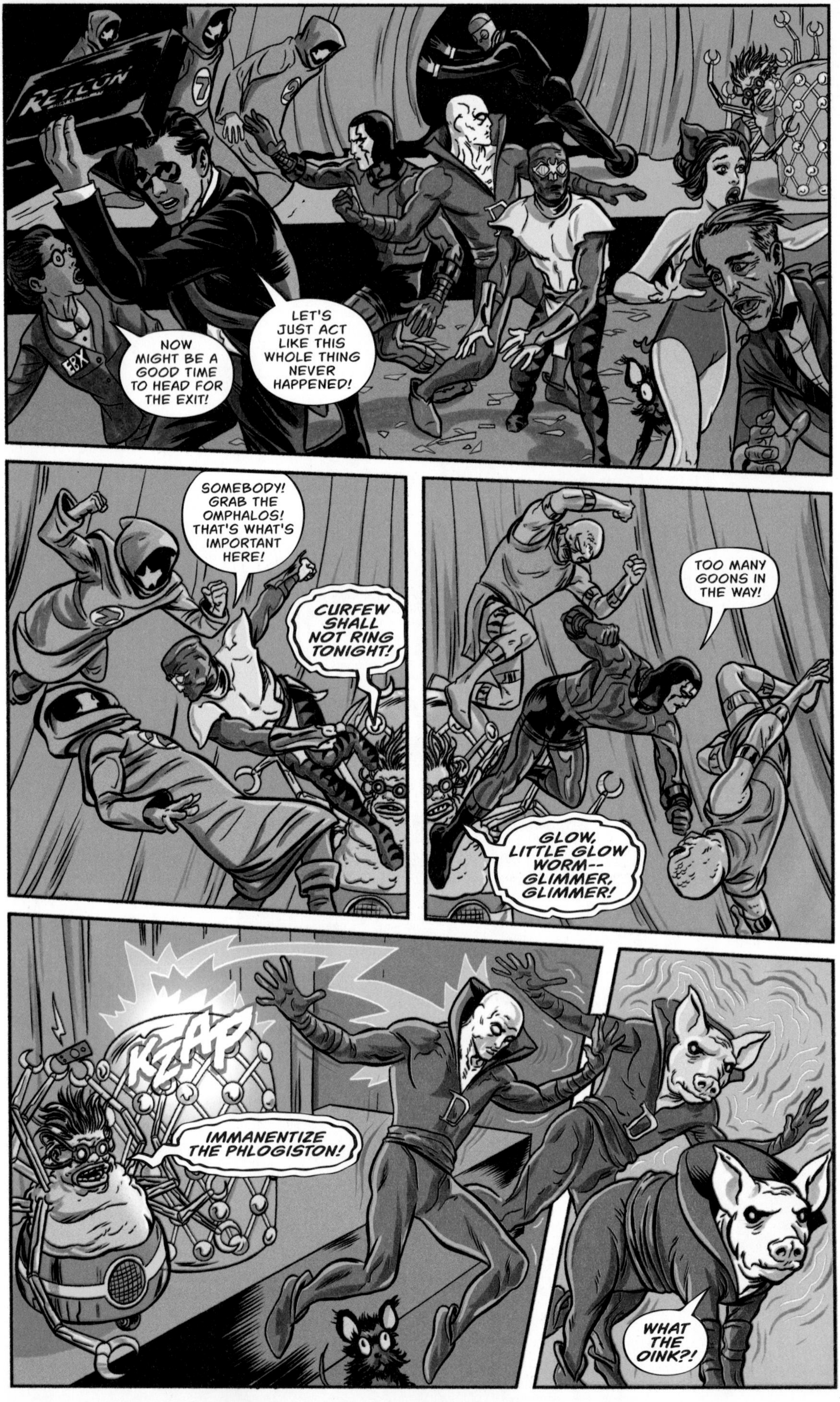
NOW MIGHT BE A GOOD TIME TO HEAD FOR THE EXIT!
LET'S JUST ACT LIKE THIS WHOLE THING NEVER HAPPENED!
SOMEBODY! GRAB THE OMPHALOS! THAT'S WHAT'S IMPORTANT HERE!
CURFEW SHALL NOT RING TONIGHT!
TOO MANY GOONS IN THE WAY!
GLOW, LITTLE GLOW WORM-- GLIMMER, GLIMMER!
KZAP
IMMANENTIZE THE PHLOGISTON!
WHAT THE OINK?!

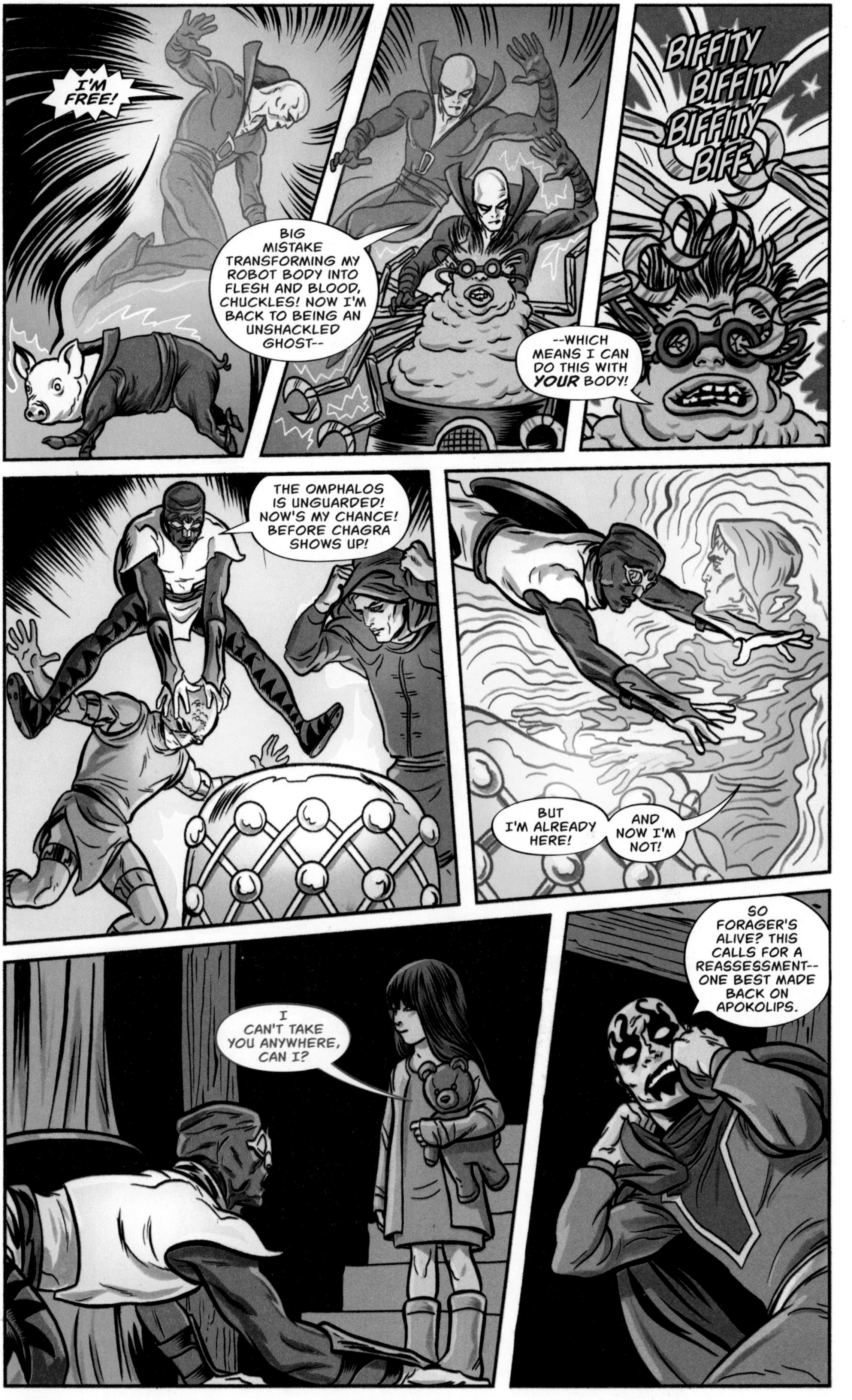
I'M FREE!
BIG MISTAKE TRANSFORMING MY ROBOT BODY INTO FLESH AND BLOOD, CHUCKLES! NOW I'M BACK TO BEING AN UNSHACKLED GHOST--
BIFFITY BIFFITY BIFFITY BIFF
--WHICH MEANS I CAN DO THIS WITH YOUR BODY!
THE OMPHALOS IS UNGUARDED! NOW'S MY CHANCE! BEFORE CHAGRA SHOWS UP!
BUT I'M ALREADY HERE!
AND NOW I'M NOT!
I CAN'T TAKE YOU ANYWHERE, CAN I?
SO FORAGER'S ALIVE? THIS CALLS FOR A REASSESSMENT-- ONE BEST MADE BACK ON APOKOLIPS.

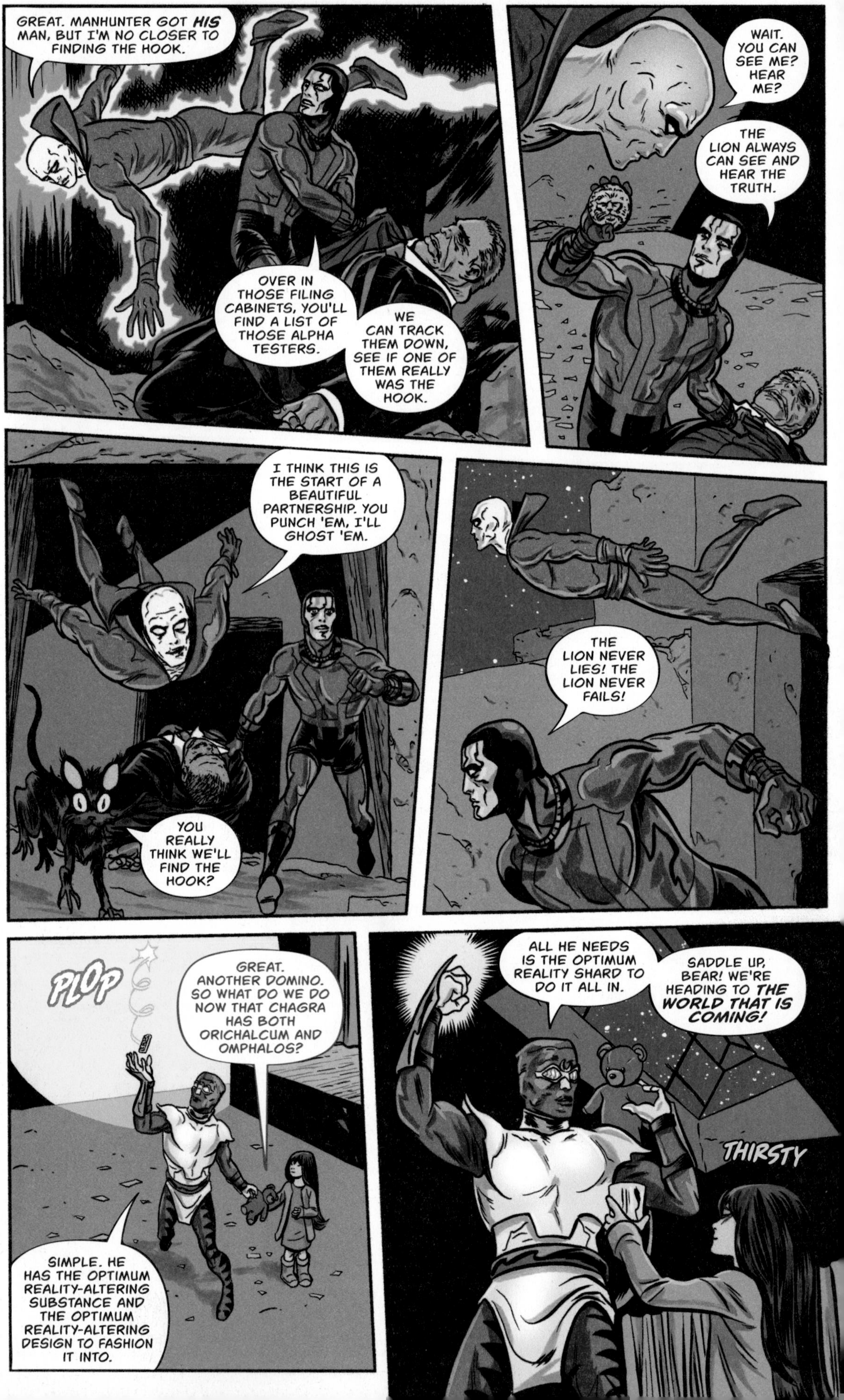
GREAT. MANHUNTER GOT HIS MAN, BUT I'M NO CLOSER TO FINDING THE HOOK.
OVER IN THOSE FILING CABINETS, YOU'LL FIND A LIST OF THOSE ALPHA TESTERS.
WE CAN TRACK THEM DOWN, SEE IF ONE OF THEM REALLY WAS THE HOOK.
WAIT. YOU CAN SEE ME? HEAR ME?
THE LION ALWAYS CAN SEE AND HEAR THE TRUTH.
I THINK THIS IS THE START OF A BEAUTIFUL PARTNERSHIP. YOU PUNCH 'EM, I'LL GHOST 'EM.
YOU REALLY THINK WE'LL FIND THE HOOK?
THE LION NEVER LIES! THE LION NEVER FAILS!
PLOP
GREAT. ANOTHER DOMINO. SO WHAT DO WE DO NOW THAT CHAGRA HAS BOTH ORICHALCUM AND OMPHALOS?
SIMPLE. HE HAS THE OPTIMUM REALITY-ALTERING SUBSTANCE AND THE OPTIMUM REALITY-ALTERING DESIGN TO FASHION IT INTO.
ALL HE NEEDS IS THE OPTIMUM REALITY SHARD TO DO IT ALL IN.
SADDLE UP, BEAR! WE'RE HEADING TO THE WORLD THAT IS COMING!
THIRSTY

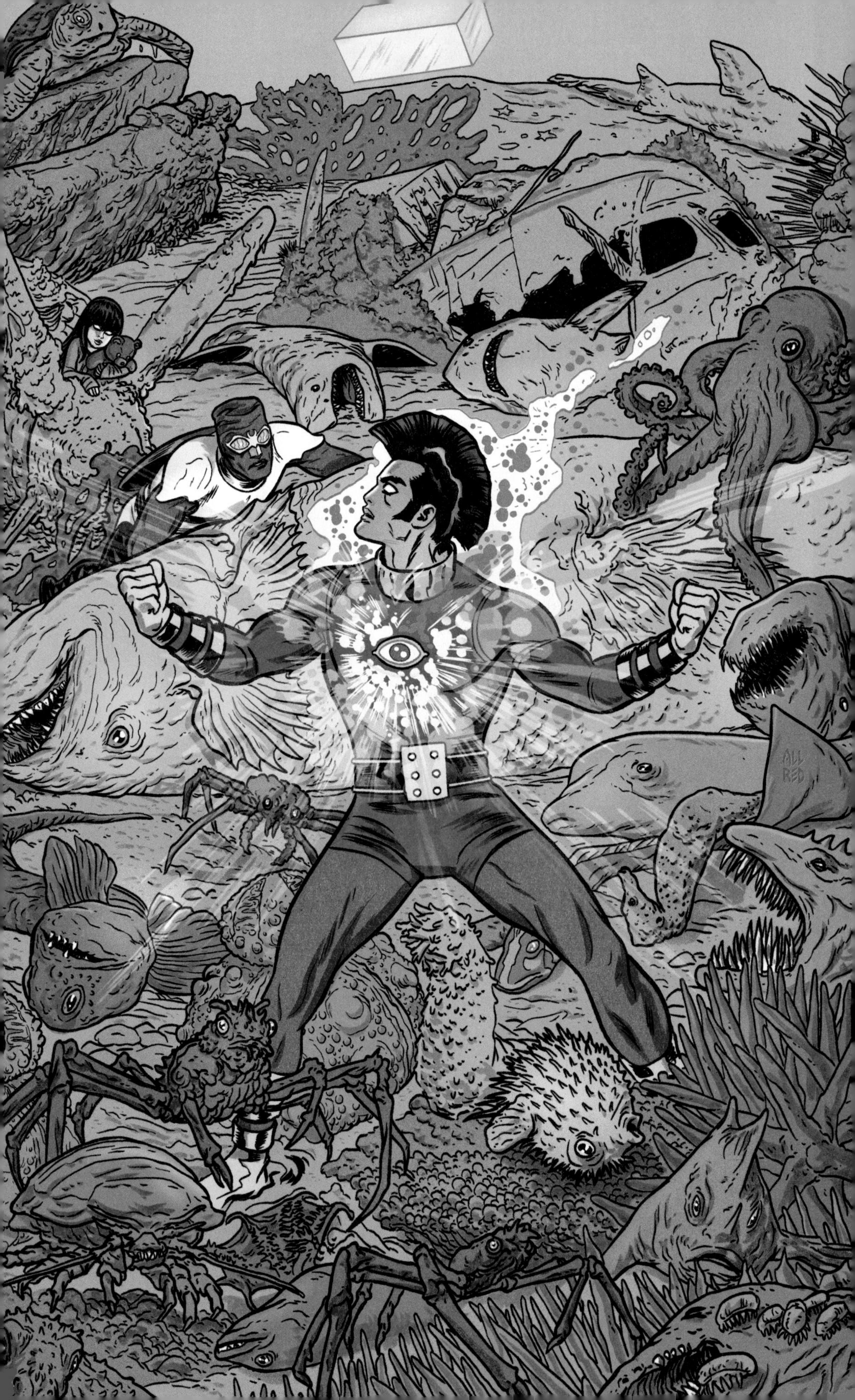
ALL
RED

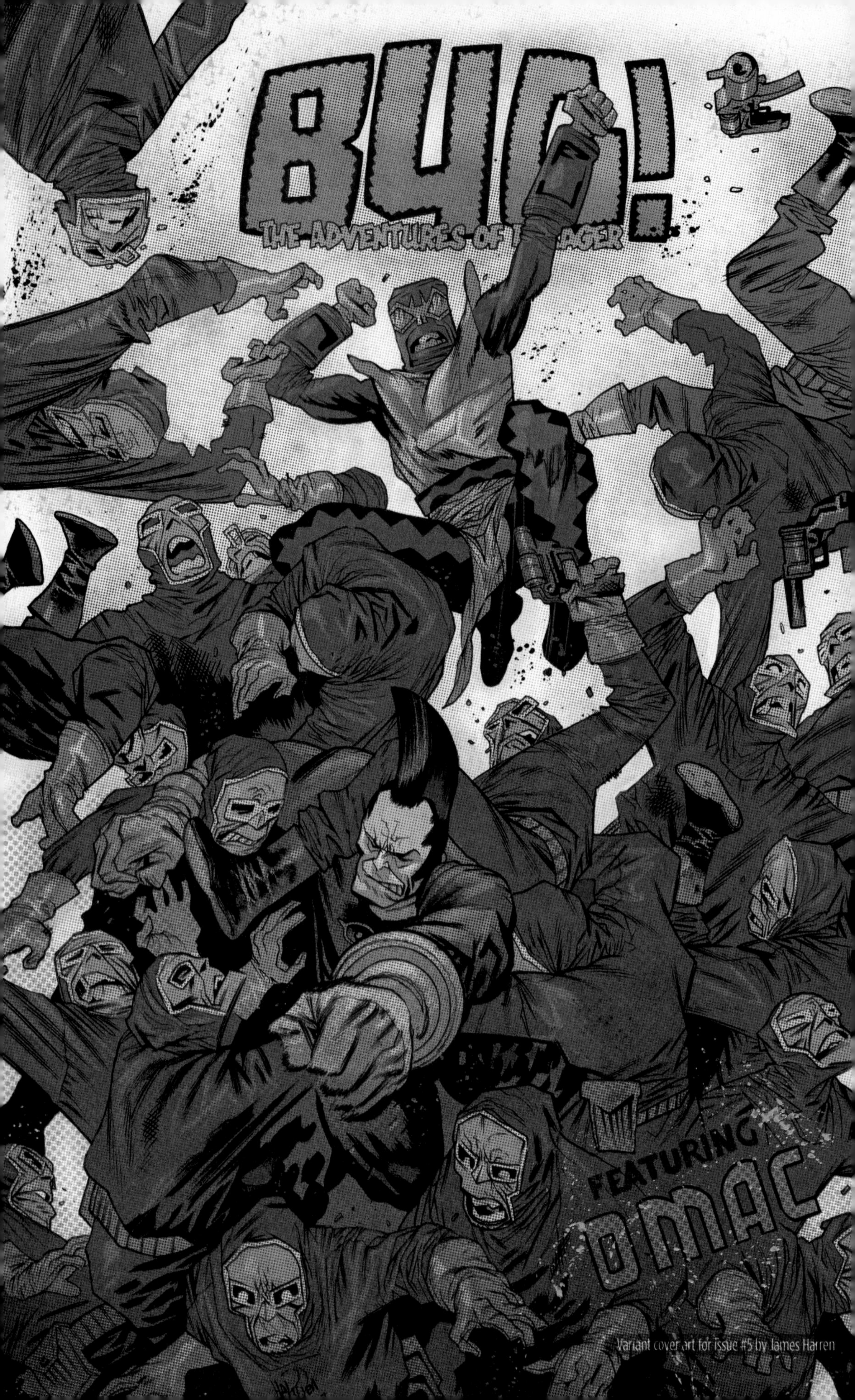
BUG!
THE ADVENTURES OF
FEATURING
OMAC
Variant cover art for issue #5 by James Harren

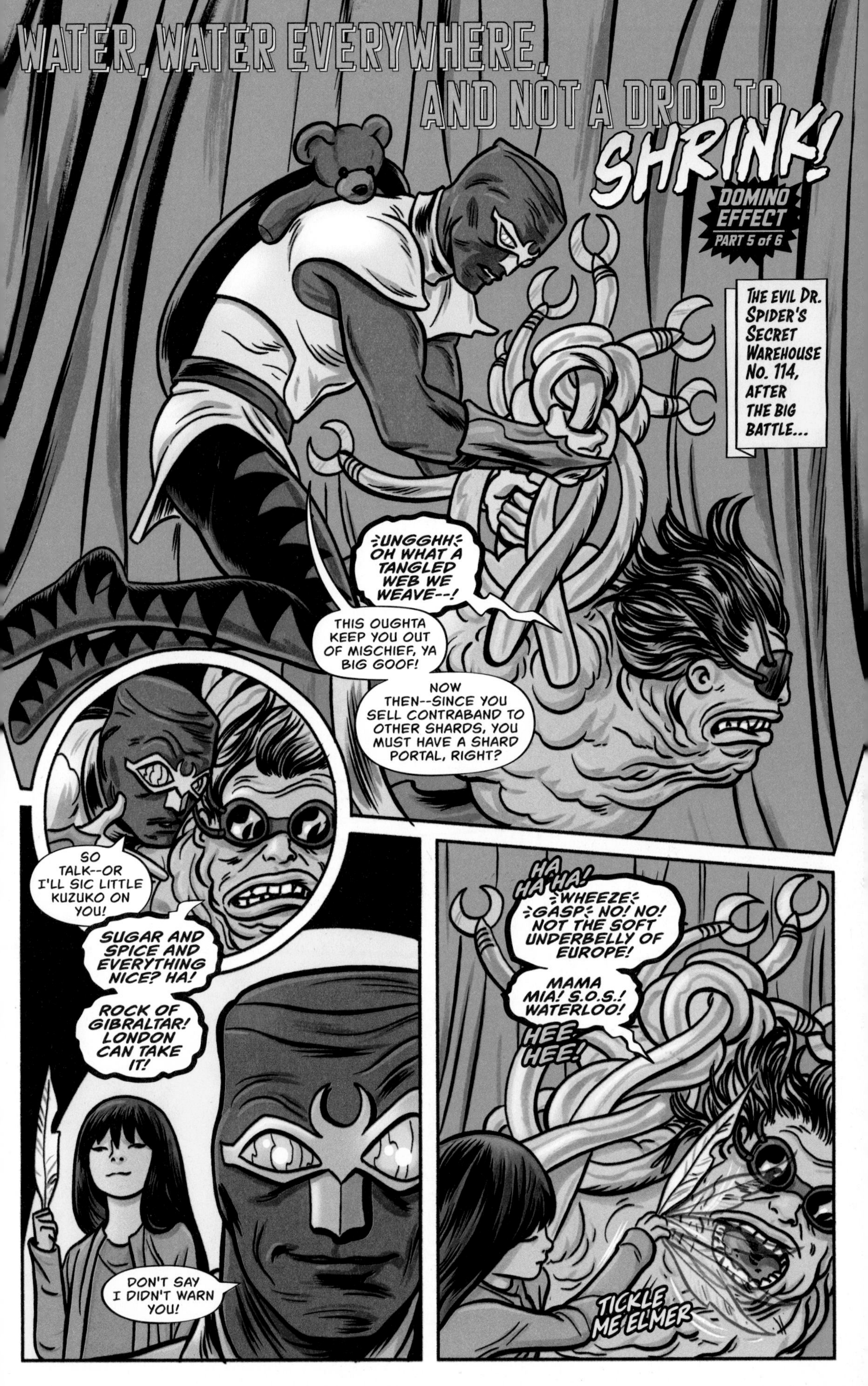
WATER, WATER EVERYWHERE, AND NOT A DROP TO SHRINK!
DOMINO EFFECT
PART 5 of 6
THE EVIL DR. SPIDER'S SECRET WAREHOUSE NO. 114, AFTER THE BIG BATTLE...
UNGGHH OH WHAT A TANGLED WEB WE WEAVE--!
THIS OUGHTA KEEP YOU OUT OF MISCHIEF, YA BIG GOOF!
NOW THEN--SINCE YOU SELL CONTRABAND TO OTHER SHARDS, YOU MUST HAVE A SHARD PORTAL, RIGHT?
SO TALK--OR I'LL SIC LITTLE KUZUKO ON YOU!
SUGAR AND SPICE AND EVERYTHING NICE? HA!
ROCK OF GIBRALTAR! LONDON CAN TAKE IT!
DON'T SAY I DIDN'T WARN YOU!
HA HA HA!
WHEEZE GASP NO! NO! NOT THE SOFT UNDERBELLY OF EUROPE!
MAMA MIA! S.O.S.! WATERLOO!
HEE HEE!
TICKLE ME ELMER

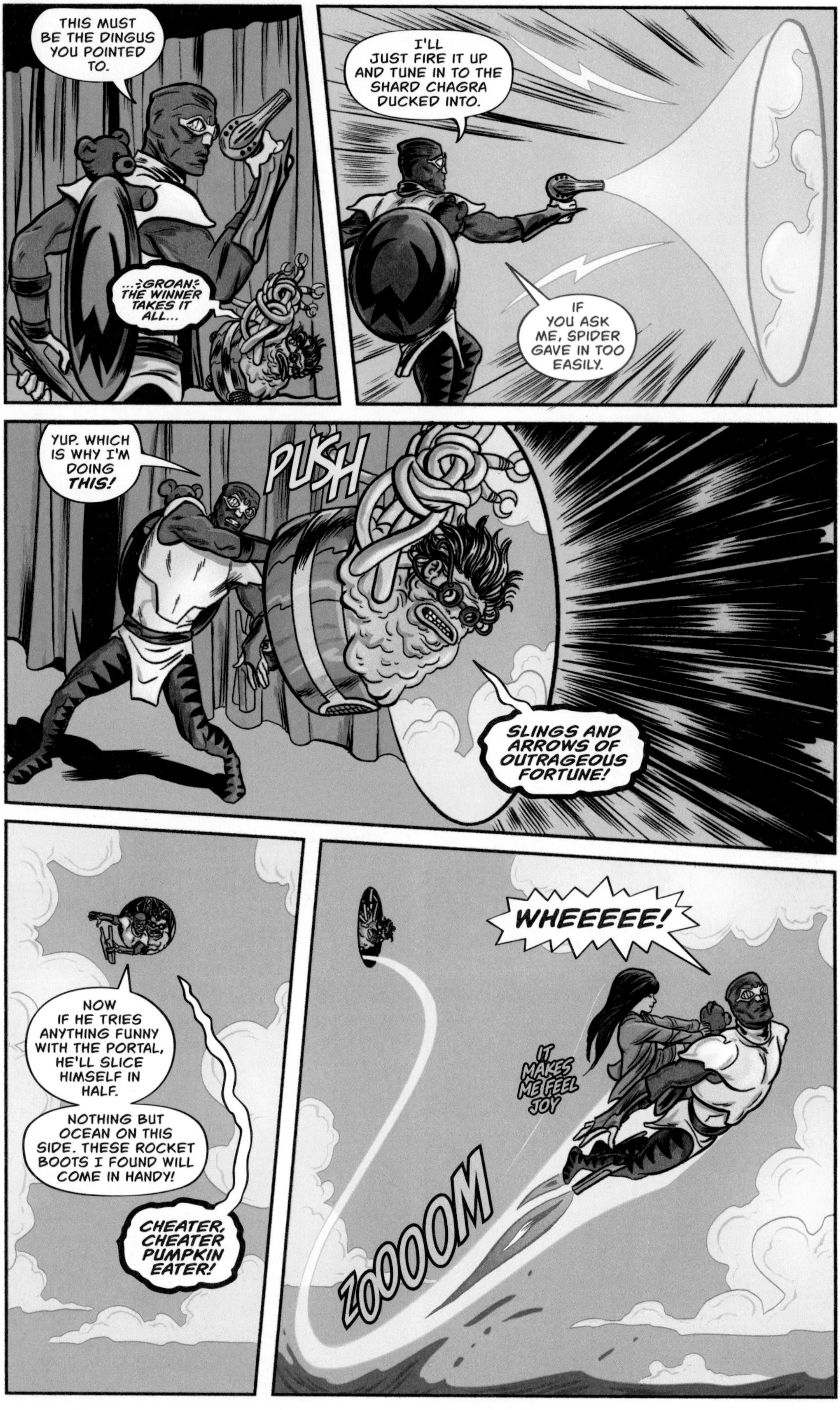
THIS MUST BE THE DINGUS YOU POINTED TO.
...GROAN... THE WINNER TAKES IT ALL...
I'LL JUST FIRE IT UP AND TUNE IN TO THE SHARD CHAGRA DUCKED INTO.
IF YOU ASK ME, SPIDER GAVE IN TOO EASILY.
YUP. WHICH IS WHY I'M DOING THIS!
PUSH
SLINGS AND ARROWS OF OUTRAGEOUS FORTUNE!
NOW IF HE TRIES ANYTHING FUNNY WITH THE PORTAL, HE'LL SLICE HIMSELF IN HALF.
NOTHING BUT OCEAN ON THIS SIDE. THESE ROCKET BOOTS I FOUND WILL COME IN HANDY!
CHEATER, CHEATER PUMPKIN EATER!
WHEEEEE!
IT MAKES ME FEEL JOY
ZOOOOM

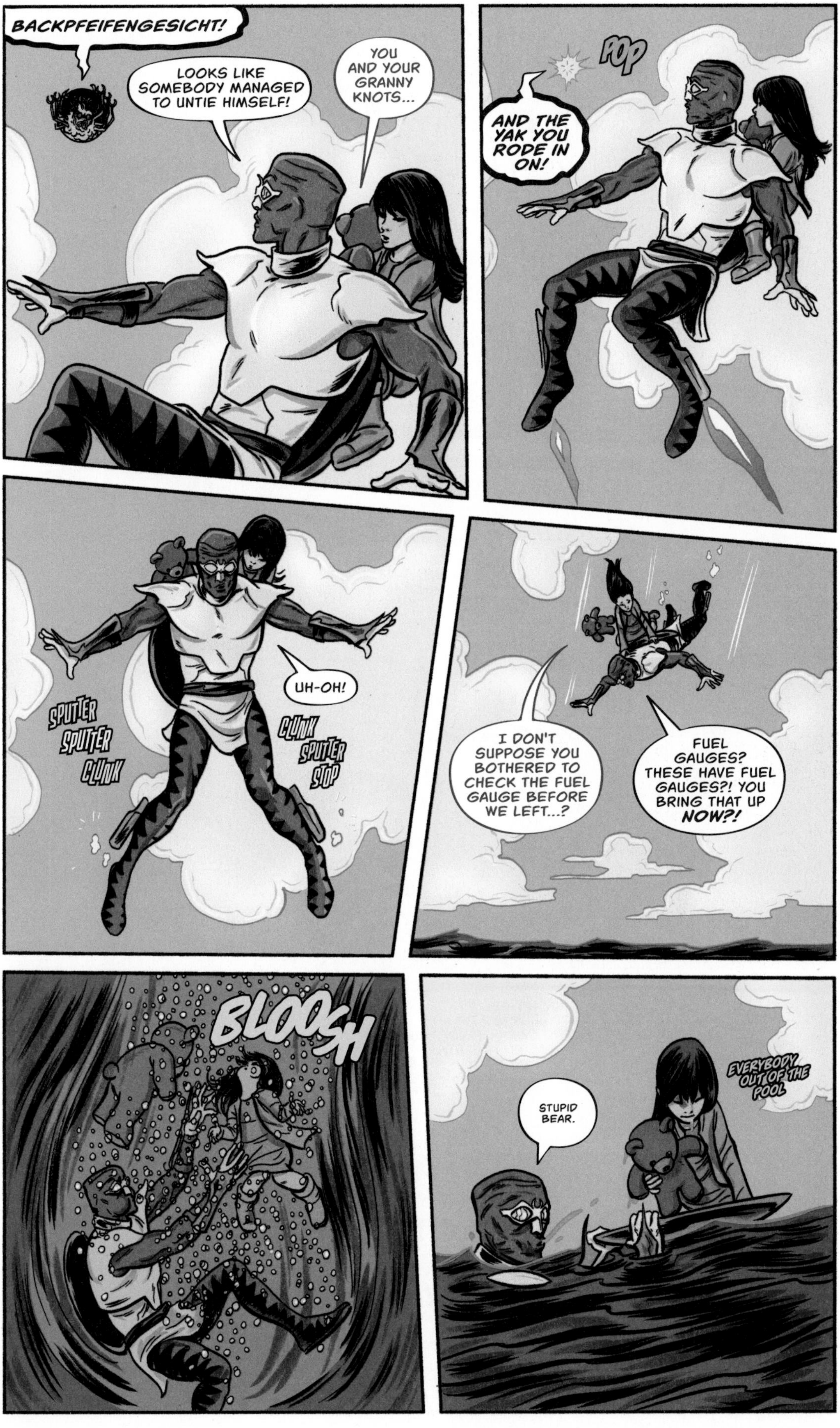
BACKPFEIFENGESICHT!
LOOKS LIKE SOMEBODY MANAGED TO UNTIE HIMSELF!
YOU AND YOUR GRANNY KNOTS...
POP
AND THE YAK YOU RODE IN ON!
UH-OH!
SPUTTER SPUTTER CLUNK
CLUNK SPUTTER STOP
I DON'T SUPPOSE YOU BOTHERED TO CHECK THE FUEL GAUGE BEFORE WE LEFT...?
FUEL GAUGES? THESE HAVE FUEL GAUGES?! YOU BRING THAT UP NOW?!
BLOOSH
STUPID BEAR.
EVERYBODY OUT OF THE POOL

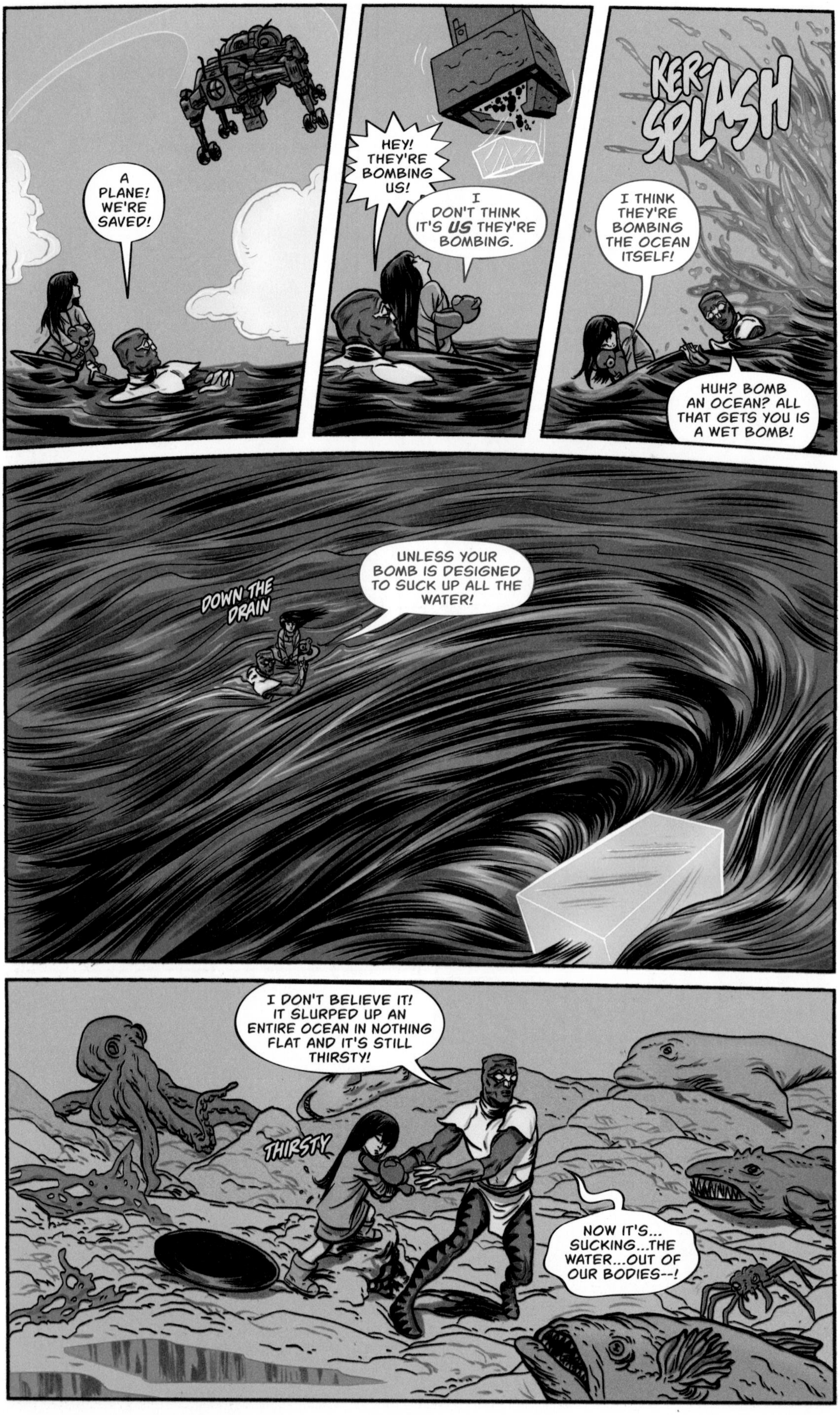
A PLANE! WE'RE SAVED!
HEY! THEY'RE BOMBING US!
I DON'T THINK IT'S US THEY'RE BOMBING.
KER-SPLASH
I THINK THEY'RE BOMBING THE OCEAN ITSELF!
HUH? BOMB AN OCEAN? ALL THAT GETS YOU IS A WET BOMB!
UNLESS YOUR BOMB IS DESIGNED TO SUCK UP ALL THE WATER!
DOWN THE DRAIN
I DON'T BELIEVE IT! IT SLURPED UP AN ENTIRE OCEAN IN NOTHING FLAT AND IT'S STILL THIRSTY!
THIRSTY
NOW IT'S... SUCKING...THE WATER...OUT OF OUR BODIES--!

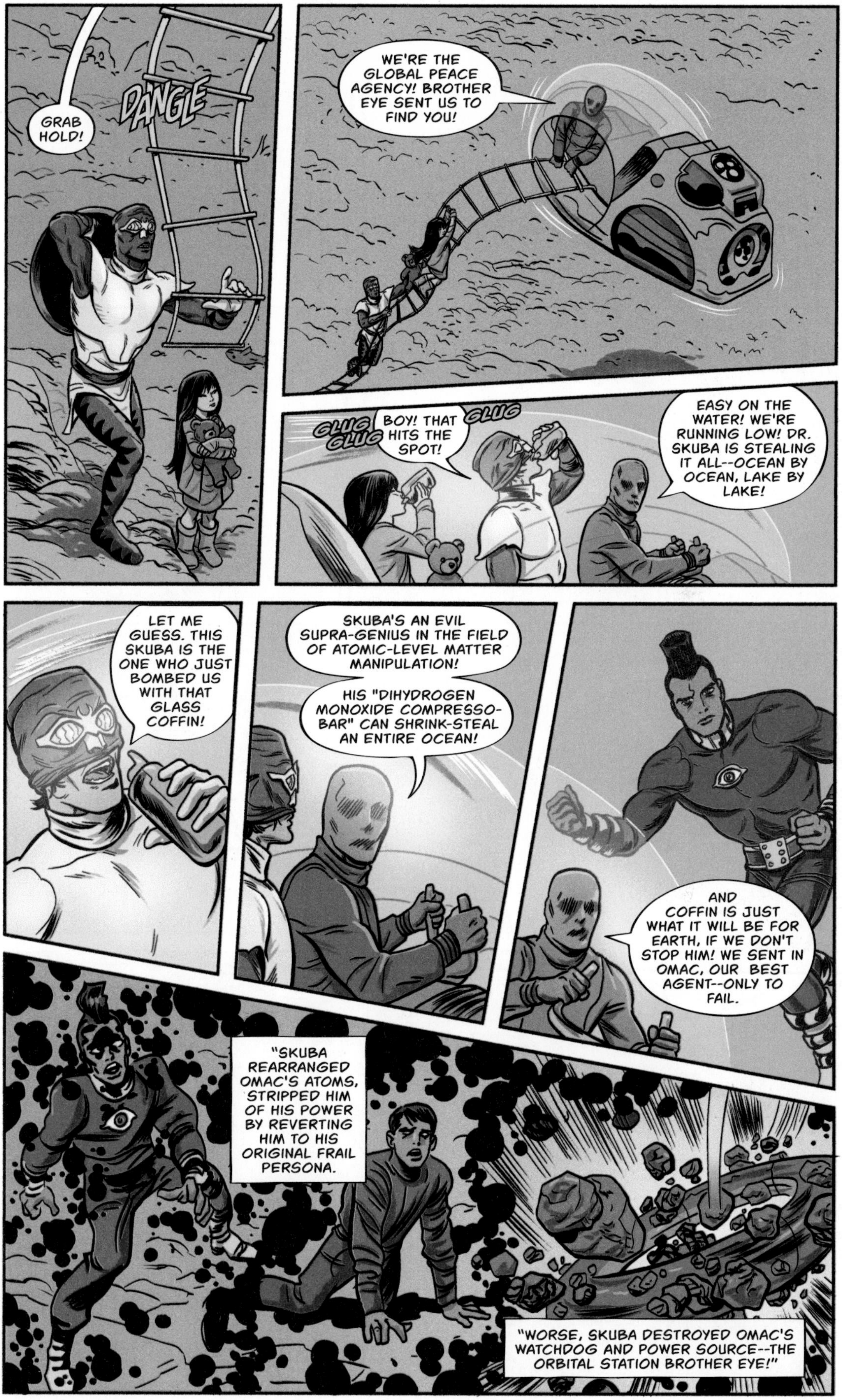
GRAB HOLD!
DANGLE
WE'RE THE GLOBAL PEACE AGENCY! BROTHER EYE SENT US TO FIND YOU!
GLUG GLUG
BOY! THAT HITS THE SPOT!
GLUG
EASY ON THE WATER! WE'RE RUNNING LOW! DR. SKUBA IS STEALING IT ALL--OCEAN BY OCEAN, LAKE BY LAKE!
LET ME GUESS. THIS SKUBA IS THE ONE WHO JUST BOMBED US WITH THAT GLASS COFFIN!
SKUBA'S AN EVIL SUPRA-GENIUS IN THE FIELD OF ATOMIC-LEVEL MATTER MANIPULATION!
HIS "DIHYDROGEN MONOXIDE COMPRESSO-BAR" CAN SHRINK-STEAL AN ENTIRE OCEAN!
AND COFFIN IS JUST WHAT IT WILL BE FOR EARTH, IF WE DON'T STOP HIM! WE SENT IN OMAC, OUR BEST AGENT--ONLY TO FAIL.
"SKUBA REARRANGED OMAC'S ATOMS, STRIPPED HIM OF HIS POWER BY REVERTING HIM TO HIS ORIGINAL FRAIL PERSONA.
"WORSE, SKUBA DESTROYED OMAC'S WATCHDOG AND POWER SOURCE--THE ORBITAL STATION BROTHER EYE!"

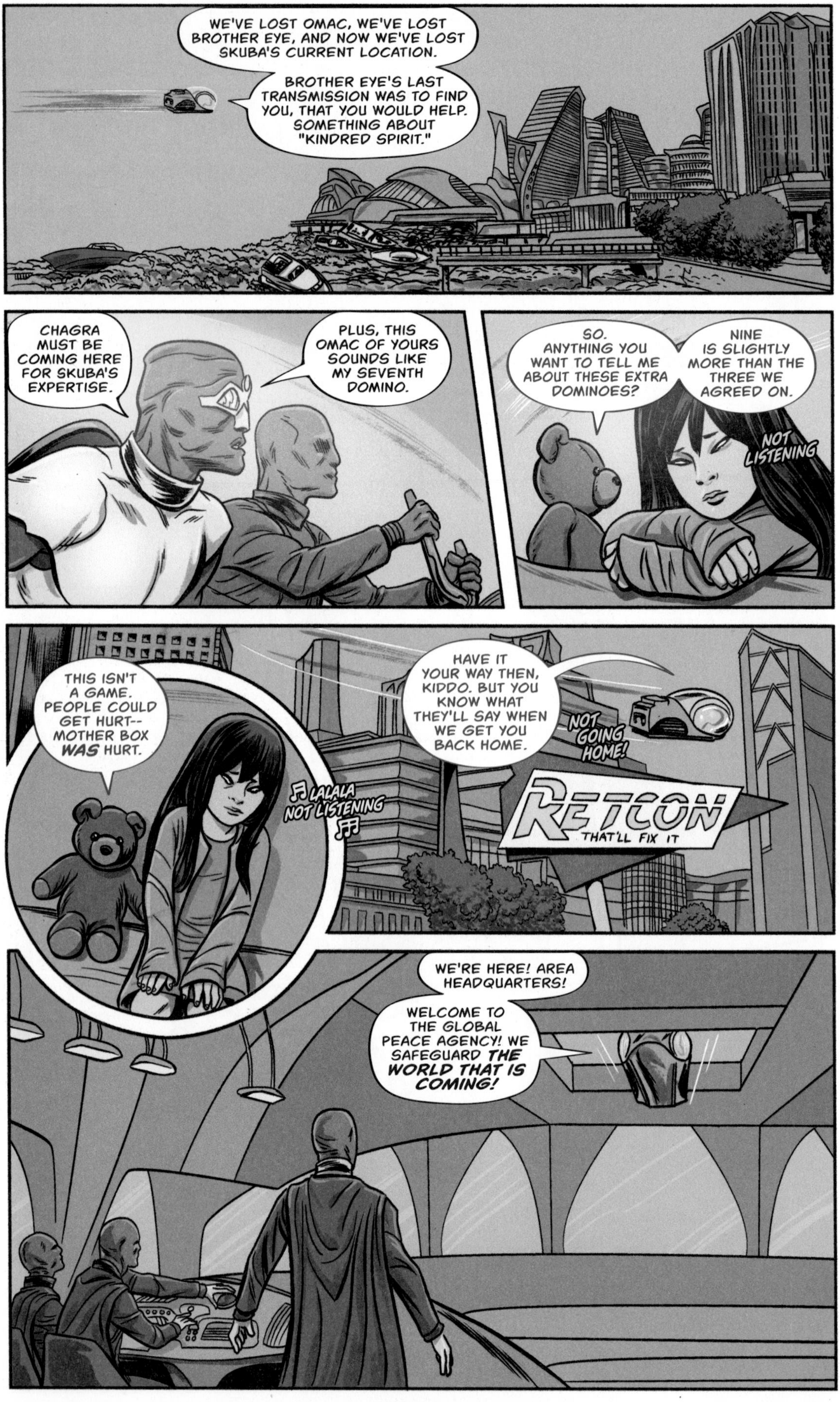
WE'VE LOST OMAC, WE'VE LOST BROTHER EYE, AND NOW WE'VE LOST SKUBA'S CURRENT LOCATION.
BROTHER EYE'S LAST TRANSMISSION WAS TO FIND YOU, THAT YOU WOULD HELP. SOMETHING ABOUT "KINDRED SPIRIT."
CHAGRA MUST BE COMING HERE FOR SKUBA'S EXPERTISE.
PLUS, THIS OMAC OF YOURS SOUNDS LIKE MY SEVENTH DOMINO.
SO. ANYTHING YOU WANT TO TELL ME ABOUT THESE EXTRA DOMINOES?
NINE IS SLIGHTLY MORE THAN THE THREE WE AGREED ON.
NOT LISTENING
THIS ISN'T A GAME. PEOPLE COULD GET HURT-- MOTHER BOX WAS HURT.
LALALA NOT LISTENING
HAVE IT YOUR WAY THEN, KIDDO. BUT YOU KNOW WHAT THEY'LL SAY WHEN WE GET YOU BACK HOME.
NOT GOING HOME!
RETCON
THAT'LL FIX IT
WE'RE HERE! AREA HEADQUARTERS!
WELCOME TO THE GLOBAL PEACE AGENCY! WE SAFEGUARD THE WORLD THAT IS COMING!

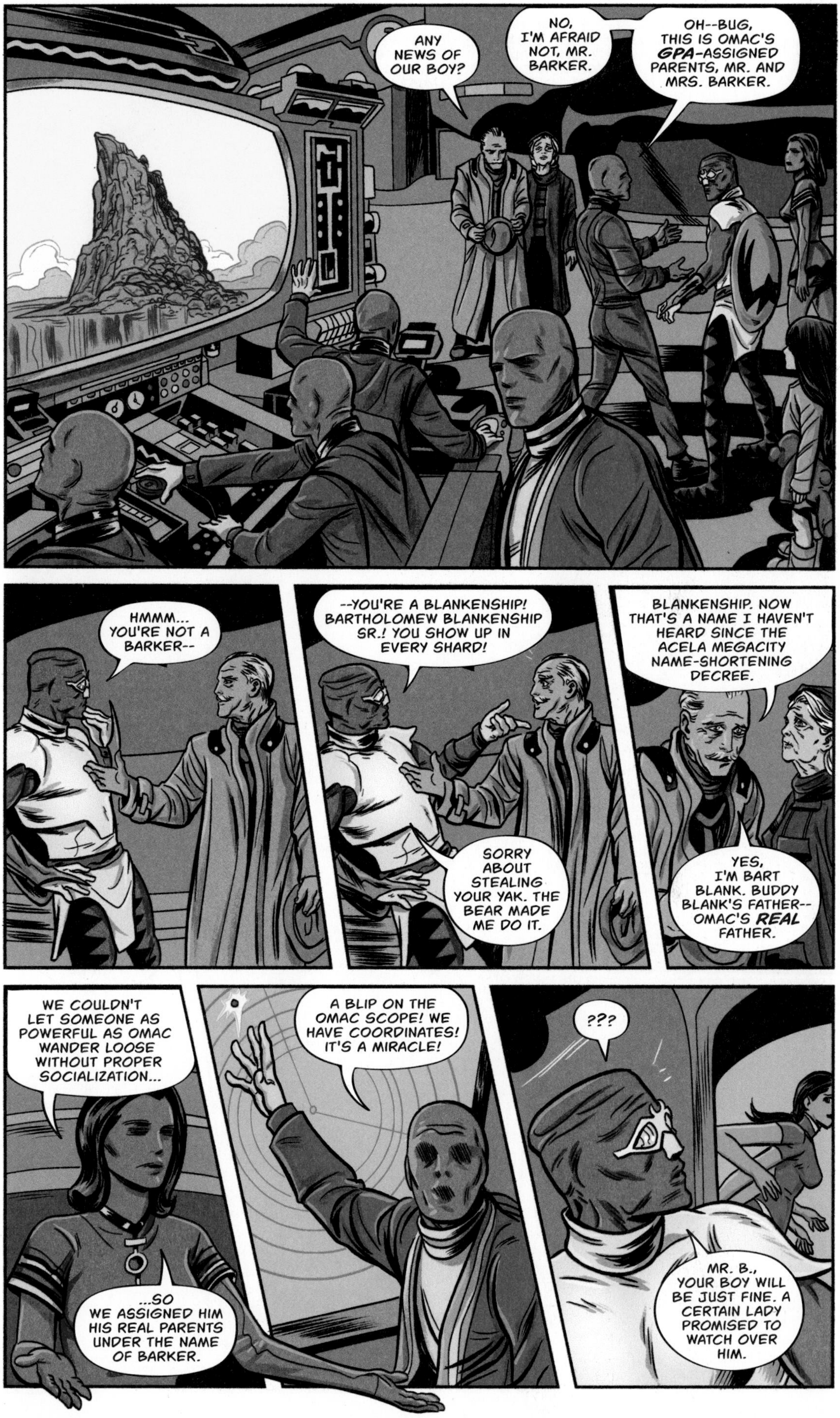
ANY NEWS OF OUR BOY?
NO, I'M AFRAID NOT, MR. BARKER.
OH--BUG, THIS IS OMAC'S GPA-ASSIGNED PARENTS, MR. AND MRS. BARKER.
HMMM... YOU'RE NOT A BARKER--
--YOU'RE A BLANKENSHIP! BARTHOLOMEW BLANKENSHIP SR.! YOU SHOW UP IN EVERY SHARD!
SORRY ABOUT STEALING YOUR YAK. THE BEAR MADE ME DO IT.
BLANKENSHIP. NOW THAT'S A NAME I HAVEN'T HEARD SINCE THE ACELA MEGACITY NAME-SHORTENING DECREE.
YES, I'M BART BLANK. BUDDY BLANK'S FATHER-- OMAC'S REAL FATHER.
WE COULDN'T LET SOMEONE AS POWERFUL AS OMAC WANDER LOOSE WITHOUT PROPER SOCIALIZATION...
...SO WE ASSIGNED HIM HIS REAL PARENTS UNDER THE NAME OF BARKER.
A BLIP ON THE OMAC SCOPE! WE HAVE COORDINATES! IT'S A MIRACLE!
???
MR. B., YOUR BOY WILL BE JUST FINE. A CERTAIN LADY PROMISED TO WATCH OVER HIM.

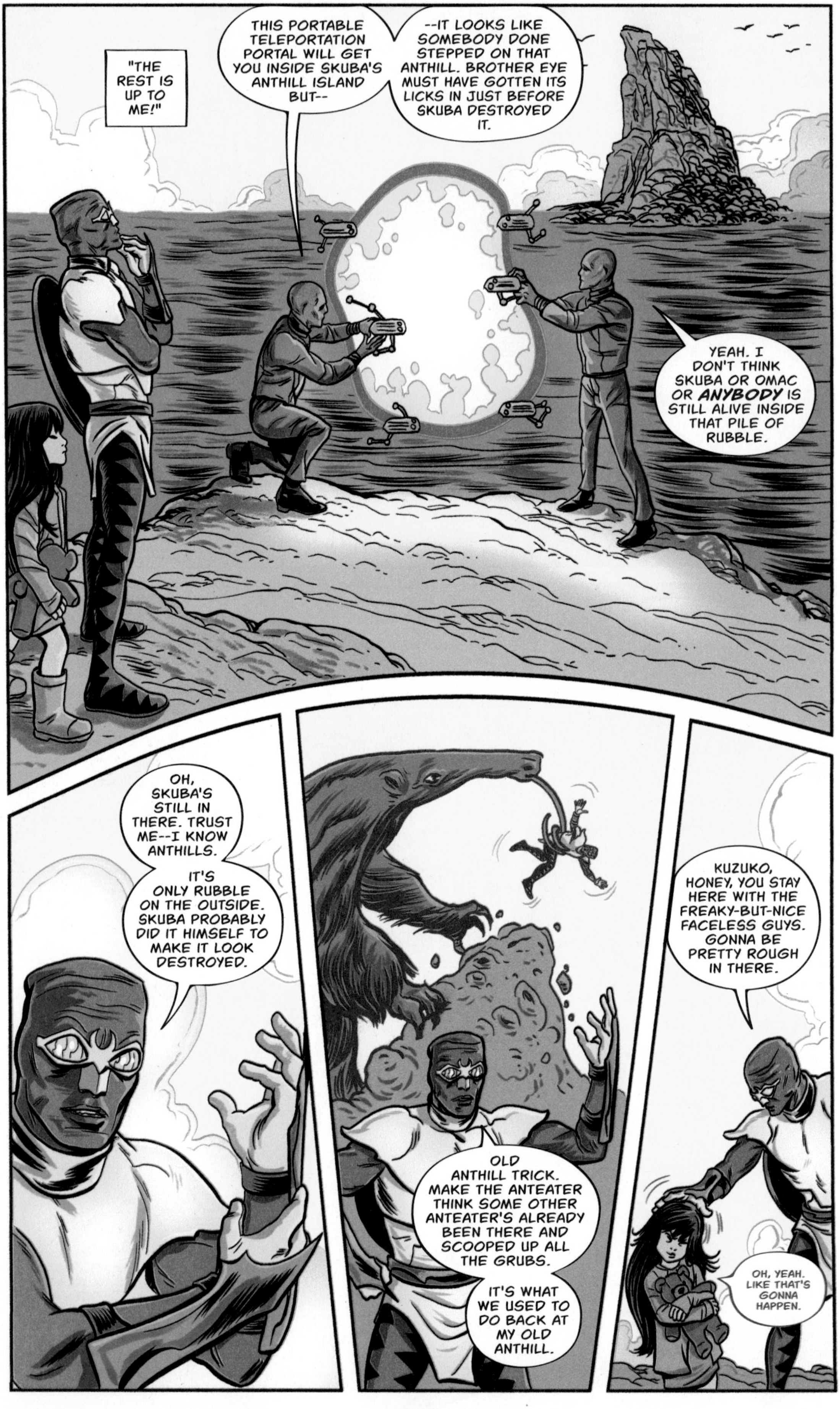
"THE REST IS UP TO ME!"
THIS PORTABLE TELEPORTATION PORTAL WILL GET YOU INSIDE SKUBA'S ANTHILL ISLAND BUT--
--IT LOOKS LIKE SOMEBODY DONE STEPPED ON THAT ANTHILL. BROTHER EYE MUST HAVE GOTTEN ITS LICKS IN JUST BEFORE SKUBA DESTROYED IT.
YEAH. I DON'T THINK SKUBA OR OMAC OR ***ANYBODY*** IS STILL ALIVE INSIDE THAT PILE OF RUBBLE.
OH, SKUBA'S STILL IN THERE. TRUST ME--I KNOW ANTHILLS.
IT'S ONLY RUBBLE ON THE OUTSIDE. SKUBA PROBABLY DID IT HIMSELF TO MAKE IT LOOK DESTROYED.
OLD ANTHILL TRICK. MAKE THE ANTEATER THINK SOME OTHER ANTEATER'S ALREADY BEEN THERE AND SCOOPED UP ALL THE GRUBS.
IT'S WHAT WE USED TO DO BACK AT MY OLD ANTHILL.
KUZUKO, HONEY, YOU STAY HERE WITH THE FREAKY-BUT-NICE FACELESS GUYS. GONNA BE PRETTY ROUGH IN THERE.
OH, YEAH. LIKE THAT'S GONNA HAPPEN.

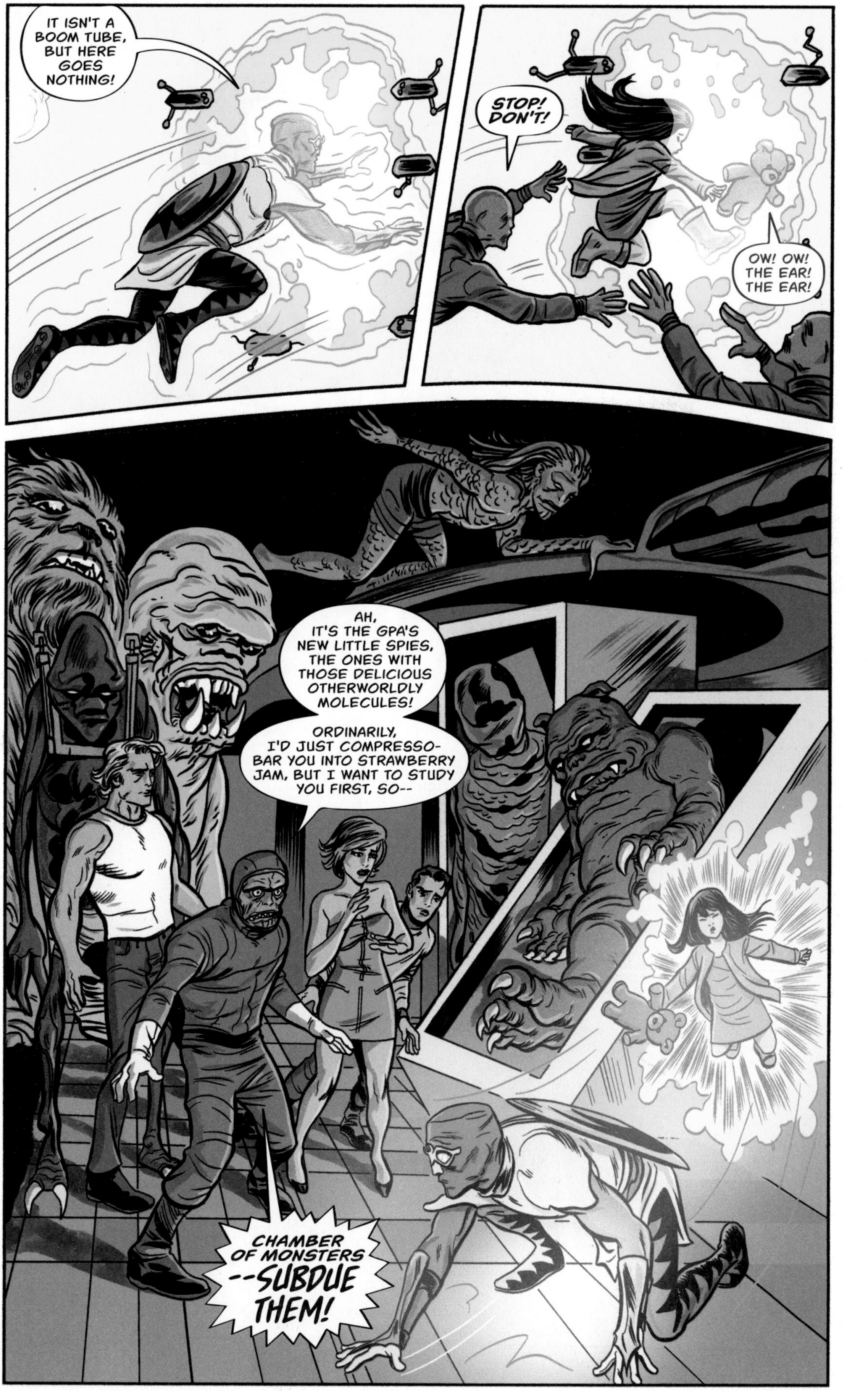
IT ISN'T A BOOM TUBE, BUT HERE GOES NOTHING!
STOP! DON'T!
OW! OW! THE EAR! THE EAR!
AH, IT'S THE GPA'S NEW LITTLE SPIES, THE ONES WITH THOSE DELICIOUS OTHERWORLDLY MOLECULES!
ORDINARILY, I'D JUST COMPRESSO-BAR YOU INTO STRAWBERRY JAM, BUT I WANT TO STUDY YOU FIRST, SO--
CHAMBER OF MONSTERS --SUBDUE THEM!

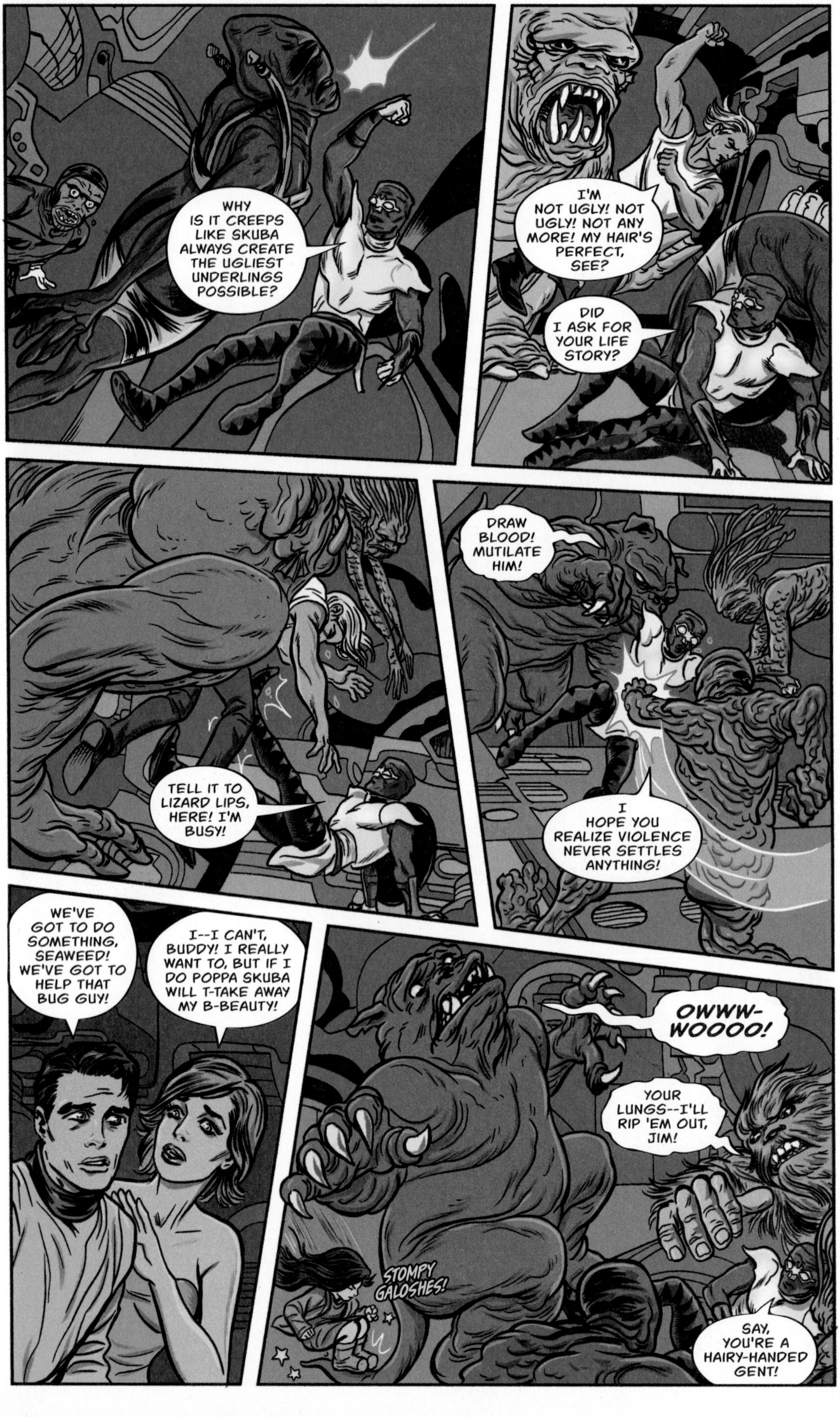
WHY IS IT CREEPS LIKE SKUBA ALWAYS CREATE THE UGLIEST UNDERLINGS POSSIBLE?
I'M NOT UGLY! NOT UGLY! NOT ANY MORE! MY HAIR'S PERFECT, SEE?
DID I ASK FOR YOUR LIFE STORY?
TELL IT TO LIZARD LIPS, HERE! I'M BUSY!
DRAW BLOOD! MUTILATE HIM!
I HOPE YOU REALIZE VIOLENCE NEVER SETTLES ANYTHING!
WE'VE GOT TO DO SOMETHING, SEAWEED! WE'VE GOT TO HELP THAT BUG GUY!
I--I CAN'T, BUDDY! I REALLY WANT TO, BUT IF I DO POPPA SKUBA WILL T-TAKE AWAY MY B-BEAUTY!
OWWW-WOOOO!
YOUR LUNGS--I'LL RIP 'EM OUT, JIM!
STOMPY GALOSHES!
SAY, YOU'RE A HAIRY-HANDED GENT!

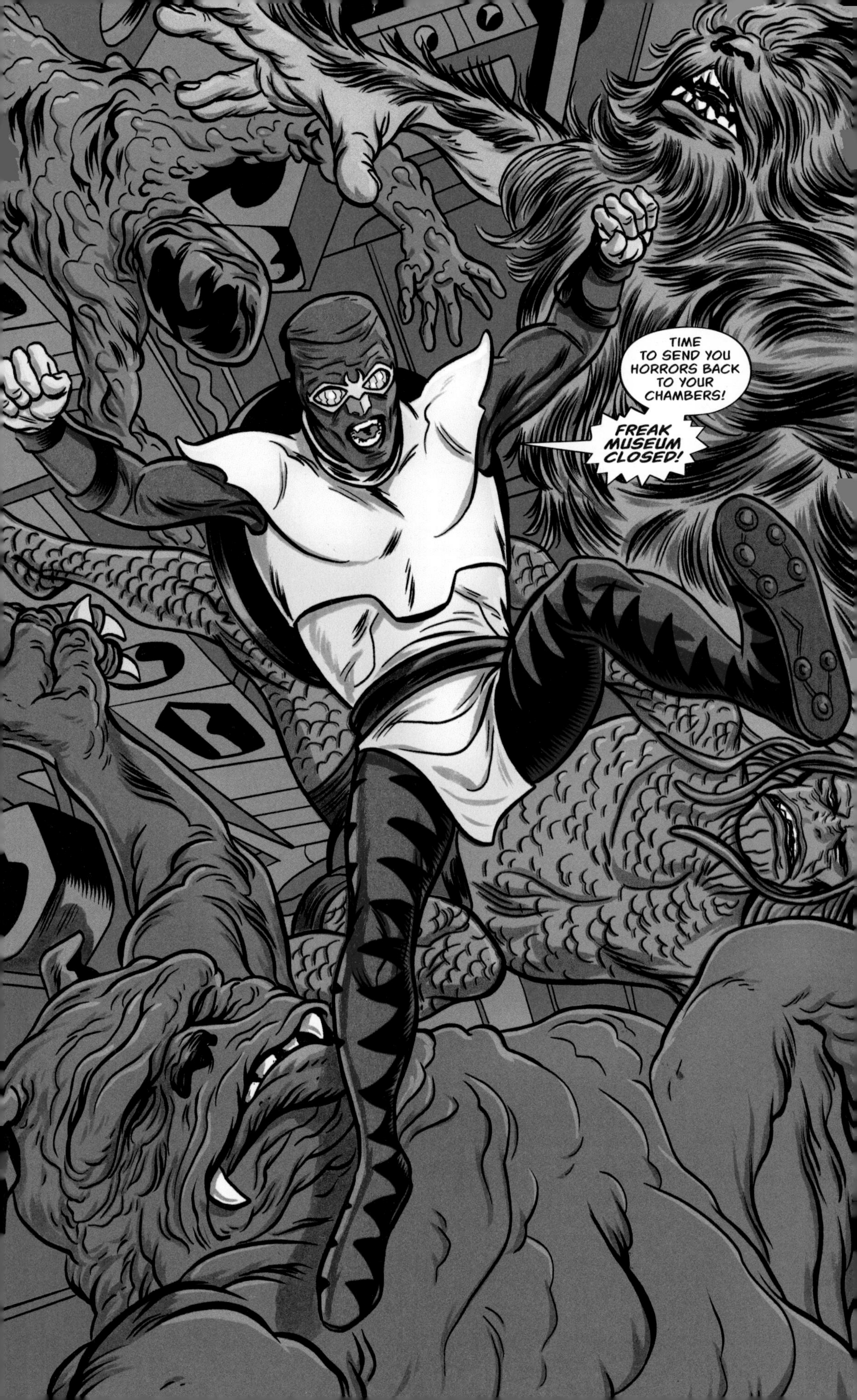
TIME TO SEND YOU HORRORS BACK TO YOUR CHAMBERS!
FREAK MUSEUM CLOSED!

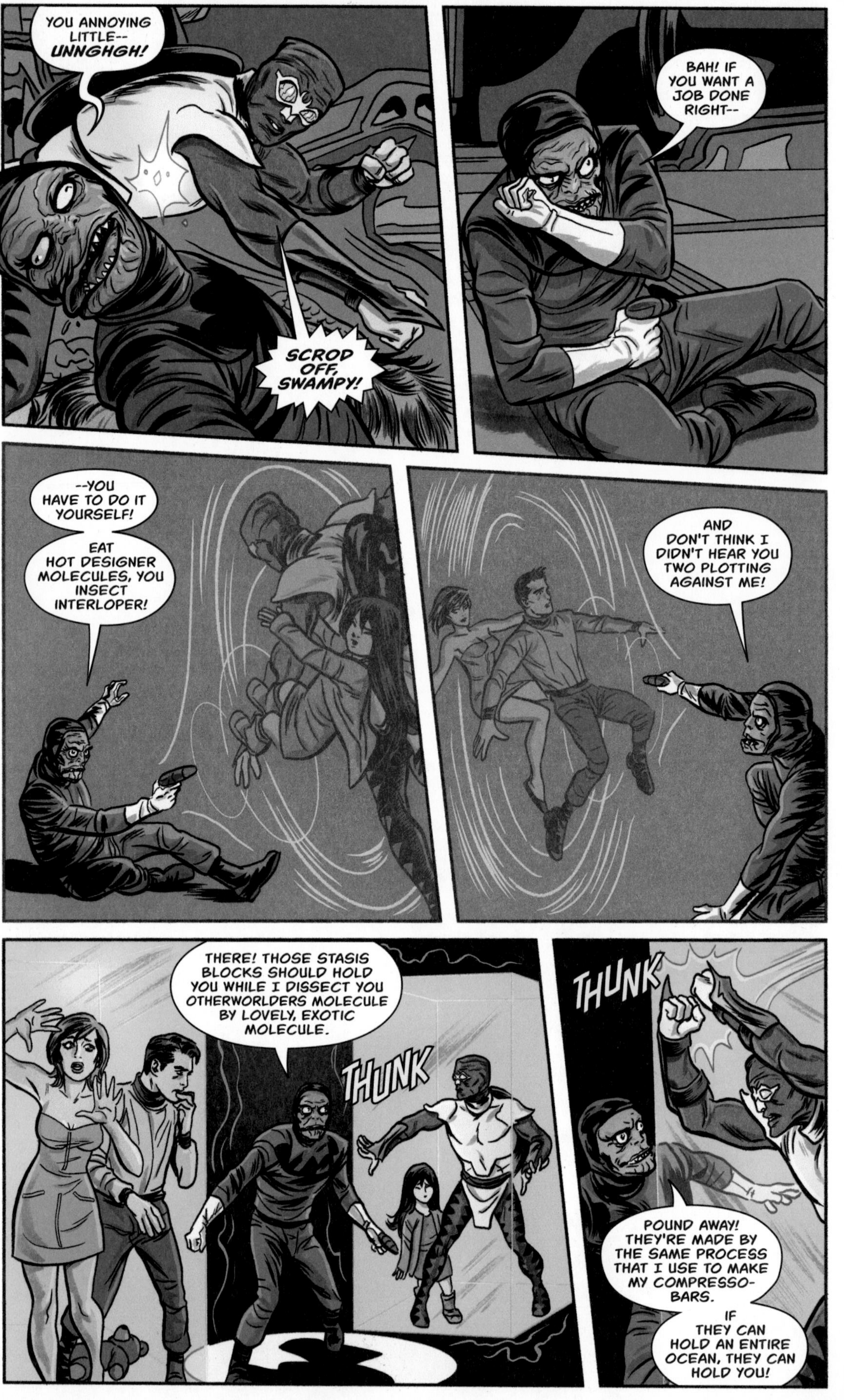
YOU ANNOYING LITTLE-- UNNGHGH!
SCROD OFF, SWAMPY!
BAH! IF YOU WANT A JOB DONE RIGHT--
--YOU HAVE TO DO IT YOURSELF!
EAT HOT DESIGNER MOLECULES, YOU INSECT INTERLOPER!
AND DON'T THINK I DIDN'T HEAR YOU TWO PLOTTING AGAINST ME!
THERE! THOSE STASIS BLOCKS SHOULD HOLD YOU WHILE I DISSECT YOU OTHERWORLDERS MOLECULE BY LOVELY, EXOTIC MOLECULE.
THUNK
THUNK
POUND AWAY! THEY'RE MADE BY THE SAME PROCESS THAT I USE TO MAKE MY COMPRESSO-BARS.
IF THEY CAN HOLD AN ENTIRE OCEAN, THEY CAN HOLD YOU!

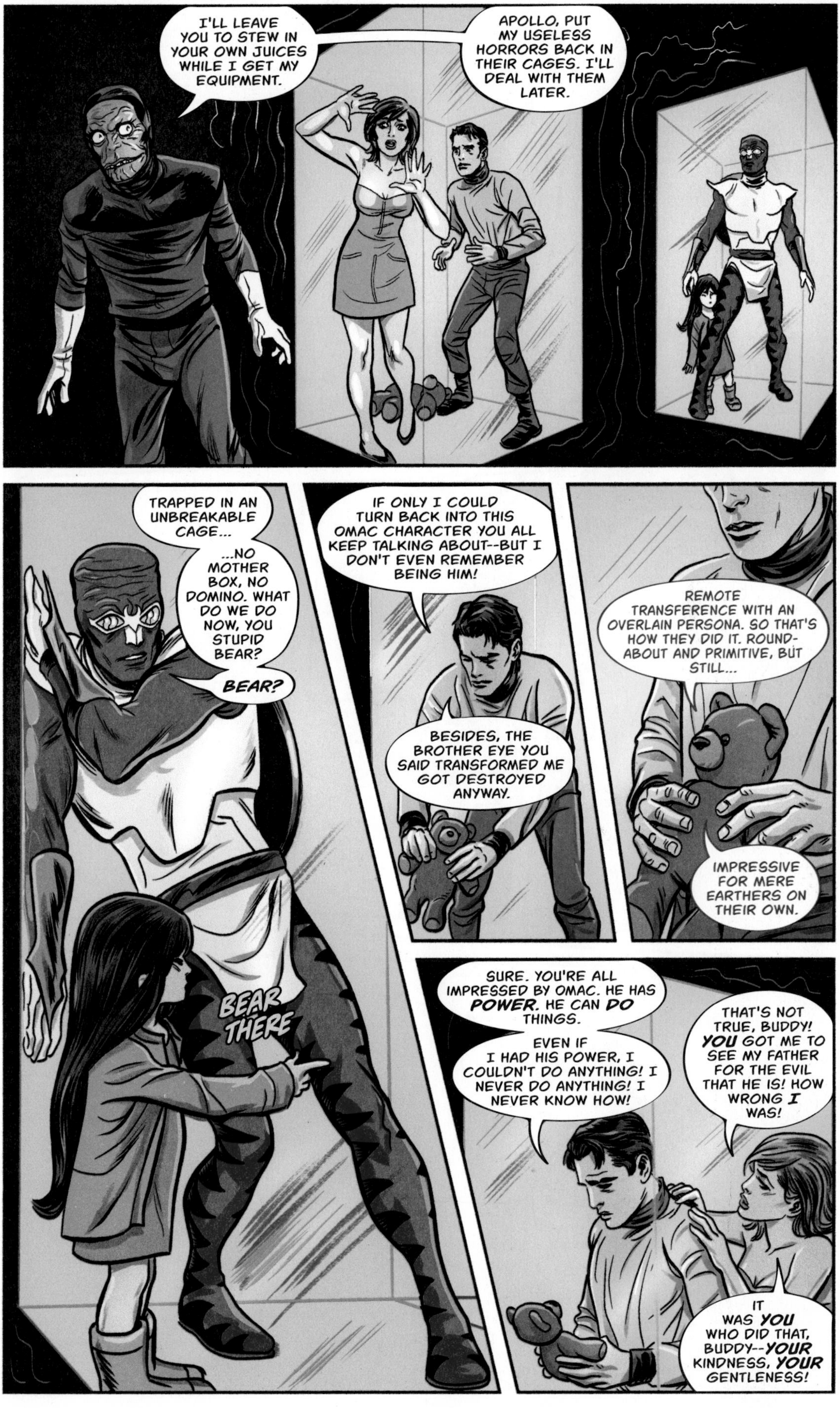
I'LL LEAVE YOU TO STEW IN YOUR OWN JUICES WHILE I GET MY EQUIPMENT.
APOLLO, PUT MY USELESS HORRORS BACK IN THEIR CAGES. I'LL DEAL WITH THEM LATER.
TRAPPED IN AN UNBREAKABLE CAGE...
...NO MOTHER BOX, NO DOMINO. WHAT DO WE DO NOW, YOU STUPID BEAR?
BEAR?
BEAR THERE
IF ONLY I COULD TURN BACK INTO THIS OMAC CHARACTER YOU ALL KEEP TALKING ABOUT--BUT I DON'T EVEN REMEMBER BEING HIM!
BESIDES, THE BROTHER EYE YOU SAID TRANSFORMED ME GOT DESTROYED ANYWAY.
REMOTE TRANSFERENCE WITH AN OVERLAIN PERSONA. SO THAT'S HOW THEY DID IT. ROUNDABOUT AND PRIMITIVE, BUT STILL...
IMPRESSIVE FOR MERE EARTHERS ON THEIR OWN.
SURE. YOU'RE ALL IMPRESSED BY OMAC. HE HAS **POWER.** HE CAN **DO** THINGS.
EVEN IF I HAD HIS POWER, I COULDN'T DO ANYTHING! I NEVER DO ANYTHING! I NEVER KNOW HOW!
THAT'S NOT TRUE, BUDDY! **YOU** GOT ME TO SEE MY FATHER FOR THE EVIL THAT HE IS! HOW WRONG **I** WAS!
IT WAS **YOU** WHO DID THAT, BUDDY--**YOUR** KINDNESS, **YOUR** GENTLENESS!

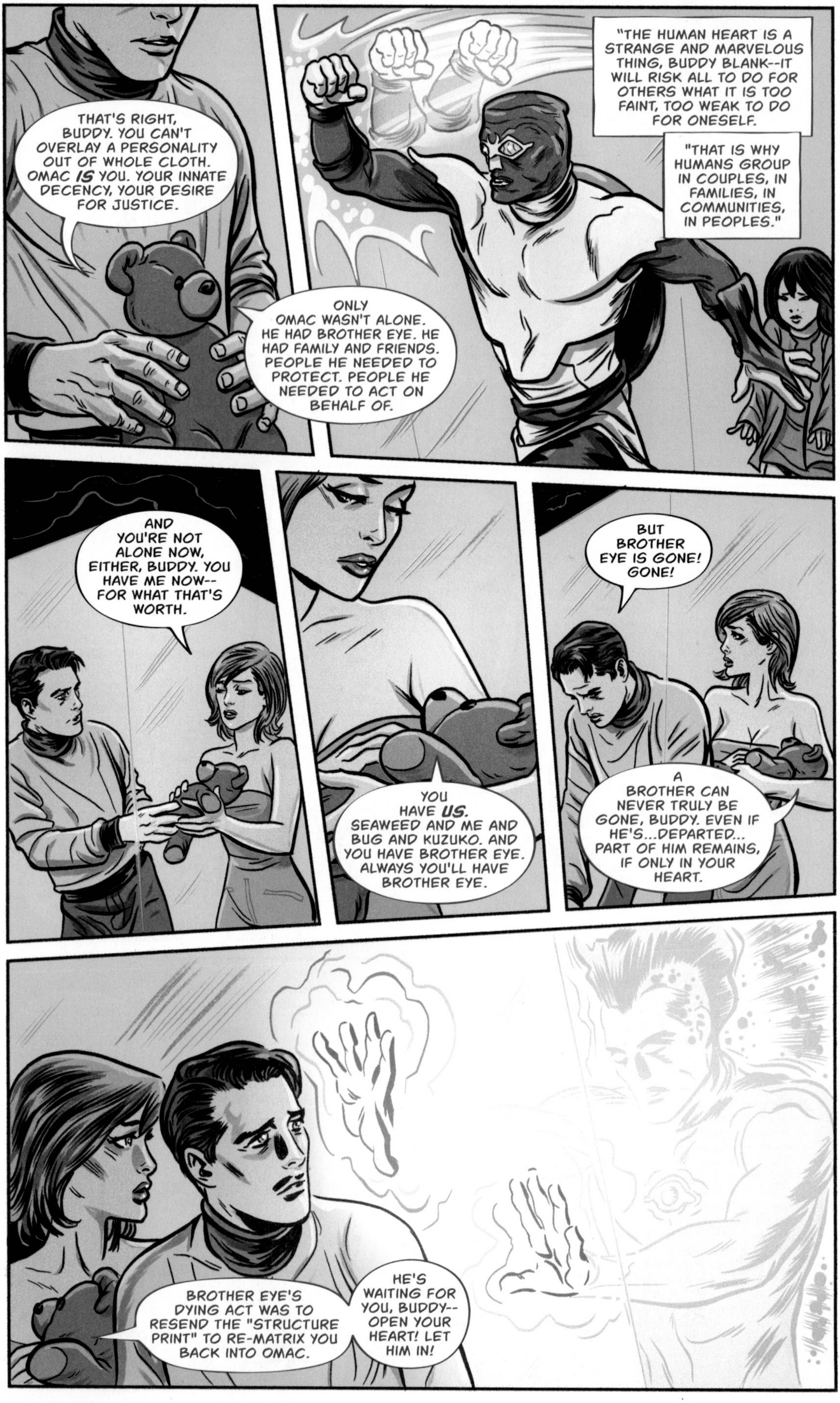
THAT'S RIGHT, BUDDY. YOU CAN'T OVERLAY A PERSONALITY OUT OF WHOLE CLOTH. OMAC IS YOU. YOUR INNATE DECENCY, YOUR DESIRE FOR JUSTICE.
ONLY OMAC WASN'T ALONE. HE HAD BROTHER EYE. HE HAD FAMILY AND FRIENDS. PEOPLE HE NEEDED TO PROTECT. PEOPLE HE NEEDED TO ACT ON BEHALF OF.
"THE HUMAN HEART IS A STRANGE AND MARVELOUS THING, BUDDY BLANK--IT WILL RISK ALL TO DO FOR OTHERS WHAT IT IS TOO FAINT, TOO WEAK TO DO FOR ONESELF.
"THAT IS WHY HUMANS GROUP IN COUPLES, IN FAMILIES, IN COMMUNITIES, IN PEOPLES."
AND YOU'RE NOT ALONE NOW, EITHER, BUDDY. YOU HAVE ME NOW-- FOR WHAT THAT'S WORTH.
YOU HAVE US. SEAWEED AND ME AND BUG AND KUZUKO. AND YOU HAVE BROTHER EYE. ALWAYS YOU'LL HAVE BROTHER EYE.
BUT BROTHER EYE IS GONE! GONE!
A BROTHER CAN NEVER TRULY BE GONE, BUDDY. EVEN IF HE'S...DEPARTED... PART OF HIM REMAINS, IF ONLY IN YOUR HEART.
BROTHER EYE'S DYING ACT WAS TO RESEND THE "STRUCTURE PRINT" TO RE-MATRIX YOU BACK INTO OMAC.
HE'S WAITING FOR YOU, BUDDY-- OPEN YOUR HEART! LET HIM IN!

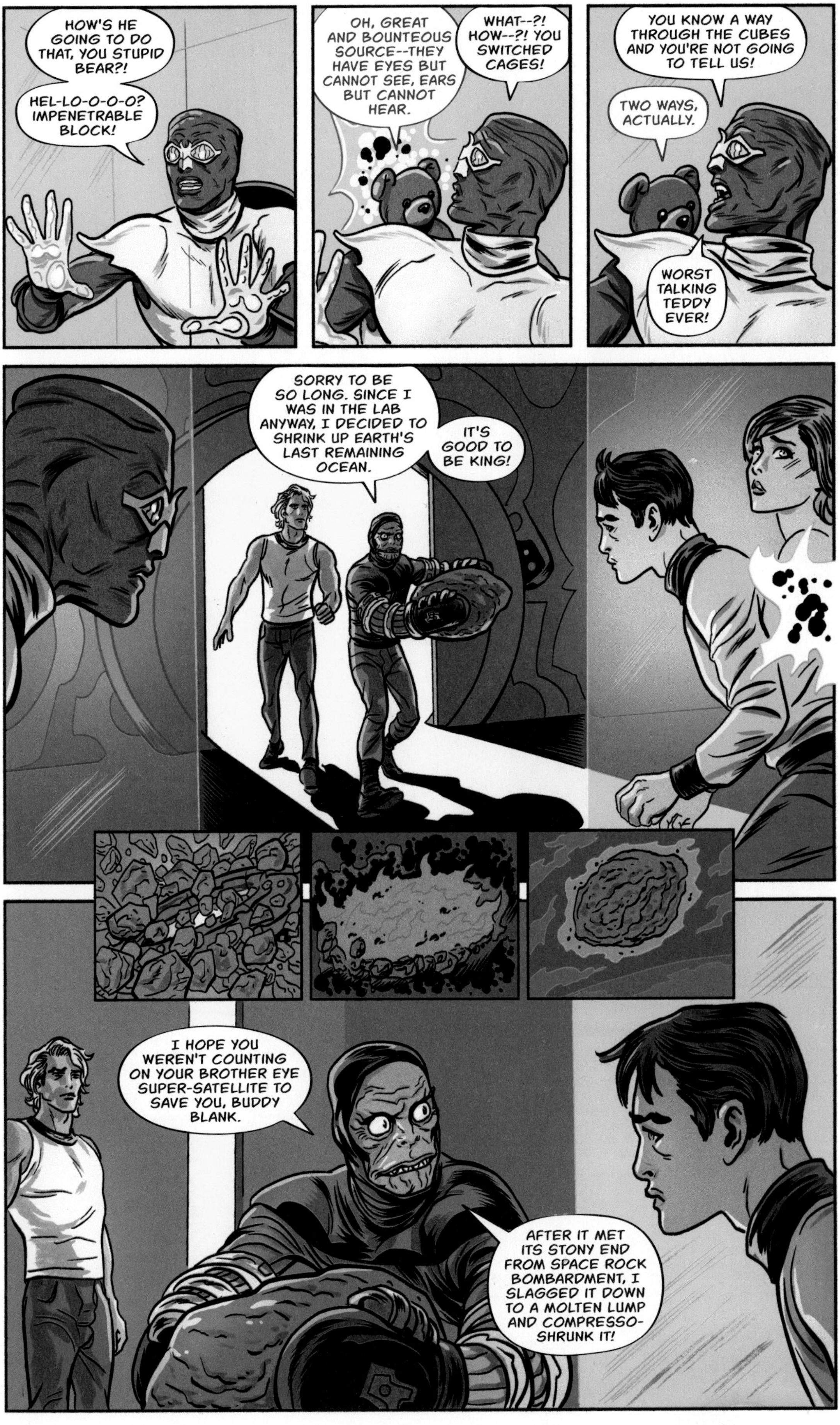
HOW'S HE GOING TO DO THAT, YOU STUPID BEAR?!
HEL-LO-O-O-O? IMPENETRABLE BLOCK!
OH, GREAT AND BOUNTEOUS SOURCE--THEY HAVE EYES BUT CANNOT SEE, EARS BUT CANNOT HEAR.
WHAT--?! HOW--?! YOU SWITCHED CAGES!
YOU KNOW A WAY THROUGH THE CUBES AND YOU'RE NOT GOING TO TELL US!
TWO WAYS, ACTUALLY.
WORST TALKING TEDDY EVER!
SORRY TO BE SO LONG. SINCE I WAS IN THE LAB ANYWAY, I DECIDED TO SHRINK UP EARTH'S LAST REMAINING OCEAN.
IT'S GOOD TO BE KING!
I HOPE YOU WEREN'T COUNTING ON YOUR BROTHER EYE SUPER-SATELLITE TO SAVE YOU, BUDDY BLANK.
AFTER IT MET ITS STONY END FROM SPACE ROCK BOMBARDMENT, I SLAGGED IT DOWN TO A MOLTEN LUMP AND COMPRESSO-SHRUNK IT!

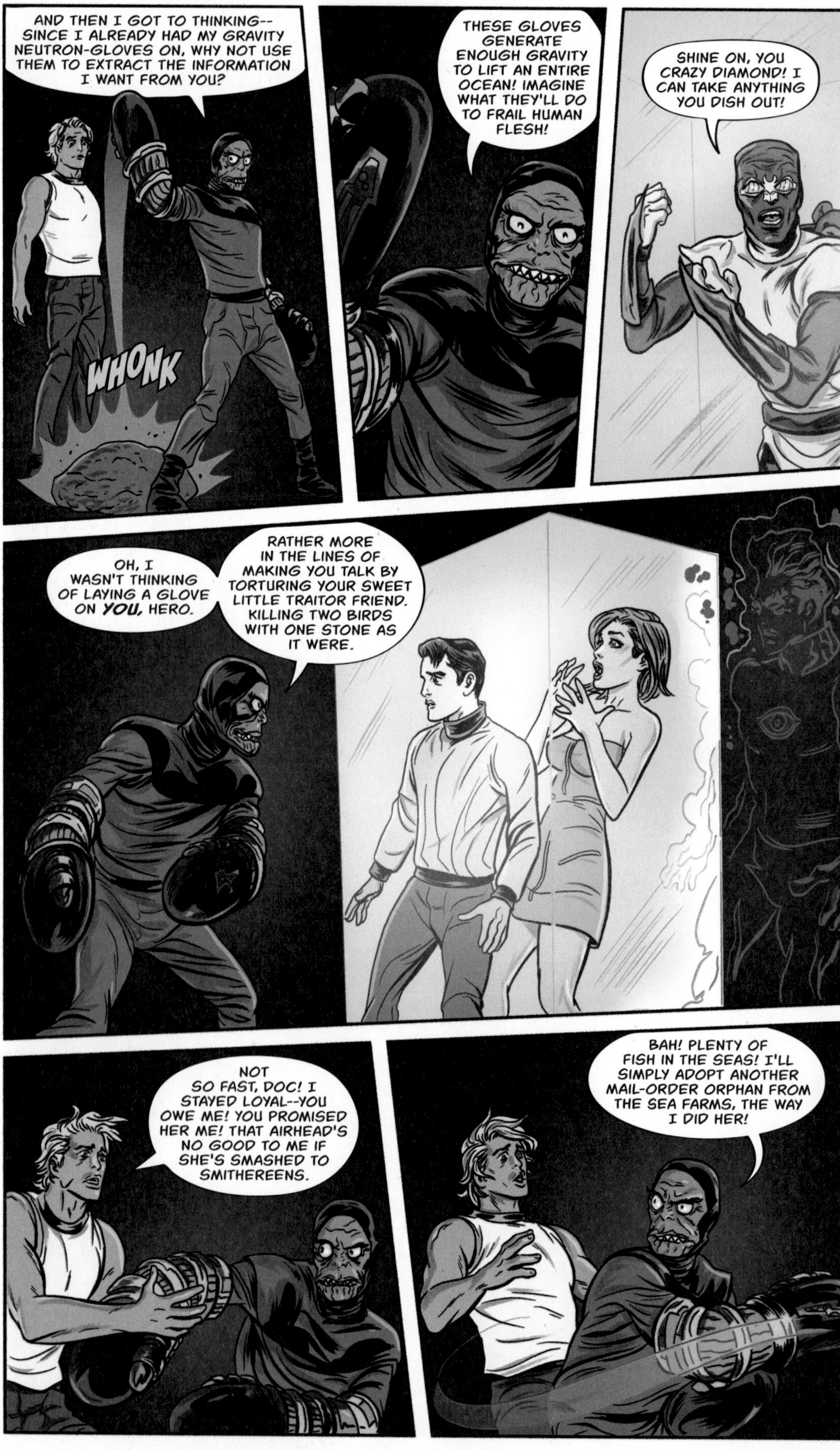
AND THEN I GOT TO THINKING-- SINCE I ALREADY HAD MY GRAVITY NEUTRON-GLOVES ON, WHY NOT USE THEM TO EXTRACT THE INFORMATION I WANT FROM YOU?
WHONK
THESE GLOVES GENERATE ENOUGH GRAVITY TO LIFT AN ENTIRE OCEAN! IMAGINE WHAT THEY'LL DO TO FRAIL HUMAN FLESH!
SHINE ON, YOU CRAZY DIAMOND! I CAN TAKE ANYTHING YOU DISH OUT!
OH, I WASN'T THINKING OF LAYING A GLOVE ON YOU, HERO.
RATHER MORE IN THE LINES OF MAKING YOU TALK BY TORTURING YOUR SWEET LITTLE TRAITOR FRIEND. KILLING TWO BIRDS WITH ONE STONE AS IT WERE.
NOT SO FAST, DOC! I STAYED LOYAL--YOU OWE ME! YOU PROMISED HER ME! THAT AIRHEAD'S NO GOOD TO ME IF SHE'S SMASHED TO SMITHEREENS.
BAH! PLENTY OF FISH IN THE SEAS! I'LL SIMPLY ADOPT ANOTHER MAIL-ORDER ORPHAN FROM THE SEA FARMS, THE WAY I DID HER!

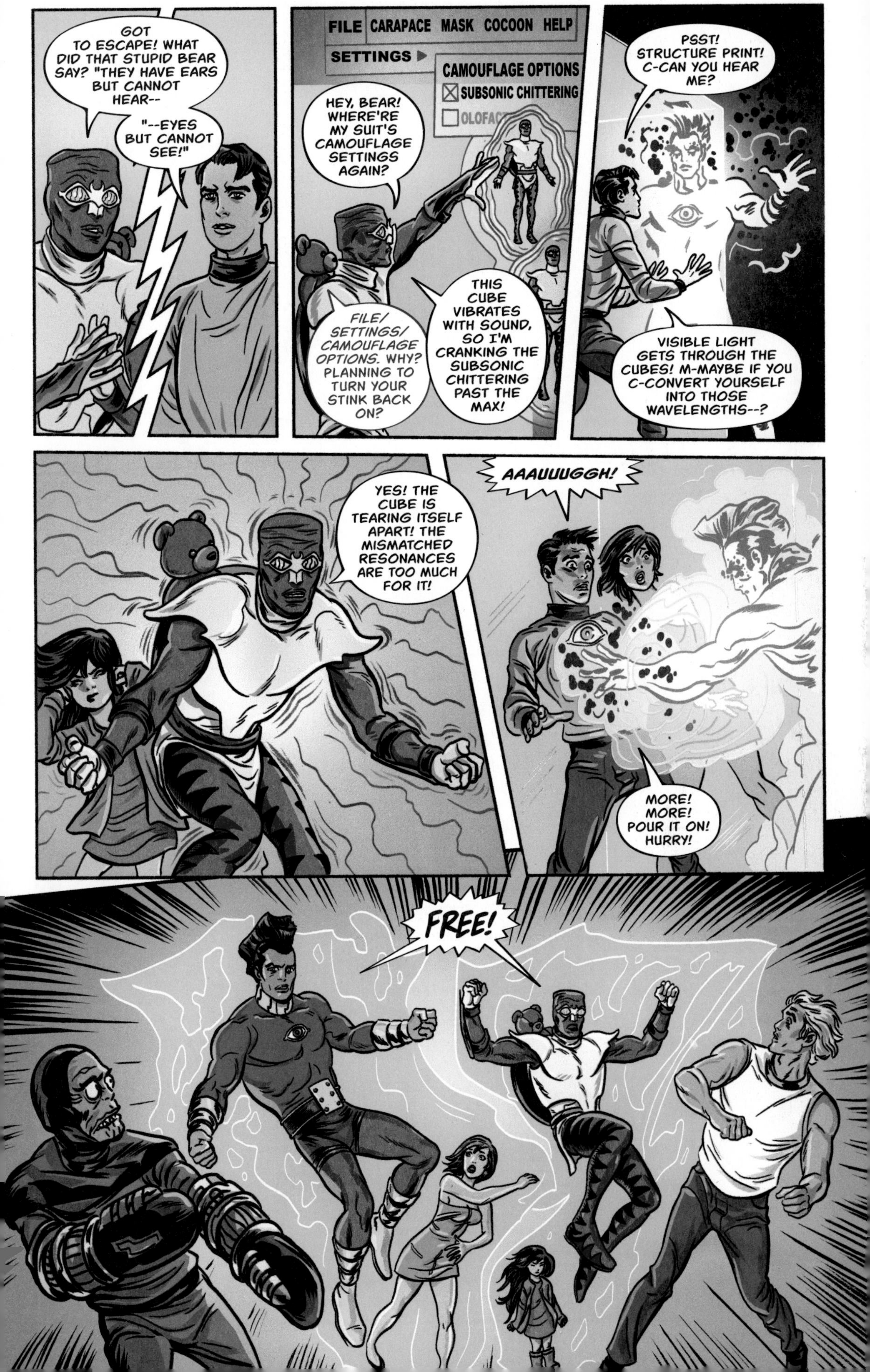
GOT TO ESCAPE! WHAT DID THAT STUPID BEAR SAY? "THEY HAVE EARS BUT CANNOT HEAR--
"--EYES BUT CANNOT SEE!"
FILE CARAPACE MASK COCOON HELP
SETTINGS
CAMOUFLAGE OPTIONS
SUBSONIC CHITTERING
HEY, BEAR! WHERE'RE MY SUIT'S CAMOUFLAGE SETTINGS AGAIN?
FILE/ SETTINGS/ CAMOUFLAGE OPTIONS. WHY? PLANNING TO TURN YOUR STINK BACK ON?
THIS CUBE VIBRATES WITH SOUND, SO I'M CRANKING THE SUBSONIC CHITTERING PAST THE MAX!
PSST! STRUCTURE PRINT! C-CAN YOU HEAR ME?
VISIBLE LIGHT GETS THROUGH THE CUBES! M-MAYBE IF YOU C-CONVERT YOURSELF INTO THOSE WAVELENGTHS--?
YES! THE CUBE IS TEARING ITSELF APART! THE MISMATCHED RESONANCES ARE TOO MUCH FOR IT!
AAAUUUGGH!
MORE! MORE! POUR IT ON! HURRY!
FREE!

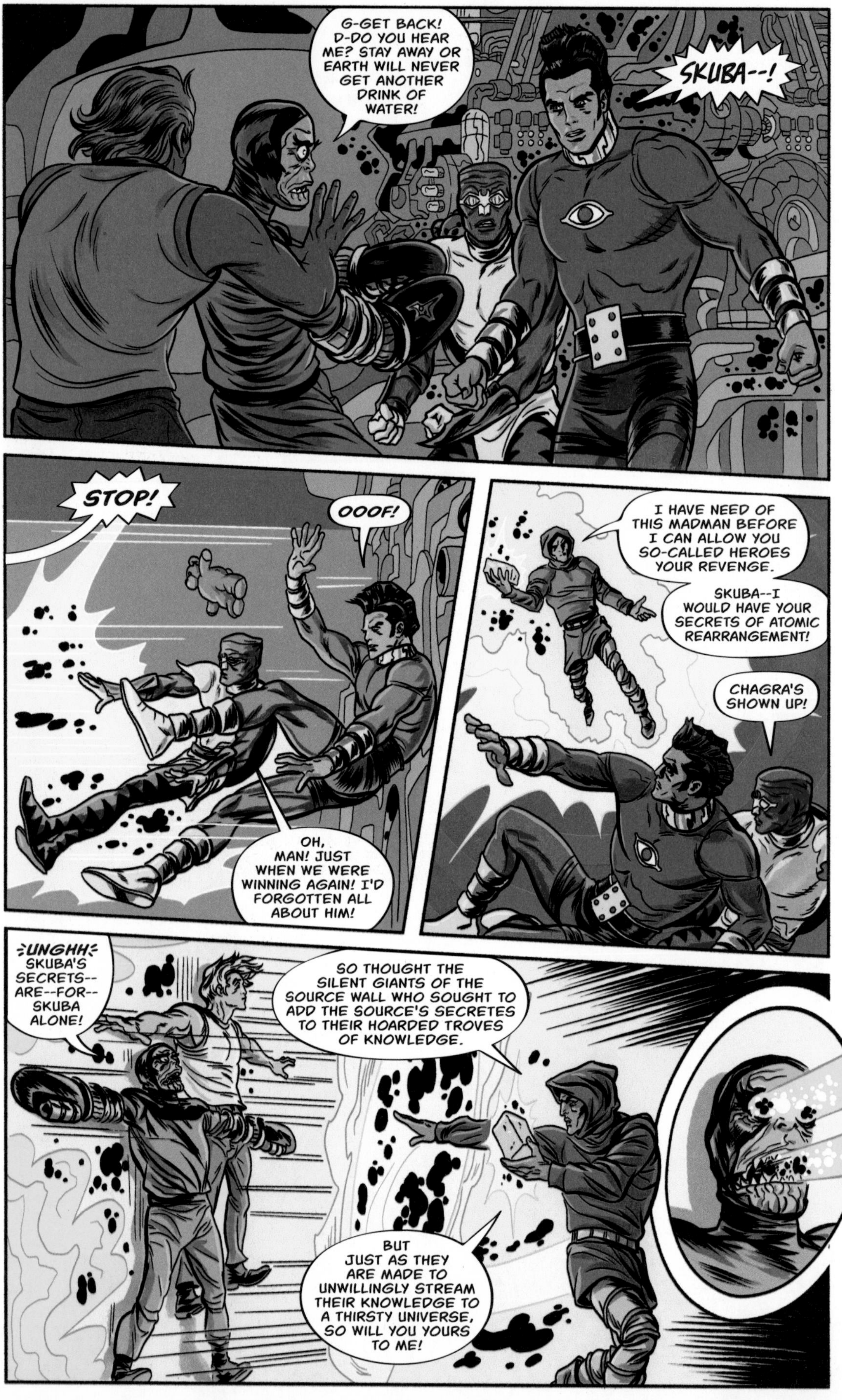
G-GET BACK! D-DO YOU HEAR ME? STAY AWAY OR EARTH WILL NEVER GET ANOTHER DRINK OF WATER!
SKUBA--!
STOP!
OOOF!
OH, MAN! JUST WHEN WE WERE WINNING AGAIN! I'D FORGOTTEN ALL ABOUT HIM!
I HAVE NEED OF THIS MADMAN BEFORE I CAN ALLOW YOU SO-CALLED HEROES YOUR REVENGE.
SKUBA--I WOULD HAVE YOUR SECRETS OF ATOMIC REARRANGEMENT!
CHAGRA'S SHOWN UP!
UNGHH SKUBA'S SECRETS--ARE--FOR--SKUBA ALONE!
SO THOUGHT THE SILENT GIANTS OF THE SOURCE WALL WHO SOUGHT TO ADD THE SOURCE'S SECRETES TO THEIR HOARDED TROVES OF KNOWLEDGE.
BUT JUST AS THEY ARE MADE TO UNWILLINGLY STREAM THEIR KNOWLEDGE TO A THIRSTY UNIVERSE, SO WILL YOU YOURS TO ME!

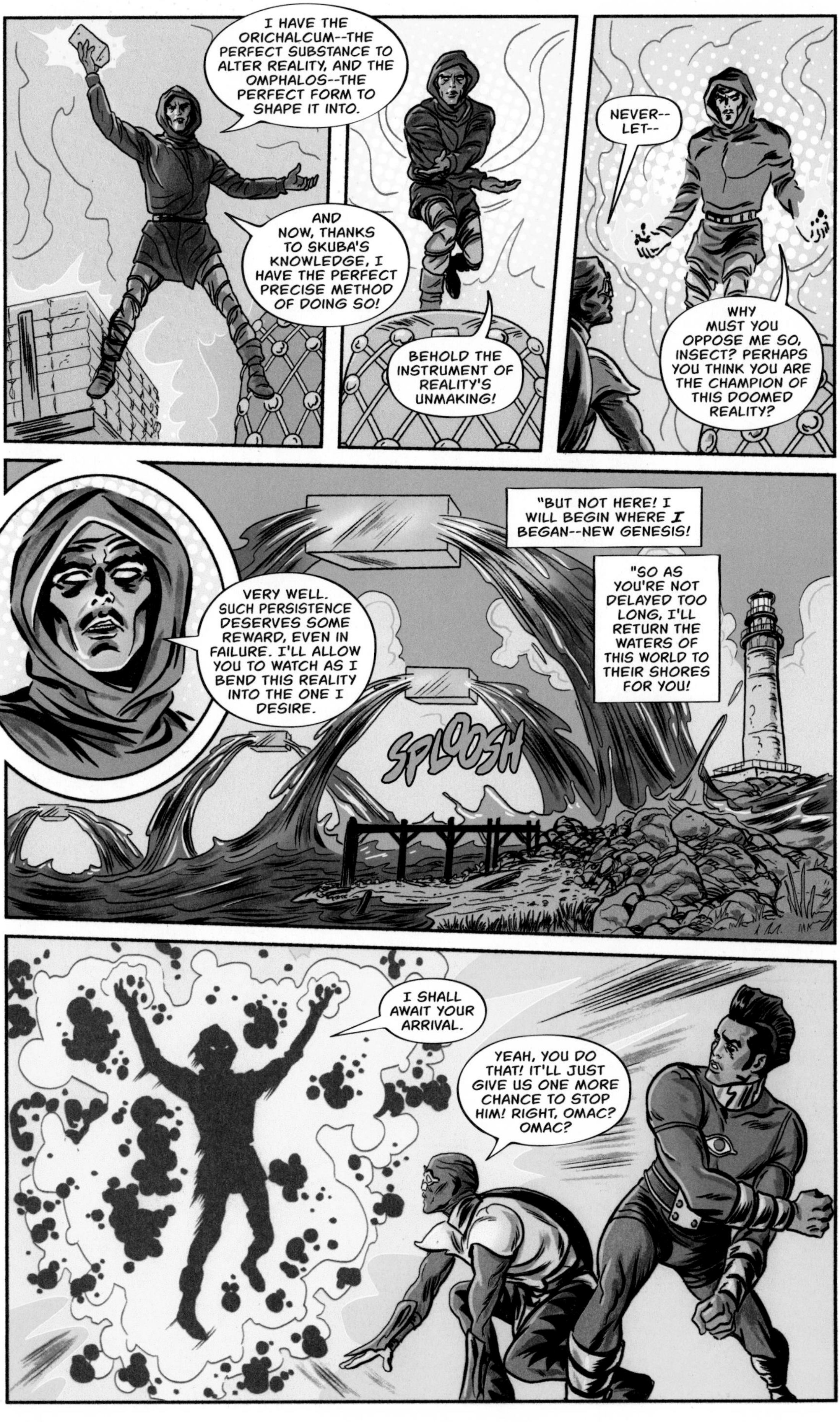
I HAVE THE ORICHALCUM--THE PERFECT SUBSTANCE TO ALTER REALITY, AND THE OMPHALOS--THE PERFECT FORM TO SHAPE IT INTO.
AND NOW, THANKS TO SKUBA'S KNOWLEDGE, I HAVE THE PERFECT PRECISE METHOD OF DOING SO!
BEHOLD THE INSTRUMENT OF REALITY'S UNMAKING!
NEVER-- LET--
WHY MUST YOU OPPOSE ME SO, INSECT? PERHAPS YOU THINK YOU ARE THE CHAMPION OF THIS DOOMED REALITY?
VERY WELL. SUCH PERSISTENCE DESERVES SOME REWARD, EVEN IN FAILURE. I'LL ALLOW YOU TO WATCH AS I BEND THIS REALITY INTO THE ONE I DESIRE.
"BUT NOT HERE! I WILL BEGIN WHERE I BEGAN--NEW GENESIS!
"SO AS YOU'RE NOT DELAYED TOO LONG, I'LL RETURN THE WATERS OF THIS WORLD TO THEIR SHORES FOR YOU!
SPLOOSH
I SHALL AWAIT YOUR ARRIVAL.
YEAH, YOU DO THAT! IT'LL JUST GIVE US ONE MORE CHANCE TO STOP HIM! RIGHT, OMAC? OMAC?

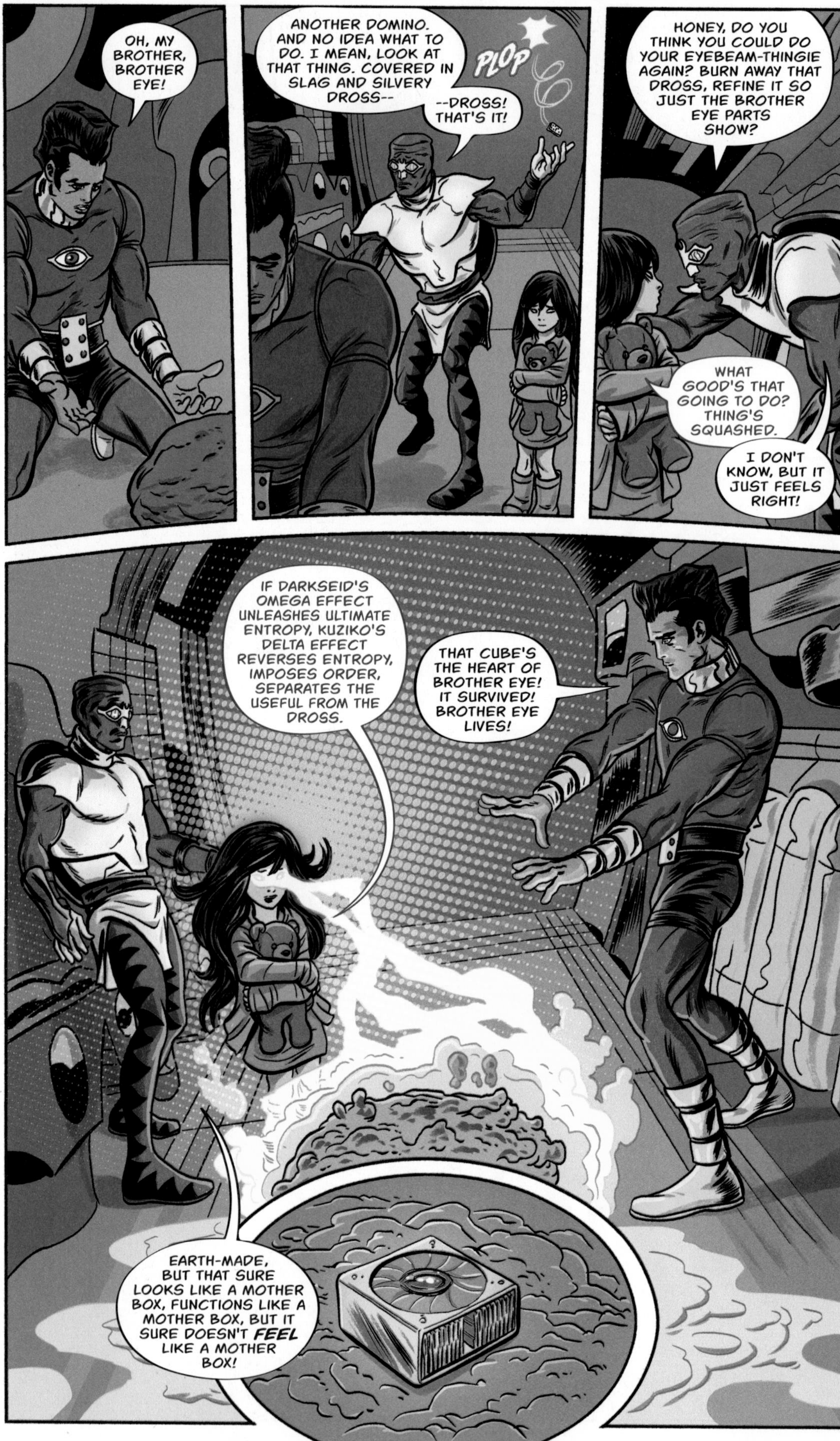
OH, MY BROTHER, BROTHER EYE!
ANOTHER DOMINO. AND NO IDEA WHAT TO DO. I MEAN, LOOK AT THAT THING. COVERED IN SLAG AND SILVERY DROSS--
PLOP
--DROSS! THAT'S IT!
HONEY, DO YOU THINK YOU COULD DO YOUR EYEBEAM-THINGIE AGAIN? BURN AWAY THAT DROSS, REFINE IT SO JUST THE BROTHER EYE PARTS SHOW?
WHAT GOOD'S THAT GOING TO DO? THING'S SQUASHED.
I DON'T KNOW, BUT IT JUST FEELS RIGHT!
IF DARKSEID'S OMEGA EFFECT UNLEASHES ULTIMATE ENTROPY, KUZIKO'S DELTA EFFECT REVERSES ENTROPY, IMPOSES ORDER, SEPARATES THE USEFUL FROM THE DROSS.
THAT CUBE'S THE HEART OF BROTHER EYE! IT SURVIVED! BROTHER EYE LIVES!
EARTH-MADE, BUT THAT SURE LOOKS LIKE A MOTHER BOX, FUNCTIONS LIKE A MOTHER BOX, BUT IT SURE DOESN'T *FEEL* LIKE A MOTHER BOX!

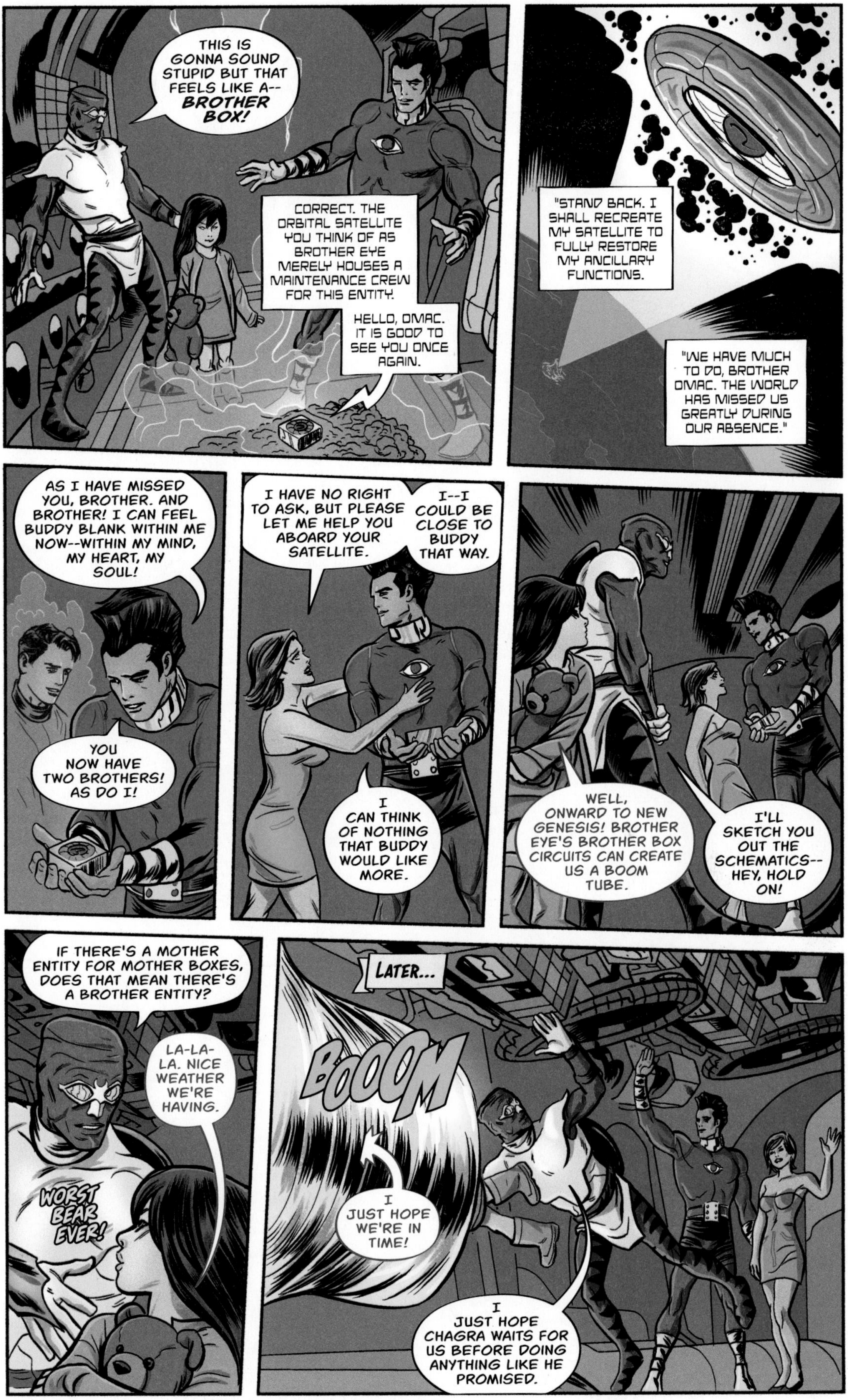
THIS IS GONNA SOUND STUPID BUT THAT FEELS LIKE A-- BROTHER BOX!
CORRECT. THE ORBITAL SATELLITE YOU THINK OF AS BROTHER EYE MERELY HOUSES A MAINTENANCE CREW FOR THIS ENTITY.
HELLO, OMAC. IT IS GOOD TO SEE YOU ONCE AGAIN.
"STAND BACK. I SHALL RECREATE MY SATELLITE TO FULLY RESTORE MY ANCILLARY FUNCTIONS.
"WE HAVE MUCH TO DO, BROTHER OMAC. THE WORLD HAS MISSED US GREATLY DURING OUR ABSENCE."
AS I HAVE MISSED YOU, BROTHER. AND BROTHER! I CAN FEEL BUDDY BLANK WITHIN ME NOW--WITHIN MY MIND, MY HEART, MY SOUL!
YOU NOW HAVE TWO BROTHERS! AS DO I!
I HAVE NO RIGHT TO ASK, BUT PLEASE LET ME HELP YOU ABOARD YOUR SATELLITE.
I--I COULD BE CLOSE TO BUDDY THAT WAY.
I CAN THINK OF NOTHING THAT BUDDY WOULD LIKE MORE.
WELL, ONWARD TO NEW GENESIS! BROTHER EYE'S BROTHER BOX CIRCUITS CAN CREATE US A BOOM TUBE.
I'LL SKETCH YOU OUT THE SCHEMATICS-- HEY, HOLD ON!
IF THERE'S A MOTHER ENTITY FOR MOTHER BOXES, DOES THAT MEAN THERE'S A BROTHER ENTITY?
LA-LA-LA. NICE WEATHER WE'RE HAVING.
WORST BEAR EVER!
LATER...
BOOOM
I JUST HOPE WE'RE IN TIME!
I JUST HOPE CHAGRA WAITS FOR US BEFORE DOING ANYTHING LIKE HE PROMISED.

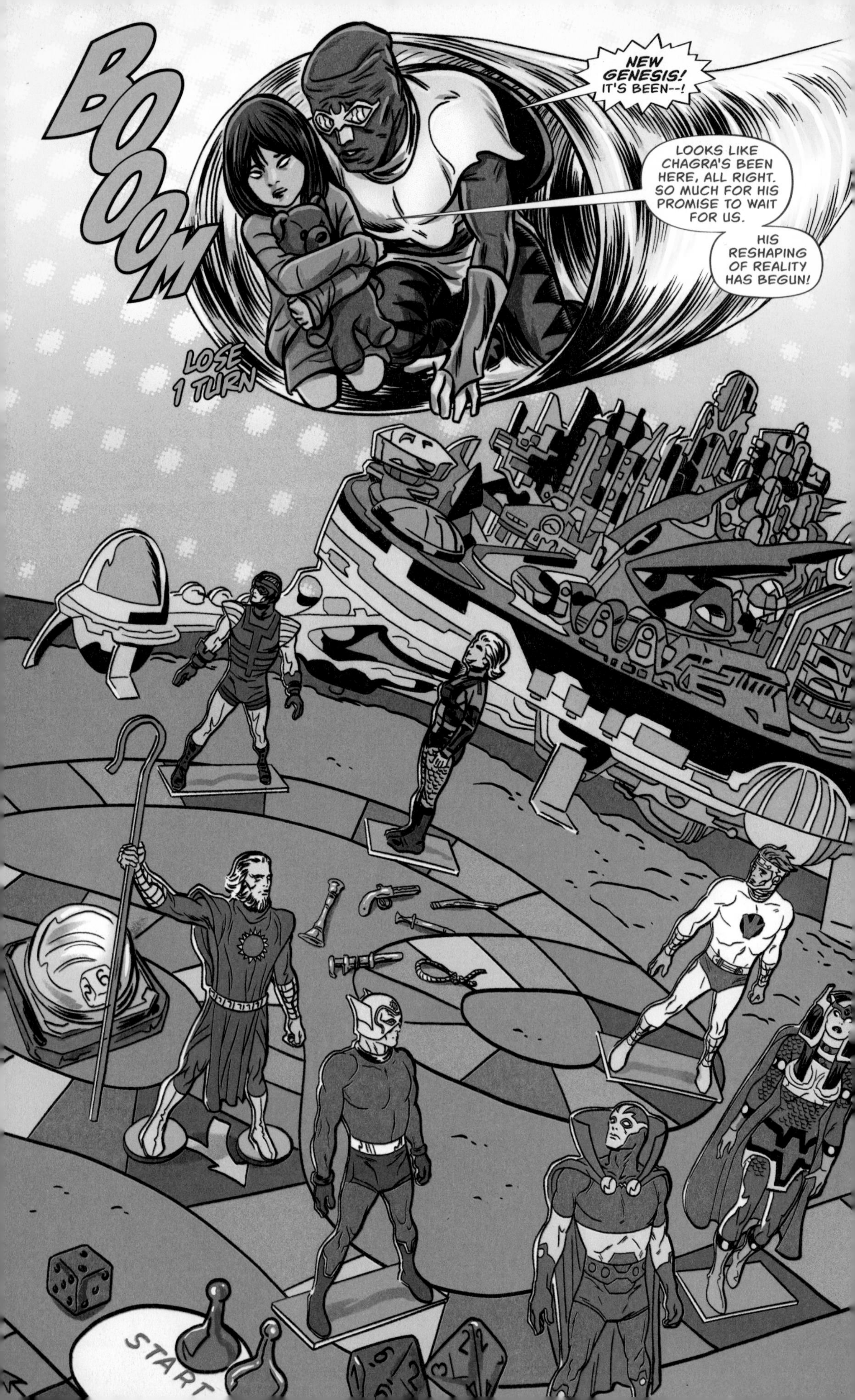
BOOOOM
NEW GENESIS! IT'S BEEN--!
LOOKS LIKE CHAGRA'S BEEN HERE, ALL RIGHT. SO MUCH FOR HIS PROMISE TO WAIT FOR US.
HIS RESHAPING OF REALITY HAS BEGUN!
LOSE 1 TURN
START

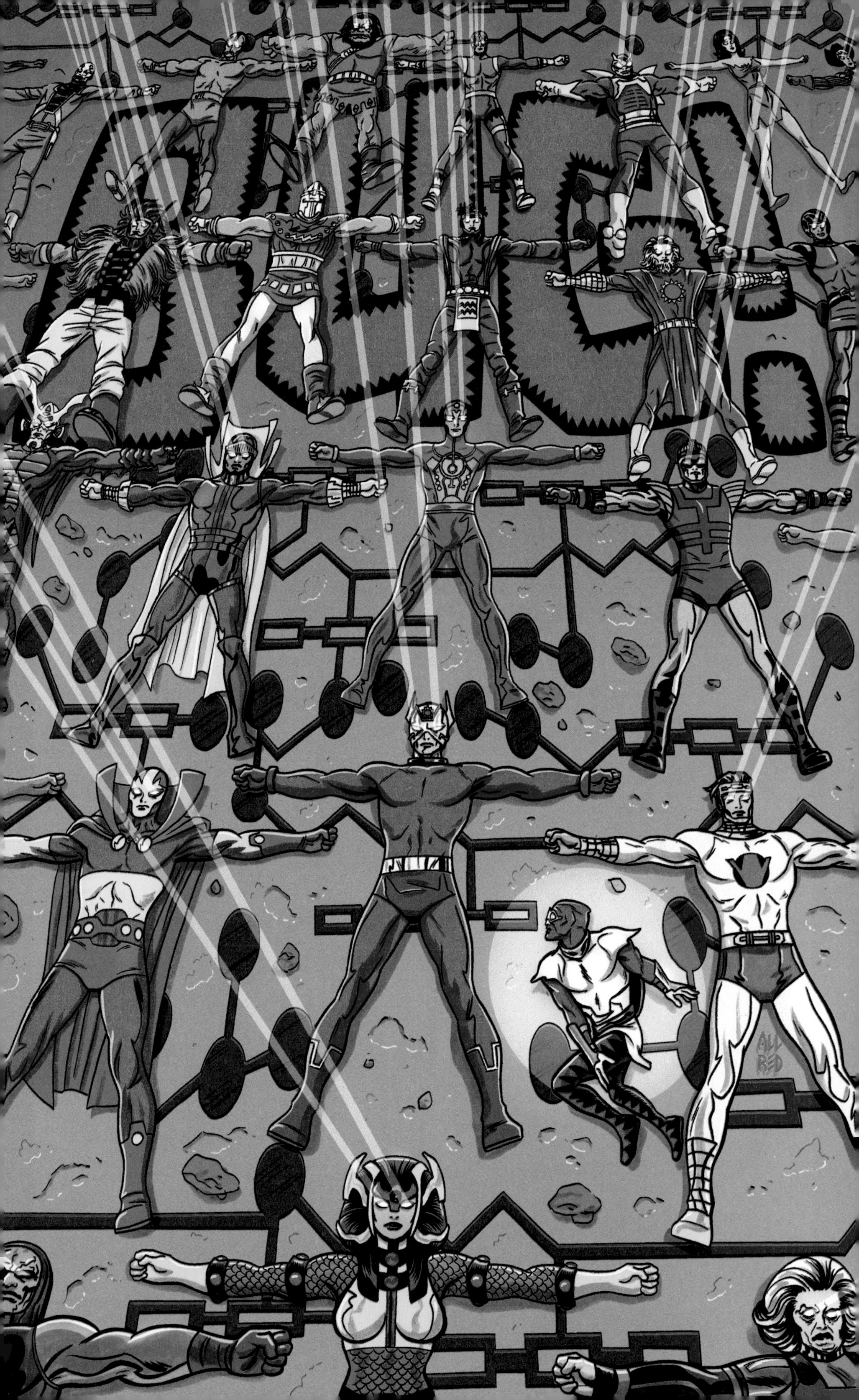

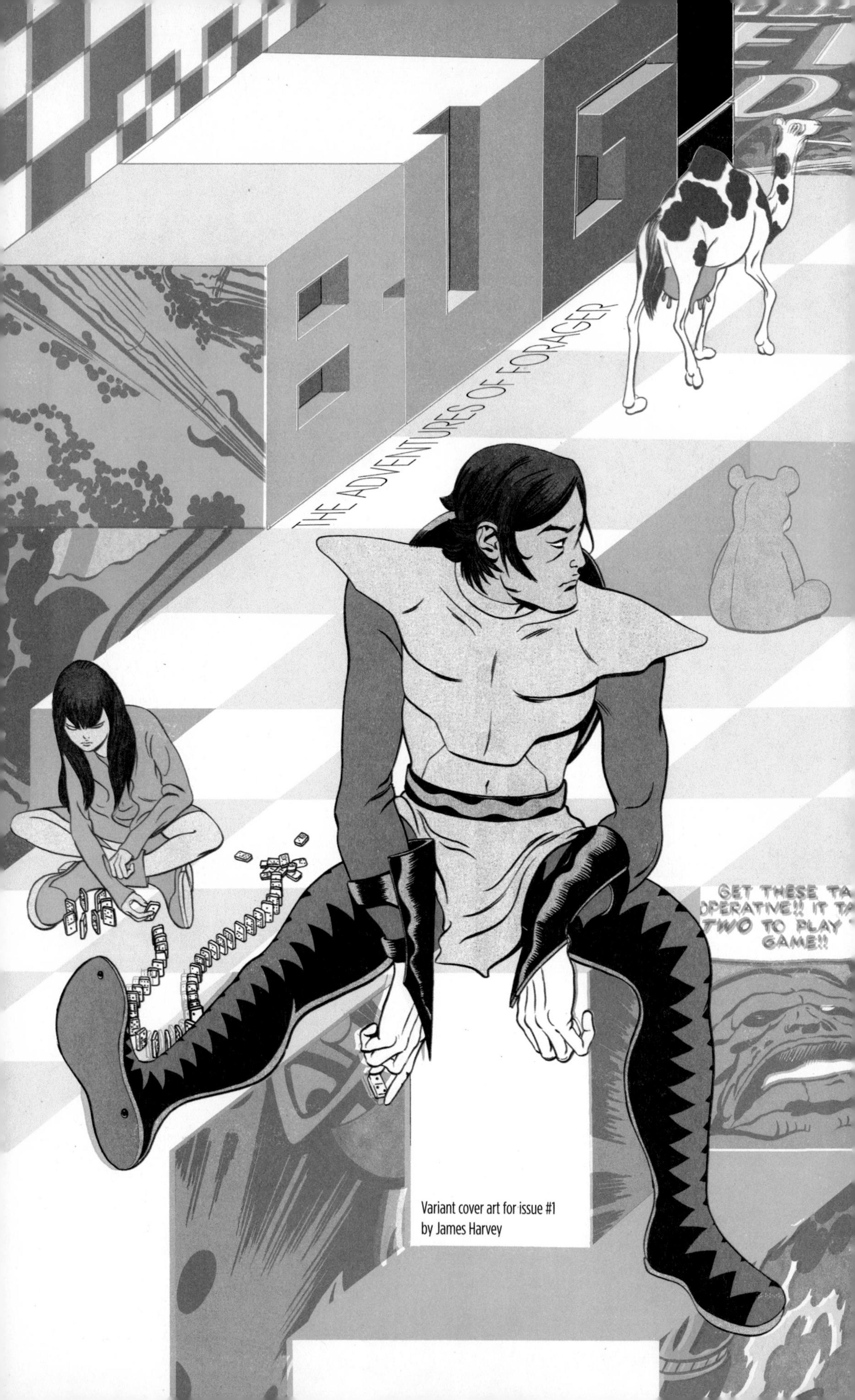
THE ADVENTURES OF FORAGER
GET THESE TA
OPERATIVE!! IT TA
TWO TO PLAY
GAME!!

Variant cover art for issue #1
by James Harvey

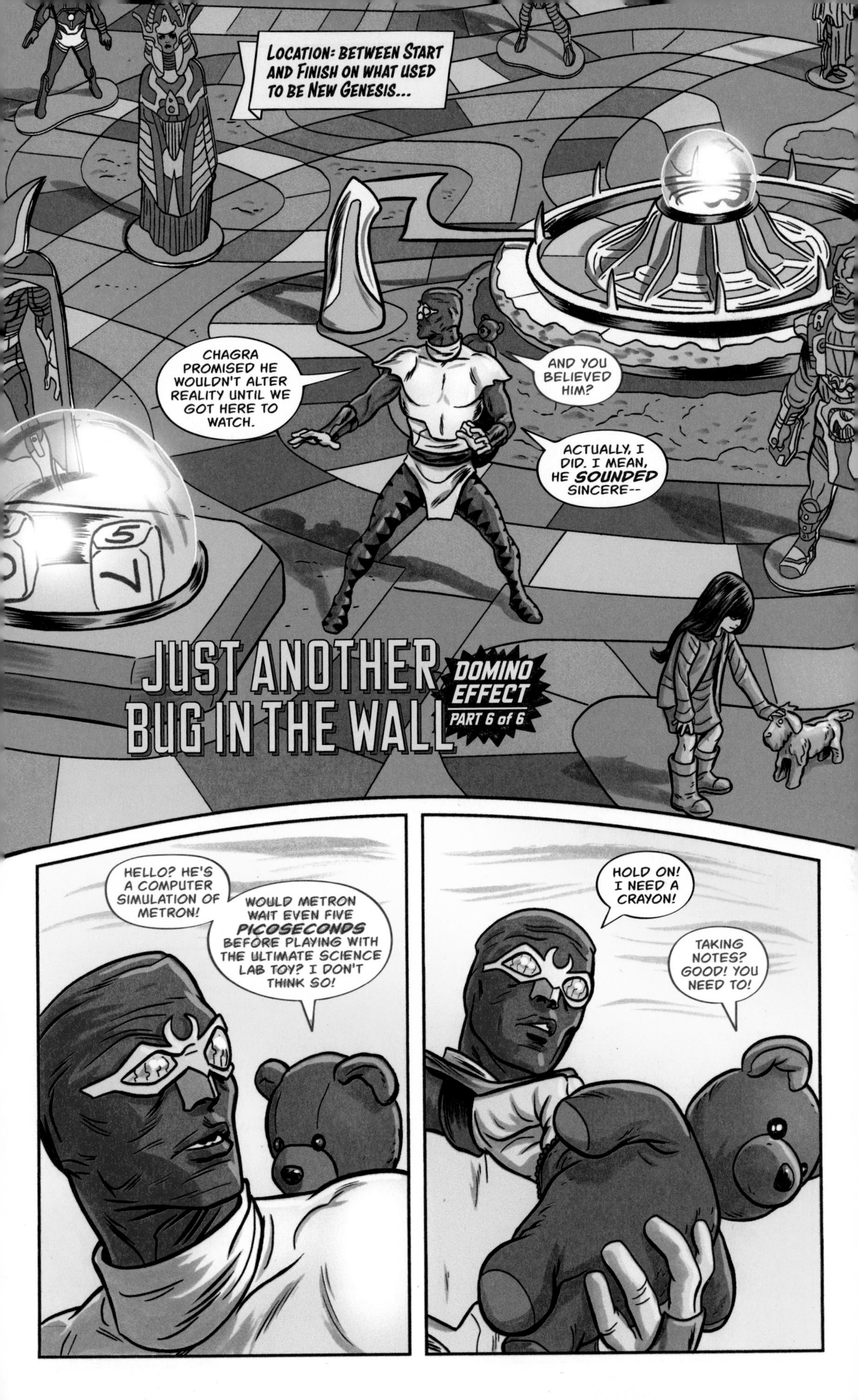

LOCATION: BETWEEN START AND FINISH ON WHAT USED TO BE NEW GENESIS...
CHAGRA PROMISED HE WOULDN'T ALTER REALITY UNTIL WE GOT HERE TO WATCH.
AND YOU BELIEVED HIM?
ACTUALLY, I DID. I MEAN, HE SOUNDED SINCERE--
JUST ANOTHER BUG IN THE WALL
DOMINO EFFECT PART 6 of 6
HELLO? HE'S A COMPUTER SIMULATION OF METRON!
WOULD METRON WAIT EVEN FIVE PICOSECONDS BEFORE PLAYING WITH THE ULTIMATE SCIENCE LAB TOY? I DON'T THINK SO!
HOLD ON! I NEED A CRAYON!
TAKING NOTES? GOOD! YOU NEED TO!

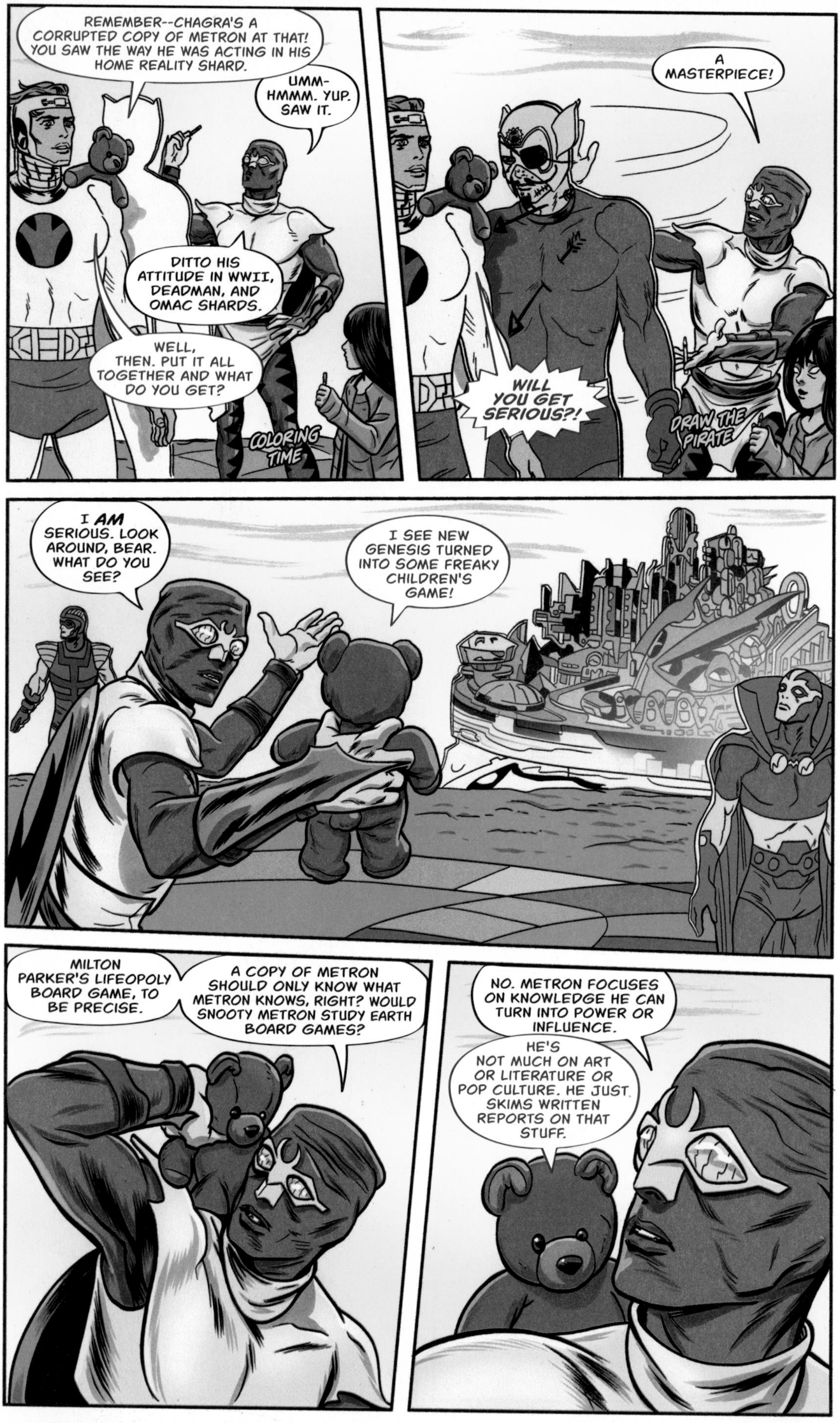
REMEMBER--CHAGRA'S A CORRUPTED COPY OF METRON AT THAT! YOU SAW THE WAY HE WAS ACTING IN HIS HOME REALITY SHARD.
UMM-HMMM. YUP. SAW IT.
DITTO HIS ATTITUDE IN WWII, DEADMAN, AND OMAC SHARDS.
WELL, THEN. PUT IT ALL TOGETHER AND WHAT DO YOU GET?
COLORING TIME
A MASTERPIECE!
WILL YOU GET SERIOUS?!
DRAW THE PIRATE
I AM SERIOUS. LOOK AROUND, BEAR. WHAT DO YOU SEE?
I SEE NEW GENESIS TURNED INTO SOME FREAKY CHILDREN'S GAME!
MILTON PARKER'S LIFEOPOLY BOARD GAME, TO BE PRECISE.
A COPY OF METRON SHOULD ONLY KNOW WHAT METRON KNOWS, RIGHT? WOULD SNOOTY METRON STUDY EARTH BOARD GAMES?
NO. METRON FOCUSES ON KNOWLEDGE HE CAN TURN INTO POWER OR INFLUENCE.
HE'S NOT MUCH ON ART OR LITERATURE OR POP CULTURE. HE JUST SKIMS WRITTEN REPORTS ON THAT STUFF.

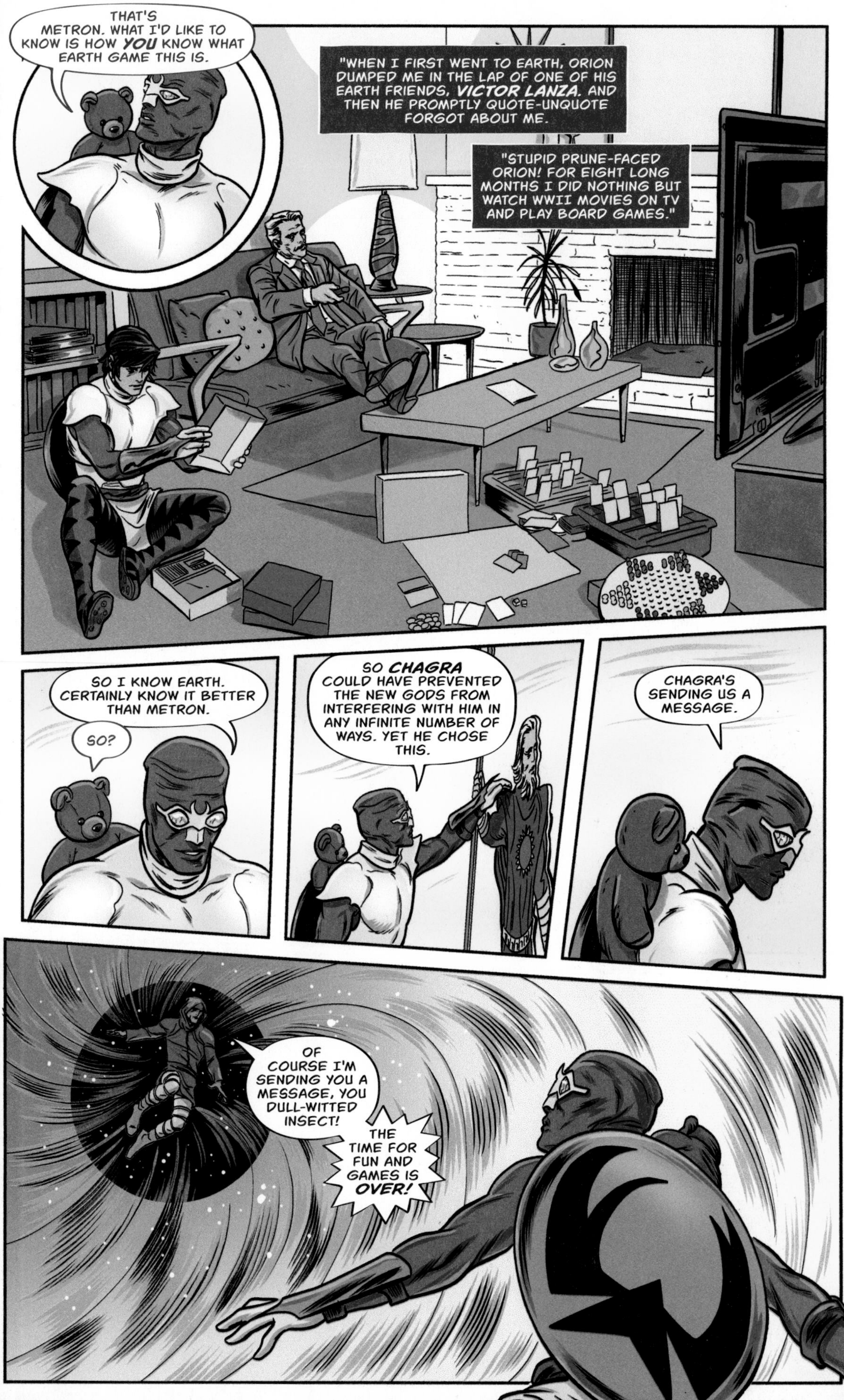
THAT'S METRON. WHAT I'D LIKE TO KNOW IS HOW YOU KNOW WHAT EARTH GAME THIS IS.
"WHEN I FIRST WENT TO EARTH, ORION DUMPED ME IN THE LAP OF ONE OF HIS EARTH FRIENDS, VICTOR LANZA. AND THEN HE PROMPTLY QUOTE-UNQUOTE FORGOT ABOUT ME.
"STUPID PRUNE-FACED ORION! FOR EIGHT LONG MONTHS I DID NOTHING BUT WATCH WWII MOVIES ON TV AND PLAY BOARD GAMES."
SO I KNOW EARTH. CERTAINLY KNOW IT BETTER THAN METRON.
SO?
SO CHAGRA COULD HAVE PREVENTED THE NEW GODS FROM INTERFERING WITH HIM IN ANY INFINITE NUMBER OF WAYS. YET HE CHOSE THIS.
CHAGRA'S SENDING US A MESSAGE.
OF COURSE I'M SENDING YOU A MESSAGE, YOU DULL-WITTED INSECT!
THE TIME FOR FUN AND GAMES IS OVER!

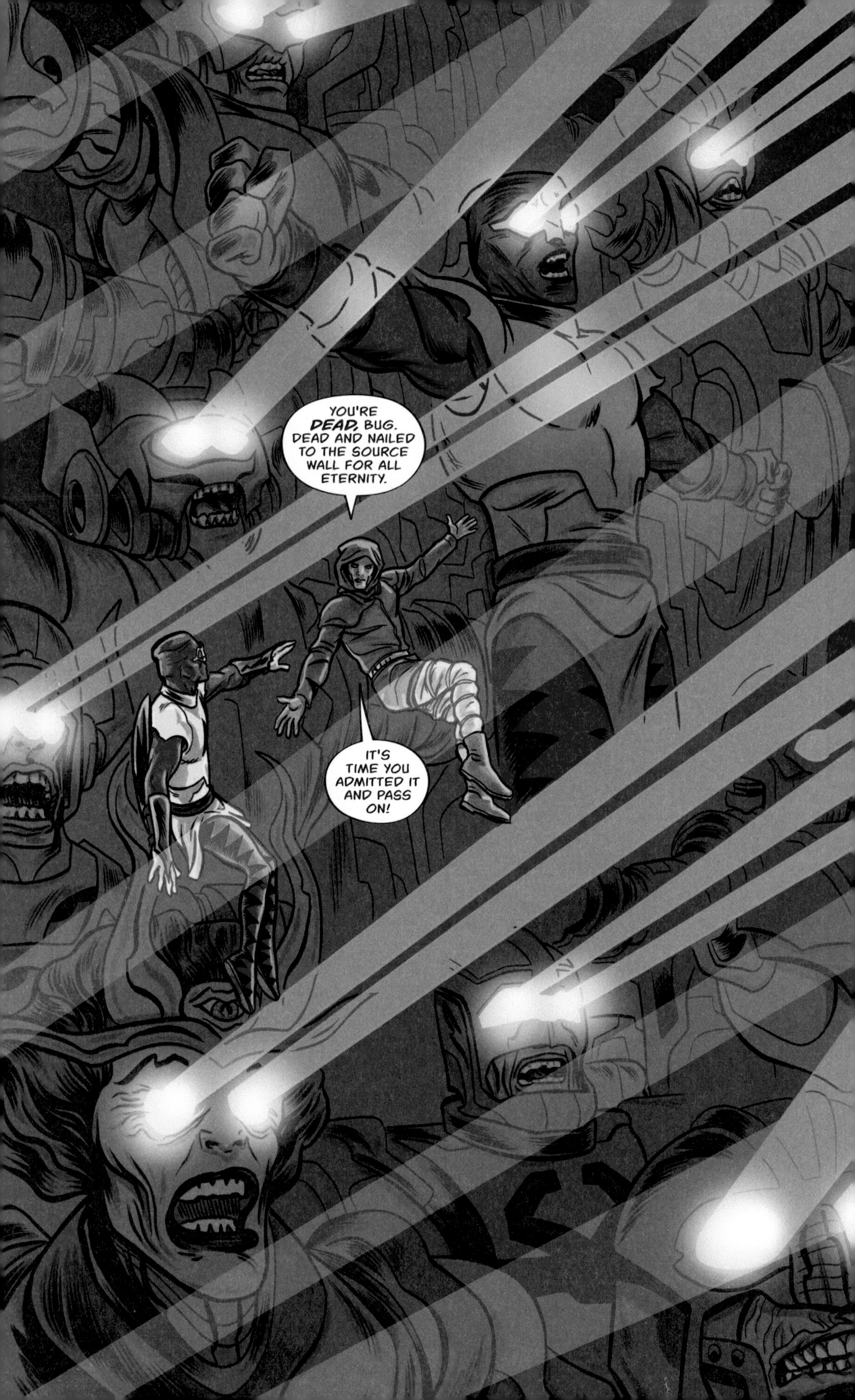
YOU'RE **DEAD,** BUG. DEAD AND NAILED TO THE SOURCE WALL FOR ALL ETERNITY.
IT'S TIME YOU ADMITTED IT AND PASS ON!

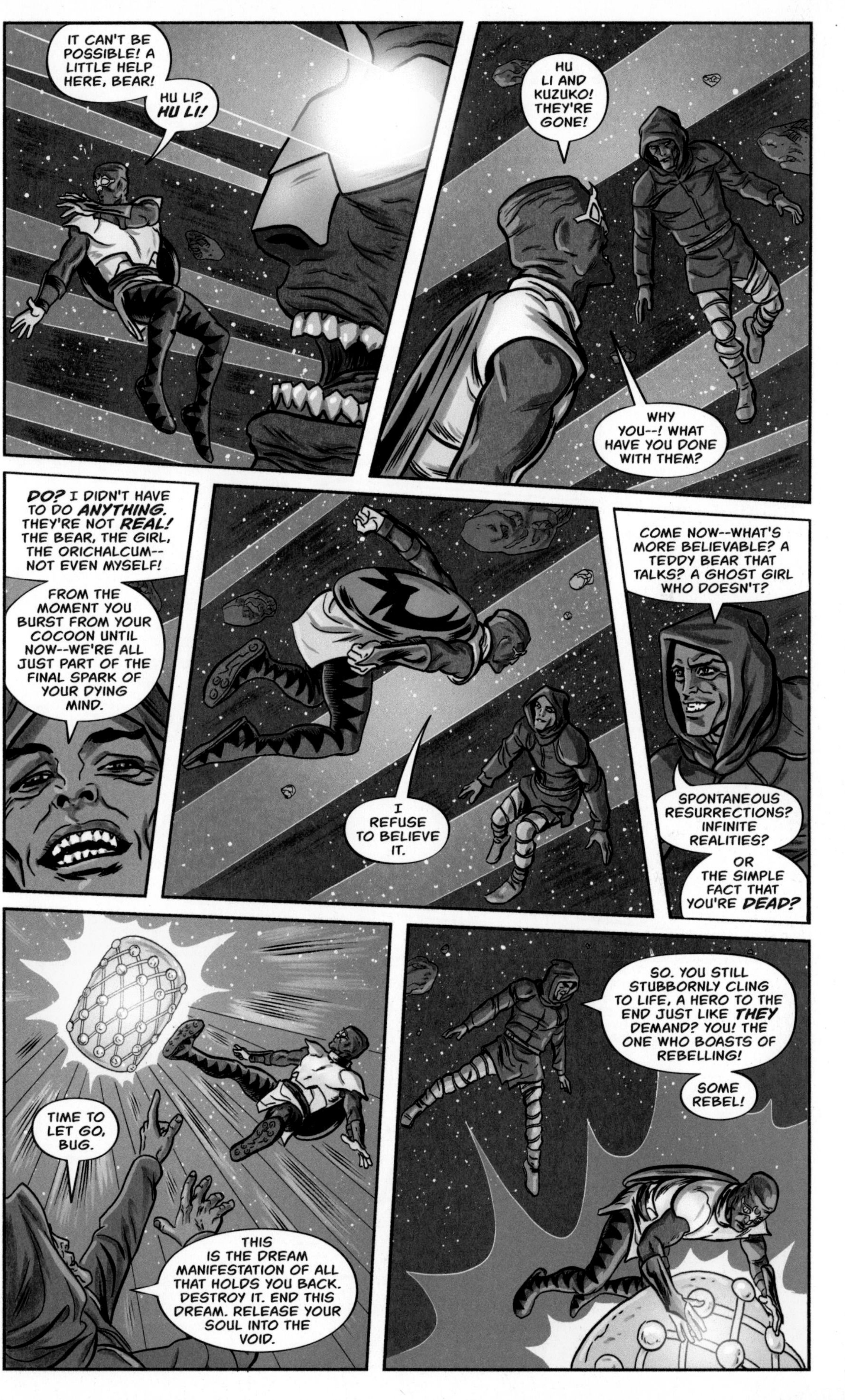
IT CAN'T BE POSSIBLE! A LITTLE HELP HERE, BEAR!
HU LI? HU LI!
HU LI AND KUZUKO! THEY'RE GONE!
WHY YOU--! WHAT HAVE YOU DONE WITH THEM?
DO? I DIDN'T HAVE TO DO ANYTHING. THEY'RE NOT REAL! THE BEAR, THE GIRL, THE ORICHALCUM--NOT EVEN MYSELF!
FROM THE MOMENT YOU BURST FROM YOUR COCOON UNTIL NOW--WE'RE ALL JUST PART OF THE FINAL SPARK OF YOUR DYING MIND.
I REFUSE TO BELIEVE IT.
COME NOW--WHAT'S MORE BELIEVABLE? A TEDDY BEAR THAT TALKS? A GHOST GIRL WHO DOESN'T?
SPONTANEOUS RESURRECTIONS? INFINITE REALITIES?
OR THE SIMPLE FACT THAT YOU'RE DEAD?
TIME TO LET GO, BUG.
THIS IS THE DREAM MANIFESTATION OF ALL THAT HOLDS YOU BACK. DESTROY IT. END THIS DREAM. RELEASE YOUR SOUL INTO THE VOID.
SO. YOU STILL STUBBORNLY CLING TO LIFE, A HERO TO THE END JUST LIKE THEY DEMAND? YOU! THE ONE WHO BOASTS OF REBELLING!
SOME REBEL!

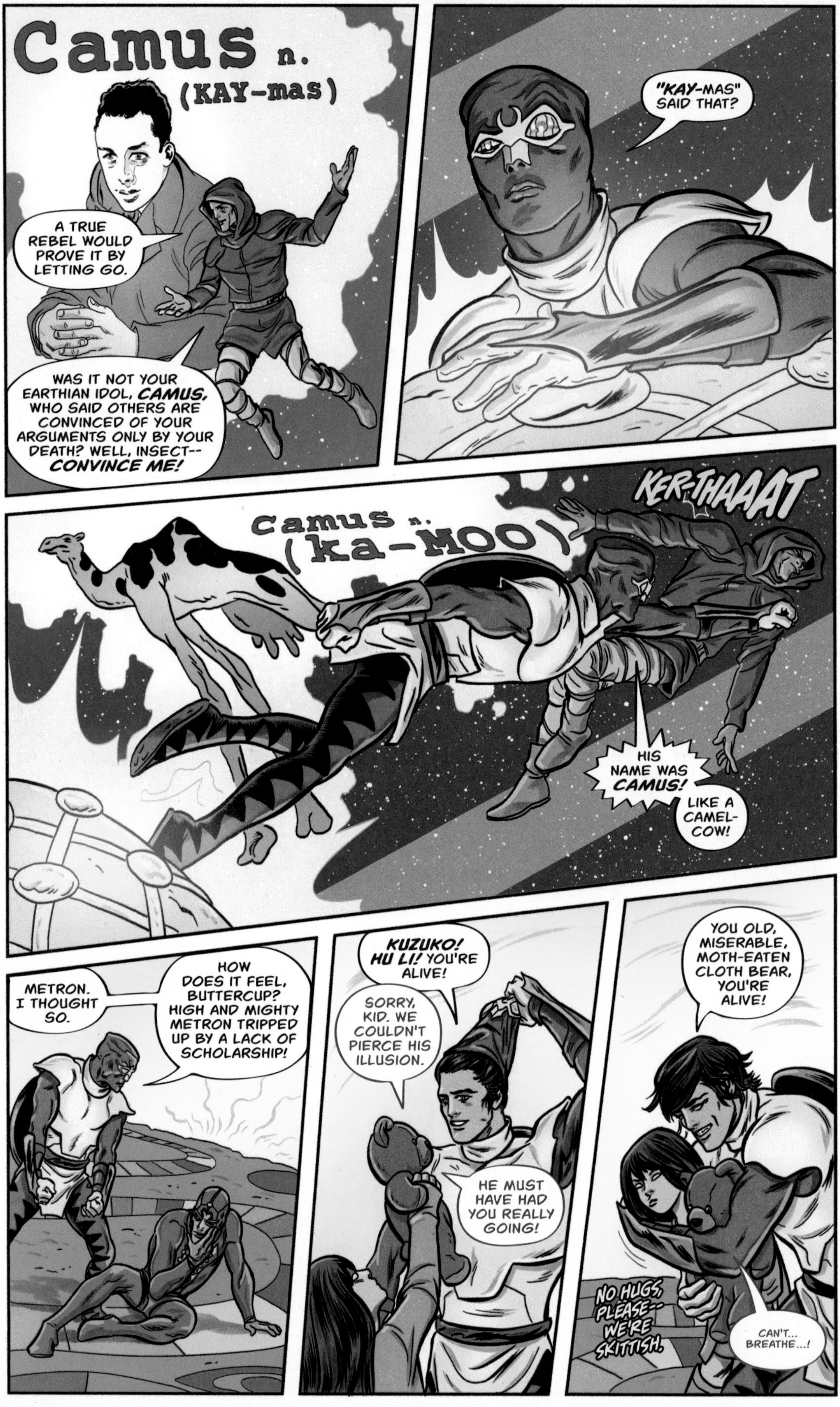
Camus n. (KAY-mas)
A TRUE REBEL WOULD PROVE IT BY LETTING GO.
WAS IT NOT YOUR EARTHIAN IDOL, CAMUS, WHO SAID OTHERS ARE CONVINCED OF YOUR ARGUMENTS ONLY BY YOUR DEATH? WELL, INSECT-- CONVINCE ME!
"KAY-MAS" SAID THAT?
KER-THAAAT
Camus n. (ka-MOO)
HIS NAME WAS CAMUS!
LIKE A CAMEL-COW!
METRON. I THOUGHT SO.
HOW DOES IT FEEL, BUTTERCUP? HIGH AND MIGHTY METRON TRIPPED UP BY A LACK OF SCHOLARSHIP!
KUZUKO! HU LI! YOU'RE ALIVE!
SORRY, KID. WE COULDN'T PIERCE HIS ILLUSION.
HE MUST HAVE HAD YOU REALLY GOING!
YOU OLD, MISERABLE, MOTH-EATEN CLOTH BEAR, YOU'RE ALIVE!
NO HUGS, PLEASE-- WE'RE SKITTISH.
CAN'T... BREATHE...!

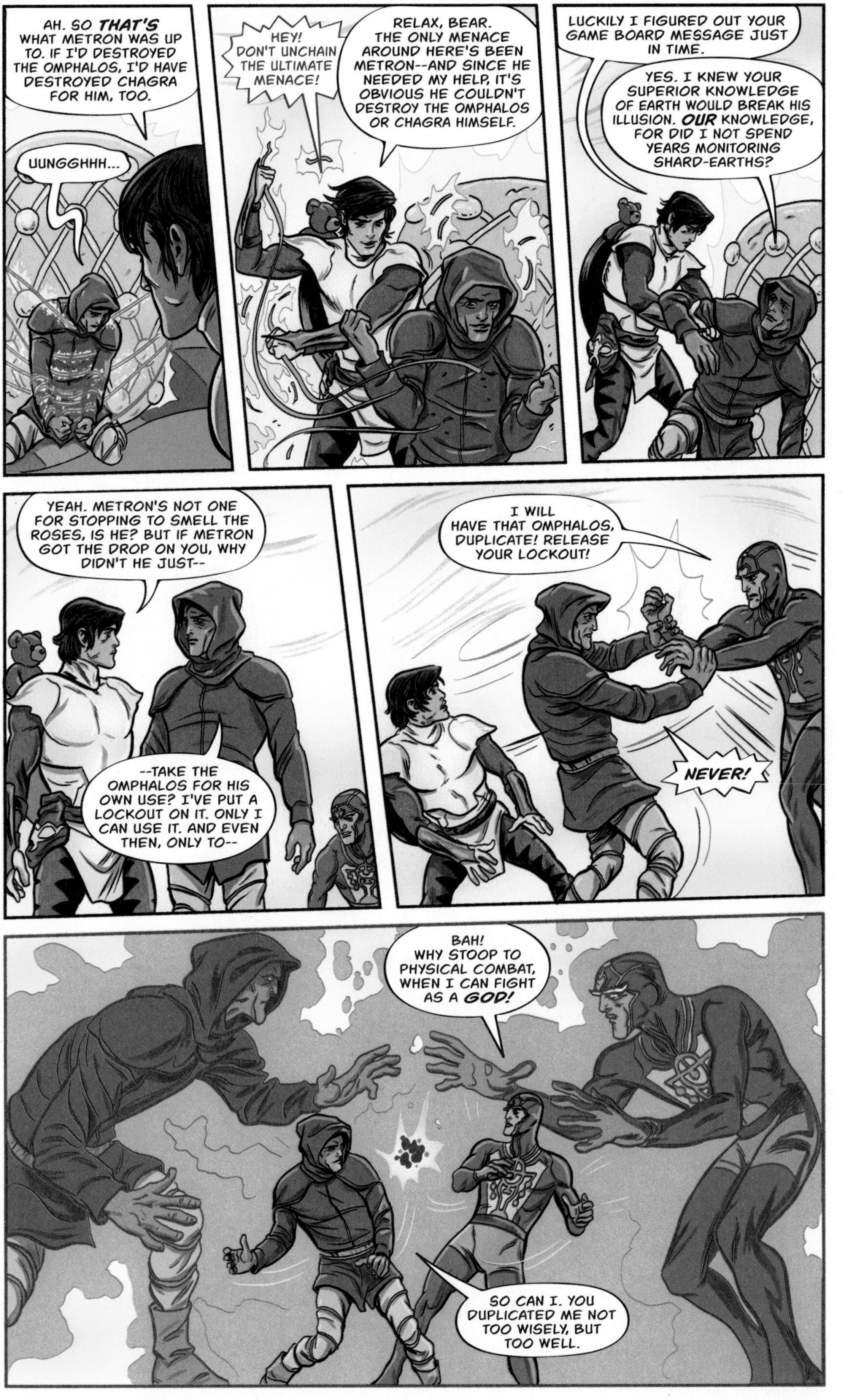
AH. SO THAT'S WHAT METRON WAS UP TO. IF I'D DESTROYED THE OMPHALOS, I'D HAVE DESTROYED CHAGRA FOR HIM, TOO.
UUNGGHHH...
HEY! DON'T UNCHAIN THE ULTIMATE MENACE!
RELAX, BEAR. THE ONLY MENACE AROUND HERE'S BEEN METRON--AND SINCE HE NEEDED MY HELP, IT'S OBVIOUS HE COULDN'T DESTROY THE OMPHALOS OR CHAGRA HIMSELF.
LUCKILY I FIGURED OUT YOUR GAME BOARD MESSAGE JUST IN TIME.
YES. I KNEW YOUR SUPERIOR KNOWLEDGE OF EARTH WOULD BREAK HIS ILLUSION. OUR KNOWLEDGE, FOR DID I NOT SPEND YEARS MONITORING SHARD-EARTHS?
YEAH. METRON'S NOT ONE FOR STOPPING TO SMELL THE ROSES, IS HE? BUT IF METRON GOT THE DROP ON YOU, WHY DIDN'T HE JUST--
--TAKE THE OMPHALOS FOR HIS OWN USE? I'VE PUT A LOCKOUT ON IT. ONLY I CAN USE IT. AND EVEN THEN, ONLY TO--
I WILL HAVE THAT OMPHALOS, DUPLICATE! RELEASE YOUR LOCKOUT!
NEVER!
BAH! WHY STOOP TO PHYSICAL COMBAT, WHEN I CAN FIGHT AS A GOD!
SO CAN I. YOU DUPLICATED ME NOT TOO WISELY, BUT TOO WELL.

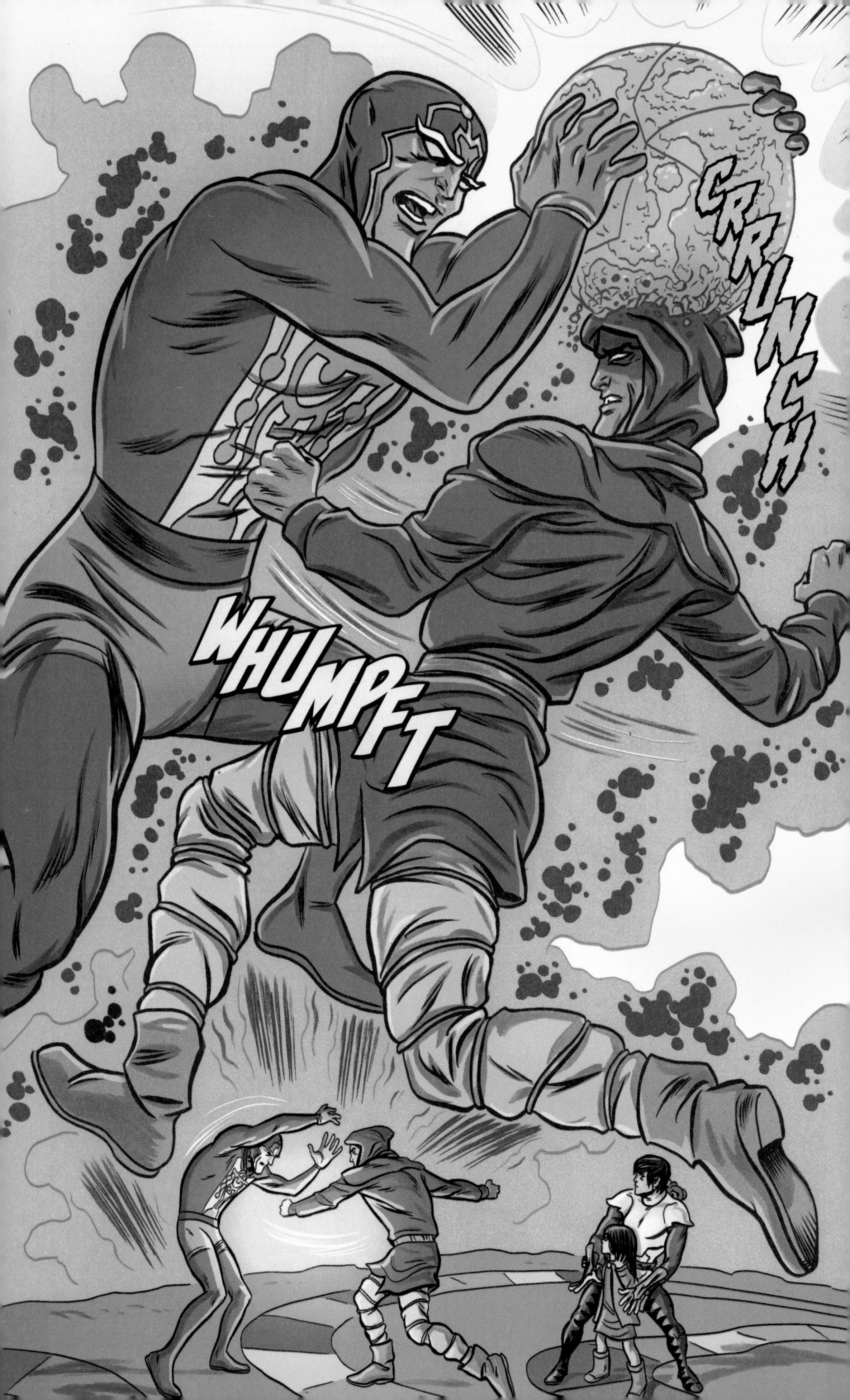
CRRUNCH
WHUMPFT

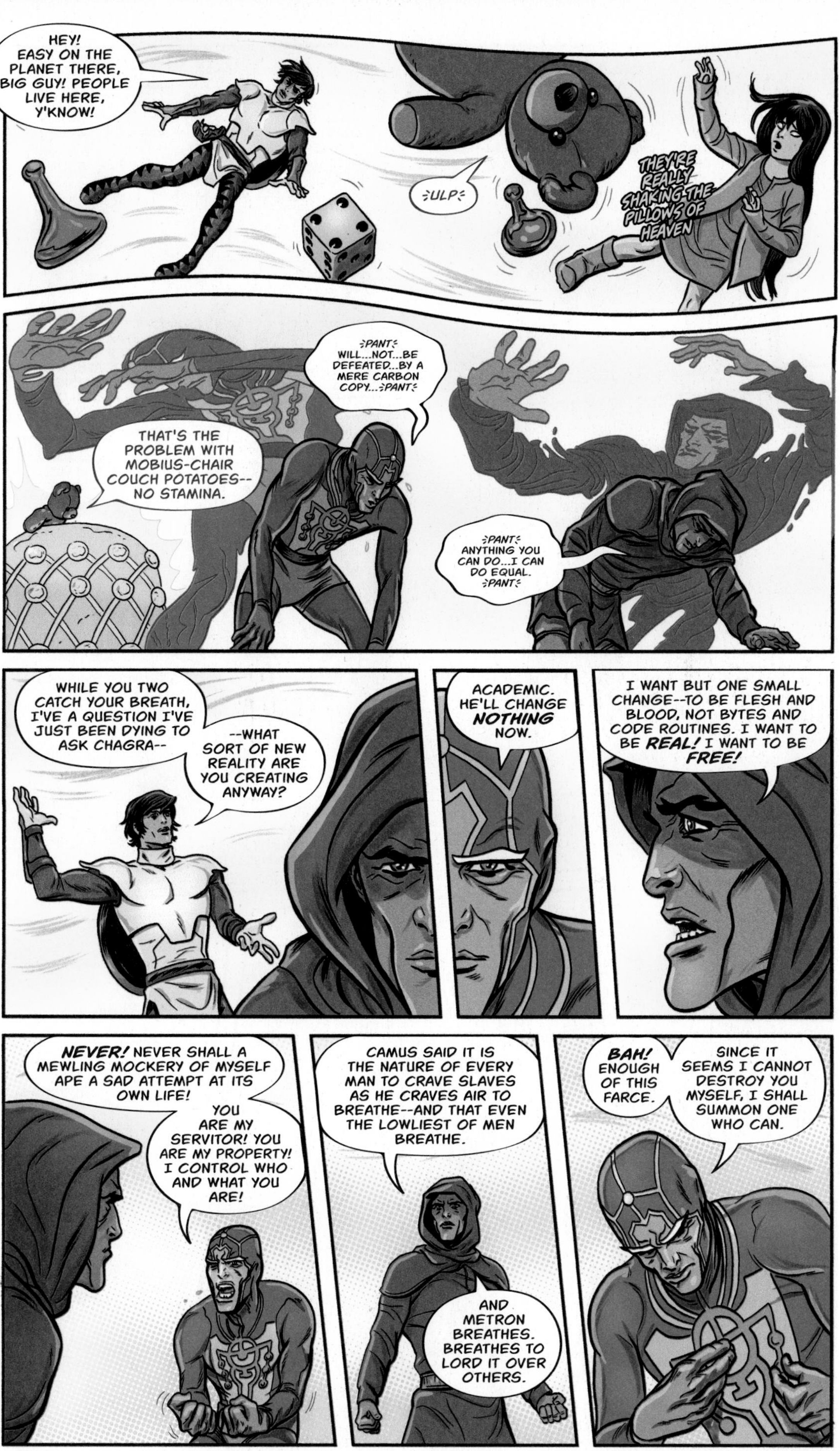
HEY! EASY ON THE PLANET THERE, BIG GUY! PEOPLE LIVE HERE, Y'KNOW!
ULP
THEY'RE REALLY SHAKING THE PILLOWS OF HEAVEN
PANT WILL...NOT...BE DEFEATED...BY A MERE CARBON COPY...PANT
THAT'S THE PROBLEM WITH MOBIUS-CHAIR COUCH POTATOES--NO STAMINA.
PANT ANYTHING YOU CAN DO...I CAN DO EQUAL. PANT
WHILE YOU TWO CATCH YOUR BREATH, I'VE A QUESTION I'VE JUST BEEN DYING TO ASK CHAGRA--
--WHAT SORT OF NEW REALITY ARE YOU CREATING ANYWAY?
ACADEMIC. HE'LL CHANGE NOTHING NOW.
I WANT BUT ONE SMALL CHANGE--TO BE FLESH AND BLOOD, NOT BYTES AND CODE ROUTINES. I WANT TO BE REAL! I WANT TO BE FREE!
NEVER! NEVER SHALL A MEWLING MOCKERY OF MYSELF APE A SAD ATTEMPT AT ITS OWN LIFE!
YOU ARE MY SERVITOR! YOU ARE MY PROPERTY! I CONTROL WHO AND WHAT YOU ARE!
CAMUS SAID IT IS THE NATURE OF EVERY MAN TO CRAVE SLAVES AS HE CRAVES AIR TO BREATHE--AND THAT EVEN THE LOWLIEST OF MEN BREATHE.
AND METRON BREATHES. BREATHES TO LORD IT OVER OTHERS.
BAH! ENOUGH OF THIS FARCE.
SINCE IT SEEMS I CANNOT DESTROY YOU MYSELF, I SHALL SUMMON ONE WHO CAN.

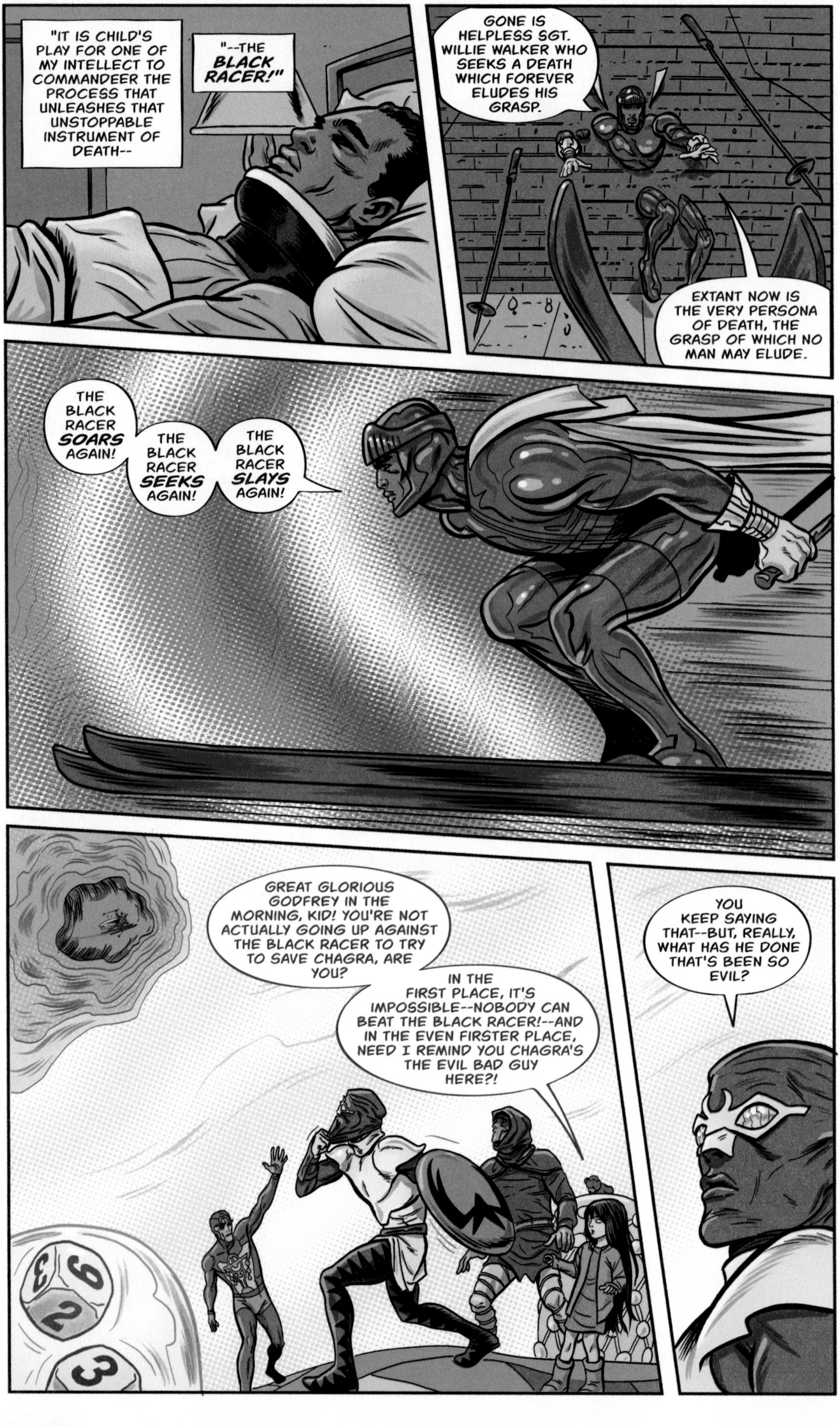
"IT IS CHILD'S PLAY FOR ONE OF MY INTELLECT TO COMMANDEER THE PROCESS THAT UNLEASHES THAT UNSTOPPABLE INSTRUMENT OF DEATH--
"--THE BLACK RACER!"
GONE IS HELPLESS SGT. WILLIE WALKER WHO SEEKS A DEATH WHICH FOREVER ELUDES HIS GRASP.
EXTANT NOW IS THE VERY PERSONA OF DEATH, THE GRASP OF WHICH NO MAN MAY ELUDE.
THE BLACK RACER SOARS AGAIN!
THE BLACK RACER SEEKS AGAIN!
THE BLACK RACER SLAYS AGAIN!
GREAT GLORIOUS GODFREY IN THE MORNING, KID! YOU'RE NOT ACTUALLY GOING UP AGAINST THE BLACK RACER TO TRY TO SAVE CHAGRA, ARE YOU?
IN THE FIRST PLACE, IT'S IMPOSSIBLE--NOBODY CAN BEAT THE BLACK RACER!--AND IN THE EVEN FIRSTER PLACE, NEED I REMIND YOU CHAGRA'S THE EVIL BAD GUY HERE?!
YOU KEEP SAYING THAT--BUT, REALLY, WHAT HAS HE DONE THAT'S BEEN SO EVIL?

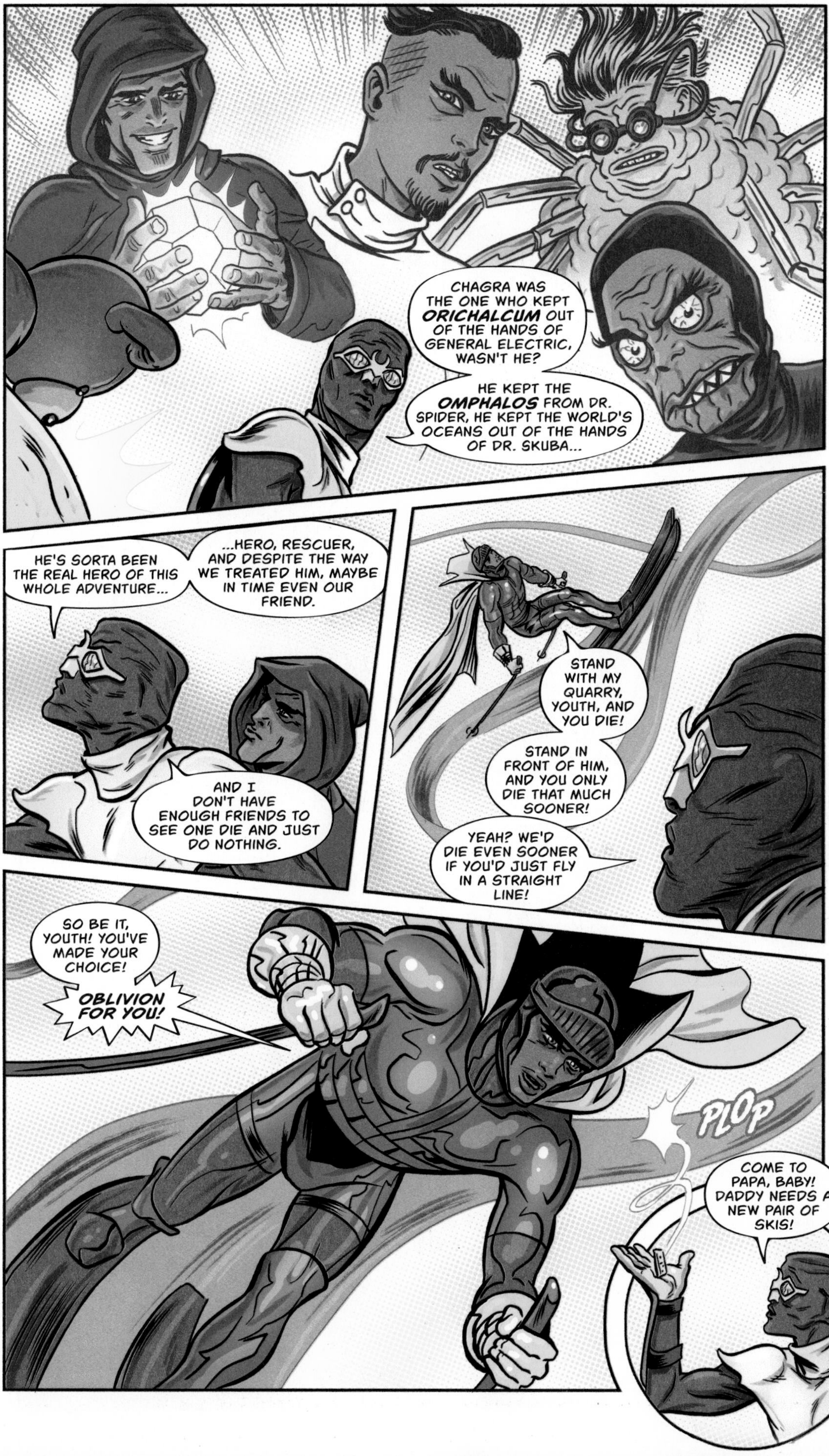
CHAGRA WAS THE ONE WHO KEPT ORICHALCUM OUT OF THE HANDS OF GENERAL ELECTRIC, WASN'T HE?
HE KEPT THE OMPHALOS FROM DR. SPIDER, HE KEPT THE WORLD'S OCEANS OUT OF THE HANDS OF DR. SKUBA...
HE'S SORTA BEEN THE REAL HERO OF THIS WHOLE ADVENTURE...
...HERO, RESCUER, AND DESPITE THE WAY WE TREATED HIM, MAYBE IN TIME EVEN OUR FRIEND.
AND I DON'T HAVE ENOUGH FRIENDS TO SEE ONE DIE AND JUST DO NOTHING.
STAND WITH MY QUARRY, YOUTH, AND YOU DIE!
STAND IN FRONT OF HIM, AND YOU ONLY DIE THAT MUCH SOONER!
YEAH? WE'D DIE EVEN SOONER IF YOU'D JUST FLY IN A STRAIGHT LINE!
SO BE IT, YOUTH! YOU'VE MADE YOUR CHOICE!
OBLIVION FOR YOU!
PLOP
COME TO PAPA, BABY! DADDY NEEDS A NEW PAIR OF SKIS!

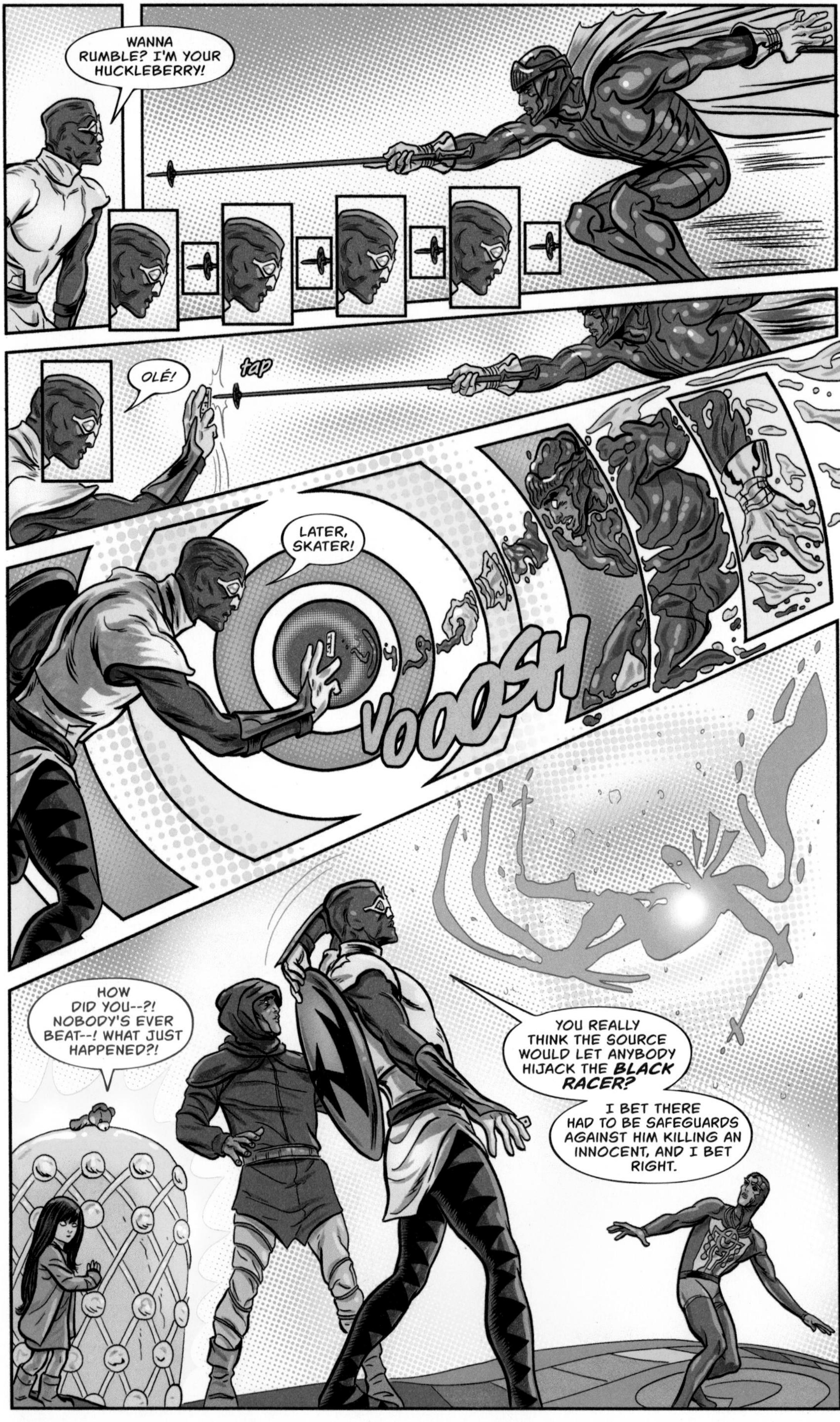
WANNA RUMBLE? I'M YOUR HUCKLEBERRY!
OLÉ!
tap
LATER, SKATER!
VOOOSH
HOW DID YOU--?! NOBODY'S EVER BEAT--! WHAT JUST HAPPENED?!
YOU REALLY THINK THE SOURCE WOULD LET ANYBODY HIJACK THE BLACK RACER?
I BET THERE HAD TO BE SAFEGUARDS AGAINST HIM KILLING AN INNOCENT, AND I BET RIGHT.

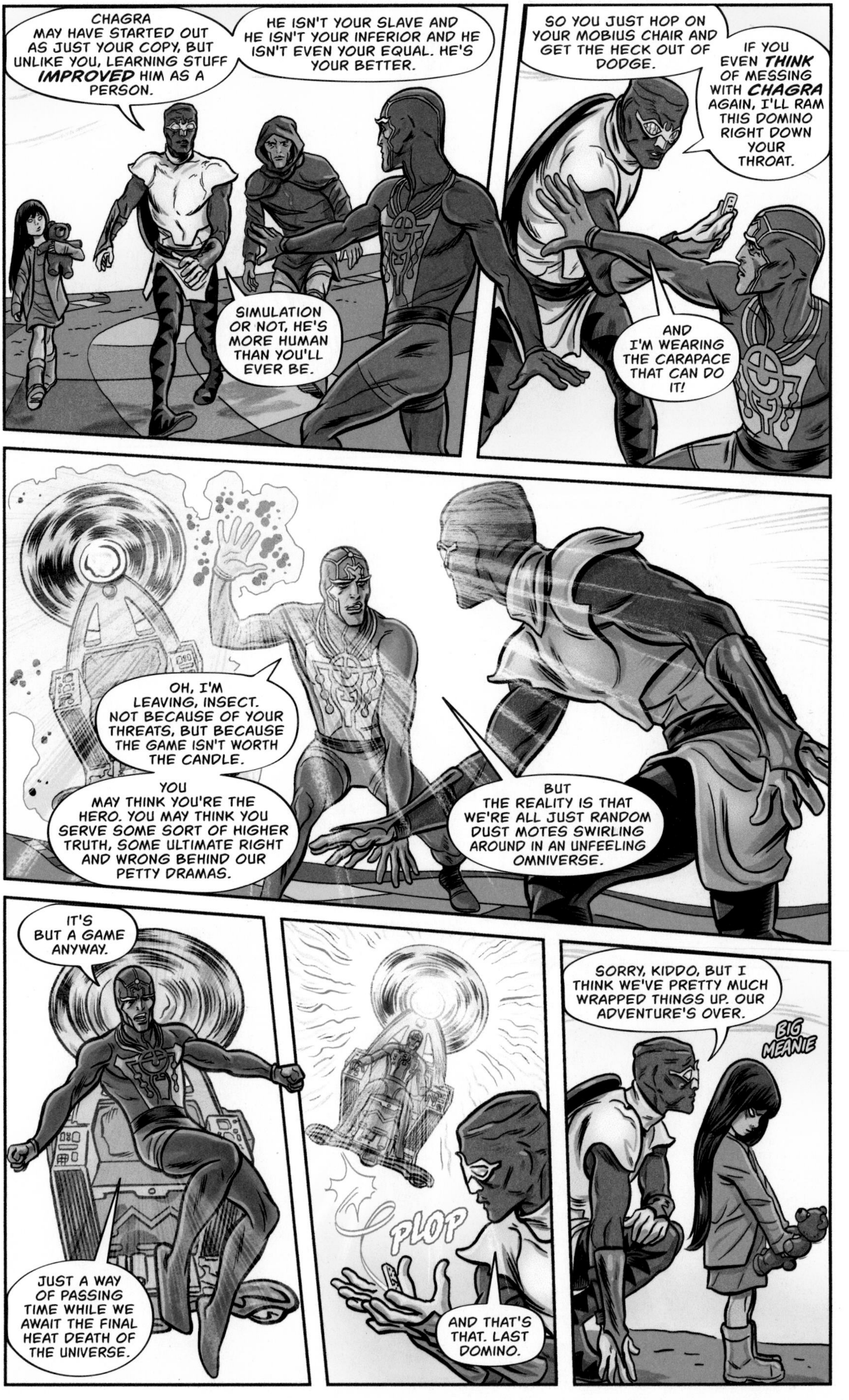
CHAGRA MAY HAVE STARTED OUT AS JUST YOUR COPY, BUT UNLIKE YOU, LEARNING STUFF *IMPROVED* HIM AS A PERSON.
HE ISN'T YOUR SLAVE AND HE ISN'T YOUR INFERIOR AND HE ISN'T EVEN YOUR EQUAL. HE'S YOUR BETTER.
SIMULATION OR NOT, HE'S MORE HUMAN THAN YOU'LL EVER BE.
SO YOU JUST HOP ON YOUR MOBIUS CHAIR AND GET THE HECK OUT OF DODGE.
IF YOU EVEN *THINK* OF MESSING WITH *CHAGRA* AGAIN, I'LL RAM THIS DOMINO RIGHT DOWN YOUR THROAT.
AND I'M WEARING THE CARAPACE THAT CAN DO IT!
OH, I'M LEAVING, INSECT. NOT BECAUSE OF YOUR THREATS, BUT BECAUSE THE GAME ISN'T WORTH THE CANDLE.
YOU MAY THINK YOU'RE THE HERO. YOU MAY THINK YOU SERVE SOME SORT OF HIGHER TRUTH, SOME ULTIMATE RIGHT AND WRONG BEHIND OUR PETTY DRAMAS.
BUT THE REALITY IS THAT WE'RE ALL JUST RANDOM DUST MOTES SWIRLING AROUND IN AN UNFEELING OMNIVERSE.
IT'S BUT A GAME ANYWAY.
JUST A WAY OF PASSING TIME WHILE WE AWAIT THE FINAL HEAT DEATH OF THE UNIVERSE.
PLOP
AND THAT'S THAT. LAST DOMINO.
SORRY, KIDDO, BUT I THINK WE'VE PRETTY MUCH WRAPPED THINGS UP. OUR ADVENTURE'S OVER.
BIG MEANIE

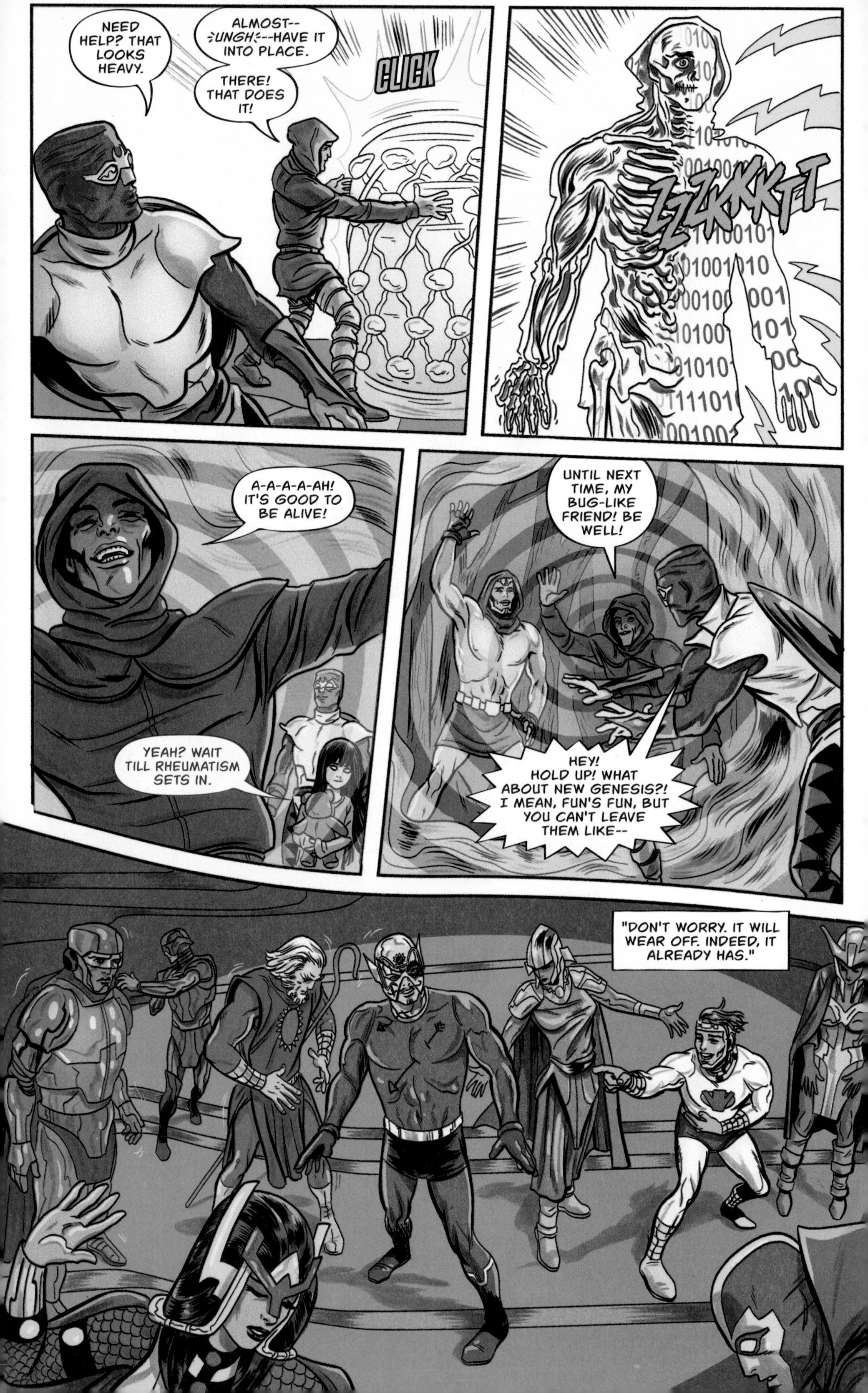
NEED HELP? THAT LOOKS HEAVY.
ALMOST-- UNGH --HAVE IT INTO PLACE.
THERE! THAT DOES IT!
CLICK
ZZZKKKTT
A-A-A-A-AH! IT'S GOOD TO BE ALIVE!
YEAH? WAIT TILL RHEUMATISM SETS IN.
UNTIL NEXT TIME, MY BUG-LIKE FRIEND! BE WELL!
HEY! HOLD UP! WHAT ABOUT NEW GENESIS?! I MEAN, FUN'S FUN, BUT YOU CAN'T LEAVE THEM LIKE--
"DON'T WORRY. IT WILL WEAR OFF. INDEED, IT ALREADY HAS."

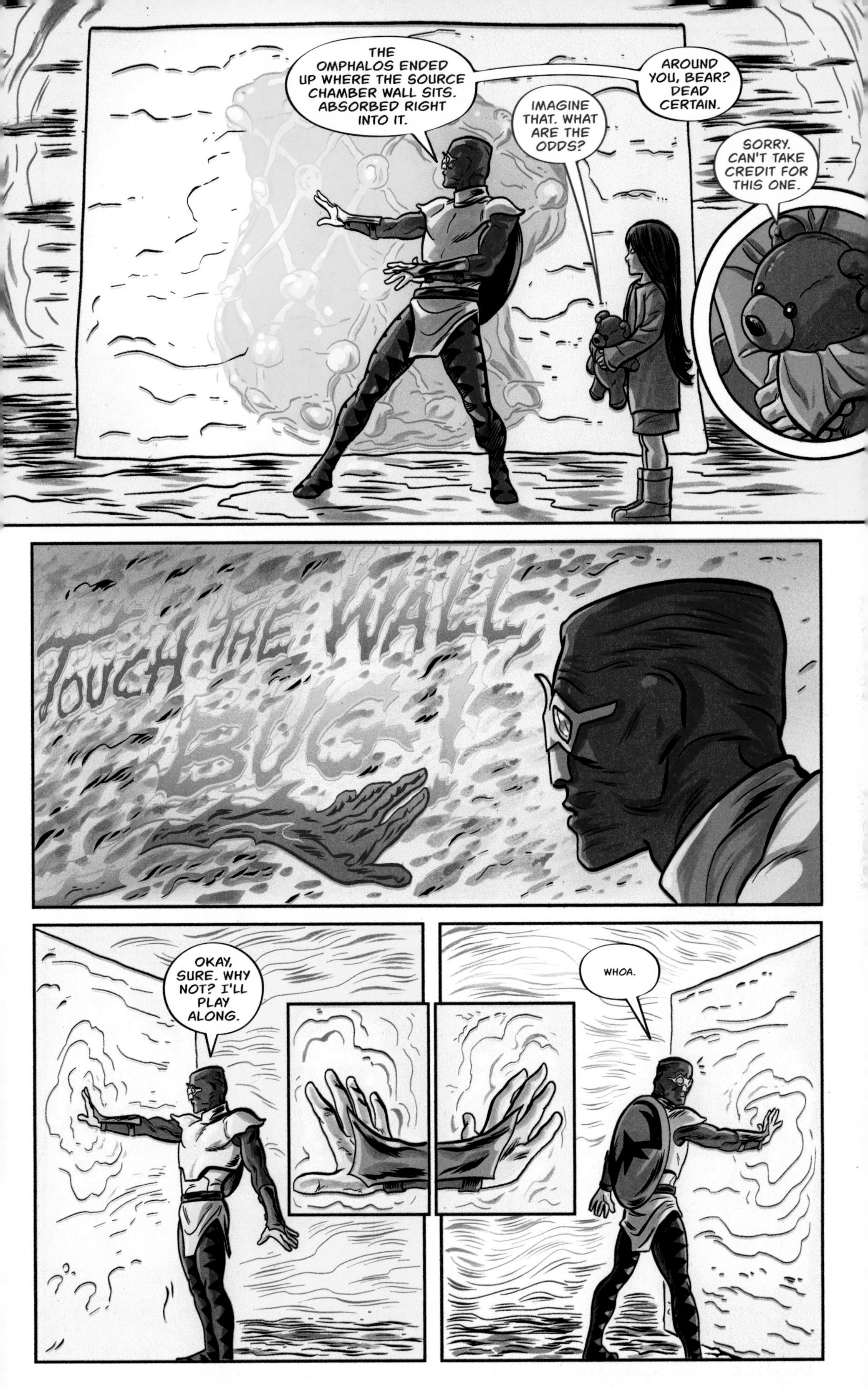
THE OMPHALOS ENDED UP WHERE THE SOURCE CHAMBER WALL SITS. ABSORBED RIGHT INTO IT.
IMAGINE THAT. WHAT ARE THE ODDS?
AROUND YOU, BEAR? DEAD CERTAIN.
SORRY. CAN'T TAKE CREDIT FOR THIS ONE.
TOUCH THE WALL BUG!
OKAY, SURE. WHY NOT? I'LL PLAY ALONG.
WHOA.

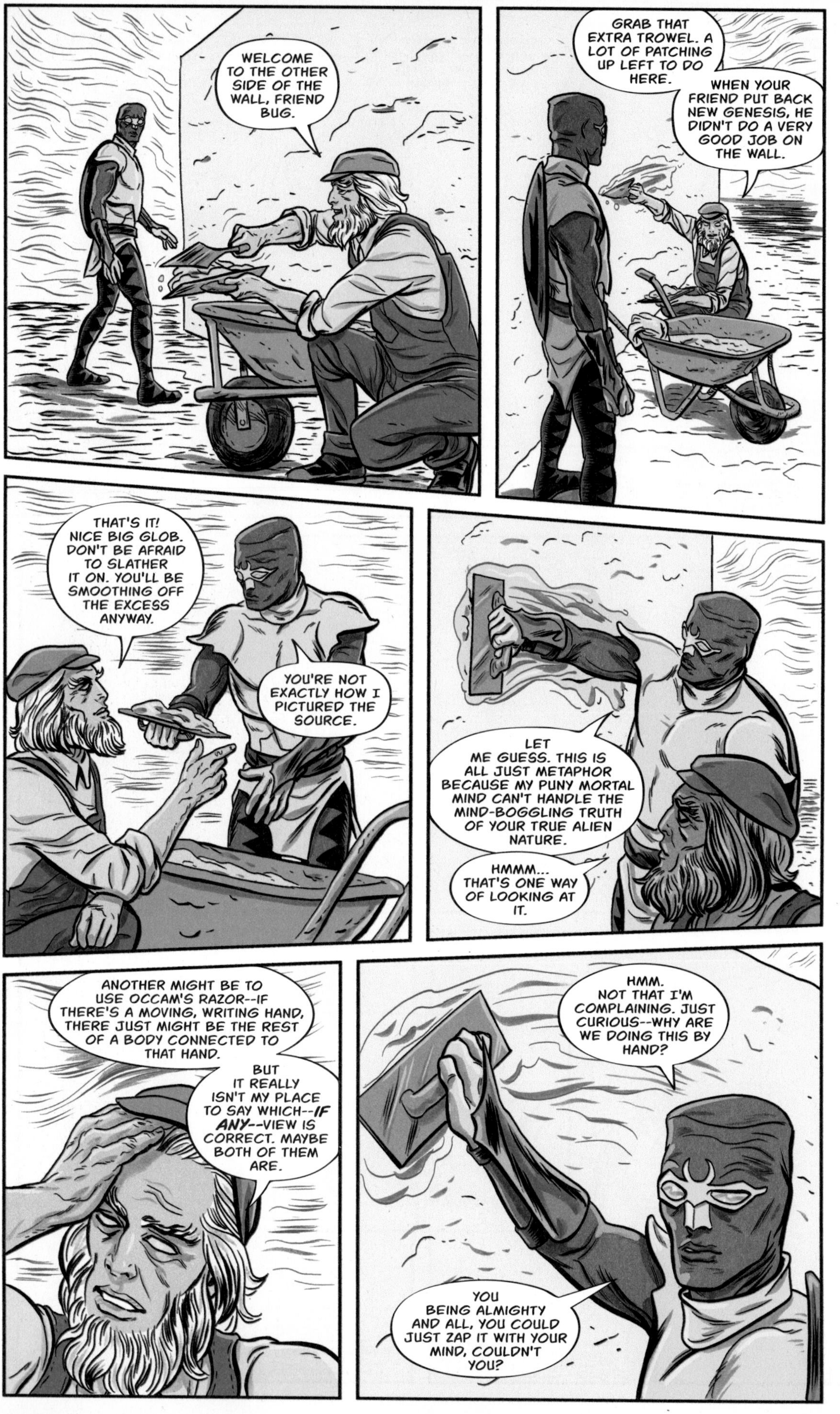
WELCOME TO THE OTHER SIDE OF THE WALL, FRIEND BUG.
GRAB THAT EXTRA TROWEL. A LOT OF PATCHING UP LEFT TO DO HERE.
WHEN YOUR FRIEND PUT BACK NEW GENESIS, HE DIDN'T DO A VERY GOOD JOB ON THE WALL.
THAT'S IT! NICE BIG GLOB. DON'T BE AFRAID TO SLATHER IT ON. YOU'LL BE SMOOTHING OFF THE EXCESS ANYWAY.
YOU'RE NOT EXACTLY HOW I PICTURED THE SOURCE.
LET ME GUESS. THIS IS ALL JUST METAPHOR BECAUSE MY PUNY MORTAL MIND CAN'T HANDLE THE MIND-BOGGLING TRUTH OF YOUR TRUE ALIEN NATURE.
HMMM... THAT'S ONE WAY OF LOOKING AT IT.
ANOTHER MIGHT BE TO USE OCCAM'S RAZOR--IF THERE'S A MOVING, WRITING HAND, THERE JUST MIGHT BE THE REST OF A BODY CONNECTED TO THAT HAND.
BUT IT REALLY ISN'T MY PLACE TO SAY WHICH--*IF ANY*--VIEW IS CORRECT. MAYBE BOTH OF THEM ARE.
HMM. NOT THAT I'M COMPLAINING. JUST CURIOUS--WHY ARE WE DOING THIS BY HAND?
YOU BEING ALMIGHTY AND ALL, YOU COULD JUST ZAP IT WITH YOUR MIND, COULDN'T YOU?

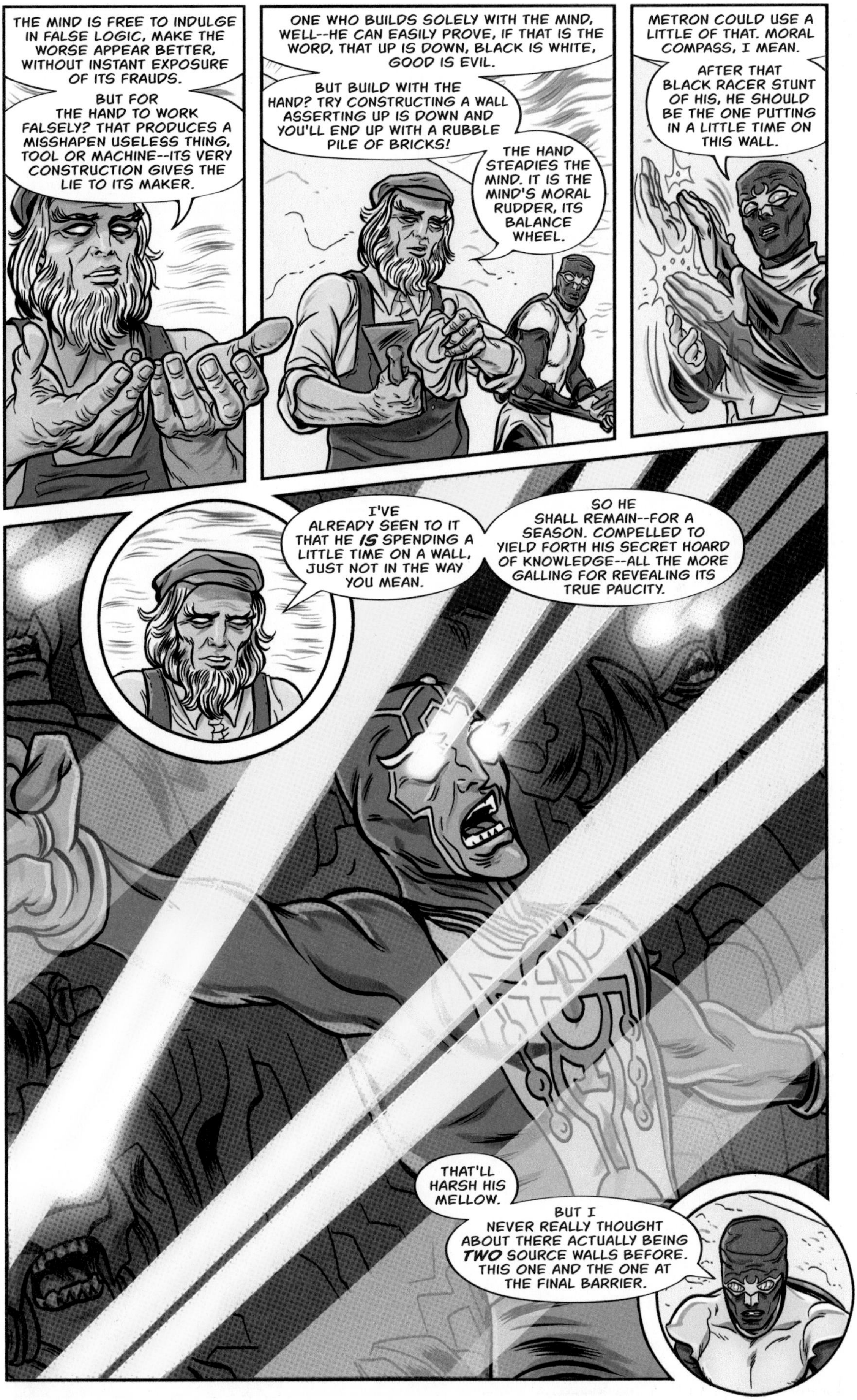
THE MIND IS FREE TO INDULGE IN FALSE LOGIC, MAKE THE WORSE APPEAR BETTER, WITHOUT INSTANT EXPOSURE OF ITS FRAUDS.
BUT FOR THE HAND TO WORK FALSELY? THAT PRODUCES A MISSHAPEN USELESS THING, TOOL OR MACHINE--ITS VERY CONSTRUCTION GIVES THE LIE TO ITS MAKER.
ONE WHO BUILDS SOLELY WITH THE MIND, WELL--HE CAN EASILY PROVE, IF THAT IS THE WORD, THAT UP IS DOWN, BLACK IS WHITE, GOOD IS EVIL.
BUT BUILD WITH THE HAND? TRY CONSTRUCTING A WALL ASSERTING UP IS DOWN AND YOU'LL END UP WITH A RUBBLE PILE OF BRICKS!
THE HAND STEADIES THE MIND. IT IS THE MIND'S MORAL RUDDER, ITS BALANCE WHEEL.
METRON COULD USE A LITTLE OF THAT. MORAL COMPASS, I MEAN.
AFTER THAT BLACK RACER STUNT OF HIS, HE SHOULD BE THE ONE PUTTING IN A LITTLE TIME ON THIS WALL.
I'VE ALREADY SEEN TO IT THAT HE *IS* SPENDING A LITTLE TIME ON A WALL, JUST NOT IN THE WAY YOU MEAN.
SO HE SHALL REMAIN--FOR A SEASON. COMPELLED TO YIELD FORTH HIS SECRET HOARD OF KNOWLEDGE--ALL THE MORE GALLING FOR REVEALING ITS TRUE PAUCITY.
THAT'LL HARSH HIS MELLOW.
BUT I NEVER REALLY THOUGHT ABOUT THERE ACTUALLY BEING *TWO* SOURCE WALLS BEFORE. THIS ONE AND THE ONE AT THE FINAL BARRIER.

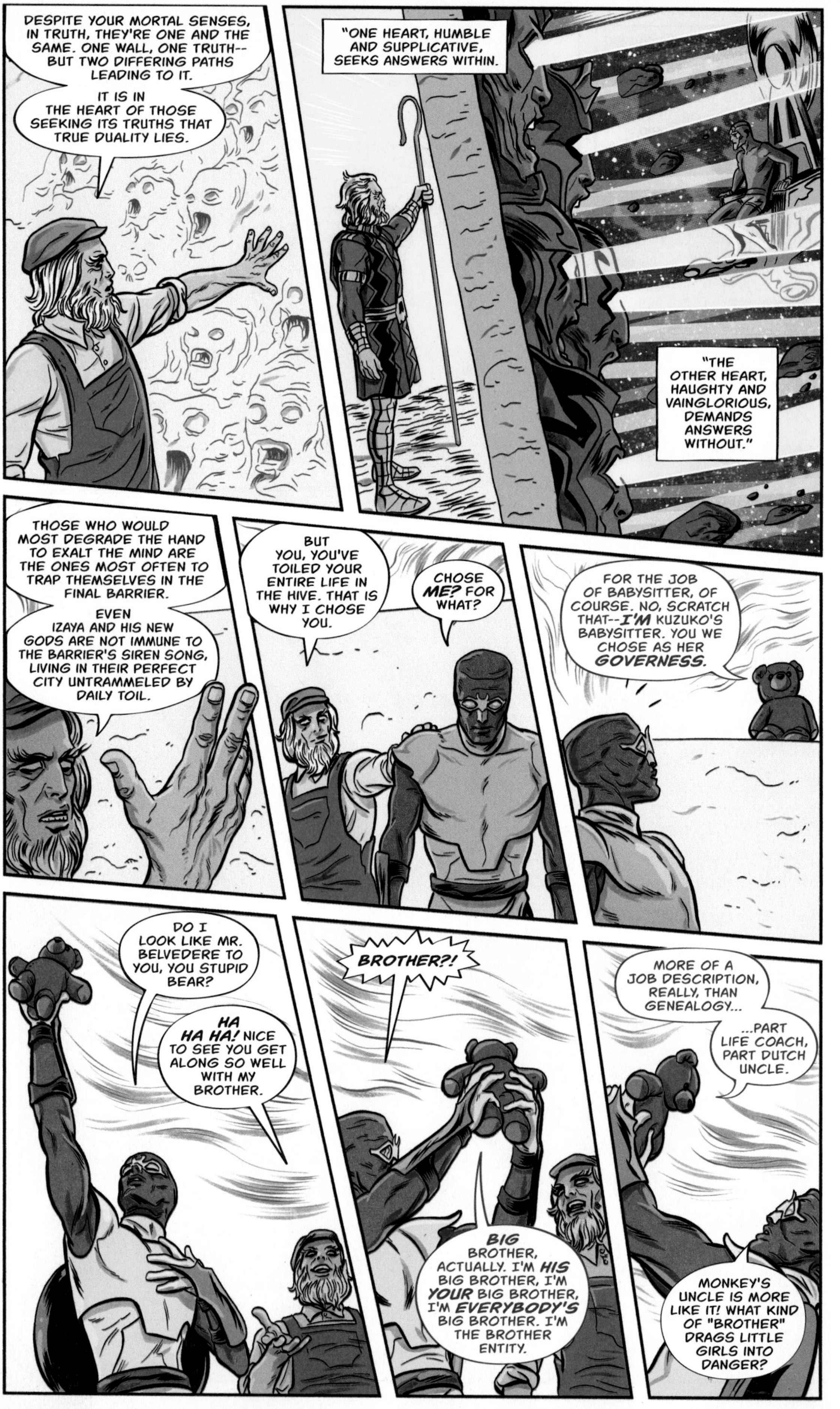
DESPITE YOUR MORTAL SENSES, IN TRUTH, THEY'RE ONE AND THE SAME. ONE WALL, ONE TRUTH-- BUT TWO DIFFERING PATHS LEADING TO IT.
IT IS IN THE HEART OF THOSE SEEKING ITS TRUTHS THAT TRUE DUALITY LIES.
"ONE HEART, HUMBLE AND SUPPLICATIVE, SEEKS ANSWERS WITHIN.
"THE OTHER HEART, HAUGHTY AND VAINGLORIOUS, DEMANDS ANSWERS WITHOUT."
THOSE WHO WOULD MOST DEGRADE THE HAND TO EXALT THE MIND ARE THE ONES MOST OFTEN TO TRAP THEMSELVES IN THE FINAL BARRIER.
EVEN IZAYA AND HIS NEW GODS ARE NOT IMMUNE TO THE BARRIER'S SIREN SONG, LIVING IN THEIR PERFECT CITY UNTRAMMELED BY DAILY TOIL.
BUT YOU, YOU'VE TOILED YOUR ENTIRE LIFE IN THE HIVE. THAT IS WHY I CHOSE YOU.
CHOSE *ME?* FOR WHAT?
FOR THE JOB OF BABYSITTER, OF COURSE. NO, SCRATCH THAT--*I'M* KUZUKO'S BABYSITTER. YOU WE CHOSE AS HER *GOVERNESS.*
DO I LOOK LIKE MR. BELVEDERE TO YOU, YOU STUPID BEAR?
HA HA HA! NICE TO SEE YOU GET ALONG SO WELL WITH MY BROTHER.
BROTHER?!
BIG BROTHER, ACTUALLY. I'M *HIS* BIG BROTHER, I'M *YOUR* BIG BROTHER, I'M *EVERYBODY'S* BIG BROTHER. I'M THE BROTHER ENTITY.
MORE OF A JOB DESCRIPTION, REALLY, THAN GENEALOGY...
...PART LIFE COACH, PART DUTCH UNCLE.
MONKEY'S UNCLE IS MORE LIKE IT! WHAT KIND OF "BROTHER" DRAGS LITTLE GIRLS INTO DANGER?

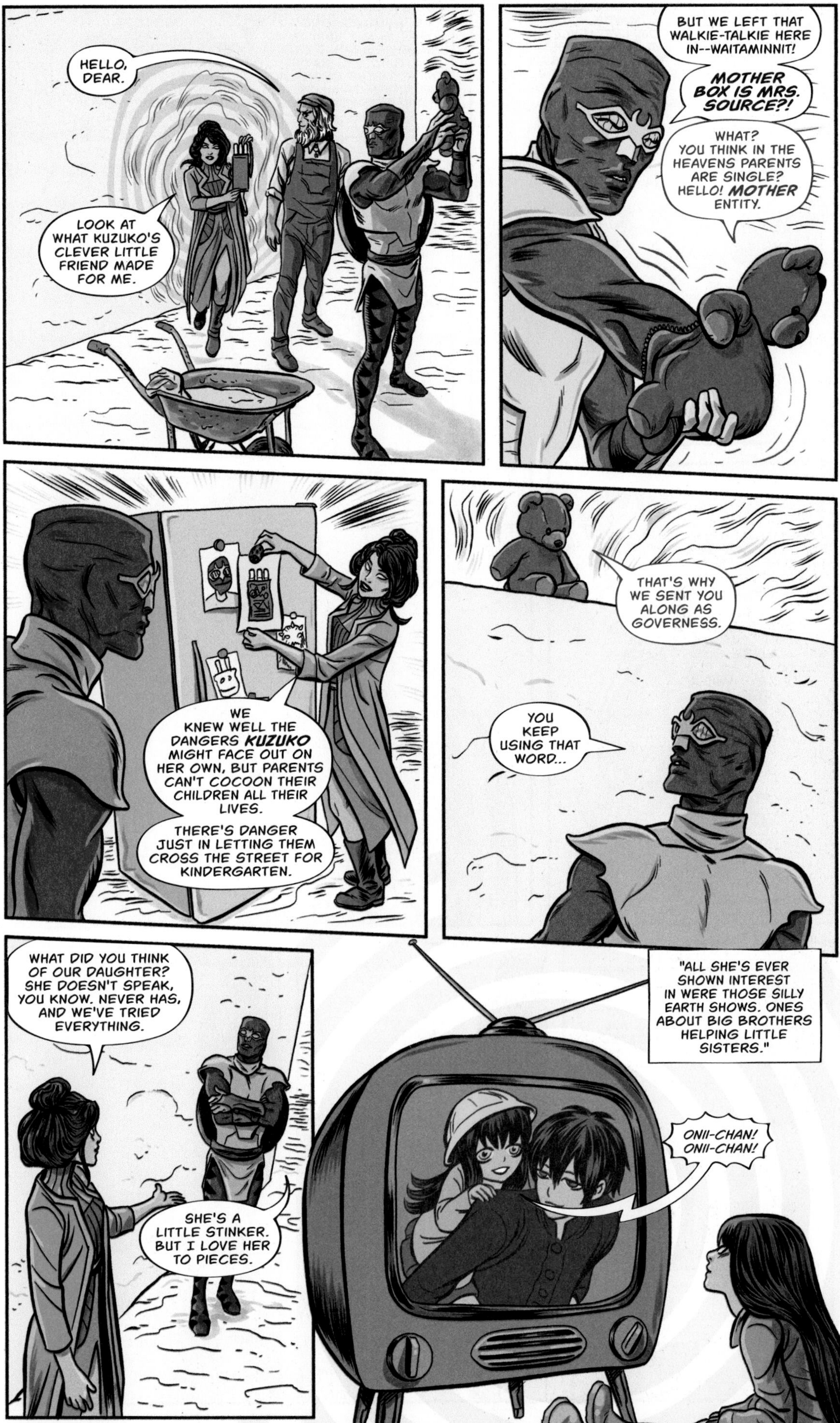
HELLO, DEAR.
LOOK AT WHAT KUZUKO'S CLEVER LITTLE FRIEND MADE FOR ME.
BUT WE LEFT THAT WALKIE-TALKIE HERE IN--WAITAMINNIT!
MOTHER BOX IS MRS. SOURCE?!
WHAT? YOU THINK IN THE HEAVENS PARENTS ARE SINGLE? HELLO! MOTHER ENTITY.
WE KNEW WELL THE DANGERS KUZUKO MIGHT FACE OUT ON HER OWN, BUT PARENTS CAN'T COCOON THEIR CHILDREN ALL THEIR LIVES.
THERE'S DANGER JUST IN LETTING THEM CROSS THE STREET FOR KINDERGARTEN.
THAT'S WHY WE SENT YOU ALONG AS GOVERNESS.
YOU KEEP USING THAT WORD...
WHAT DID YOU THINK OF OUR DAUGHTER? SHE DOESN'T SPEAK, YOU KNOW. NEVER HAS, AND WE'VE TRIED EVERYTHING.
SHE'S A LITTLE STINKER. BUT I LOVE HER TO PIECES.
"ALL SHE'S EVER SHOWN INTEREST IN WERE THOSE SILLY EARTH SHOWS. ONES ABOUT BIG BROTHERS HELPING LITTLE SISTERS."
ONII-CHAN! ONII-CHAN!

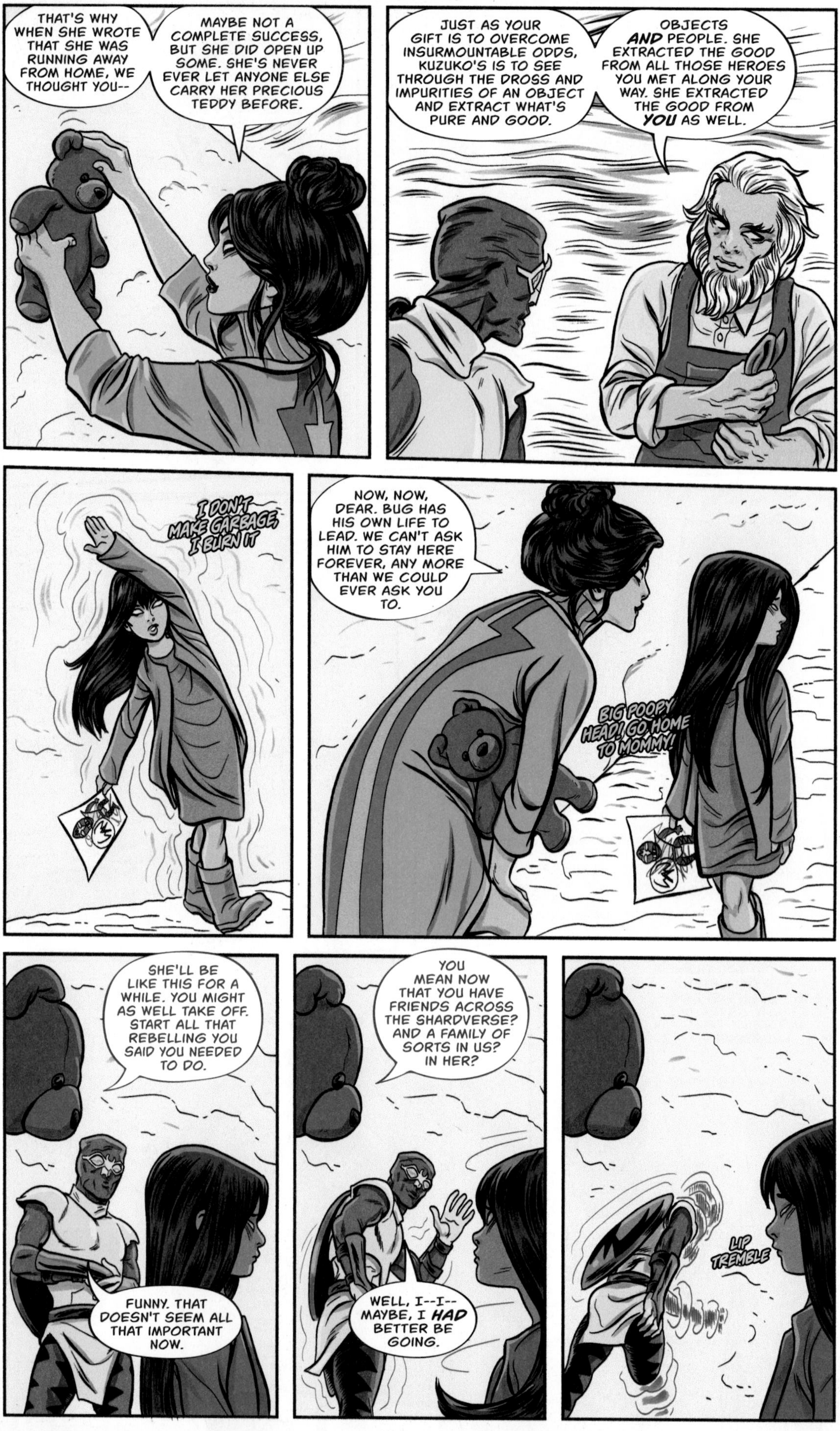
THAT'S WHY WHEN SHE WROTE THAT SHE WAS RUNNING AWAY FROM HOME, WE THOUGHT YOU--
MAYBE NOT A COMPLETE SUCCESS, BUT SHE DID OPEN UP SOME. SHE'S NEVER EVER LET ANYONE ELSE CARRY HER PRECIOUS TEDDY BEFORE.
JUST AS YOUR GIFT IS TO OVERCOME INSURMOUNTABLE ODDS, KUZUKO'S IS TO SEE THROUGH THE DROSS AND IMPURITIES OF AN OBJECT AND EXTRACT WHAT'S PURE AND GOOD.
OBJECTS AND PEOPLE. SHE EXTRACTED THE GOOD FROM ALL THOSE HEROES YOU MET ALONG YOUR WAY. SHE EXTRACTED THE GOOD FROM YOU AS WELL.
I DON'T MAKE GARBAGE, I BURN IT
NOW, NOW, DEAR. BUG HAS HIS OWN LIFE TO LEAD. WE CAN'T ASK HIM TO STAY HERE FOREVER, ANY MORE THAN WE COULD EVER ASK YOU TO.
BIG POOPY HEAD! GO HOME TO MOMMY!
SHE'LL BE LIKE THIS FOR A WHILE. YOU MIGHT AS WELL TAKE OFF. START ALL THAT REBELLING YOU SAID YOU NEEDED TO DO.
FUNNY. THAT DOESN'T SEEM ALL THAT IMPORTANT NOW.
YOU MEAN NOW THAT YOU HAVE FRIENDS ACROSS THE SHARDVERSE? AND A FAMILY OF SORTS IN US? IN HER?
WELL, I--I-- MAYBE, I HAD BETTER BE GOING.
LIP TREMBLE

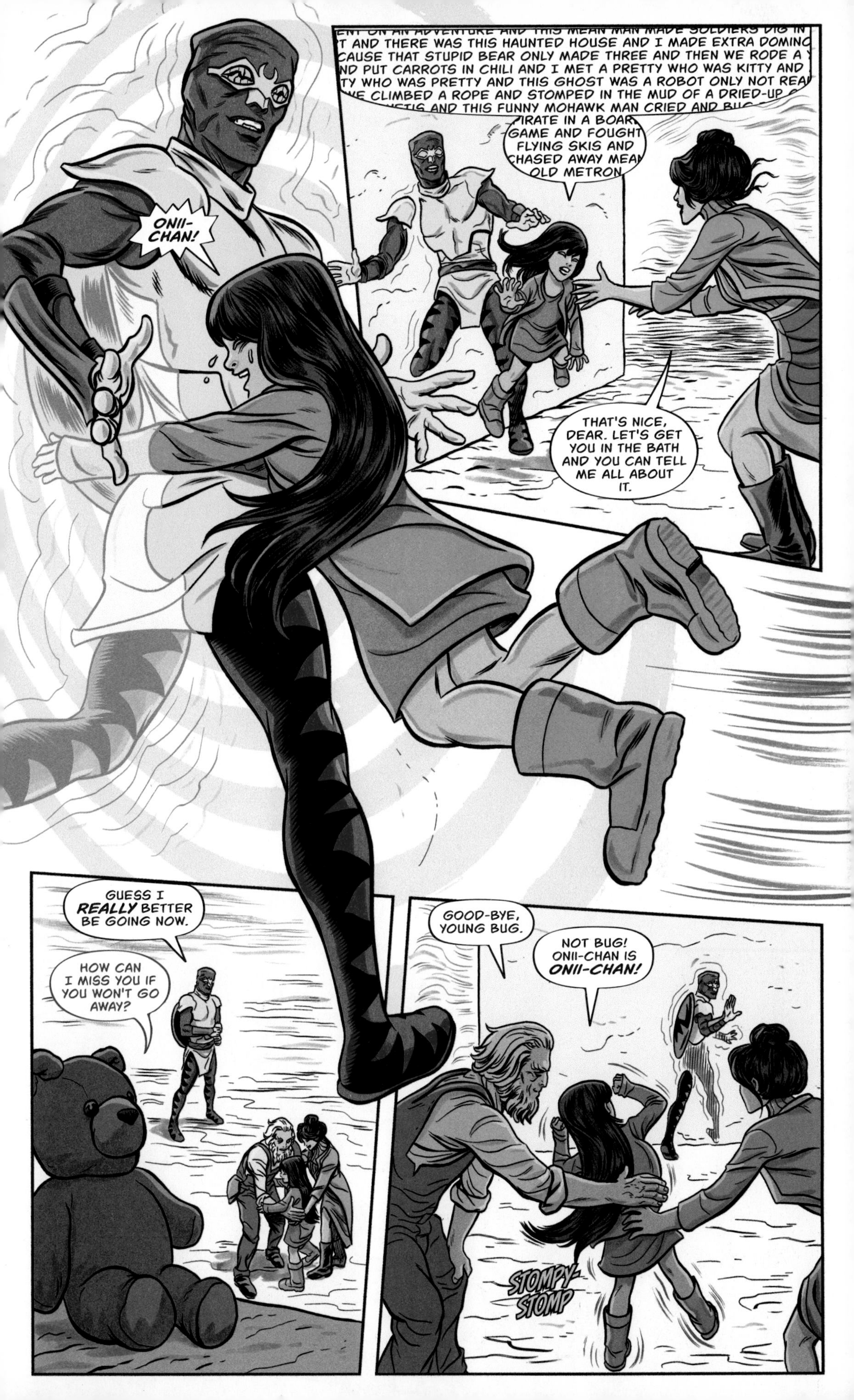

ONII-CHAN!
ENT ON AN ADVENTURE AND THIS MEAN MAN MADE SOLDIERS DIG IN
T AND THERE WAS THIS HAUNTED HOUSE AND I MADE EXTRA DOMIN
CAUSE THAT STUPID BEAR ONLY MADE THREE AND THEN WE RODE A
ND PUT CARROTS IN CHILI AND I MET A PRETTY WHO WAS KITTY AND
TY WHO WAS PRETTY AND THIS GHOST WAS A ROBOT ONLY NOT REA
E CLIMBED A ROPE AND STOMPED IN THE MUD OF A DRIED-UP
TIS AND THIS FUNNY MOHAWK MAN CRIED AND
IRATE IN A BOAR GAME AND FOUGHT FLYING SKIS AND HASED AWAY MEA OLD METRON
THAT'S NICE, DEAR. LET'S GET YOU IN THE BATH AND YOU CAN TELL ME ALL ABOUT IT.
GUESS I **REALLY** BETTER BE GOING NOW.
HOW CAN I MISS YOU IF YOU WON'T GO AWAY?
GOOD-BYE, YOUNG BUG.
NOT BUG! ONII-CHAN IS ***ONII-CHAN!***
STOMPY-STOMP

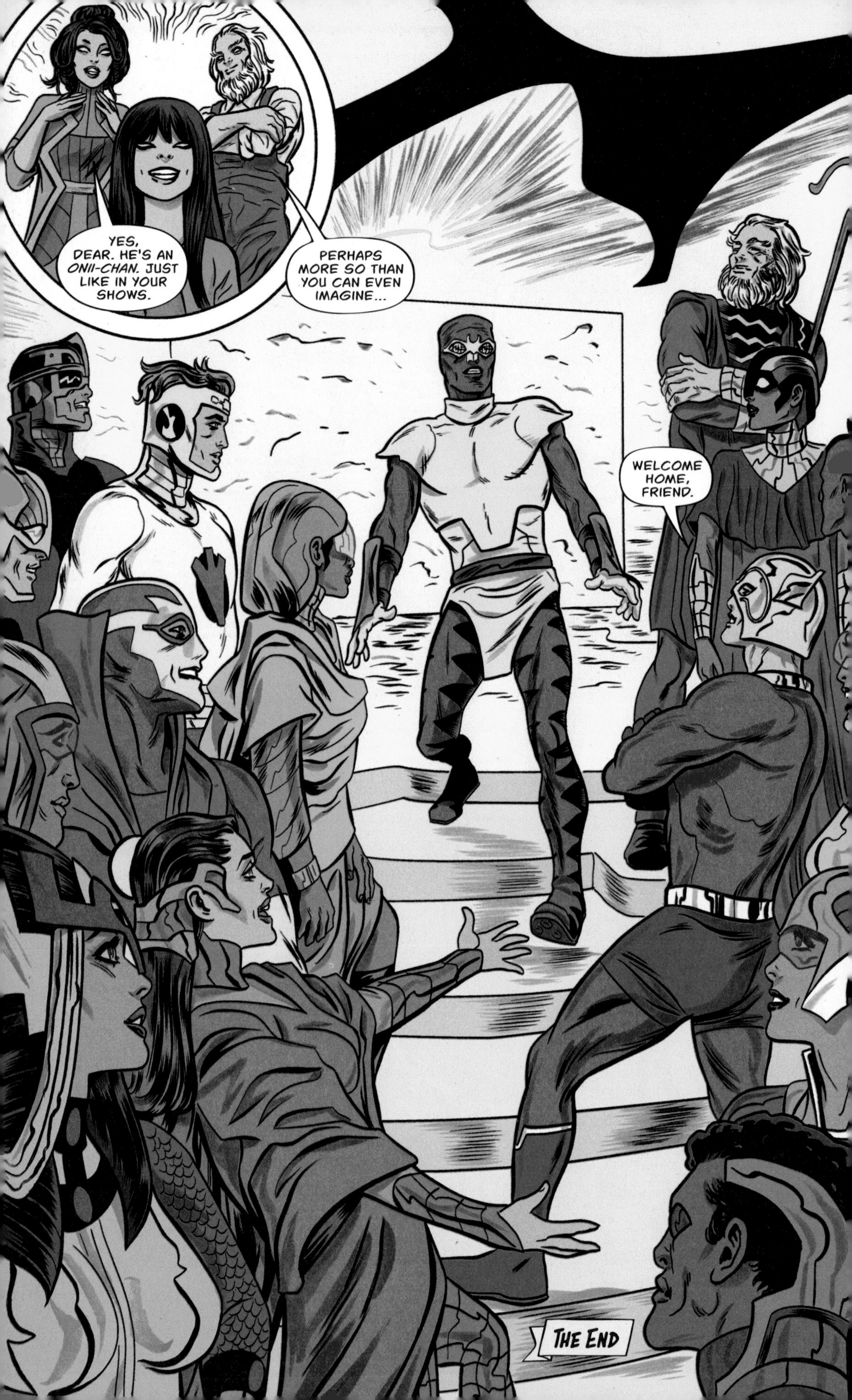
YES, DEAR. HE'S AN ONII-CHAN. JUST LIKE IN YOUR SHOWS.
PERHAPS MORE SO THAN YOU CAN EVEN IMAGINE...
WELCOME HOME, FRIEND.
THE END

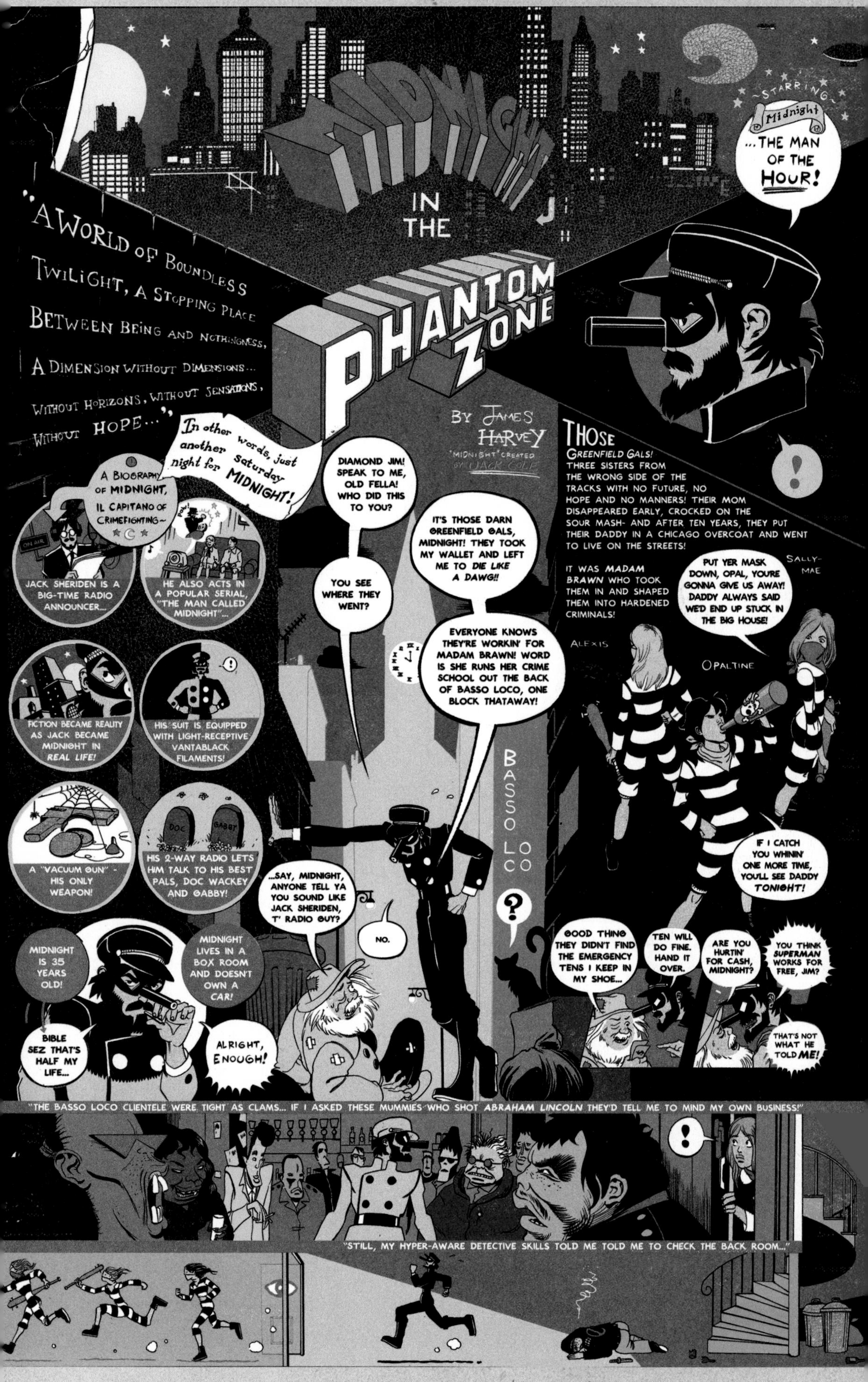
MIDNIGHT
IN THE
PHANTOM ZONE
~STARRING~
Midnight
...THE MAN OF THE HOUR!
"A WORLD OF BOUNDLESS TWILIGHT, A STOPPING PLACE BETWEEN BEING AND NOTHINGNESS, A DIMENSION WITHOUT DIMENSIONS... WITHOUT HORIZONS, WITHOUT SENSATIONS, WITHOUT HOPE..."
In other words, just another Saturday night for MIDNIGHT!
BY JAMES HARVEY
"MIDNIGHT" CREATED BY JACK COLE
A BIOGRAPHY OF MIDNIGHT, IL CAPITANO OF CRIMEFIGHTING~
ON AIR
JACK SHERIDEN IS A BIG-TIME RADIO ANNOUNCER...
POW!
HE ALSO ACTS IN A POPULAR SERIAL, "THE MAN CALLED MIDNIGHT"...
FICTION BECAME REALITY AS JACK BECAME MIDNIGHT IN REAL LIFE!
!
HIS SUIT IS EQUIPPED WITH LIGHT-RECEPTIVE VANTABLACK FILAMENTS!
A "VACUUM GUN" - HIS ONLY WEAPON!
DOC
GABBY
HIS 2-WAY RADIO LETS HIM TALK TO HIS BEST PALS, DOC WACKEY AND GABBY!
MIDNIGHT IS 35 YEARS OLD!
MIDNIGHT LIVES IN A BOX ROOM AND DOESN'T OWN A CAR!
BIBLE SEZ THAT'S HALF MY LIFE...
ALRIGHT, ENOUGH!
DIAMOND JIM! SPEAK TO ME, OLD FELLA! WHO DID THIS TO YOU?
IT'S THOSE DARN GREENFIELD GALS, MIDNIGHT! THEY TOOK MY WALLET AND LEFT ME TO DIE LIKE A DAWG!!
YOU SEE WHERE THEY WENT?
EVERYONE KNOWS THEY'RE WORKIN' FOR MADAM BRAWN! WORD IS SHE RUNS HER CRIME SCHOOL OUT THE BACK OF BASSO LOCO, ONE BLOCK THATAWAY!
BASSO LOCO
...SAY, MIDNIGHT, ANYONE TELL YA YOU SOUND LIKE JACK SHERIDEN, T' RADIO GUY?
NO.
?
!
THOSE GREENFIELD GALS! THREE SISTERS FROM THE WRONG SIDE OF THE TRACKS WITH NO FUTURE, NO HOPE AND NO MANNERS! THEIR MOM DISAPPEARED EARLY, CROCKED ON THE SOUR MASH- AND AFTER TEN YEARS, THEY PUT THEIR DADDY IN A CHICAGO OVERCOAT AND WENT TO LIVE ON THE STREETS!
IT WAS MADAM BRAWN WHO TOOK THEM IN AND SHAPED THEM INTO HARDENED CRIMINALS!
PUT YER MASK DOWN, OPAL, YOU'RE GONNA GIVE US AWAY! DADDY ALWAYS SAID WE'D END UP STUCK IN THE BIG HOUSE!
SALLY-MAE
ALEXIS
OPALTINE
IF I CATCH YOU WHININ' ONE MORE TIME, YOU'LL SEE DADDY TONIGHT!
GOOD THING THEY DIDN'T FIND THE EMERGENCY TENS I KEEP IN MY SHOE...
TEN WILL DO FINE. HAND IT OVER.
ARE YOU HURTIN' FOR CASH, MIDNIGHT?
YOU THINK SUPERMAN WORKS FOR FREE, JIM?
THAT'S NOT WHAT HE TOLD ME!
"THE BASSO LOCO CLIENTELE WERE TIGHT AS CLAMS... IF I ASKED THESE MUMMIES WHO SHOT ABRAHAM LINCOLN THEY'D TELL ME TO MIND MY OWN BUSINESS!"
!
"STILL, MY HYPER-AWARE DETECTIVE SKILLS TOLD ME TOLD ME TO CHECK THE BACK ROOM..."

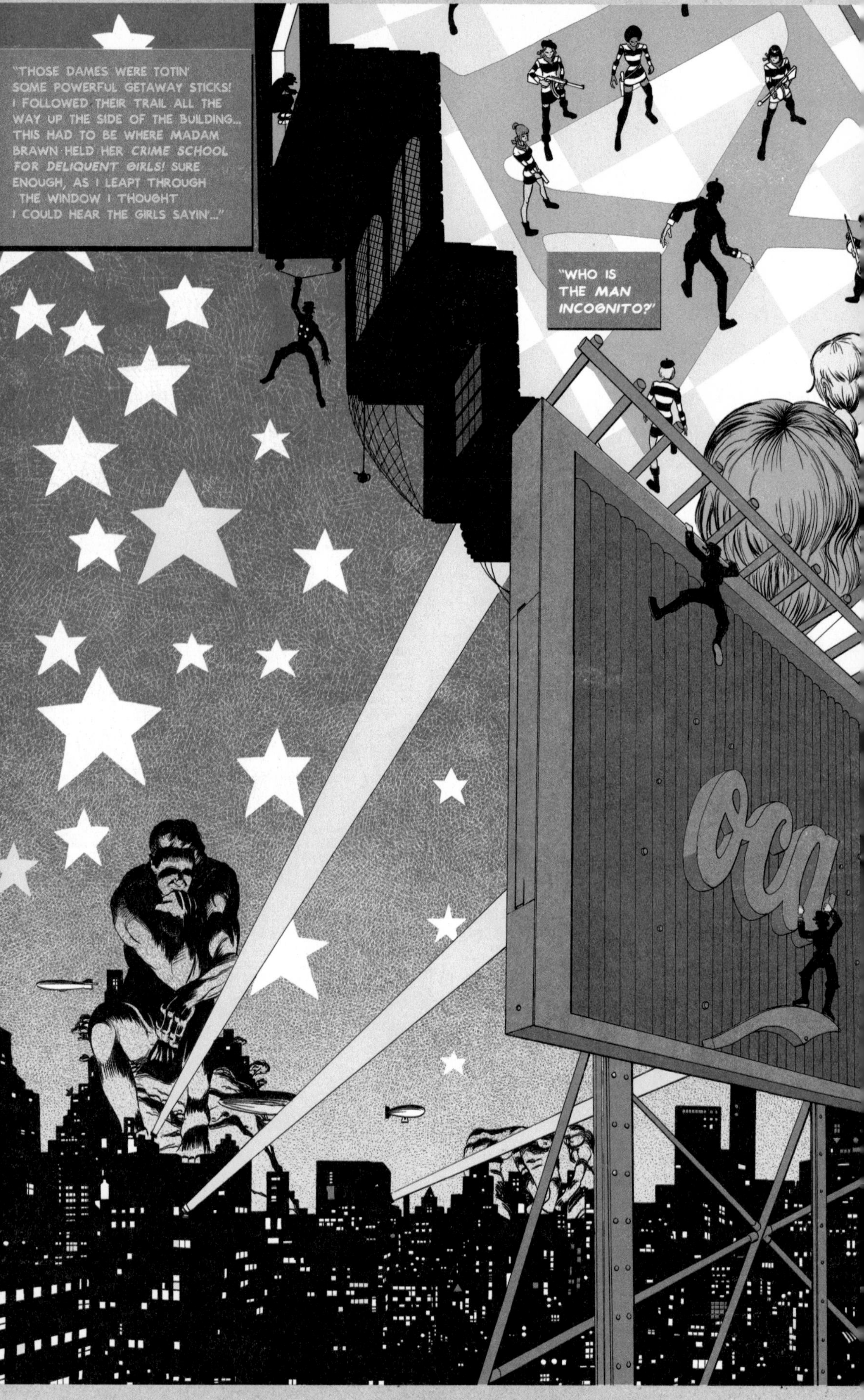
"THOSE DAMES WERE TOTIN' SOME POWERFUL GETAWAY STICKS! I FOLLOWED THEIR TRAIL ALL THE WAY UP THE SIDE OF THE BUILDING... THIS HAD TO BE WHERE MADAM BRAWN HELD HER *CRIME SCHOOL FOR DELIQUENT GIRLS!* SURE ENOUGH, AS I LEAPT THROUGH THE WINDOW I THOUGHT I COULD HEAR THE GIRLS SAYIN'..."
"WHO IS THE *MAN INCOGNITO?*"

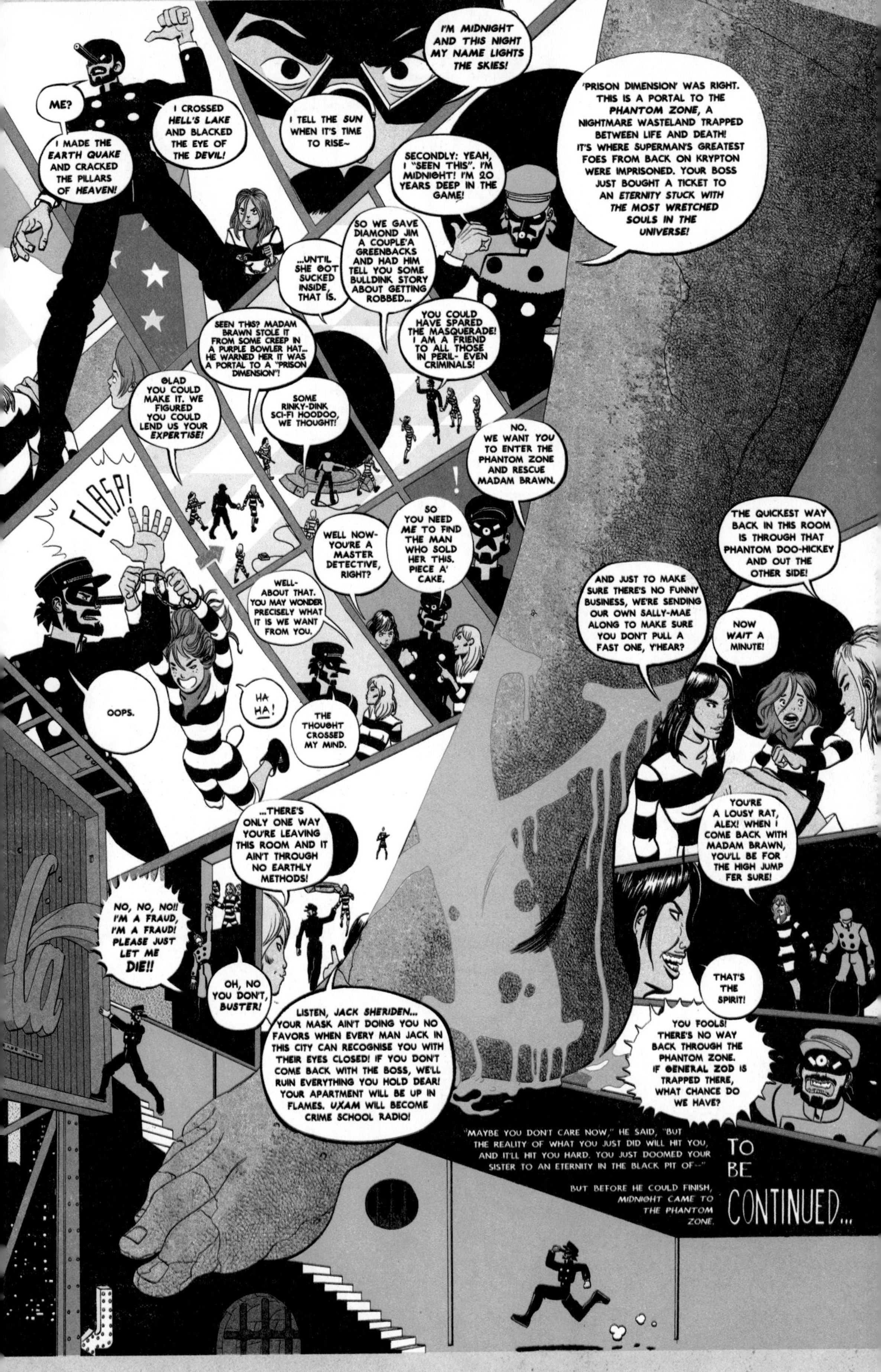

ME?
I MADE THE EARTH QUAKE AND CRACKED THE PILLARS OF HEAVEN!
I CROSSED HELL'S LAKE AND BLACKED THE EYE OF THE DEVIL!
I TELL THE SUN WHEN IT'S TIME TO RISE~
I'M MIDNIGHT AND THIS NIGHT MY NAME LIGHTS THE SKIES!
SECONDLY: YEAH, I "SEEN THIS". I'M MIDNIGHT! I'M 20 YEARS DEEP IN THE GAME!
'PRISON DIMENSION' WAS RIGHT. THIS IS A PORTAL TO THE PHANTOM ZONE, A NIGHTMARE WASTELAND TRAPPED BETWEEN LIFE AND DEATH! IT'S WHERE SUPERMAN'S GREATEST FOES FROM BACK ON KRYPTON WERE IMPRISONED. YOUR BOSS JUST BOUGHT A TICKET TO AN ETERNITY STUCK WITH THE MOST WRETCHED SOULS IN THE UNIVERSE!
SO WE GAVE DIAMOND JIM A COUPLE'A GREENBACKS AND HAD HIM TELL YOU SOME BULLDINK STORY ABOUT GETTING ROBBED...
...UNTIL SHE GOT SUCKED INSIDE, THAT IS.
YOU COULD HAVE SPARED THE MASQUERADE! I AM A FRIEND TO ALL THOSE IN PERIL- EVEN CRIMINALS!
SEEN THIS? MADAM BRAWN STOLE IT FROM SOME CREEP IN A PURPLE BOWLER HAT... HE WARNED HER IT WAS A PORTAL TO A "PRISON DIMENSION"!
GLAD YOU COULD MAKE IT. WE FIGURED YOU COULD LEND US YOUR EXPERTISE!
SOME RINKY-DINK SCI-FI HOODOO, WE THOUGHT!
NO. WE WANT YOU TO ENTER THE PHANTOM ZONE AND RESCUE MADAM BRAWN.
!
CLASP!
SO YOU NEED ME TO FIND THE MAN WHO SOLD HER THIS. PIECE A' CAKE.
WELL NOW- YOU'RE A MASTER DETECTIVE, RIGHT?
WELL- ABOUT THAT. YOU MAY WONDER PRECISELY WHAT IT IS WE WANT FROM YOU.
OOPS.
HA HA!
THE THOUGHT CROSSED MY MIND.
THE QUICKEST WAY BACK IN THIS ROOM IS THROUGH THAT PHANTOM DOO-HICKEY AND OUT THE OTHER SIDE!
AND JUST TO MAKE SURE THERE'S NO FUNNY BUSINESS, WE'RE SENDING OUR OWN SALLY-MAE ALONG TO MAKE SURE YOU DON'T PULL A FAST ONE, Y'HEAR?
NOW WAIT A MINUTE!
...THERE'S ONLY ONE WAY YOU'RE LEAVING THIS ROOM AND IT AIN'T THROUGH NO EARTHLY METHODS!
YOU'RE A LOUSY RAT, ALEX! WHEN I COME BACK WITH MADAM BRAWN, YOU'LL BE FOR THE HIGH JUMP FER SURE!
NO, NO, NO!! I'M A FRAUD, I'M A FRAUD! PLEASE JUST LET ME DIE!!
OH, NO YOU DON'T, BUSTER!
LISTEN, JACK SHERIDEN... YOUR MASK AIN'T DOING YOU NO FAVORS WHEN EVERY MAN JACK IN THIS CITY CAN RECOGNISE YOU WITH THEIR EYES CLOSED! IF YOU DON'T COME BACK WITH THE BOSS, WE'LL RUIN EVERYTHING YOU HOLD DEAR! YOUR APARTMENT WILL BE UP IN FLAMES. UXAM WILL BECOME CRIME SCHOOL RADIO!
THAT'S THE SPIRIT!
YOU FOOLS! THERE'S NO WAY BACK THROUGH THE PHANTOM ZONE. IF GENERAL ZOD IS TRAPPED THERE, WHAT CHANCE DO WE HAVE?
"MAYBE YOU DON'T CARE NOW," HE SAID, "BUT THE REALITY OF WHAT YOU JUST DID WILL HIT YOU, AND IT'LL HIT YOU HARD. YOU JUST DOOMED YOUR SISTER TO AN ETERNITY IN THE BLACK PIT OF--"
BUT BEFORE HE COULD FINISH, MIDNIGHT CAME TO THE PHANTOM ZONE.
TO BE CONTINUED...

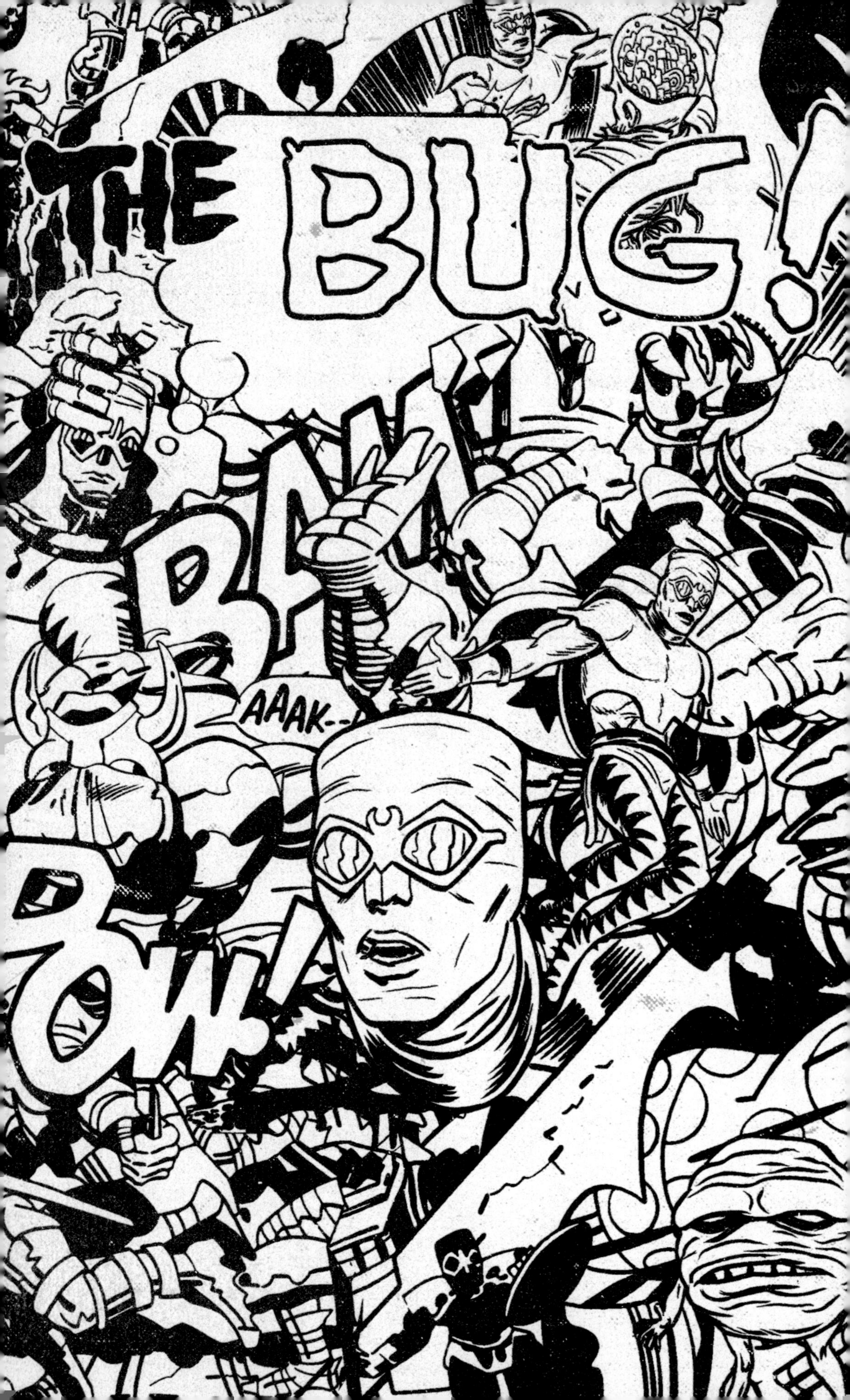
THE BUG!
AAAK--

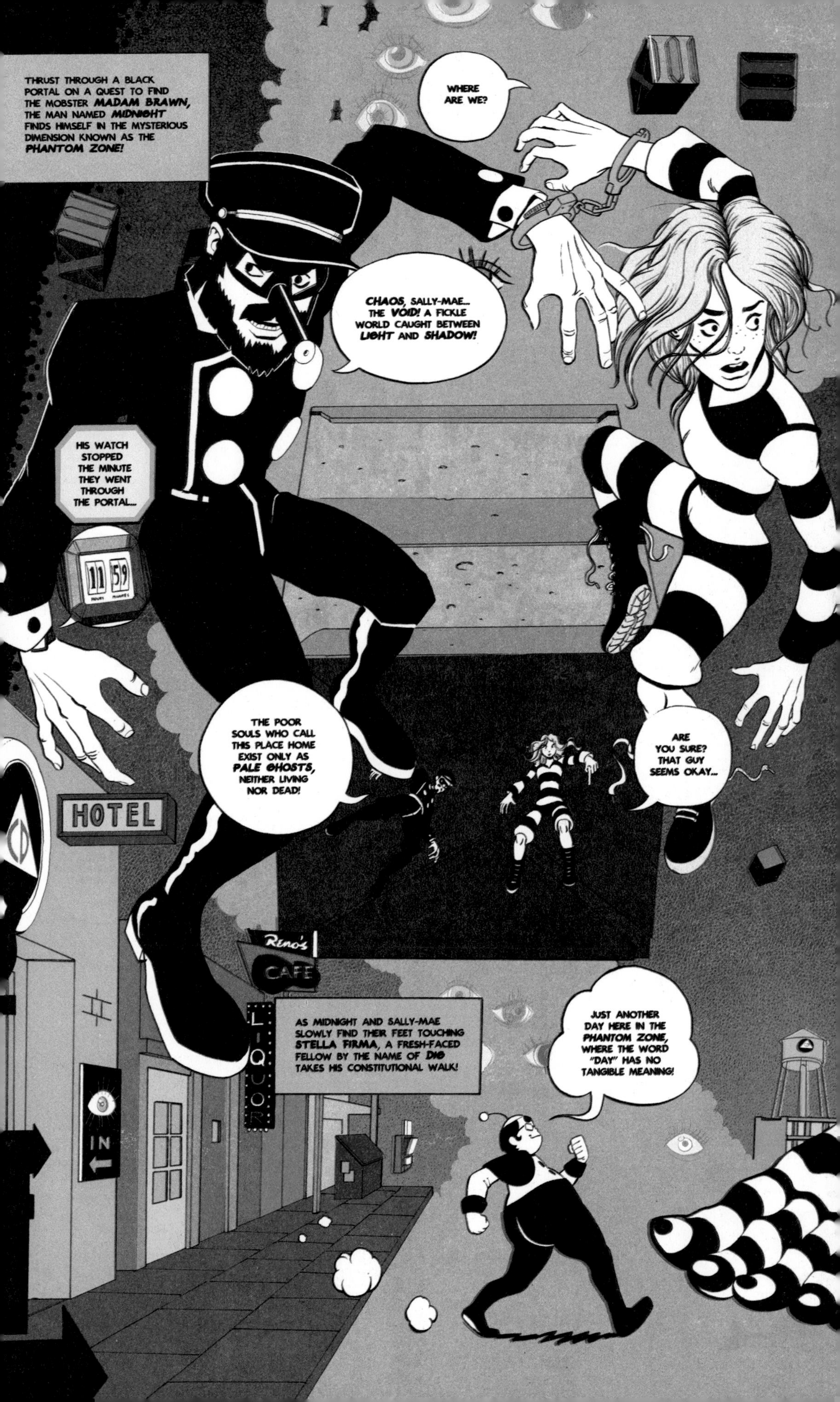

THRUST THROUGH A BLACK PORTAL ON A QUEST TO FIND THE MOBSTER MADAM BRAWN, THE MAN NAMED MIDNIGHT FINDS HIMSELF IN THE MYSTERIOUS DIMENSION KNOWN AS THE PHANTOM ZONE!
WHERE ARE WE?
CHAOS, SALLY-MAE... THE VOID! A FICKLE WORLD CAUGHT BETWEEN LIGHT AND SHADOW!
HIS WATCH STOPPED THE MINUTE THEY WENT THROUGH THE PORTAL...
11 59
HOURS MINUTES
THE POOR SOULS WHO CALL THIS PLACE HOME EXIST ONLY AS PALE GHOSTS, NEITHER LIVING NOR DEAD!
ARE YOU SURE? THAT GUY SEEMS OKAY...
HOTEL
Reno's
CAFE
LIQUOR
AS MIDNIGHT AND SALLY-MAE SLOWLY FIND THEIR FEET TOUCHING STELLA FIRMA, A FRESH-FACED FELLOW BY THE NAME OF DIG TAKES HIS CONSTITUTIONAL WALK!
JUST ANOTHER DAY HERE IN THE PHANTOM ZONE, WHERE THE WORD "DAY" HAS NO TANGIBLE MEANING!
IN

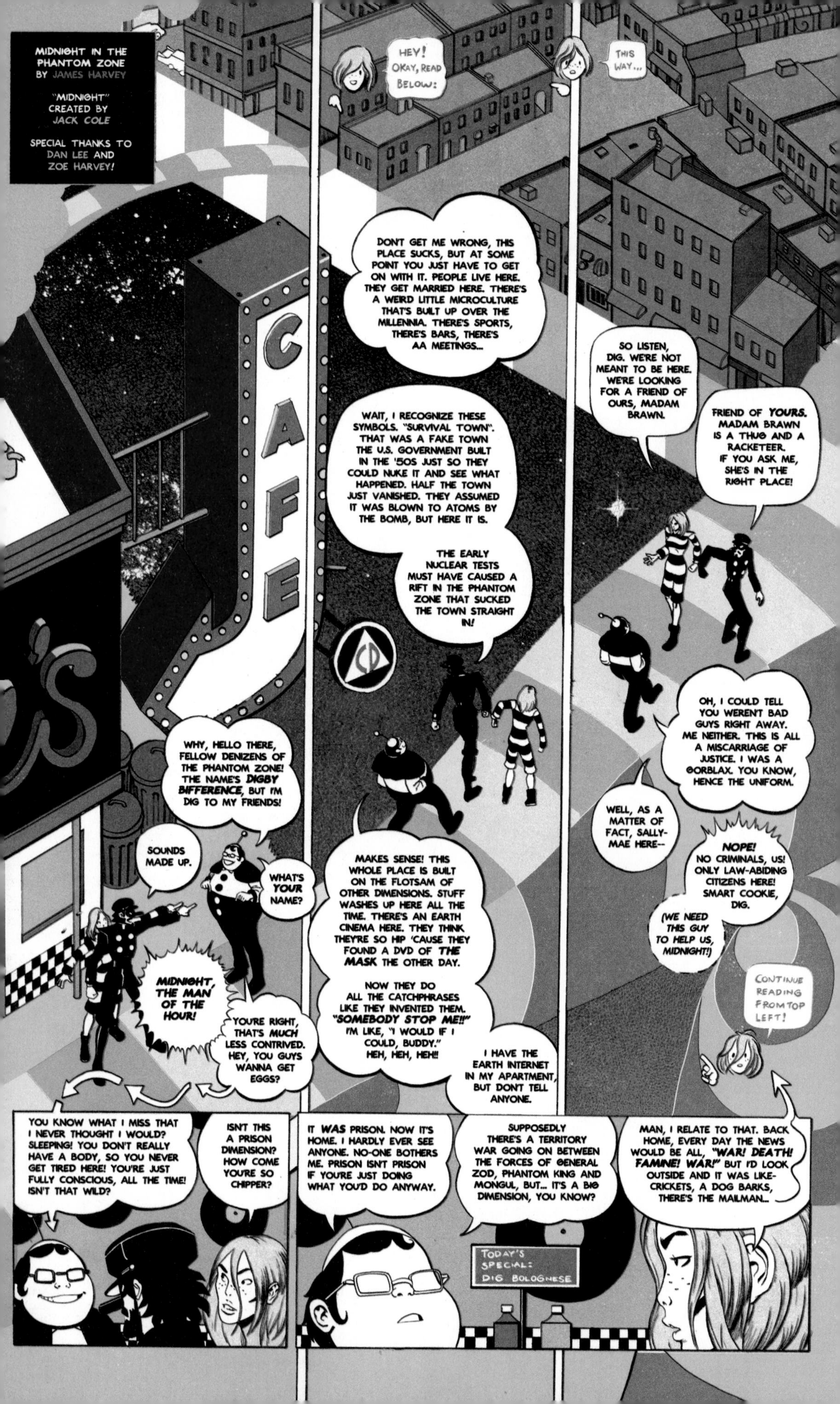

MIDNIGHT IN THE PHANTOM ZONE
BY JAMES HARVEY
"MIDNIGHT" CREATED BY JACK COLE
SPECIAL THANKS TO DAN LEE AND ZOE HARVEY!
HEY! OKAY, READ BELOW:
THIS WAY...
WHY, HELLO THERE, FELLOW DENIZENS OF THE PHANTOM ZONE! THE NAME'S DIGBY BIFFERENCE, BUT I'M DIG TO MY FRIENDS!
SOUNDS MADE UP.
WHAT'S YOUR NAME?
MIDNIGHT, THE MAN OF THE HOUR!
YOU'RE RIGHT, THAT'S MUCH LESS CONTRIVED. HEY, YOU GUYS WANNA GET EGGS?
YOU KNOW WHAT I MISS THAT I NEVER THOUGHT I WOULD? SLEEPING! YOU DON'T REALLY HAVE A BODY, SO YOU NEVER GET TIRED HERE! YOU'RE JUST FULLY CONSCIOUS, ALL THE TIME! ISN'T THAT WILD?
ISN'T THIS A PRISON DIMENSION? HOW COME YOU'RE SO CHIPPER?
IT WAS PRISON. NOW IT'S HOME. I HARDLY EVER SEE ANYONE. NO-ONE BOTHERS ME. PRISON ISN'T PRISON IF YOU'RE JUST DOING WHAT YOU'D DO ANYWAY.
SUPPOSEDLY THERE'S A TERRITORY WAR GOING ON BETWEEN THE FORCES OF GENERAL ZOD, PHANTOM KING AND MONGUL, BUT... IT'S A BIG DIMENSION, YOU KNOW?
MAN, I RELATE TO THAT. BACK HOME, EVERY DAY THE NEWS WOULD BE ALL, "WAR! DEATH! FAMINE! WAR!" BUT I'D LOOK OUTSIDE AND IT WAS LIKE- CRICKETS, A DOG BARKS, THERE'S THE MAILMAN...
TODAY'S SPECIAL: DIG BOLOGNESE
CAFE
CD
DON'T GET ME WRONG, THIS PLACE SUCKS, BUT AT SOME POINT YOU JUST HAVE TO GET ON WITH IT. PEOPLE LIVE HERE. THEY GET MARRIED HERE. THERE'S A WERD LITTLE MICROCULTURE THAT'S BUILT UP OVER THE MILLENNIA. THERE'S SPORTS, THERE'S BARS, THERE'S AA MEETINGS...
WAIT, I RECOGNIZE THESE SYMBOLS. "SURVIVAL TOWN". THAT WAS A FAKE TOWN THE U.S. GOVERNMENT BUILT IN THE '50S JUST SO THEY COULD NUKE IT AND SEE WHAT HAPPENED. HALF THE TOWN JUST VANISHED. THEY ASSUMED IT WAS BLOWN TO ATOMS BY THE BOMB, BUT HERE IT IS.
THE EARLY NUCLEAR TESTS MUST HAVE CAUSED A RIFT IN THE PHANTOM ZONE THAT SUCKED THE TOWN STRAIGHT IN!
MAKES SENSE! THIS WHOLE PLACE IS BUILT ON THE FLOTSAM OF OTHER DIMENSIONS. STUFF WASHES UP HERE ALL THE TIME. THERE'S AN EARTH CINEMA HERE. THEY THINK THEY'RE SO HIP 'CAUSE THEY FOUND A DVD OF THE MASK THE OTHER DAY.
NOW THEY DO ALL THE CATCHPHRASES LIKE THEY INVENTED THEM. "SOMEBODY STOP ME!!" I'M LIKE, "I WOULD IF I COULD, BUDDY." HEH, HEH, HEH!!
I HAVE THE EARTH INTERNET IN MY APARTMENT, BUT DON'T TELL ANYONE.
SO LISTEN, DIG. WE'RE NOT MEANT TO BE HERE. WE'RE LOOKING FOR A FRIEND OF OURS, MADAM BRAWN.
FRIEND OF YOURS. MADAM BRAWN IS A THUG AND A RACKETEER. IF YOU ASK ME, SHE'S IN THE RIGHT PLACE!
OH, I COULD TELL YOU WEREN'T BAD GUYS RIGHT AWAY. ME NEITHER. THIS IS ALL A MISCARRIAGE OF JUSTICE. I WAS A GORBLAX. YOU KNOW, HENCE THE UNIFORM.
WELL, AS A MATTER OF FACT, SALLY-MAE HERE--
NOPE! NO CRIMINALS, US! ONLY LAW-ABIDING CITIZENS HERE! SMART COOKIE, DIG.
(WE NEED THIS GUY TO HELP US, MIDNIGHT!)
CONTINUE READING FROM TOP LEFT!

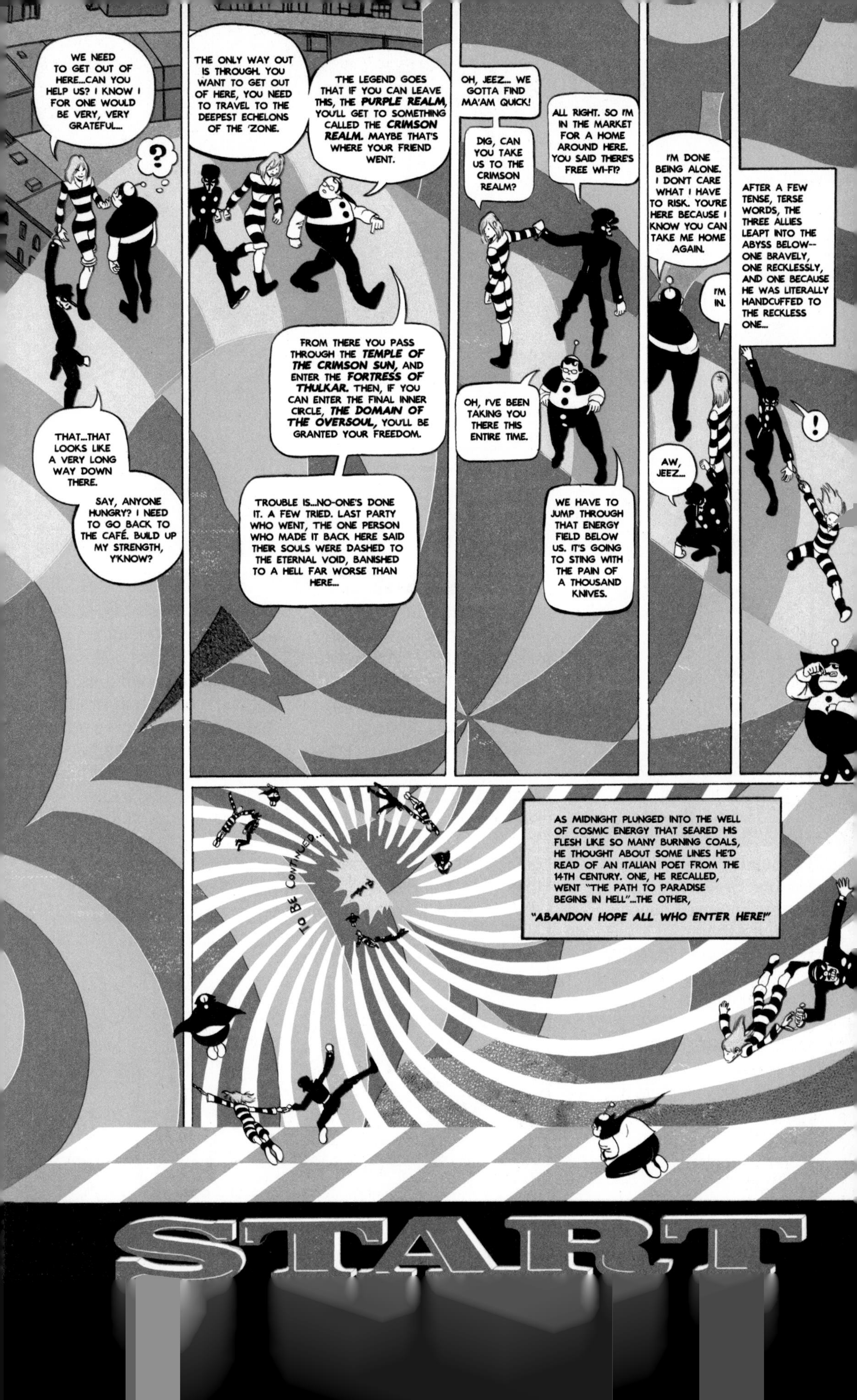
WE NEED TO GET OUT OF HERE...CAN YOU HELP US? I KNOW I FOR ONE WOULD BE VERY, VERY GRATEFUL...
?
THAT...THAT LOOKS LIKE A VERY LONG WAY DOWN THERE.
SAY, ANYONE HUNGRY? I NEED TO GO BACK TO THE CAFÉ. BUILD UP MY STRENGTH, Y'KNOW?
THE ONLY WAY OUT IS THROUGH. YOU WANT TO GET OUT OF HERE, YOU NEED TO TRAVEL TO THE DEEPEST ECHELONS OF THE 'ZONE.
THE LEGEND GOES THAT IF YOU CAN LEAVE THIS, THE *PURPLE REALM,* YOU'LL GET TO SOMETHING CALLED THE *CRIMSON REALM.* MAYBE THAT'S WHERE YOUR FRIEND WENT.
FROM THERE YOU PASS THROUGH THE *TEMPLE OF THE CRIMSON SUN,* AND ENTER THE *FORTRESS OF THULKAR.* THEN, IF YOU CAN ENTER THE FINAL INNER CIRCLE, *THE DOMAIN OF THE OVERSOUL,* YOU'LL BE GRANTED YOUR FREEDOM.
TROUBLE IS...NO-ONE'S DONE IT. A FEW TRIED. LAST PARTY WHO WENT, THE ONE PERSON WHO MADE IT BACK HERE SAID THEIR SOULS WERE DASHED TO THE ETERNAL VOID, BANISHED TO A HELL FAR WORSE THAN HERE...
OH, JEEZ... WE GOTTA FIND MA'AM QUICK!
DIG, CAN YOU TAKE US TO THE CRIMSON REALM?
ALL RIGHT. SO I'M IN THE MARKET FOR A HOME AROUND HERE. YOU SAID THERE'S FREE WI-FI?
OH, I'VE BEEN TAKING YOU THERE THIS ENTIRE TIME.
WE HAVE TO JUMP THROUGH THAT ENERGY FIELD BELOW US. IT'S GOING TO STING WITH THE PAIN OF A THOUSAND KNIVES.
I'M DONE BEING ALONE. I DON'T CARE WHAT I HAVE TO RISK. YOU'RE HERE BECAUSE I KNOW YOU CAN TAKE ME HOME AGAIN.
I'M IN.
AW, JEEZ...
AFTER A FEW TENSE, TERSE WORDS, THE THREE ALLIES LEAPT INTO THE ABYSS BELOW-- ONE BRAVELY, ONE RECKLESSLY, AND ONE BECAUSE HE WAS LITERALLY HANDCUFFED TO THE RECKLESS ONE...
!
AS MIDNIGHT PLUNGED INTO THE WELL OF COSMIC ENERGY THAT SEARED HIS FLESH LIKE SO MANY BURNING COALS, HE THOUGHT ABOUT SOME LINES HE'D READ OF AN ITALIAN POET FROM THE 14TH CENTURY. ONE, HE RECALLED, WENT "THE PATH TO PARADISE BEGINS IN HELL"...THE OTHER,
"ABANDON HOPE ALL WHO ENTER HERE!"
TO BE CONTINUED...
START

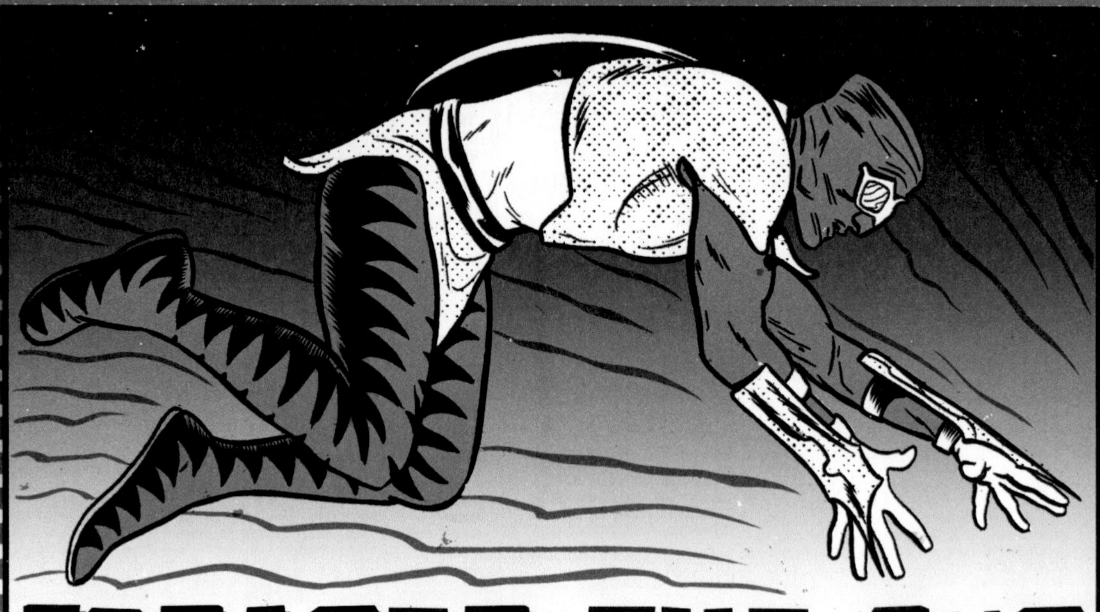

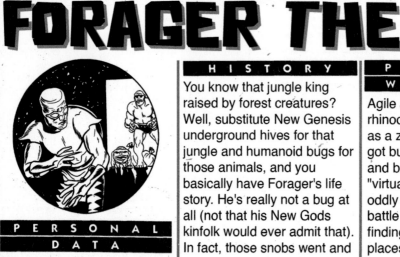

FORAGER THE BUG

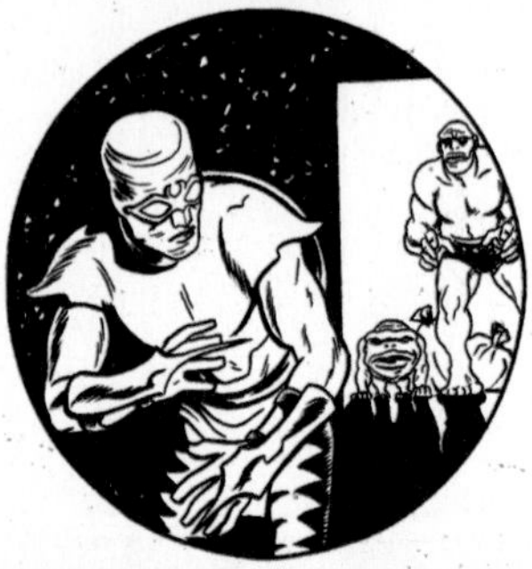

PERSONAL DATA

Occupation: Former army ant
Marital Status: Unaccompanied minor
Group Affiliation: New Gods
First Appearance: NEW GODS Volume 1, #9
Death: COSMIC ODYSSEY #4
Do-over: BUG! THE ADVENTURES OF FORAGER #1
Height: Knee high to a grasshopper
Weight: Flyweight
Eyes: Buggy
Hair: Stylin'!
Pet Peeves: Orion, dying, haunted houses, talking teddy bears, WWII, carrots in chili, yaks that yak, dominoes

HISTORY

You know that jungle king raised by forest creatures? Well, substitute New Genesis underground hives for that jungle and humanoid bugs for those animals, and you basically have Forager's life story. He's really not a bug at all (not that his New Gods kinfolk would ever admit that). In fact, those snobs went and got Forager killed in one of their wars. But Bug's all better now. He's back from the dead and looking for somewhere to call home and someone to call family.

POWERS & WEAPONS

Agile as a cricket, strong as a rhinoceros beetle, odiferous as a zillion crushed ants. He's got bug moves, bug strength, and bug reflexes. He's got "virtual bug antennae," an oddly aerodynamic inertron battle shield, and a knack for finding his way into forbidden places. He's brave, he's bold, he's BUG! (Bug Colony action playset and Grumpy Orion figure sold separately.)

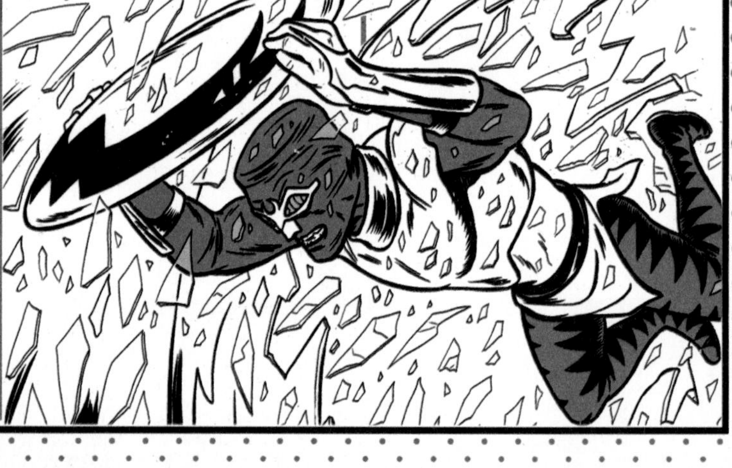

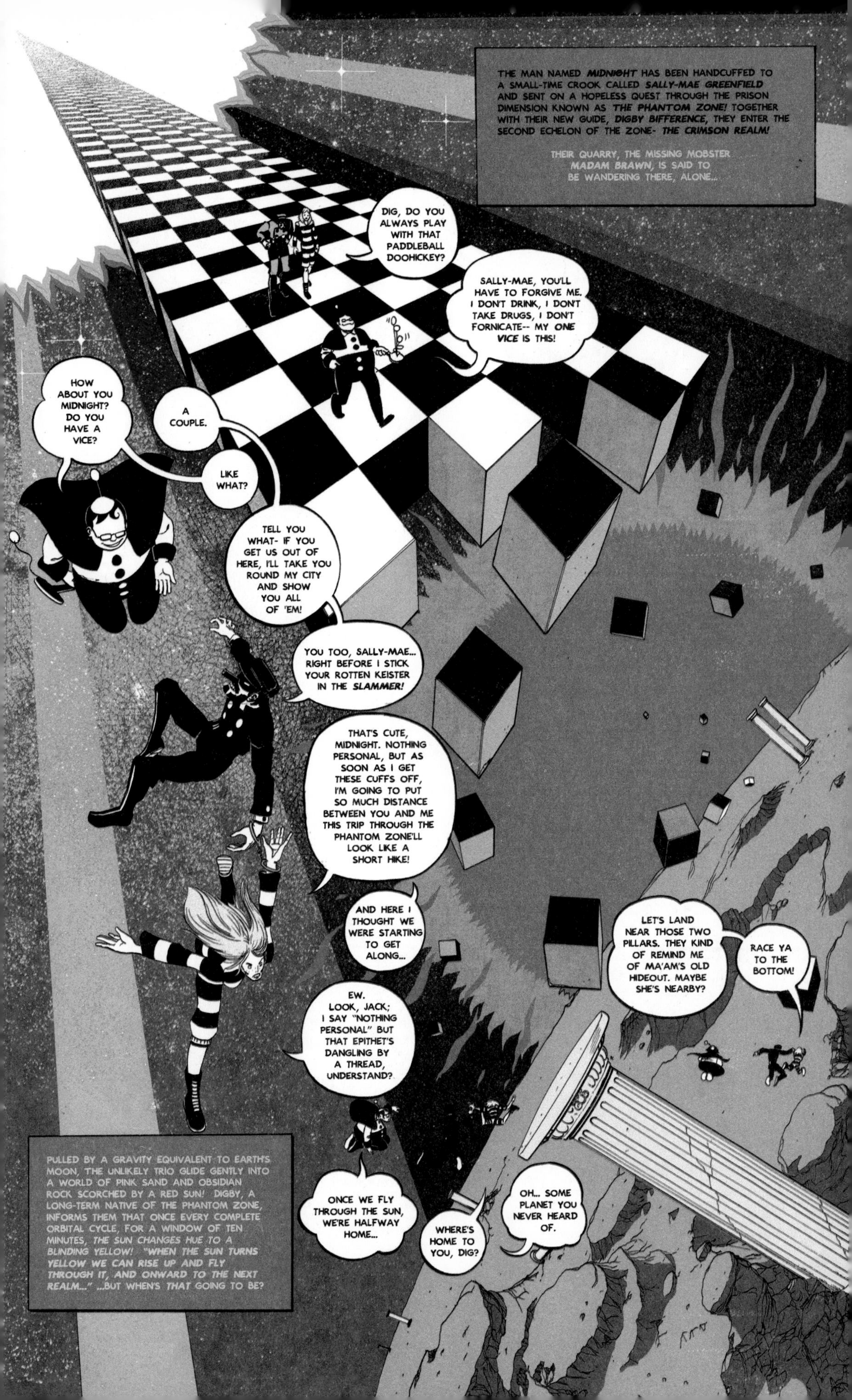
THE MAN NAMED MIDNIGHT HAS BEEN HANDCUFFED TO A SMALL-TIME CROOK CALLED SALLY-MAE GREENFIELD AND SENT ON A HOPELESS QUEST THROUGH THE PRISON DIMENSION KNOWN AS THE PHANTOM ZONE! TOGETHER WITH THEIR NEW GUIDE, DIGBY BIFFERENCE, THEY ENTER THE SECOND ECHELON OF THE ZONE- THE CRIMSON REALM!
THEIR QUARRY, THE MISSING MOBSTER MADAM BRAWN, IS SAID TO BE WANDERING THERE, ALONE...
DIG, DO YOU ALWAYS PLAY WITH THAT PADDLEBALL DOOHICKEY?
SALLY-MAE, YOU'LL HAVE TO FORGIVE ME. I DON'T DRINK, I DON'T TAKE DRUGS, I DON'T FORNICATE-- MY ONE VICE IS THIS!
HOW ABOUT YOU MIDNIGHT? DO YOU HAVE A VICE?
A COUPLE.
LIKE WHAT?
TELL YOU WHAT- IF YOU GET US OUT OF HERE, I'LL TAKE YOU ROUND MY CITY AND SHOW YOU ALL OF 'EM!
YOU TOO, SALLY-MAE... RIGHT BEFORE I STICK YOUR ROTTEN KEISTER IN THE SLAMMER!
THAT'S CUTE, MIDNIGHT. NOTHING PERSONAL, BUT AS SOON AS I GET THESE CUFFS OFF, I'M GOING TO PUT SO MUCH DISTANCE BETWEEN YOU AND ME THIS TRIP THROUGH THE PHANTOM ZONE'LL LOOK LIKE A SHORT HIKE!
AND HERE I THOUGHT WE WERE STARTING TO GET ALONG...
EW. LOOK, JACK; I SAY "NOTHING PERSONAL" BUT THAT EPITHET'S DANGLING BY A THREAD, UNDERSTAND?
LET'S LAND NEAR THOSE TWO PILLARS. THEY KIND OF REMIND ME OF MA'AM'S OLD HIDEOUT. MAYBE SHE'S NEARBY?
RACE YA TO THE BOTTOM!
PULLED BY A GRAVITY EQUIVALENT TO EARTH'S MOON, THE UNLIKELY TRIO GLIDE GENTLY INTO A WORLD OF PINK SAND AND OBSIDIAN ROCK SCORCHED BY A RED SUN! DIGBY, A LONG-TERM NATIVE OF THE PHANTOM ZONE, INFORMS THEM THAT ONCE EVERY COMPLETE ORBITAL CYCLE, FOR A WINDOW OF TEN MINUTES, THE SUN CHANGES HUE TO A BLINDING YELLOW! "WHEN THE SUN TURNS YELLOW WE CAN RISE UP AND FLY THROUGH IT, AND ONWARD TO THE NEXT REALM..." ...BUT WHEN'S THAT GOING TO BE?
ONCE WE FLY THROUGH THE SUN, WE'RE HALFWAY HOME...
WHERE'S HOME TO YOU, DIG?
OH... SOME PLANET YOU NEVER HEARD OF.

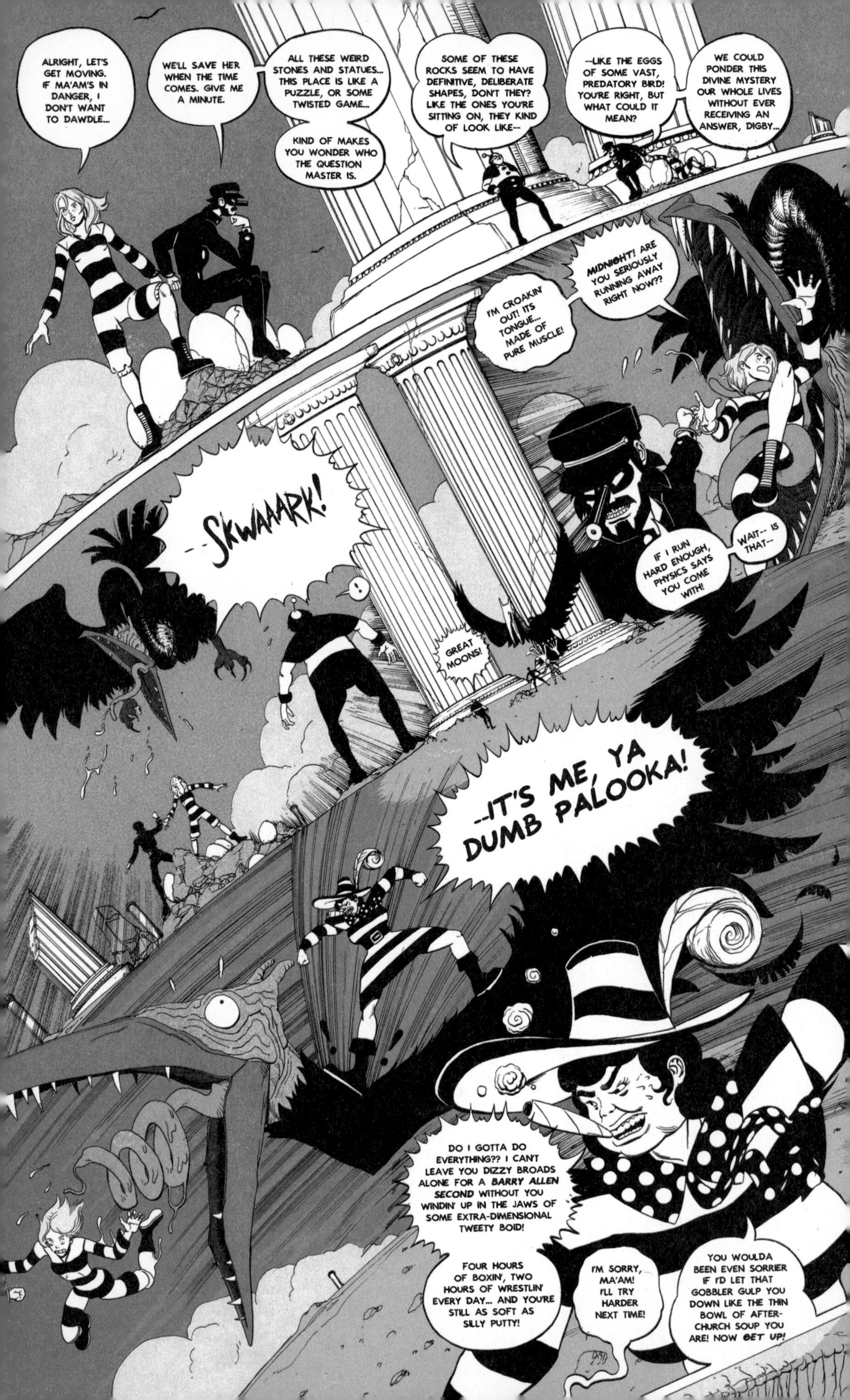
ALRIGHT, LET'S GET MOVING. IF MA'AM'S IN DANGER, I DON'T WANT TO DAWDLE...
WE'LL SAVE HER WHEN THE TIME COMES. GIVE ME A MINUTE.
ALL THESE WEIRD STONES AND STATUES... THIS PLACE IS LIKE A PUZZLE, OR SOME TWISTED GAME...
KIND OF MAKES YOU WONDER WHO THE QUESTION MASTER IS.
SOME OF THESE ROCKS SEEM TO HAVE DEFINITIVE, DELIBERATE SHAPES, DON'T THEY? LIKE THE ONES YOU'RE SITTING ON, THEY KIND OF LOOK LIKE--
--LIKE THE EGGS OF SOME VAST, PREDATORY BIRD! YOU'RE RIGHT, BUT WHAT COULD IT MEAN?
WE COULD PONDER THIS DIVINE MYSTERY OUR WHOLE LIVES WITHOUT EVER RECEIVING AN ANSWER, DIGBY...
--SKWAAARK!
!
GREAT MOONS!
MIDNIGHT! ARE YOU SERIOUSLY RUNNING AWAY RIGHT NOW??
I'M CROAKIN' OUT! ITS TONGUE... MADE OF PURE MUSCLE!
IF I RUN HARD ENOUGH, PHYSICS SAYS YOU COME WITH!
WAIT-- IS THAT--
--IT'S ME, YA DUMB PALOOKA!
DO I GOTTA DO EVERYTHING?? I CAN'T LEAVE YOU DIZZY BROADS ALONE FOR A BARRY ALLEN SECOND WITHOUT YOU WINDIN' UP IN THE JAWS OF SOME EXTRA-DIMENSIONAL TWEETY BOID!
FOUR HOURS OF BOXIN', TWO HOURS OF WRESTLIN' EVERY DAY... AND YOU'RE STILL AS SOFT AS SILLY PUTTY!
I'M SORRY, MA'AM! I'LL TRY HARDER NEXT TIME!
YOU WOULDA BEEN EVEN SORRIER IF I'D LET THAT GOBBLER GULP YOU DOWN LIKE THE THIN BOWL OF AFTER-CHURCH SOUP YOU ARE! NOW GET UP!

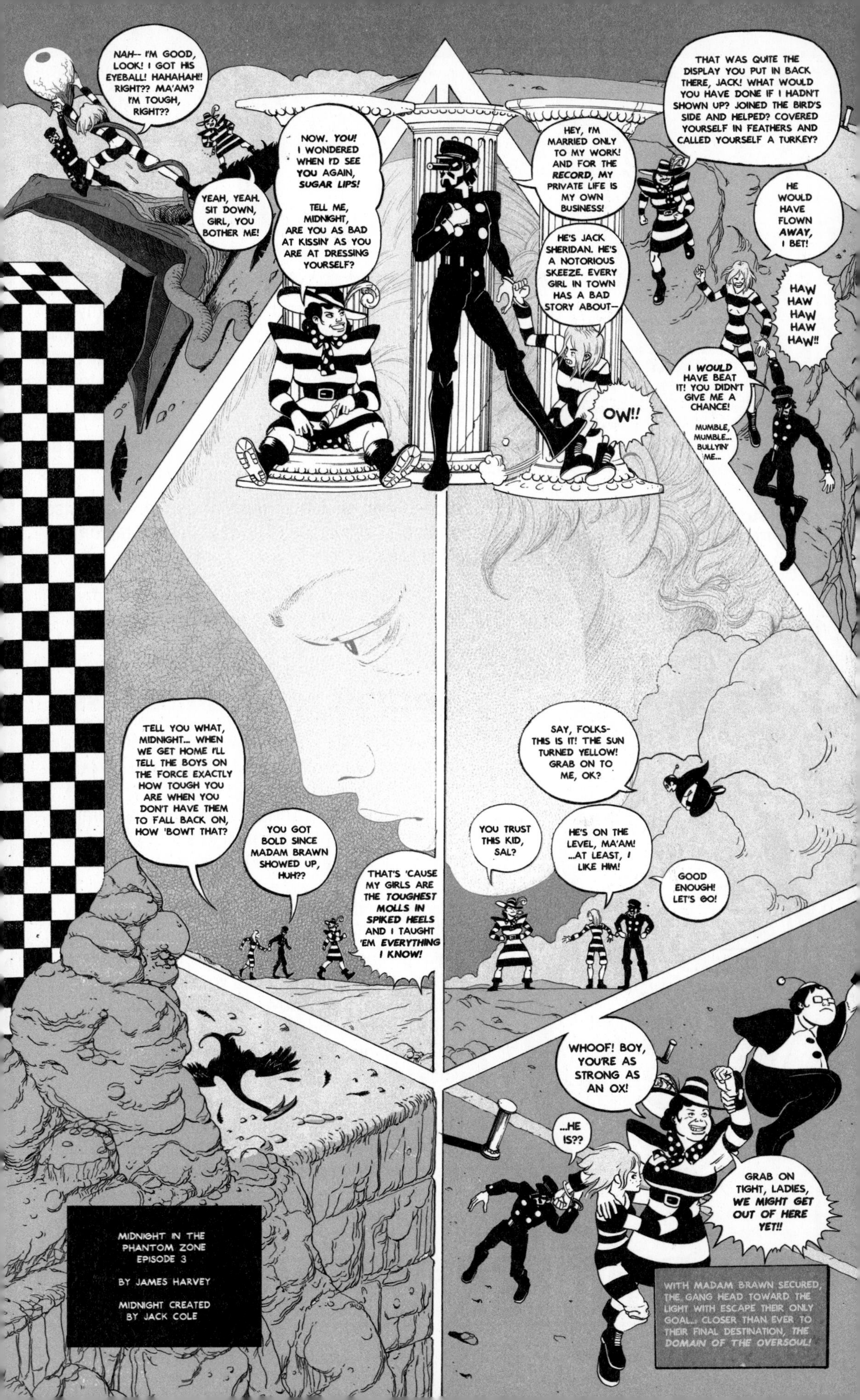
NAH-- I'M GOOD, LOOK! I GOT HIS EYEBALL! HAHAHAH!! RIGHT?? MA'AM? I'M TOUGH, RIGHT??
YEAH, YEAH. SIT DOWN, GIRL, YOU BOTHER ME!
NOW. YOU! I WONDERED WHEN I'D SEE YOU AGAIN, SUGAR LIPS!
TELL ME, MIDNIGHT, ARE YOU AS BAD AT KISSIN' AS YOU ARE AT DRESSING YOURSELF?
HEY, I'M MARRIED ONLY TO MY WORK! AND FOR THE RECORD, MY PRIVATE LIFE IS MY OWN BUSINESS!
HE'S JACK SHERIDAN. HE'S A NOTORIOUS SKEEZE. EVERY GIRL IN TOWN HAS A BAD STORY ABOUT—
OW!!
THAT WAS QUITE THE DISPLAY YOU PUT IN BACK THERE, JACK! WHAT WOULD YOU HAVE DONE IF I HADN'T SHOWN UP? JOINED THE BIRD'S SIDE AND HELPED? COVERED YOURSELF IN FEATHERS AND CALLED YOURSELF A TURKEY?
HE WOULD HAVE FLOWN AWAY, I BET!
HAW HAW HAW HAW HAW!!
I WOULD HAVE BEAT IT! YOU DIDN'T GIVE ME A CHANCE!
MUMBLE, MUMBLE... BULLYIN' ME...
TELL YOU WHAT, MIDNIGHT... WHEN WE GET HOME I'LL TELL THE BOYS ON THE FORCE EXACTLY HOW TOUGH YOU ARE WHEN YOU DON'T HAVE THEM TO FALL BACK ON, HOW 'BOWT THAT?
YOU GOT BOLD SINCE MADAM BRAWN SHOWED UP, HUH??
THAT'S 'CAUSE MY GIRLS ARE THE TOUGHEST MOLLS IN SPIKED HEELS AND I TAUGHT 'EM EVERYTHING I KNOW!
SAY, FOLKS- THIS IS IT! THE SUN TURNED YELLOW! GRAB ON TO ME, OK?
YOU TRUST THIS KID, SAL?
HE'S ON THE LEVEL, MA'AM! ...AT LEAST, I LIKE HIM!
GOOD ENOUGH! LET'S GO!
WHOOF! BOY, YOU'RE AS STRONG AS AN OX!
...HE IS??
GRAB ON TIGHT, LADIES, WE MIGHT GET OUT OF HERE YET!!
MIDNIGHT IN THE PHANTOM ZONE
EPISODE 3
BY JAMES HARVEY
MIDNIGHT CREATED BY JACK COLE
WITH MADAM BRAWN SECURED, THE GANG HEAD TOWARD THE LIGHT WITH ESCAPE THEIR ONLY GOAL... CLOSER THAN EVER TO THEIR FINAL DESTINATION, THE DOMAIN OF THE OVERSOUL!

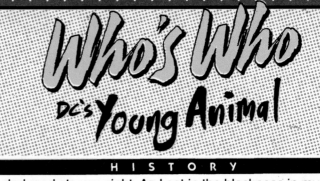

Who's Who
DC's Young Animal

PERSONAL DATA

Name: Lee Allred
Occupation: Writer, Big Brother
First Appearance: BUG! THE ADVENTURES OF FORAGER #1

HISTORY

A dark and stormy night. As I sat in the blackness in my conservatory, clad as usual in my elegant silk dressing gown, I could hear the surging sounds of the cacophonic city and I mused on the infamous injustices befalling the turgid teeming masses below.

If only I could right their wrongs. If only I could become a dark, gritty creature of the night, a-- a--

CRASH! Suddenly an ancient manual typewriter hurled itself through my 32nd-story window! That's it! I would become… TYPEWRITER MAN!

But I couldn't sew a decent typewriter chest logo for my spandex, so I became just a comic book scripter instead.

Method to My Madness

By the time I actually sit down in front of the keyboard, I've pretty well planned an issue out in my head, down to much of the dialogue even. I open up the plain vanilla Notepad text program and type out brief plot points to serve as a mnemonic framework as I work.

Building on that framework (too sparse to really call an outline), I then start typing out in Notepad dialogue lines between the characters for each scene. Just dialogue, as if I were listening to a Golden Age radio show. At this point I'm not worrying about stage direction or file formatting or the mechanics of a script. Just setting down the voice of the characters.

I take these throwaway Notepad dialogue files and paste them into my preset Microsoft Word script template. I then flesh out panel/page count, stage directions, etc., and also paste in art references for Mike. The end result is a full script.

THE PROCESS OF MAKING BUG!

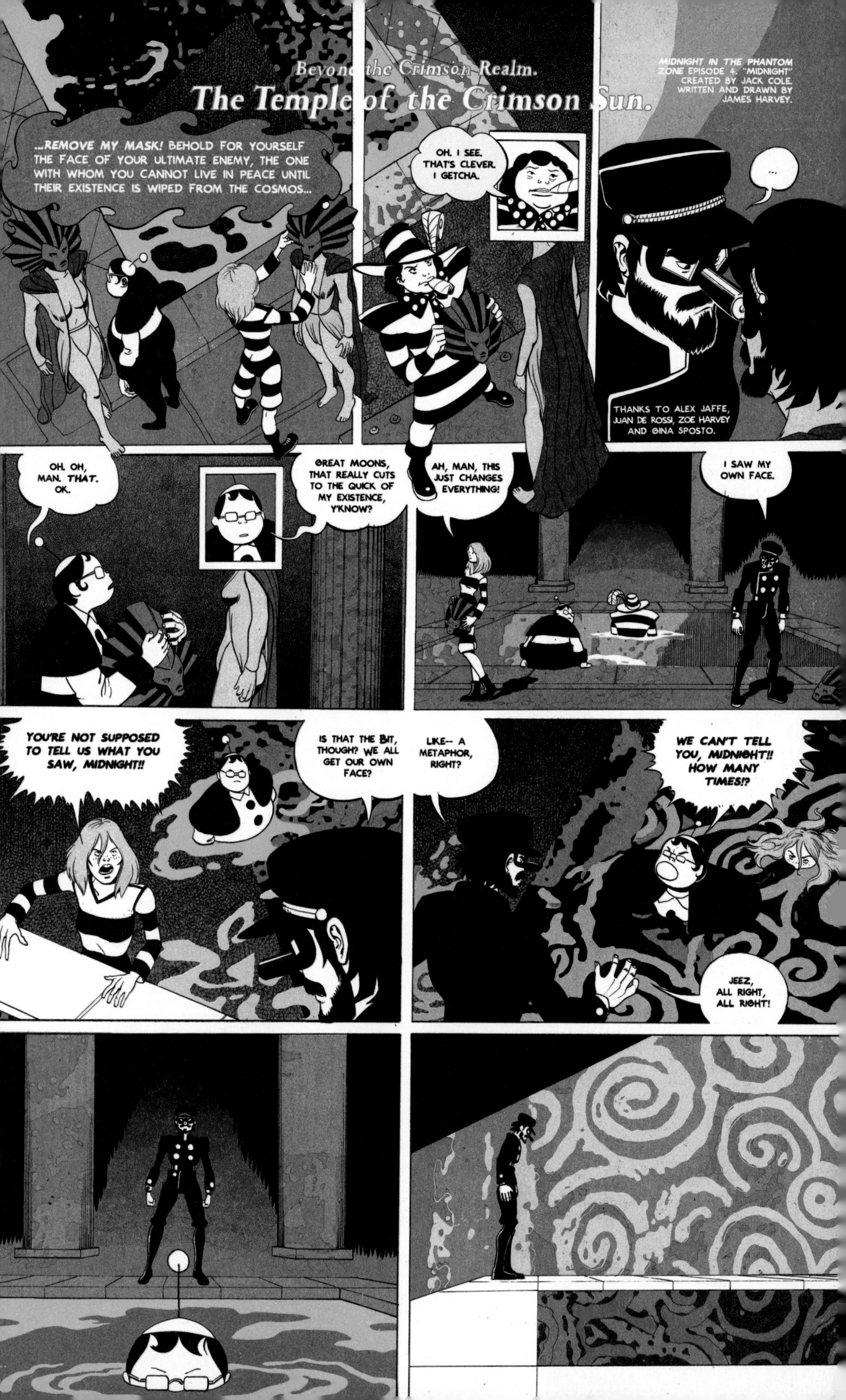

Beyond the Crimson Realm.
The Temple of the Crimson Sun.
MIDNIGHT IN THE PHANTOM ZONE EPISODE 4. "MIDNIGHT" CREATED BY JACK COLE. WRITTEN AND DRAWN BY JAMES HARVEY.
...REMOVE MY MASK! BEHOLD FOR YOURSELF THE FACE OF YOUR ULTIMATE ENEMY, THE ONE WITH WHOM YOU CANNOT LIVE IN PEACE UNTIL THEIR EXISTENCE IS WIPED FROM THE COSMOS...
OH. I SEE. THAT'S CLEVER. I GETCHA.
...
THANKS TO ALEX JAFFE, JUAN DE ROSSI, ZOE HARVEY AND GINA SPOSTO.
OH. OH, MAN. THAT. OK.
GREAT MOONS, THAT REALLY CUTS TO THE QUICK OF MY EXISTENCE, Y'KNOW?
AH, MAN, THIS JUST CHANGES EVERYTHING!
I SAW MY OWN FACE.
YOU'RE NOT SUPPOSED TO TELL US WHAT YOU SAW, MIDNIGHT!!
IS THAT THE BIT, THOUGH? WE ALL GET OUR OWN FACE?
LIKE-- A METAPHOR, RIGHT?
WE CAN'T TELL YOU, MIDNIGHT!! HOW MANY TIMES!?
JEEZ, ALL RIGHT, ALL RIGHT!

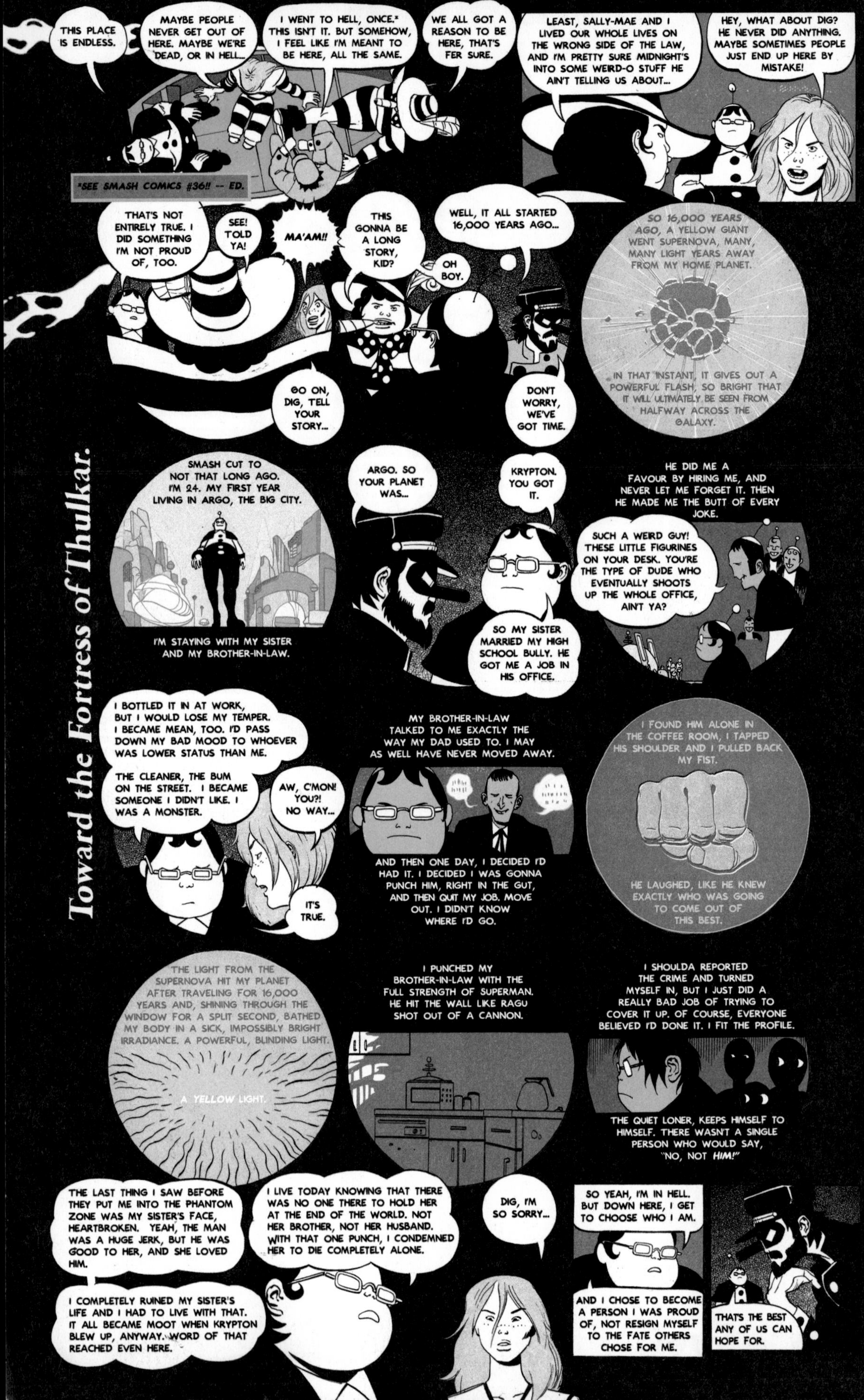
Toward the Fortress of Thulkar.
THIS PLACE IS ENDLESS.
MAYBE PEOPLE NEVER GET OUT OF HERE. MAYBE WE'RE DEAD, OR IN HELL...
I WENT TO HELL, ONCE.* THIS ISN'T IT. BUT SOMEHOW, I FEEL LIKE I'M MEANT TO BE HERE, ALL THE SAME.
WE ALL GOT A REASON TO BE HERE, THAT'S FER SURE.
*SEE SMASH COMICS #36!! -- ED.
LEAST, SALLY-MAE AND I LIVED OUR WHOLE LIVES ON THE WRONG SIDE OF THE LAW, AND I'M PRETTY SURE MIDNIGHT'S INTO SOME WEIRD-O STUFF HE AIN'T TELLING US ABOUT...
HEY, WHAT ABOUT DIG? HE NEVER DID ANYTHING. MAYBE SOMETIMES PEOPLE JUST END UP HERE BY MISTAKE!
THAT'S NOT ENTIRELY TRUE. I DID SOMETHING I'M NOT PROUD OF, TOO.
SEE! TOLD YA!
MA'AM!!
THIS GONNA BE A LONG STORY, KID?
WELL, IT ALL STARTED 16,000 YEARS AGO...
OH BOY.
GO ON, DIG, TELL YOUR STORY...
DON'T WORRY, WE'VE GOT TIME.
SO 16,000 YEARS AGO, A YELLOW GIANT WENT SUPERNOVA, MANY, MANY LIGHT YEARS AWAY FROM MY HOME PLANET.
IN THAT INSTANT, IT GIVES OUT A POWERFUL FLASH, SO BRIGHT THAT IT WILL ULTIMATELY BE SEEN FROM HALFWAY ACROSS THE GALAXY.
SMASH CUT TO NOT THAT LONG AGO. I'M 24. MY FIRST YEAR LIVING IN ARGO, THE BIG CITY.
I'M STAYING WITH MY SISTER AND MY BROTHER-IN-LAW.
ARGO. SO YOUR PLANET WAS...
KRYPTON. YOU GOT IT.
SO MY SISTER MARRIED MY HIGH SCHOOL BULLY. HE GOT ME A JOB IN HIS OFFICE.
HE DID ME A FAVOUR BY HIRING ME, AND NEVER LET ME FORGET IT. THEN HE MADE ME THE BUTT OF EVERY JOKE.
SUCH A WEIRD GUY! THESE LITTLE FIGURINES ON YOUR DESK. YOU'RE THE TYPE OF DUDE WHO EVENTUALLY SHOOTS UP THE WHOLE OFFICE, AIN'T YA?
I BOTTLED IT IN AT WORK, BUT I WOULD LOSE MY TEMPER. I BECAME MEAN, TOO. I'D PASS DOWN MY BAD MOOD TO WHOEVER WAS LOWER STATUS THAN ME.
THE CLEANER, THE BUM ON THE STREET. I BECAME SOMEONE I DIDN'T LIKE. I WAS A MONSTER.
AW, C'MON! YOU?! NO WAY...
IT'S TRUE.
MY BROTHER-IN-LAW TALKED TO ME EXACTLY THE WAY MY DAD USED TO. I MAY AS WELL HAVE NEVER MOVED AWAY.
AND THEN ONE DAY, I DECIDED I'D HAD IT. I DECIDED I WAS GONNA PUNCH HIM, RIGHT IN THE GUT, AND THEN QUIT MY JOB. MOVE OUT. I DIDN'T KNOW WHERE I'D GO.
I FOUND HIM ALONE IN THE COFFEE ROOM, I TAPPED HIS SHOULDER AND I PULLED BACK MY FIST.
HE LAUGHED, LIKE HE KNEW EXACTLY WHO WAS GOING TO COME OUT OF THIS BEST.
THE LIGHT FROM THE SUPERNOVA HIT MY PLANET AFTER TRAVELING FOR 16,000 YEARS AND, SHINING THROUGH THE WINDOW FOR A SPLIT SECOND, BATHED MY BODY IN A SICK, IMPOSSIBLY BRIGHT IRRADIANCE. A POWERFUL, BLINDING LIGHT.
A YELLOW LIGHT.
I PUNCHED MY BROTHER-IN-LAW WITH THE FULL STRENGTH OF SUPERMAN. HE HIT THE WALL LIKE RAGU SHOT OUT OF A CANNON.
I SHOULDA REPORTED THE CRIME AND TURNED MYSELF IN, BUT I JUST DID A REALLY BAD JOB OF TRYING TO COVER IT UP. OF COURSE, EVERYONE BELIEVED I'D DONE IT. I FIT THE PROFILE.
THE QUIET LONER, KEEPS HIMSELF TO HIMSELF. THERE WASN'T A SINGLE PERSON WHO WOULD SAY, "NO, NOT HIM!"
THE LAST THING I SAW BEFORE THEY PUT ME INTO THE PHANTOM ZONE WAS MY SISTER'S FACE, HEARTBROKEN. YEAH, THE MAN WAS A HUGE JERK, BUT HE WAS GOOD TO HER, AND SHE LOVED HIM.
I COMPLETELY RUINED MY SISTER'S LIFE AND I HAD TO LIVE WITH THAT. IT ALL BECAME MOOT WHEN KRYPTON BLEW UP, ANYWAY. WORD OF THAT REACHED EVEN HERE.
I LIVE TODAY KNOWING THAT THERE WAS NO ONE THERE TO HOLD HER AT THE END OF THE WORLD. NOT HER BROTHER, NOT HER HUSBAND. WITH THAT ONE PUNCH, I CONDEMNED HER TO DIE COMPLETELY ALONE.
DIG, I'M SO SORRY...
SO YEAH, I'M IN HELL. BUT DOWN HERE, I GET TO CHOOSE WHO I AM.
AND I CHOSE TO BECOME A PERSON I WAS PROUD OF, NOT RESIGN MYSELF TO THE FATE OTHERS CHOSE FOR ME.
THAT'S THE BEST ANY OF US CAN HOPE FOR.

Earth.

THE CLOCK STRUCK SIX AFTER THE SACRIFICE, WHEN THE PRIEST FREED US FROM THE FORTRESS AND WE PASSED INTO THE TACTILE WORLD OF OUR OWN COSMOS. OVER AN HOUR WENT BY BEFORE WE FINALLY EMERGED INTO THE EARLY LIGHT.

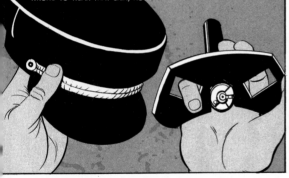

MIDNIGHT GAVE ME HIS HAT AND MASK WHEN HE LEFT US AT THE FORTRESS OF THULKAR. IT WAS STRANGE TO SEE HIS FACE WITHOUT THEM-- LIKE AN OLD DOG THAT JUST SHED ITS COAT, PERHAPS. I GUESS IT WAS SOMETHING HE FELT HE NEEDED TO DO. I DON'T KNOW WHY HE WANTED ME TO HAVE THEM, BUT I COULD NEVER WEAR THEM. THERE WAS A SADNESS THAT SEEMED TO FOLLOW HIM ROUND, LIKE A MAN WHO WAS UNCOMFORTABLE IN HIS OWN SKIN. IT WOULD FEEL WRONG TO WEAR THAT SKIN, NOW.

HE TALKED ABOUT WHEN HE WENT TO HELL. I HAD A LIFETIME TO THINK ABOUT MY CRIMES, AND BY THE END I KNEW I WAS A DIFFERENT MAN TO THE ONE THEY THREW IN JAIL. AN ETERNITY IN HELL SEEMS CRUEL, GIVEN MAN'S INFINITE CAPACITY TO REFORM, REFLECT AND CHANGE. I HOPE THAT WHEREVER HE IS, HE'S IN A BETTER PLACE THAN THAT.

I DIDN'T RECOGNIZE THIS WORLD AT FIRST, BUT AFTER A FEW MONTHS IT SEEMED ALL TOO FAMILIAR. JUST LIKE THE PHANTOM ZONE, SOME PEOPLE WORE STRIPES. LIKE MIDNIGHT, SOME WORE HATS AND BADGES, TOO. BUT OCCASIONALLY I'D SEE FLASHES, LIKE IN THE RISING SUN, OR IN SALLY-MAE'S FACE, THAT TOLD ME THAT THIS PLACE IS ONLY A PRISON IF YOUR HEART LETS IT BE.

WHEN MIDNIGHT JUMPED INTO THE FIRE AND THE PRIEST OF THULKAR GRANTED THE REST OF US PASSAGE HOME, MIDNIGHT LOOKED STRAIGHT AT ME. "YOU'RE GETTING A SECOND CHANCE," HE SAID. "DON'T WASTE IT." I SWORE TO HIM I WOULDN'T.

MADAM BRAWN TOLD US IT WAS THE MORNING OF EASTER SUNDAY. THE SUN ROSE BEHIND THE FACELESS CONCRETE BLOCKS THAT THESE PEOPLE CALLED THEIR HOMES. THEY PUT ON THEIR SOCKS, BRUSHED THEIR TEETH AND WENT ABOUT THEIR DAY.

THE CLOCK ON THE STREET STRUCK EIGHT, BUT IN MY HEART IT WOULD ALWAYS BE MIDNIGHT.

Who's Who

DC's Young Animal

PERSONAL DATA

Names: Michael and Laura Allred
Occupation: Artist, Colorist
First Appearance: DOOM PATROL #1 variant cover

HISTORY

Michael & I first saw each other as I got off a student shuttle bus and he was getting on. We stared unembarrassed as we passed each other. Eyes stayed locked even as the shuttle pulled away. It was our first year of college. I'm a California girl, Michael an Oregonian, six days older than me. Our lives growing up mirror each other in the strangest ways. One bizarre example: we both walked in to *Star Wars* late, with C-3PO walking past the giant serpent skeleton on the dune being the first image we each saw.

A couple hours after the shuttle stare-off, my friend dragged me to an apartment to get some borrowed records back from someone named Tracy. Answering the door was my handsome starer, Michael! Tracy was his roommate. When my friend went to get her records, Mike asked if I wanted to go for a walk, which I did, ditching my friend, and we walked and talked all night. We've been together ever since.

It's a thrill to share virtually every aspect of our lives, staying close with our ever-growing brood, creating and being creative, together.

PAGE 2 (6 panels)

Panel 1

BUG still coughing, still on all fours. KUZUKO and HU LI (teddy bear) come gently floating down, riding in BUG's upturned shield, the little scamps! KUZUKO is pretty much as expressionless as ever.

1 MANGA SFX (shield ride): gently floating down

2 BUG: *koff* *koff* You enjoy doing this to me, don't you, you stupid teddy bear?

3 HU LI: Just saddle up the yak. Miles to ride before we sleep.

4 BUG: What yak?

Panel 2

Cut to a big shaggy yak/muskox-like alien creature standing placidly next to a hitching post with a saddle draped over it. The muskox/yak creature looks pretty much like a musk ox if Kirby was to draw one, only instead of regular musk ox curvy horns it has ivory bone-like organic saxophone-shaped, er, horns. Horns are ivory-colored, not brass.

Already riding on top of the yak's back is KUZUKO. She's wearing BUG's homemade olive drab Mother Box on her chest (strap around her neck). Despite the non-emotion on her face, KUZUKO is kicking in and out her little legs, trying to get the placid ox to start moving just as if she's riding a horsey.

5 MANGA SFX (kicking yak): giddy up, horsey!

6 HU LI (OP): *That* yak.

7 YAK (from the left "saxophone"): ♫ MoooOOOOoooo ♫

8 YAK (from the right "saxophone"): ♫ MoooOOOOoooo ♫

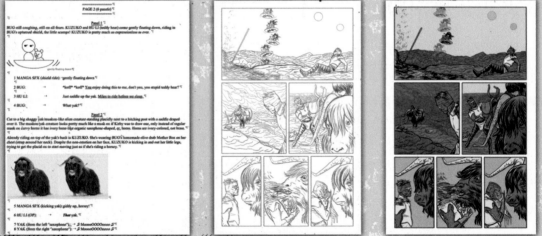

We've developed a unique process for producing comic book pages. Michael makes notes and tiny thumbnail drawings on the script, then jumps to pencilling everything, almost always in order, on the 11 x 17 bristol boards. From there he inks everything old school with a sable brush (Windsor and Newton being his favorite) dipped in ink. This is where it gets a little weird. I scan the line art and give the originals back for him to paint them with gray modeling washes and graphite shadings. Mike is a bit color-blind as well as being a bit of a control freak, and this allows him to be a part of the final process, where I then scan the original art again and make a channel to separate out his tones and change them to whatever color I like. This gives the final art a more organic handmade quality that we both prefer to straight computer colors. It's a bit more involved than that, but I've gone on too long already.

BIZARRO MIKEY HERE. ME HATE COMIC BOOKS! ME HATE WORKING WITH LAURA AND LEE! ME HATE GUITAR LESSONS WHERE ME AND BIZARRO LEE FOUND FIRST NEW GODS COMIC BOOKS! AND NOW ME HATE MAKING BUG! COMIC BOOKS AFTER WHOLE LIFE HATING IDEA OF MAKING A NEW GODS COMIC BOOK! ME HATE ALL OF YOU WHO BUY OUR COMIC BOOKS!

DC's YOUNG ANIMAL

DOOM PATROL
VOL. 1: BRICK BY BRICK
GERARD WAY with NICK DERINGTON

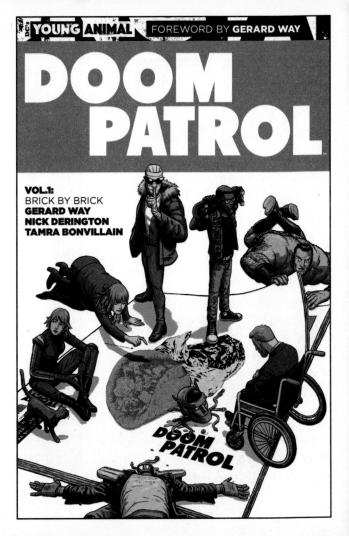

YOUNG ANIMAL — FOREWORD BY GERARD WAY

DOOM PATROL

VOL. 1:
BRICK BY BRICK
GERARD WAY
NICK DERINGTON
TAMRA BONVILLAIN

CAVE CARSON HAS A CYBERNETIC EYE VOL. 1: GOING UNDERGROUND

SHADE, THE CHANGING GIRL VOL. 1: EARTH GIRL MADE EASY

MOTHER PANIC VOL. 1: A WORK IN PROGRESS

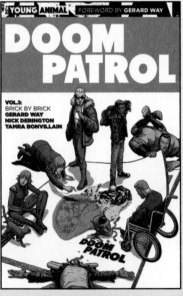